The **Canadian Press**

STYLEBOOK

A GUIDE FOR WRITING AND EDITING

14th edition

Patti Tasko
Editor

The Canadian Press
The Last Word. First.

36 King St. East, Toronto, Ontario M5C 2L9
416-364-0321 www.cp.org

Copyright © 2006 The Canadian Press
1st edition 1940
2nd edition 1947
3rd edition 1954
4th edition 1957
5th edition 1966
6th edition 1974
7th edition 1983
8th edition 1989
9th edition 1992
10th edition 1995
11th edition 1999
12th edition 2002
13th edition 2004
14th edition 2006

Library and Archives Canada Cataloguing in Publication

The Canadian Press stylebook : a guide for writing and editing /
Patti Tasko, editor. -- 14th ed.

Includes bibliographical references and index.
ISBN 0-920009-38-7

1. Journalism--Style manuals. 2. Canadian Press--Handbooks, manuals, etc.
I. Tasko, Patti II. Canadian Press

PN4783.C35 2006   808'.06607   C2006-902250-X

Design and cover art by Sean Vokey, The Canadian Press.

Printed in Canada.

Contents

Legal

The working journalist

Tools and technical guides

Illustrating the news

The CP news report

Introduction

The *CP Stylebook* began life as a modest little pamphlet more than a half-century ago. It was a sort of operator's manual for staff at The Canadian Press, Canada's national news agency.

It has blossomed since then into a comprehensive reference work used in newsrooms and business offices across Canada. It is required reading in university and college media courses.

Through its many editions, the stylebook has increasingly taken on the concerns of a wide variety of editors and writers outside the news media who work with words and need a standard Canadian reference. The language should be understandable to anyone who picks it up.

The stylebook has been organized into these main sections:

Policies: The standards that guide the work of collecting and distributing news. Basic journalism ethics, but also specific help with sensitive areas like racism, sexism, misquotes and anonymous sources.

General: Hard news and soft news, from news analysis to foreign reporting and sports coverage. The different types of basic news stories.

Legal: Libel. Copyright. Court coverage. Police searches of the newsroom. Contempt. The rights — and limitations — that govern the everyday work of reporters and editors.

The working journalist: Communicating clearly. Down-to-earth advice on writing and editing, with common pitfalls identified and lots of examples to illustrate each point. A how-to guide for access-to-information laws. Writing and editing for online readers.

Tools and technical guides: Organized alphabetically, this is the section that editors can consult for advice on punctuation, capitalization and other grammatical elements, as well as guidance on how to write about every topic from Aboriginal Peoples to Weather. Also includes a section on tricky words.

Illustrating the news: Pictures on the page. Practical information about getting photos and graphics into print.

The CP news report: A how-to-read-the-wire guide. Sets out procedures for advisories, packaging the news, coding and slugging of copy, the handling of corrections and other important elements of the agency's news report.

News releases: Writing and editing pointers for those trying to make news.

White space is provided throughout for notes and observations – particularly helpful at publications that modify or expand on CP style.

What's new

This 14th edition has been extensively updated to reflect the priorities and sensitivities of today's world, as well as the needs of writers and editors, no matter their medium. Lots of details change, but the emphasis on getting real people and real pocketbook issues into the news, in a readable style, remains.

In this edition you will find the following changes to style:

1.   CP's currency style has changed. It is now **US$500, C$800**. See page 192.

2.   For satellite names, CP follows industry style: **Anik F1, Anik F2**. This is an exception to our general rule on using a hyphen when a figure follows a letter. See page 201.

3.   The abbreviation for the military title lieutenant now is always **Lt.** Previously we used **Lieut.** except when it was part of a combining form. Now it is **Lt. John Brown** and **Lt.-Col. Sue Smith**.

4.   For clarity, CP recommends using italics, when technically possible, for the titles of compositions, including books, movies and songs. If italics cannot be used, then quote marks are put around the titles. See page 305.

Readers and editors of the CP Wire will also be interested in the following changes:

1.   Caution notes replace Borderline slugs for alerting readers to obscenity and possibly offensive material in news stories. See pages 18 and 32.

2.   Details on such new story formats as BizFlashes and QuickHits and changes to existing formats can be found in the chapters **Business news**, page 44, and **Slugs and Coding**, page 427.

3.   CP will now carry credit lines at the bottom of stories on those occasions when a reporter makes a significant contribution but is not in the location of the placeline. See page 420.

4.   All items must carry a headline to help databases process and display our news. See page 434.

CP's basic style changes cautiously: evolution, not revolution. While this edition contains many changes of emphasis and detail, there are few departures from long-standing fundamentals. CP continually assesses its style to keep it up to date and sensible. Suggestions for improvement are always welcome.

Patti Tasko, Editor

ptasko@cp.org

What is CP?

There is probably no other organization that has made such an ongoing contribution to Canadian life and yet has such a low public profile. Since CP was founded in 1917, the news agency has been instrumental in telling Canadians about themselves. It has shaped the way Canadians see the world. It has played a crucial role in the growth of the country's news industry.

Canadians who read a newspaper over morning coffee, listen to a radio newscast on the drive to work, check their Blackberrys for news headlines at lunch, watch the TV news before bed and pick up weekend sports scores on the Internet would likely be surprised to discover a lot of that information came from The Canadian Press.

News from CP and its broadcast division, Broadcast News, is carried by almost every daily newspaper in Canada. It is used by hundreds of radio and television stations, from national all-news, sports and business channels to tiny stations in remote corners of the country. The logo (CP) appears on web portals and sites. Hockey and basketball fans can see CP headlines on television tickers at the Air Canada Centre in Toronto. They are on screens in elevators. Reports are picked up by other news agencies that rely on CP to cover Canada for the world. They are e-mailed to Canada's newsmakers, who are well aware of CP's reach.

Some days the sweep of CP's reach is glaringly obvious. The day after the funeral of former prime minister Pierre Trudeau, readers in every major city in Canada saw a CP picture of his son Justin Trudeau, mourning beside his coffin, in their newspaper. Some days the reach creeps up on people. Average Canadians, quoted or photographed by CP for a story, are often amazed to discover the number of places where their face or name will turn up.

CP was created by newspaper publishers to provide a flow of news across the sparsely populated regions of the country. Before 1917, newspapers exchanged news within regional associations and received international news from The Associated Press on north-south telegraph circuits. But there was no ready means of sending news east and west across Canada.

Then the First World War came along, and publishers were desperate to receive news of Canada's troops in Europe. Part of CP's early financing was a $50,000 federal grant to pay for telegraph circuits linking the Maritimes to Quebec and Ontario and the Prairies to British Columbia. The government offered to help because of CP's potential to serve the cause of national unity during the war.

That funding ended in 1924 by mutual agreement and CP's founding publishers voted never again to risk the appearance of compromise by accepting government money for any news purpose.

What is CP? It is a news agency, co-operatively owned by the media companies that own Canada's daily newspapers. These 95 or so newspapers elect a board of directors that controls CP. They also pay fees to the agency based on circulation and contribute news of their area to the common pool.

Since its early days this exchange of news via CP has been at the heart of the co-operative. CP is the only major news agency in the world that uses voluntary newspaper contributions as a key ingredient in its news report.

How does the exchange work? The Montreal Gazette, for instance, takes on the responsibility of covering a major court case in its city for the co-operative. In return it gets coverage from the Halifax Chronicle-Herald about a waterfront strike. CP is the conduit, compiling reports from member papers and ensuring that the important news of the day is covered and delivered in time for deadlines that span six time zones.

From the beginning, CP has had reporters and editors based in bureaus across the country. But they cannot possibly cover the country to the extent that Canada's newspapers can, from Port Alberni on Vancouver Island to St. John's, N.L., from Whitehorse in the Yukon to Windsor, Ont. Add into this mix news stories shared by the hundreds of radio and television stations that are clients of CP and BN. The result is a Canadian news report that is unmatched for its depth, breadth, timeliness and diversity.

The CP report is not limited to Canadian news, but also includes full coverage from around the world. The bulk of the international report originates with The Associated Press. CP World Desk editors fight their way through a massive file of AP news every day, round-the-clock, looking for stories of particular interest to Canadians. A CP bureau in Washington as well as a network of stringers, supplement this report.

A French-language service was established in 1951. In addition to providing an important service to French-language members, this service also serves as an important pipeline of news from Quebec. The best elements of this are translated into English for CP members and the best elements of CP are translated into French for the Presse Canadienne service. This ensures that Quebecers are not isolated by language from important news from English Canada and that newspapers, radio and TV broadcasters in English Canada, likewise, are not isolated from important stories and issues in Quebec.

Since the early days of public and private radio, CP has served the broadcasting industry. An early task was preparing scripts for Lorne Greene and other well-known voices who read the latest dispatches from Second World War battlefronts over the fledgling Canadian Broadcasting Corp.

Currently, CP's Broadcast News provides service to private television and radio broadcasters as well as audio to Internet sites and wireless services. BN microphone flashes are a common sight at major events as material is collected for the hourly newscasts and other information programming.

On the technical side, in 1973 CP became the first news organization in Canada to make extensive use of word processors to write and edit stories. In the mid-1980s, CP and BN switched from land circuits to satellite for delivery of stories, photos and audio reports. In 1997 the news agency started delivering news reports over the Internet to member newspapers and commercial subscribers. The following year a French-language service was added "en ligne" as well.

Past generations of CP journalists who practised their craft to the click of Morse code and the beat of teletype machines would find the modern CP newsroom a strange beast indeed. But some things would still feel comfortably familiar. It continues to be an organization driven by a quest for first-rate journalism. CP's mission hasn't changed. The goal continues to be to keep Canadians informed and help them understand and experience their world more fully. CP tells people the story of their country, every day, in all forms and from all corners of the land. In the 21st century of the global village the stories of our nation are a cornerstone of who we are and will become.

President

Notes

Why CP style is the way it is

A new Internet domain may crack down on cybersquatting and offer more choice for web names.

Several words in that sentence would not have made sense to an average reader a generation ago. Most of today's readers would find the phrasing normal in a news report.

That's one of the reasons why stylebooks are needed. If the World Wide Web turns up in a business-page story and again on lifestyles pages, the capitalization should be the same in both cases. Otherwise, it is annoying and possibly confusing for the reader.

English is a fluid language, but it's bound by complicated rules of grammar. Working reporters and editors don't have time to research decisions on vocabulary and capitalization and grammar every time a problem arises. A stylebook presents such decisions in a logical, handy form.

Whimsy is found in every stylebook. But style decisions overall are based on sound reasons. Most are basic grammar and common sense, with the stylebook simply a reminder. Other decisions involve choosing from among a range of valid alternatives, and at that point a number of factors come into play.

Among the ones that have influenced CP style over the decades:

Preferences of Canadian newspapers

Newspapers own The Canadian Press and most of them follow CP style in their handling of local news. It's only common sense to accept their preferences. If there's an important style change being considered, the papers are consulted. The majority preference becomes CP style.

For example, CP became the first western news agency to drop the courtesy titles **Mr., Mrs., Miss** and **Ms.** from all copy. Over the years, the use of such titles had become erratic — sometimes used on news pages but not in sports sections, for instance. Most papers agreed the rules needed change, and the soundest course was to drop all such titles. Some papers continue to use them, either throughout the paper or in particular sections.

More recently, CP adopted the "our" spelling for words of more than one syllable in which the "u" is not pronounced. CP had written with **color** and **rigor** for 80 years, and felt the "or" spelling was an established Canadian option. But "our" was the spelling preferred by many readers and taught in most Canadian schools. A significant number of CP's member newspapers had already adopted the "our" spelling. A survey CP conducted showed that 77 per cent of its member newspapers wanted CP to use this style as well. So we started writing with **colour** and **rigour**.

The complete list of "our" words can be found in the *Stylebook's* companion volume, *Caps and Spelling.*

Consistency

A style that is full of exceptions is difficult to use. One goal of this stylebook is to keep exceptions to a minimum.

Maintaining consistency can be troublesome. New words crop up all the time, and often a certain style becomes commonplace – even if it is inconsistent with similar uses. That's why people write T-shirt, but e-mail. CP style tries to maintain consistency as much as it is possible given the influence of common usage.

Popular usage

News reporting is meant to inform the public, not to score points with language purists. Outdated expressions can get in the way of that goal. Some of the changes in the meaning of words may not be for the better, but if most readers are led to believe that **presently** means **right now**, rather than **soon**, there's no point in using the word in a news story and risking misunderstanding.

CP won't be the first to accept the misuse of a word, and occasionally we're a bit stubborn about changes that seem to debase the language. But eventually a misused form can take on a life of its own and CP bows to the inevitable. We have reluctantly accepted the word **gender** in such phrases as **gender politics** or **gender equality** although **sexual equality** makes more basic sense. (**Gender** is primarily the word used by grammarians to distinguish between masculine, feminine and neuter words; **sex** is what distinguishes males from females.)

Sensitivity

Today's perfectly normal word can be tomorrow's flagrant example of sexism, racism or other abuse. In particular, people who feel put upon by society are likely to reject labels that seem to limit their potential or lock them into hurtful self-images.

People who are identified by certain words (**cripple, housewife, Indian**) can easily believe that the language is insensitive and prefer another description (**disabled person, stay-at-home mom, aboriginal**). In time, those labels may also fall out of favour.

CP believes that people's preferences should be respected when new forms are adopted by a significant number of those concerned and become familiar to the general public. But we don't want to be faddish, accepting words for routine use that are so *sensitive* that they have little clear meaning left — expressions like **developmentally challenged**. Nor will we go along casually with new labels that are politically controversial among the people most concerned.

Words like **spokesman** and **chairman** cause resentment, understandably, when applied to women. CP uses **spokeswoman** and **chairwoman**, as well as such forms as **salesperson**, **chairperson** and **spokesperson** when the sex of the individual is unknown. But the clumsy term **alderperson** does not seem to have gained wide acceptance, so CP prefers an alternative such as **councillor**.

CP's goal is to carefully think out our style decisions and come to a decision that is agreeable to both the public and those who use our stylebooks. However, our main influence is readers and what works for them. We don't expect everyone to agree with all of our style decisions, but we do welcome input and feedback from everyone.

CP policies

Principles

When The Canadian Press was founded in 1917, it was for one reason: to serve the newspapers that owned it, and through them, the Canadian public. For decades, the only contact CP had with the public was through its member newspapers. But rapid changes in the communications industry have changed the way CP fulfils its mandate of keeping Canadians informed.

CP serves almost every daily newspaper in Canada, providing reliable and relevant news, photos and graphics. But beyond the traditional printed word, CP's role in new media continues to expand. Regardless of whether Canadians are getting their news from the Internet, cable TV or news tickers on all-news television channels, there's a good chance much of the information comes from The Canadian Press. CP is truly Canada's No. 1 source for news – in French and English. News gathering is an imprecise science, but CP's formula is the envy of other news services around the world: a dedicated staff in bureaus and correspondent points across the country and in London and Washington; a working partnership with member newspapers; a connection to hundreds of TV and radio newsrooms through Broadcast News; and stringers around the world.

There's a difference between providing information and telling Canadians what is happening in their vast country – and how events beyond our borders affect them. Context and perspective are fundamental parts of the CP report. It's the goal of all CP reporters and editors to focus on real people – not just institutions – to show in human terms how events affect our lives. It's a busy world out there so every CP story needs to convince the reader that they should devote the time to read it. If the story doesn't strive to be interesting or tell the reader why they should care, the page will be turned or the channel changed.

Although our role continues to evolve, the principles that guide our work are unchanged. Everything that we do must be honest, unbiased and unflinchingly fair. We deal with facts that are demonstrable, supported by sources that are reliable and responsible. We pursue with equal vigour all sides of a story.

Accuracy is fundamental. Discovery of a mistake calls for immediate correction. Corrections to stories already published or broadcast must not be grudging or stingy. They must be written in a spirit of genuinely wanting to right a wrong in the fairest and fullest manner.

Our work is urgent. Speed must be a primary objective of a news service committed to the deadlines of newspapers and broadcasters in six time zones. Online news has no deadlines – or more precisely, the deadline is right now. But being reliable is always more important than being fast.

Good taste is a constant consideration. Some essential news is essentially repellent. Its handling need not be.

Staff responsibility

Responsibility for upholding CP standards rests with our reporters, editors and supervisors. So much individuality is involved in reporting, writing and editing news that it is impossible to have precise rules covering every eventuality. Being guided by proven practices is the surest way of meeting the standards that Canadians have come to expect from CP.

Among the most important of these practices:

1. Investigate fully before transmitting any story or identifying any individual in a story where there is the slightest reason for doubt. When in doubt cut it out. But never make this an excuse for ditching an angle without thorough checking. The doubt must be an honest doubt, arrived at after examination of all the facts.

Conservative Leader Stephen Harper speaks to media outside the House of Commons in May 2005. Journalists will have a point of view, but it must not get in the way of balanced reporting.

(CP—Jonathan Hayward)

2. Cite competent authorities and sources as the origin of any information open to question. Have proof available for publication in the event of a denial.

3. Be impartial when handling any news affecting parties or matters in controversy. Give fair representation to all sides at issue.

4. Stick to the facts without editorial opinion or comment. Reporters' opinions are not wanted in CP copy. Their observations are. So are accurate backgrounding and authoritative interpretation essential to the reader's understanding of complicated issues.

5. Admit errors promptly, frankly. Public distrust of the media is profound and troubling. The distrust is fed by inaccuracy, carelessness, indifference to public sentiment, automatic cynicism about those in public life, perceived bias or unfairness and other sins suggesting arrogance.

6. CP can help overcome such public attitudes through scrupulous care for facts and unwavering dedication to fairness. We must not be quick to dismiss criticism and complaints, a trait journalists refuse to accept in others.

7. The power of news stories to injure can reach both the ordinary citizen and the corporate giant. CP's integrity and sensitivity demand that supervisors and staff respond sympathetically and quickly when an error has been made. It doesn't matter whether the complaint comes from a timid citizen acting alone or from a powerful figure's battery of lawyers.

8. Every story shown to be erroneous and involving a corrective must be drawn to the attention of supervisory staff. Each bureau is responsible for the copy it files whether it is written by its staff or by travelling staffers assigned to special events.

Ethical behaviour

Part of our responsibility as journalists is to ensure we don't do anything that demeans the craft or weakens our credibility. Because we deliver the bad news about politicians who turn dirty, caregivers who abuse their trust and business people who discard ethics for gain, we must observe stringent ethical practices, and be seen to be doing so.

It is impossible to raise all potential ethical challenges in this book. But the following guiding principles are offered in the spirit of wanting to advance, not restrain, our work.

1. Pride in yourself and in the practice of journalism nourishes ethical behaviour.

2. CP policy is to pay its way. Staff should not accept anything that might compromise our integrity or credibility.

3. CP does not pay newsmakers for interviews, to take their pictures or to film or record them.

4. CP reporters do not misrepresent themselves to get a story. They always identify themselves as journalists.

Impartiality

Impartiality is somewhat like exercise. You have to work out regularly to build tone and strength.

The best exercise for impartiality is to stop regularly and ask yourself: "Am I being as impartial, honest and fair as I can be?"

Some other guides to impartiality:

Parties in controversy, whether in politics or law or otherwise, receive fair consideration. Statements issued by conflicting interests merit equal prominence, whether combined in a single story or used at separate times.

But always try to get opposing sides for simultaneous publication.

If an attack by one group or person on another has been covered, any authoritative answer is also carried. If a proper source cannot be reached, say so, and keep trying.

When a comparative unknown expresses controversial views, question his or her expertise on the subject. If there is no expertise, or the individual does not have an official position that puts weight behind the views, consider carefully whether the report should be carried.

Quotations

Quotes are the lifeblood of any story. They put rosiness into the cheeks of the palest stories. They add credibility, immediacy and punch.

They can also bring grief to writers and editors who play loose with them. Some news organizations permit liberties with quotes. CP takes a somewhat stern approach to any tampering with just what was said.

In general, we quote people verbatim and in standard English. We correct slips of grammar that are obvious slips and that would be needlessly embarrassing. We remove verbal mannerisms such as *ah*'s, routine vulgarities and meaningless repetitions. Otherwise we do not revise quotations.

While we don't routinely use abnormal spellings and grammar to indicate dialects or mispronunciations, they can have a place in helping to convey atmosphere.

Cleaning up this quote from a concerned unionized fisherman would have taken some of the heart out of the story:

"We don't want our money took to Toronto and not spent on behalf of our members," said Eric Miller. "The few dollars that I makes, I want it spent on behalf of my family, my friends and my brothers and sisters in Newfoundland."

Quotes containing bafflegab are routinely paraphrased in plain English, no matter how eminent the speaker.

Other points to remember about handling quotes:

1. Getting exact quotes without shorthand or tape is not easy. When there is risk that a quote is not exact, for whatever reason, a paraphrase is safest.

2. When exactness is essential — if it's one person's word against another's — quote verbatim.

3. When a speaker uses what is obviously a wrong word, check back when possible. When a quote does not make sense, check back with the speaker or ditch it.

4. Misquotes result not only from tampering or carelessness. Failure to place a quote in context can have the same eroding effect on credibility. For instance: **"If our tax revenues allow it, I'll repave all secondary highways"** should not be parlayed into the bare reported statement that the speaker promised to repave all secondary highways.

Similarly, failure to indicate tone can skew a quote. A speaker's jocular comment may need to be reported with an explanatory **she said with a smile**. There are other occasions when the bare words benefit from addition of a brief description: **"I'm not guilty,"** **he said, glowering at the jury.**

5. When clear and concise, a full quote is preferred to a partial quote. But a partial quote can be useful for spicing a lead, setting off a controversial statement or giving the flavour of a speaker.

6. Make only cosmetic changes to quotations from a text: changing spelling and capitalization to CP style, for example.

7. If words are left out of a text or middle of a quotation, show the omission with an ellipsis. Note: **Ellipses are best avoided. Prefer other devices, such as paraphrases or partial quotes.**

8. Long bracketed explanations and paraphrases should not be inserted at the beginning or end of a quote.

Not: "(The new program) is imaginative, realistic and worth the time and money invested," Scott said.

But: The new program "is imaginative, realistic and worth the time and money invested," Scott said.

9. Guard against attributing one person's quote to several speakers.

Not: Most retailers surveyed condemned the new tax, saying that "it will mean working half a day a week for the government."

10. Do not include in a quote words that the speaker could not have spoken.

Not: Davis said he "was delighted that the prize is going to the American."

But: Davis said he was "delighted that the prize is going to the American."

Davis's words were "I'm (not was) delighted."

➤ See **Slang**, page 310.

11. Do not alter audio clips except to make sound clearer and reduce line noise. Within a clip, edit only to remove pauses and stumbles.

Language

A reminder to be careful with translations. We should not imply that someone is speaking English when he is not.

In interviews and speeches, make clear what language is being used unless it is obvious. At a news conference where both French and English are used, specify when French was the original language. When reporting the shouts of a crowd or the wording of protest signs that are in other languages, specify that a translation is involved.

Readers are entitled to know when a direct or indirect quote is based on translation rather than the exact words used.

Obscenity

Casual obscenity, blasphemy and vulgarity are not wanted in the news report. Four-letter words shouted from a crowd or muttered by an angry demonstrator add nothing useful to a story. CP's news stories are used by a wide variety of media, and some, especially broadcasters who may rip and read a CP story, do not want obscenities in copy.

There are few exceptions. A prominent figure who uses obscene language in a public situation is one. An interview subject may use obscenities in such a way that leaving them out would paint a false picture. Or a quote that includes a vulgarity might be the most effective way to connote certain emotions. But these are the exceptions, not the rule. Always consider other ways of getting across this element of the story before resorting to the use of obscenities.

Obscenities or vulgar language should always be flagged with a **Caution note** that contains the obscenity:

CAUTION: Note language (fuck) in para 3.

Note: When such a note is required on CP copy moving to broadcasters, include it in the **Update** line so it appears on the broadcast wire.

When an obscenity or vulgarity must be reported, do not use the prissy device of replacing some letters of the offensive words with hyphens, or use an euphemism such as **effing** or **f-word**. Put the questionable language in a separate paragraph that can be readily deleted by editors who do not want to use it.

Sensitive subjects

Potential for offence lurks in every news story. Age, race, sex, disabilities, religion – all are often pertinent to the news but must be handled thoughtfully.

Use fairness, sensitivity and good taste when identifying age, colour, creed, nationality, personal appearance, religion, sex and any other heading under which a person or group may feel slighted.

Aboriginal Peoples

In Canada, there are status (or reserve) Indians, non-status Indians (living outside reserves), Métis (people of mixed European and native origin) and Inuit. Collectively, they are known variously as Aboriginal Peoples, original peoples, aboriginals, indigenous peoples, the First Nations (for those who live on reserves) and other variations.

Some points concerning Aboriginal Peoples:

1. CP uses uppercase for **Aboriginal Peoples**, which includes all Indian, Métis and Inuit people in Canada. **First Nations** is also uppercase. Other variations – **indigenous people, aboriginals** (except for Aboriginals of Australia), **native peoples** – are lowercase.

2. In all references, be guided by the preference of those concerned.

3. Use **Indian** with discretion. Some people object to it because it originated with the European explorers' misconception that they had landed in India. Others, especially status Indians, prefer it to be used.

4. Use **native** advisedly. **Aboriginal** and **First Nations** are more specific and are preferred by many in the community.

5. Where reasonable, prefer the actual name of the community – Cree, Mohawk, Blackfoot, Ojibwa – to a generality. For band names, use the spelling the band prefers, which is also the spelling used by the federal government.

6. The word tribe in its original sense was reserved for primitive peoples. Some natives use it casually and it need not be entirely avoided. But **community, people, nation, band, language group** are alternatives.

➤ See **Aboriginal Peoples**, page 199.

Age

Often age is relevant as part of a personal description or for identification. Ages also help readers to relate to people in news stories.

In general, give a person's age rather than imprecise and possibly derogatory terms such as **senior citizen, retiree, elderly** or **middle-aged.**

Put the age in the lead only when it is significant, such as in obituaries or when an 85-year-old is cycling across the country, or when a three-year-old child is missing. Guard against the formula lead — **a 30-year-old dentist; a 52-year-old fisherman; a 23-year-old convict** . . .

Writing **Mario Lalonde, 30,** is usually preferable to the more cumbersome **30-year-old Mario Lalonde.**

If age is missing for an obituary, give an indication of it from the person's activities, such as year of graduation or year of retirement.

Infant describes a baby that is no more than a few months old; a **baby** is a child who is not yet walking. **Toddler** describes a child around the age of two, while a **preschooler** is between the ages of three and five. Males up to 16 are called **boys** and females to that age are **girls.** Use a phrase like **young people** for those of both sexes who are somewhat older.

First names may be used in subsequent references for those under 18, except in sports stories.

Youth in general includes both sexes: **the youth of Canada.** Applied to individuals, it usually means males. Try to avoid the latter use.

Disabilities

Be accurate, clear and sensitive when describing a person with a disability, handicap, illness or disease. They are people first; their disability is only one part of their humanity and most would say it is the least important part.

Mention a disability only if it is pertinent. Never dismiss someone with an unqualified **disabled, crippled** or the like. Write **Romanov, whose hands are twisted with arthritis,** . . . And perhaps indicate to what extent a person has overcome a disability or how she copes with it: **Girushi uses a wheelchair once she leaves her studio.**

Be specific. **Afflicted with** suggests pain and suffering. It doesn't always apply. Nor does **suffering.** People who use wheelchairs are not necessarily **confined** to them. **Crippling** can be a temporary or permanent condition. People may be **deaf, slightly deaf** or **hard of hearing; blind** or have **poor eyesight.** A **patient** is someone under a doctor's care or in hospital. **Victim** connotes helplessness. A child who is **mentally handicapped** (slow) is not necessarily **mentally disturbed** (ill). Epileptics have **seizures,** not **fits.**

While it is important to be specific for clarity, there are also some terms that may be used in the scientific community that are not as acceptable in casual use. **Mentally retarded** is a valid medical description, yet many dislike it because of the schoolyard insults associated with the term.

Don't define people by their disorders: **the disabled, the blind, the handicapped.** Writing **people with disabilities** emphasizes the human beings and not the disabilities.

Race and ethnicity

CP news reports should reflect the ethnic diversity of Canada in a natural way, free of explicit or unconscious racism.

Identify a person by race, colour, national origin or immigration status only when it is truly pertinent. It is appropriate to report that a woman facing deportation is Polish. Similarly, the victim of hate mail may be referred to as a Jew. A full description, including but not limited to colour, may be used if a person wanted by police is at large.

The appearance of racial minorities in news reports should not be confined to accounts of cultural events, racial tension or crime. A Korean shopkeeper's reaction to a sales tax is just as valid as a Scottish stockbroker's. Include comments from various groups in matters of public interest such as federal taxes or national surveys on general topics.

Remember that what is obvious to a university-educated Christian of British stock might need explanation for persons from a variety of other backgrounds. And it should not be taken for granted that a Muslim ceremony needs explanation while a Roman Catholic mass does not.

Race and ethnicity are pertinent when it motivates an incident or when it helps explain the emotions of those in confrontation. Thus references to race or ethnic background are relevant in reports of racial controversy, immigration difficulties, language discussions and so on.

When an incident cuts across ethnic lines, say so, as when a sizable number of Canadian-born individuals join Chinese immigrants demonstrating against immigration procedures.

That a man found guilty of shoplifting is, say, an aboriginal is usually irrelevant and he should not be identified as such.

Race is pertinent in reporting an accomplishment unusual in a particular race: for example, if a Canadian of Chinese origin is named to the Canadian Football Hall of Fame.

Beware of playing up inflammatory statements at the expense of the main story. Be certain that a spokesman indeed speaks for a community or organization, and give a brief description of that organization, its aims and number of members.

Don't always turn to the same minority spokespeople and organizations for reaction. This can give unwarranted standing to groups that don't necessarily reflect the full range of views of their communities.

Let people speak for themselves. In particular, avoid stories about aboriginal people in which all or most of the talk is provided by white bureaucrats.

Arguing that humour was intended is no defence for a racial slur.

Use racially derogatory terms like **Paki** and **nigger** only when part of a direct quotation and when essential to the story. Flag such a story:

CAUTION: Note racial slur in para 15.

Names of races

1. Capitalize the proper names of nationalities, peoples, races and tribes.

Aboriginal Peoples, Arab, Caucasian, French-Canadian, Inuit, Jew, Latin, Negro, Asian, Cree

2. Note that **black** and **white** do not name races and are lowercase.

3. The term **black** is acceptable in all references in Canada and the United States. In the United States **African-American** is also used; in Canada **African-Canadian** is used by some people but not by others. In the United States there is a National Association for the Advancement of Colored People, usually identified as the NAACP.

4. There is usually no need to use hyphenated descriptions such as **Polish-Canadian** or **Jamaican-Canadian**, given they may put an inappropriate emphasis on the person's ethnic background. But these descriptions can be used if the individual prefers it and it is relevant.

Sexism

Treat the sexes equally and without stereotyping. A woman's marital or family status — single, married, divorced, grandmother — is pertinent only to explain a personal reference or to round out a profile. The test always is: Would this information be used if the subject were a man?

Referring to a woman gratuitously as **attractive, leggy** or **well-endowed** is as inappropriate as describing a man as **a hunk, hairy-chested** or **having great buns**. But there are stories beyond the routine in which it is appropriate to describe someone's appearance.

Never assume that **a family of four** always consists of a man, a woman and their two children. Don't write as if every **married couple** consists of a man and a woman.

Shoppers (not **housewives**) are paying more.

When writing in general terms prefer **police officer** or **constable** to **policeman**, **firefighter** to **fireman**, **mail carrier** to **mailman**, **flight attendant** to **stewardess**.

But if sex is pertinent, masculine and feminine forms are proper: **postman**, **policewoman**, **air steward**.

Use only established feminine variants ending in **-woman**.

Write **businesswoman**, **Frenchwoman**, **spokeswoman** but not **journeywoman**, **linewoman**, **defencewoman**.

Avoid other feminine variants unless they are so well established that a substitute rings false.

Thus it is proper to describe a woman as a **hostess**, **masseuse**, **princess**, **seamstress** or as an **author**, **comedian**, **Jew**, **murderer**, **poet**, **sculptor**. **Actor** and **actress** are both acceptable.

Avoid cumbersome coinages like **alderperson**. **Chairperson**, **salesperson** and **spokesperson** are in general use and can be used.

There is not an entirely satisfactory substitute for **fisherman**, although **fisher**, **fish harvester**, **fish industry worker**, **fishing licensees** or the phrase **fishermen and women** are all possibilities.

Some readers find the use of **he (him, his)** as a word of common or indeterminate gender to be sexist. **His or her** and the like can be used but may prove awkward. In that case reword the sentence if possible. Instead of: **Whoever is promoted will have $50 added to his or her pay**, write: **Whoever is promoted will get a $50 raise**. As a last resort, **they (them, their)** is an increasingly acceptable alternative to **he (him, his)**.

Often a plural construction solves the sex problem: **Retired officers are not usually referred to by their former rank**. **Not**: **A retired officer is not usually referred to by his or her former rank**.

The generic **man** is regarded by some as excluding women. Instead of **man** or **mankind**, you can write **people**, **human beings**, **humanity**, **human race**. Alternatives to **manmade** include **artificial**, **constructed**, **manufactured**, **synthetic**. But don't get carried away. To write **human energy** or **human resources** to avoid **manpower**, or **person-eating tiger** to avoid **man-eating tiger** is being hypersensitive.

Michael Hendricks, left, and Rene Leboeuf celebrate their marriage iin a Montreal courtroom in April 2004. The terms husband and wife can exclude some married couples.

(CP—Paul Chiasson)

Other issues

1. **Gay** is usually preferred as an alternative for homosexual men and is also commonly used for women, although **lesbian** is preferred by many women. Follow an individual's preference when it is known. Use **sexual orientation,** not **sexual preference**; gay people do not view their sexuality as an option. Don't refer to a gay **lifestyle** or suggest that the majority of homosexuals routinely live unorthodox lives; most don't. Language is still evolving on what to call the individuals in a same-sex relationship or marriage. Follow their preference if it is known. **Partner, husband** and **wife** are all acceptable options depending on preference.

2. When writing about abortion, the terms **pro-life** and **pro-choice** can be used if they are preferred by the person or organization involved. Be aware, however, that pro-life also includes those opposed to euthanasia. When writing about this subject in a general way, it is better to use a specific, neutral phrase, such as **abortion-rights advocates** or **opponents of abortion**.

Sources

Cultivating knowledgeable sources who can provide the background and insight necessary for delivering a complete story is the trademark of the excellent reporter.

Without good sources — be they the town clerk in the small northern mining town, or the fast-moving executive assistant to a cabinet minister — CP cannot hope to craft a comprehensive daily picture of life in Canada and the world.

Getting and keeping good sources is hard work. It involves patient telephone work plus breaking free from our desks to get out and meet people.

CP reporters, editors and supervisors are encouraged to pull back from the front lines occasionally to spend time with people who know what's happening in the world beyond our own limited horizons. Special efforts should be made to develop contacts in non-urban areas, ethnic communities and other places beyond the bright spotlight of big-city journalism.

It is the job of journalists to meet a variety of people. We should all take a special interest in people and listen to what they have to say. Developing good sources is a way of living to the committed journalist.

When dealing with sources, remember that many people are not used to dealing with the media. Ensure they understand they are being quoted, and their words or picture may appear in many newspapers.

A cardinal rule with sources is to avoid close personal involvement. There is nothing wrong with social contact with sources, but close personal relationships can lead to conflicts of interest.

Unnamed sources

The public interest is best served when someone with facts or opinions to make public is identified by the press by name and qualifications. Readers need to see named sources to help them decide on the credibility and importance of the information.

Regular use of unnamed sources weakens our news reports. CP should be firm in discouraging the quoting of sources who want to hide their identities. Leaks, especially in government and business, are sometimes designed to undermine new policies or to damage rivals.

There are of course many situations when people with information important to the public insist on concealing their identity for understandable reasons. CP would be foolish, and in some cases irresponsible, never to grant anonymity in news copy, but it can show leadership in working to stop misuse of unnamed sources.

Some guidelines:

1. Push sources hard to understand that putting their names to what they say is important to freedom of information. This is especially important in dealings with public servants who demand anonymity in routine circumstances.

2. Beat reporters should regularly test the willingness of their sources to be named.

3. Information from unnamed sources should be confirmed whenever possible by one or two other sources (always respecting the original source's anonymity, of course). Try to get supporting documentation. One-source stories are rarely acceptable these days.

4. Reporters writing stories containing unnamed sources must be able to demonstrate: (a) The information is of genuine public interest; (b) The information can be verified by at least one other source, even if unnamed; (c) The source is known to them; (d) There is no real possibility that the source is using CP for selfish purposes; (e) Normal standards of fairness and balance are followed.

5. Bureau supervisors must be consulted before a story with unnamed sources is released. Names of sources will be given to Head Office when requested.

6. Direct quotes should be avoided unless the actual words have unusual significance. This is especially important when opinion is being expressed and the sources might be tempted to use bolder language than if they were being named.

7. If the source is presenting one side of a controversy, the opposing side's views must be sought and presented fairly in the original story.

8. Do not say a person declined comment if this person is also an unnamed source in the story.

We don't have to tie every bit of information to a named source. Naming the airline employee who hands out a list of dead and injured in a plane crash adds nothing to the story. The government official who provides routine background or uncontestable fact need not always be named.

But always note names, just in case. And a reminder that prudent reporters always store their notes and tapes in safekeeping for one year at least. In extremely important matters, tapes and notes should be kept indefinitely.

Government officials often insist on anonymity at information briefings, such as in the locked room where reporters write federal or provincial budget stories in advance of delivery. CP abides by such restrictions if necessary, but will not go along with deliberate misrepresentation, such as when a cabinet minister wishes to pass as a civil servant.

Statements from such briefings should not be passed off as general knowledge or undisputed fact. The reader should be told as much as possible about the source and the circumstances should be described.

It is not unheard of for a source to give information confidentially, then deny it by name. If CP feels obliged to carry such a denial, it will identify the original source as the person denying it, provided we are confident the original story accurately reflected the source's information. Consult Head Office before proceeding.

Ethics and sources

When we do promise anonymity we must scrupulously respect that pledge. But it cannot be absolute and it is only fair to tell potential sources so. The courts may require reporters to disclose sources.

Verbal contracts with sources are enforceable in court. Make sure both you and your source understand precisely what that agreement is before you get the information. Do not make promises you cannot keep.

For instance, you can promise not to identify the source in your story and to not willingly make the identity known beyond your employer. You cannot promise to protect the source from any damages that result if the name does become known, through accident or through court order.

CP will not require or advise an employee to balk at the court's direction. It will provide counsel who can advise the employee and who will seek to persuade the court that the public interest does not require disclosure, or who will plead for a closed hearing.

Sources also should know that reporters must identify their sources to their supervisors. This could include anyone from a bureau News Editor to the President. This does not mean that everyone in the chain of command must know. A staffer in a delicate circumstance may go directly to the Editor-in-Chief or the President.

In extreme circumstances the President might have to inform the Chairman of the Board of a CP source because the member newspapers are legally responsible with CP for the CP news they publish.

If a source must be disclosed beyond the level of the President, senior management will make a concerted effort to advise the originating staffer in advance.

There may be cases where 100 per cent confidentiality is essential on an extremely sensitive news tip and CP is unable to confirm the information with other sources. In such a case senior management will consult the originating staffer. If the problem is insurmountable, CP will not carry the material.

Good reporting dictates that readers be given as much information as possible about the unnamed source's background. This helps readers judge why the story is worth their attention. Qualifications ascribed to the unnamed source must never be misleading. A bit of thought should produce a description helpful to the reader yet protective of the source.

It may be necessary to consult the source about the wording of such a description so the story can inform the reader without revealing the identity.

Other details should be clarified with sources. May all material be used, or must some be treated as only for the reporter's information and guidance (called *background* or *deep background* in the jargon of officialdom)? Are direct quotes permissible or only paraphrases?

Some phrases like **off the record** can have different meanings to different people. Be sure everyone is operating under the same meanings. Consult Head Office when someone proposes unusual restraints.

Some informants may provide information that may be attributed by name, then insist on anonymity for additional information. Attributing this confidential information is tricky: it would be misleading to specify that it came from someone else (**another Finance Department official, who asked for anonymity, said**). Usually it is preferable to rely on phrasing such as **It was also learned.**

Other guides to dealing with unnamed sources:

1. Don't use the unnamed sources of others as if they were CP's. Unnamed sources in stories picked up from newspapers or broadcast should be specifically tied to the paper or broadcaster: **The News quoted an unidentified official in the Energy Department as saying** . . .

2. Stories should specify that the source requested anonymity and explain why.

3. Spokespeople and officials should not be confused. A spokesperson puts forward the position of others; an official actually helps formulate that position.

4. Where a fictitious name is being used — for instance, in the case of a juvenile in trouble or a family on welfare — or where a composite person is created to represent a variety of similar individuals, the artifice must be explained promptly. It is a device that cannot be used often without losing impact.

Involving Head Office

Stories from unnamed sources pack much potential for harm against an individual or an institution. Thoughtless journalism damages careers, personal lives, companies and public faith in the media. It also can hurt CP's reputation and its legal position in any suits that might arise.

Safeguards have been designed to help ensure that major stories with potential for harm get plenty of thoughtful evaluation before being rushed into print.

Bureaus with major news breaks involving unnamed sources and with legal and ethical implications must follow these steps:

1.   Have counsel review the story.

2.   After legal checks, the bureau supervisor must set up a telephone conference with the Editor-in-Chief and a Main Desk editor.

3.   The conference will answer questions such as:

(a) Who are the sources? How credible are they? What motives exist for a leak of information? Can further verification be obtained?

(b) What public good will the story serve? What are the legal risks? What ethical considerations are involved?

4.   Every opportunity to respond must be given to the person or institution involved. Where conscientious effort does not produce a response, the story must detail the attempts made and the reasons why no response was provided.

A final caution: The source who does not want to be named in copy will rarely be available for CP's defence in the event of court action. This could leave us with no defence and lacking any ability to prove what we distributed for public consumption.

Describing unnamed sources

News sources given anonymity should be identified as specifically as possible.

Sources said is bare bones and lacks credibility. Also don't use the hackneyed or meaningless phrases **political observers** and **senior officials** and adjectives like **key, informed, veteran**.

Use specifics that give readers reason to read and believe the story: **An industry source who has been involved in the negotiations, a west European diplomat familiar with the case, a Finance Department official who worked on the draft.**

Internet sources

The Internet can be a quick source for a vast array of information in the form of raw data, official records and e-mail.

There is no special protection when reporting information obtained online. And online sources can easily lie about their identity. Verify information obtained online just as vigorously as that obtained from other sources.

Make sure the domain type (.edu, .gov, .com) is appropriate for the information provided on the website. Sites set up by professional groups are generally more reliable than personal ones. Sources for information should be clearly stated. Check to make sure the information is current.

The same copyright rules apply to material from websites as traditional print publications. Material from websites must be fully credited when paraphrased and enclosed in quotation marks when carried word for word. Guard against accidentally cutting and pasting words that are not your own into copy without proper attribution.

Get permission from the source before publishing quotations from e-mail. Specify in the story that the quote came from an e-mail.

Material from websites must be fully credited. Stick to authoritative sites.

Diverse sources

A balanced news report will provide a full range of voices and perspectives. Comments from these groups should not be limited to particular "special interest" topics such as child care or multiculturalism, but also the economy, sports, science, the law and all other news areas. Reporters should make a conscious effort to make sure their lists of sources include people that represent the diverse Canadian population.

Taste and tough calls

The media should do their work with compassion, good taste and respect for individual privacy. On the other hand, some media are only too happy to feed the appetite from some segments of the public for gore and salacious detail.

How far to go in informing the public is a dilemma faced every day.

Do we publish the photos of people jumping off the top floors of the burning World Trade Center? Some newspapers did, arguing that the dramatic illustrations made the enormity of the tragedy real on a human level. Others did not, arguing the pictures were just too horrific.

Some editors considered photos of people jumping off the World Trade Center on Sept. 11, 2001, too horrific to publish. Others used them as a graphic representation of the terror of those trapped in the towers.

(AP Photo)

Were the bounds of decency overstepped by publishing the photos of U.S. soldiers abusing Iraqi prisoners at the Abu Ghraib prison in Baghdad?

Was it offensive to publish pictures of the burned bodies of four foreigners hung from a bridge in Iraq? Was there any journalistic justification for carrying photos showing body parts strewn on the ground after the bombing of a train in Spain?

What about republishing an editorial cartoon that many Muslims consider an insult to their religion but that was also the catalyst for violent protests?

These are tough calls, with strongly felt opinions on each side.

At CP we approach each tough call thoughtfully, relying on our experience, good taste and news judgment to help us make the right decision. We weigh carefully what the public needs to know and wants to know against what some might consider repugnant.

CP acts as both retailer and wholesaler of news, and this can sometimes influence how such decisions are made. We reach the public directly through some of our services, such as CP Online and Command News, our public database. Here, our decisions directly affect what is seen and we must act accordingly. We also provide material to newspapers and expect that their staff will apply their own standards before deciding whether to publish it. We must not act as their censors, rejecting material based on standards that are more stringent than they, or their reading public, are willing to accept.

That said, it is our job to select and edit, and we must not abandon journalistic standards and principles on the premise that the final gatekeepers are other editors.

Some guidelines:

1.   An individual's grief is private. CP respects privacy and does not exploit grief to enhance the news.

2.   Before covering any funeral, we must ask ourselves: What possible important information will we gain for the public by intruding on this intensely private event?

➤ See **Obituaries**, page 68.

3.   Flag questionable stories and photos with a **Caution** note that the material might offend some readers.

CAUTION: Note contents in paras 5-8 may be considered offensive.

4.   When dealing with grieving sources, be respectful and understanding. Don't push your way in. Most people are willing to share their thoughts in situations involving grief, provided there is legitimate public interest. Don't ask people how they feel about a loss.

5.   Public interest must also be carefully weighed when deciding whether to publish the identity of a victim. Details of some crimes are so graphic that naming the victim can only cause more anguish to the innocent party. This can be especially harmful when publishing the victim's name serves no public purpose and adds nothing to the story.

Terrorism, hostage-takings

No news story is worth someone's life. Going for the scoop at any cost when lives are at stake belongs to a time long past.

Police officers surround a man who has taken a woman at gunpoint in front of Union Station in Toronto during rush-hour. CP has a clear policy on handling breaking news on hostage-takings.

(CP—Derek Oliver)

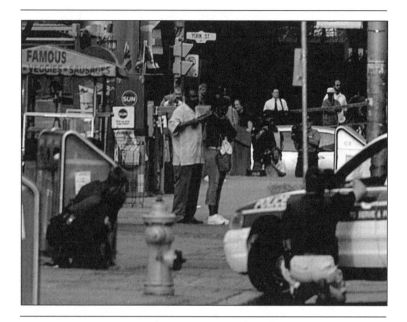

That's why we treat terrorist incidents and hostage-takings with extreme caution: They are life-and-death situations.

We have a responsibility to report the news but we have an even greater responsibility to ensure that our actions in news-gathering and reporting do not endanger human lives.

We do not want to become an open publicity line for lawbreakers or give unwitting support to destructive or violent causes.

Some guidelines:

1.   Notify police immediately when you receive a phone call, fax or note about an unpublicized hostage-taking or other threatening act. Make all information available to police.

2.   Do not move a story before checking a senior editorial supervisor at Head Office.

3.   If the story is approved, write that the information was given to **a news organization** without naming CP. Naming CP would risk having it become an outlet for terrorist publicity.

4.   Never telephone the terrorists or their hostages without the approval of a senior editorial supervisor at Head Office. If approval is received, consult the same supervisor again before

moving a story.

5.   Do not detail police or security countermeasures or any other information that might aid the terrorists.

6.   We will not tailor or distribute demands or platforms from organizations without Head Office approval. Head Office will not give approval without consulting police or government, or both.

7.   Translate the language of terrorists and police for readers: use plain English such as **note** and **kill** for **communique** and **execute**.

8.   Terrorism is an international phenomenon, and there can be pressure on CP to match extensive coverage provided by American and other foreign networks or news agencies. Carefully weigh the need to inform the public against the risk of encouraging more such acts. Consult supervisors about the quantity of material moved, especially on services that go directly to the public such as cable and CP Online, and the detail that should be provided.

9. Photo coverage from Canada and abroad should be monitored carefully to ensure that terrorists are not being glamorized, that victims are not being endangered and that the incidents are not being sensationalized.

10. News of ongoing hostage-taking or other terrorist incidents in Canada should not be transmitted on cable, broadcast services or CP Online without the approval of a senior supervisor, to guard against the possibility that such reports are being monitored by those involved.

11. Keep members and clients informed through advisories when these policy restraints affect coverage of an incident.

Defining terrorism

For decades the United Nations has been attempting to agree on what exactly the term should mean. The events of Sept. 11, 2001, put the issue on front pages. Slamming hijacked passenger jets into office towers seems to be accepted by almost everyone as terrorism. But there are often discrepancies in the way the media define and interpret other activities. Sometimes the word **terrorist** is used; other times **militant**, **guerrilla** or even **freedom fighter**. The perceptions of an activity can certainly be influenced by the choice of language – "One person's terrorist is another person's freedom fighter," as the saying goes.

Most definitions of terrorism incorporate the idea that it involves the use of violence or threat of violence to attain political, ideological or religious goals. Some specify that it is perpetuated against civilian, not military, targets. For journalists, the best advice is to be specific in the choice of terms used, and to guard against automatically labelling one side the terrorists, which makes the other side automatically the good guys. We do not shy away from the word **terrorist**, but we do use it with caution. There are always more neutral words available. Terms such as **bombers, gunmen** and **killers** also offer the advantage of being more specific.

Scare stories

The number of terror scare stories took a quantum leap after Sept. 11, 2001 – buildings evacuated, border points closed, flights cancelled, sometimes over such things as a package left unattended. Many of these incidents were not news.

Before treating such a story as news, ask:

1. Is there anything to the scare? If an office building is cleared for a suspicious package that turns out to be someone's forgotten lunch, then there is no story. If the suspicious package turns out to contain a dangerous substance, then there is likely a story. Wait to see which it is.

2. Is the reaction to a scare such as a bomb threat newsworthy in itself? A plant being evacuated for a short time is not news. An airport that is shut down for hours is.

Internet viruses

The reality of our wired world means Internet viruses, or even the threat of them, can cause widespread concern among Canadians who depend on computers to live their lives. News organizations can provide a valuable service in ensuring reports on new viruses are distributed quickly. This reporting should be done without glorifying the cyberterrorists who create these viruses. The same rules for reporting on other supposed threats apply to coverage of Internet viruses. Stories should only be carried if there is proof that a virus poses an unusual or significant threat.

General

Analyses

The CP News Analysis tests the best qualities that reporters and editors can bring to the news report.

The writer must know the subject intimately to give the reader an informed, intelligent and reasoned assessment of the issues involved. Readers look to the CP News Analysis for a clear and unbiased understanding of what has happened or may happen – and why.

An analysis cannot be done off the cuff. It demands careful forethought and discussion with a number of outside experts. Familiarity and comfort with the underlying issues is a must for the writer.

Most important: an analysis is not a soapbox. It can focus on a single perspective or point of view, but that perspective must be dispassionate and logical. Opposing views must not be neglected.

Some guidelines:

1.   The CP News Analysis is usually built around a single thesis: the new tax will have little effect on consumer spending; the Opposition leader's staff is hurting her image. The thesis is supported by material marshalled in logical order. Objections can be noted, experts cited and secondary angles explored a bit. But the analysis should never lose sight of the main theme by jumbling it with distractions.

2.   The analysis should open the reader's eyes, not belabour the obvious. Worthwhile analyses can be built on an unconventional viewpoint, a perspective that hasn't been explored much in the past, a prediction that seems calm when others are confused or even hysterical.

3.   The analysis should strike the right balance and tone in the first paragraph. It should not be cute or hyper. Get right to the point:

CP News Analysis
By Bruce Cheadle

OTTAWA (CP) — When it's raining abuse, maintain a sunny disposition.

Conservative Leader Stephen Harper stuck to his playbook in Monday night's federal election debate, striking a world-wearing, good-natured pose under a barrage of criticism from Liberal Leader Paul Martin.

In a spirited debate marked by sharp exchanges among all four party leaders, Harper was notable for his stubborn grin and calm demeanour.

4. The CP News Analysis is not a substitute for the CP Backgrounder. The analysis focuses more on perspective than on factual background while the backgrounder leans more toward straight-ahead treatment of the major issues in a complex news story.

5. Analyses do not float a writer's pet theory. They do not pass judgment. They do not offer the writer's solutions. These are CP News Analyses and writers should consider every line of them from that perspective. CP must be able to stand behind every word of every analysis. That means editorializing — or anything that can be construed as editorializing — is out.

Unacceptable: The question that Liberals asked, so ineffectually, during an eight-week campaign suddenly is now pertinent to every Canadian.

Acceptable: The question that Liberals asked, and was so often dismissed, during an eight-week campaign suddenly is now pertinent to every Canadian.

Never try to build a case with adjectival powder when mortar in the form of facts and thoughtful opinion is lacking. Keep digging or abandon the story as a lost cause.

6. Keep loaded phrases and words out of analyses. They can turn a sound argument into instant rhetoric — and send a reader away.

Unacceptable: The decision to impose the GST during a recession was based strictly on political considerations, but it will haunt government candidates in the next election. (Two errors: CP is speculating on motivation and CP is making a hard prediction.)

Acceptable: Opposition MPs see pure political strategy behind the decision to impose the GST two years before an election even if it worsens the recession. Among government MPs, there is fear that even two years won't be long enough to soften voters' anger about the new tax. (The information is the same, but the sources for it are people in a position to say.)

7. Many analyses lend themselves to human touches. In a piece dealing with a major corporate shakeup, for example, a reader might wonder what elements in a new chief executive officer's background particularly qualify her for the top job. Who are the political winners and losers in a federal throne speech? What is the likely impact of a cabinet shuffle on the new or shifted ministers' prospects in the next election?

8. The one-voice *analysis* has no place in the CP news report. Instead, analyses should attempt to synthesize opinion and be as well sourced as news stories. They should give the reader a

sense of the sources who have been consulted, even if they must be unnamed. In an analysis on aboriginal issues, for example, it makes a big difference whether the issues are looked at through the eyes of academics or aboriginals themselves.

9.   Avoid over-attribution — a constant **he said, she said**. Often a general line early in an analysis can help.

> . . . **interviews with several senior Conservative party members.**

This gives the reader a sense that the writer has done his homework.

10. The CP writer's own observations and conclusions can be helpful in shaping some analyses. For example, a reporter who has covered a major environmental story from its beginnings to a key development months later should have the background and understanding to assess the situation fairly and from all perspectives. More often, however, the analysis flows from exhaustive research, an uncluttered understanding of the issues involved and solid contact with sources on all sides of those issues.

11. Analyses should be written as close as possible to the news event to heighten their impact and increase play.

12. A writer assigned to an analysis on a fixed time event, such as an election night, should not be assigned other duties. He or she will require an uncluttered mind (and desk) to concentrate on the event and its meaning for readers.

In these cases, it should usually be possible to rough out a couple of potential analyses based on different outcomes. If, for example, it appears possible that a minority government could be elected, some obvious questions could be explored in advance. How will the leading party hold power? What alliances might be made? How will the minority status affect the ruling party's election promises? What has been the experience of other minority governments? Is another election likely soon?

13. No analysis should be distributed without being seen by a senior supervisor such as a News Editor or Bureau Chief.

14. Copy should be slugged **CP News Analysis**. There should always be a double keyword slug — one word indicating the subject, the other identifying the piece as an analysis. The label **CP News Analysis** is intended to be publishable. It goes directly above the writer's byline and below the headline.

FedElxn-Analysis

Tory minority set to start work on changing Canada's political culture

CP News Analysis
By Bruce Cheadle

OTTAWA (CP) — . . .

CP Backgrounders

When it's time to pull a maze of news threads together or to stand back from a particularly confusing story, the CP Backgrounder is the vehicle of choice — and a welcome friend to the reader.

Above all, the CP Backgrounder gives the reader the answers to basic questions: What's really going on here? What does it mean to me and my families and my neighbours?

CP Backgrounders differ from CP News Analyses. Essentially, the analysis builds a structure of interpretation upon a foundation of factual material. The backgrounder focuses on the foundation stones through an orderly assembly of factual detail and perspective.

The backgrounder provides historical context, sets out the whys and wherefores of a complicated issue in the news, explores legal questions or lists the pocketbook impact of the development under review.

Where appropriate, the backgrounder will also quote knowledgeable authorities — or everyday people with first-hand experience in similar circumstances — about future implications for the lives of readers.

A strong sense of a key player's human side is usually needed to give the reader an understanding of the personalities involved.

There is no practical limit to the kinds of situations that can be served by a well-thought-out backgrounder:

• How researchers are exploring Parkinson's disease after actor Michael J. Fox reveals he has it.

• How Prairie farmers are coping with a string of bad luck: drought, debt, coyotes and grasshoppers.

• How the premier has pulled her party together at the last minute to head into an election, with the story focusing on her persuasive personality and political savvy.

• Why some major corporations are lopping off subsidiaries after years of bigger-is-better thinking.

• What's behind a new NHL rule on face masks, reviewing a rash of facial injuries from a doctor's perspective.

Effective backgrounders can often be worked up on matters that might otherwise receive only passing attention in the spot news report.

An example:

Business interests, local residents and nature lovers are locked in a battle over a proposed tourism development in the North. What is at stake? Why are the various sides in conflict? How have the battle lines been drawn?

The story could include interesting sketches of people on each side of the dispute, description and history of the area being fought over and some sense of the values being promoted — a rare breeding ground for song birds versus jobs in a high unemployment area, for example.

The writing approach to such stories is as wide open as the imagination of the writer. It often helps to focus on a specific element in a many-sided situation or on a single human being directly involved. The story should not read like a spot news item — refer only briefly to the hard news angle that has provoked the Backgrounder.

Be wary of the grab-bag lead that tries to gather in a large number of major components. It is an approach that rarely works.

Point form can be especially effective in setting out key issues or background to give the reader some fast and tidy context.

A backgrounder on the Atlantic provinces, for instance, could hit points like this high up in the story:

• The four provinces have 194 legislature members and 34,000 civil servants for a population of 2.2 million. Alberta, with a population of 2.4 million, has 83 legislature members and 12,000 civil servants.

• Newfoundland and Labrador gets 47 cents of every government dollar from the federal treasury; P.E.I. 46 cents; New Brunswick and Nova Scotia 39 cents each.

• The cap on federal transfer payments has already cut $400 million from the amount the region had been counting on, and more cuts seem certain.

Style

The label **CP Backgrounder** is intended to be publishable. It goes directly above the writer's byline and below the headline.

Parkinson's-Backgrounder

Scientists have found no test, no cure for Parkinson's disease
CP Backgrounder
By Helen Branswell
TORONTO (CP) — . . .

Business news

Business news is about companies, industry, trade, commerce, finance and the economy. But ultimately it concerns people — their jobs, mortgages, bank accounts, investments and long-term prosperity.

Changes in economic conditions affect people. And people's behaviour can influence the economy.

• The merger of two companies, for example, may combine their strengths and improve production efficiency. But it may also mean lost jobs.

• Consumers continuing to spend despite signs of an impending recession may temporarily delay the start of the downturn.

• Higher interest rates could mean a higher Canadian dollar, which benefits someone travelling abroad but hurts exporters. Closer to home, higher interest rates may mean a bigger monthly mortgage payment, but savings in the bank may earn a bit more interest.

Business news deals with fluctuations in financial markets. As much as possible, business stories should explain what the price movements indicate. To what extent do they reflect investors' perception of economic conditions or a company's prospects? How much of the change is affected by political events? By sheer speculation? Is there a herd mentality at work? How about the interplay of greed and fear?

Like other news, business news occurs within the context of society. Bottom lines can be affected by developments in areas not traditionally associated with business. Environmental concerns, new standards of ethics and morality, the spread of disease, an aging population — these are some of the factors that can affect a company's prospects.

Similarly, business news in Canada is affected by what goes on elsewhere. A war in the Middle East could improve the economic outlook of oil-producing western provinces. The discovery of a cheaper and better substitute overseas may hurt the prospects of Canadian producers of, say, lumber or steel. Eventually, people who work in these industries feel the effect.

Business reporting

There is a great appetite for timely business news among newspapers, broadcasters, Internet news services, so-called day traders on the stock market and the corporate world. There are many news sources and services, all competing to be first with their stories.

CP's goal is to be the fastest provider of the largest Canadian business file in the country, one that is of use to both average readers and those who work in the finance industry. But while there's a premium on getting the story first, accuracy must always be the top priority. The business community is the biggest rumour mill around, and a rumour picked up by a media outlet can have a great effect on stock prices. Be careful. Check reports with more than one source.

Discard the assumption that business writing has to be staid, uninteresting and faceless. Business stories are often dynamic and colourful, driven by compelling personalities making their way through a constantly changing economic landscape.

Business writers should keep in mind the two kinds of readers: general readers who want to keep up with what is happening in the business world; and business readers who want information on investments, the economy and developments in fields related to their own. But both audiences appreciate easy-to-read stories that are free of jargon.

Graphics can cover background or related information for which there is no room in a business story.

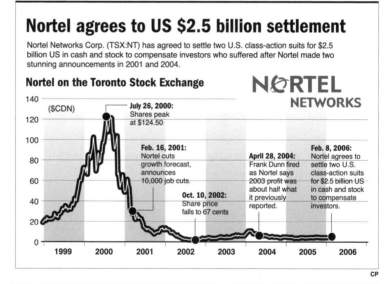

Nortel agrees to US $2.5 billion settlement

Nortel Networks Corp. (TSX:NT) has agreed to settle two U.S. class-action suits for $2.5 billion US in cash and stock to compensate investors who suffered after Nortel made two stunning announcements in 2001 and 2004.

Nortel on the Toronto Stock Exchange

N⊘RTEL
NETWORKS

($CDN)

July 26, 2000: Shares peak at $124.50

Feb. 16, 2001: Nortel cuts growth forecast, announces 10,000 job cuts.

Oct. 10, 2002: Share price falls to 67 cents

April 28, 2004: Frank Dunn fired as Nortel says 2003 profit was about half what it previously reported.

Feb. 8, 2006: Nortel agrees to settle two U.S. class-action suits for $2.5 billion US in cash and stock to compensate investors.

1999 2000 2001 2002 2003 2004 2005 2006

CP

Common pitfalls

• Check all figures. One extra digit can throw a number off completely. A single letter turns million into billion.

• Watch accounting terms. Net operating income and net income, for example, can be quite different things.

• Watch percentages. A statement that a company's profit is up 50 per cent isn't helpful without the raw numbers: $150 is 50 per cent more than $100, and $1.5 million is 50 per cent more than $1 million. Include actual figures.

• Don't make readers do the math in stories that compare numbers such as unemployment reports or corporate earnings. Include the current figure, the percentage increase or decrease, and last year's figure.

- Be wary of corporate self-interest in all aspects of business reporting. Remember that securities analysts are not unbiased observers of a company or sector. They work in an industry whose main job is to promote stock trading.

- Companies often use polls to increase brand awareness and market new products. Ask yourself if the poll provides newsworthy information. Question statistics to ensure they are not being used selectively by companies and lobby groups to advance their interests.

- Don't get bogged down with numbers. Use numbers that tell the reader something, such as net profit or revenues or earnings per share. Don't load the story with secondary figures such as cash flow or capital spending unless they are important to the news peg.

- Verify corporate identities. Some companies have similar names but are not directly related, or one may be a subsidiary of another. Appliance-maker **Camco Inc.** and uranium producer **Cameco Corp.** are in entirely different lines of business.

- Keep up to date with corporate name changes; **Molson Inc.**, for example, now is **Molson-Coors Inc.** after its merger with the U.S. brewer. In stories, make a reference to what the company used to be called if the change was recent or the new name is not easily recognizable. Product names are also bought and sold – check with the company concerned.

- Be careful when using the term **bankruptcy.** A troubled company can ask a court for bankruptcy protection from creditors as it restructures and carries out business as usual. That doesn't mean it's bankrupt, although it can be called insolvent. If a court-monitored restructuring can't be done, creditors can petition the company into bankruptcy, which means its assets will be sold and the firm will go out of business.

Some suggestions

- Keep human faces high in the story whenever possible. It's a way of saying a corporate development affects people in real life. For example, if **Really Clean Inc.** announced a layoff of 150 employees, an effective approach to the story might be:

James Lee walked home from work to save bus fare. He and 140 of his co-workers at Really Clean received layoff notices Friday.

- Always ask how any development is likely to affect the reader. Some events, such as World Trade Organization negotiations, may have no immediate impact on readers but their long-term impact can be significant, affecting the Canadian economy and such things as egg and butter prices. Reforms in China may not directly affect Canada, but they may help boost the Chinese economy and lift demand for oil, lumber, minerals and other products imported from Canada.

- When doing stories about economic predictions – especially bank and corporate forecasts of the coming year – try to include the previous year's forecast and how accurate it was. That helps readers decide how much weight to give the report.

• Concepts such as unemployment are hard to define statistically and can be measured differently in Canada and other countries. In Canada, the jobless numbers released each month don't include part-time workers or discouraged workers – people who have given up looking for work. That means the true jobless rate may be higher than the official count.

• Keep long corporate names or unfamiliar acronyms out of the first paragraph. Instead, use a short name that may be readily recognized, or a quick explanation of the type of business. The full name can be included a bit later in the story.

• It sometimes helps to mention a company's best-known products. For example: **Scott Paper, the company that makes White Swan tissue** . . .

• Complex corporate relationships, company holdings or a corporate history might best be laid out in a sidebar, a chart or a QuickFacts box. This allows the story to deal with the impact of a development.

• Translate business jargon into plain English. If a technical term must be included, explain what it means. Even readers with a lot of business knowledge appreciate accessible writing.

Tips for CP writers and editors

• Business stories on interest rates, company shutdowns, expansions or big shifts in stock markets and the dollar frequently find their way on to general news pages. Such stories should be double-filed as a business and general news items, with a note alerting editors: **Eds: Moves Business and General. Avoid duplication.** A business designator only should be used for all other items: routine company reports and annual meetings, a new twist in options trading, corporate takeovers, personal finance copy and the like.

• Some companies and organizations make the same announcement in two or more cities, or make a telephone conference call available to reporters from across the continent in hopes of getting many stories written on the same subject. As well, a company president will visit several places within a few days, delivering the same message to different groups. CP should avoid duplicating coverage of the same event. However, watch for regional angles that might be presented in one place only. If in doubt, check the archives or consult with the Business Editor or Main Desk.

• National reports can also yield important regional stories. Statistics Canada job figures that show British Columbia leading the country in growth could be developed by the regional bureau into a broader story explaining what's behind the numbers.

• Include stock symbols in the **Index** line of slugging and in brackets in the body of stories about companies listed on Canadian exchanges. This is valued information for readers who follow investment news closely.

- Good illustrations for business pages can be hard to come by and therefore are in great demand. Reporters should think about possibilities for a good graphic or photograph when they get their business-news assignment, so graphics editors can start planning. If a steel company is expected to report sharply lower year-end earnings in the next few days, alert the photo desk so a photographer can be sent out to get a shot of workers leaving the plant. This gives editors a livelier picture to work with than might otherwise be available on deadline. Annual meetings can be a good source of people pictures, whether of a reclusive chairman or an angry shareholder. Corporate websites can provide charts and other illustrations.

Business terms

Bonds, debentures
The buyer of **bonds** or **debentures** is a creditor who lends money to the company for a fixed term at an agreed interest rate.

Debentures are unsecured promises to repay the loan. Corporate **bonds** are ordinarily secured by fixed assets. Although government securities are often called bonds, they are actually debentures – guaranteed by the government but without assets being pledged. If a company goes out of business, secured creditors' claims on its assets have priority over claims of other creditors and preferred shareholders, who in turn are ahead of common shareholders.

Cash flow
Refers to a company's cash resources. Unlike earnings, cash flow includes interest, taxes, depreciation and amortization. Cash flow shows investors the company's ability to pay dividends and finance expansion.

Consolidated statement
A financial statement that includes the results of subsidiary companies. This is usually done when the parent company owns 50 per cent or more of a subsidiary. For example, when Imasco Ltd. of Montreal issues financial reports, it consolidates results from its major operating units – Imperial Tobacco, the Shoppers Drug Mart chain, Canada Trust and real estate developer Genstar.

Extraordinary items
Year-over-year comparisons of net profit can be distorted in a year when, for example, plants and equipment are sold or the value of investments or assets is written down because they have lost market value. A big layoff or restructuring will also dramatically affect a company's bottom line because of severance and restructuring costs. In general, focus on the figures that give a true picture of a company's performance. BCE Inc. might say it had an annual profit of $1.4 billion from operations but wrote off $2.9 billion in assets, posting a net loss of $1.5 billion. But that doesn't mean BCE is in trouble, since the writeoff was an accounting measure and not a loss of cash.

For a meaningful comparison from year to year, it is usually necessary to look as well at **net profit** before **extraordinary** items, generally referred to as operating profit or profit from operations. Whenever possible, try for longer-term comparisons such as a five-year range or average. Figures should be given for comparable earlier periods.

Financing

Equity financing means raising money through the sale of common shares. The buyer becomes a part-owner of the company.

Debt financing means raising money through bonds and debentures. The buyer lends money to the company, which promises to repay the amount in the future with interest.

Net profit, net income, net earnings

The three terms means the same thing – a company's profit (or loss) after all expenses and taxes have been paid. It is out of net profit that dividends are paid – first to preferred shareholders, then to common shareholders.

Net operating profit

Money earned from a company's operations – the sale of its products or services. It should not be confused with net profit, which includes both income from operations and non-operating sources like rents, interest and investments.

Net earnings per share

Obtained by deducting from net profit any amount paid to preferred shareholders, and dividing the resulting amount by the number of common shares outstanding. It is a key figure that investors, analysts and other players in the financial industry consider in determining the performance of a company. Companies often take a beating in the stock market when their earnings per share fall short of analysts' predictions.

Revenues

A company's overall sales and money earned from other sources. This should not be mistaken for profits. The cost of doing business, including wages, is subtracted to get profits.

Share, stock

A part-ownership of a company obtained by providing capital to the business. Common shareholders have the right to vote in the company. If the company performs well, shareholders benefit from the rise in the value of the shares. The term a share refers to a common share unless otherwise stated.

Preferred shares entitle the holder to a fixed dividend from net profit before common shareholders are paid. Preferred shares generally carry no voting privileges as long as promised dividends are paid.

Company meetings and reports

Some Canadian companies have played important roles in the country's economic development. Other firms have been the economic bedrock of their community. Some occupy pivotal positions in their sector of the economy. Others have high name recognition among consumers who use their products. The financial health and future plans of these businesses are often news of wide interest.

Company meetings and reports can provide information on how these companies are doing and where they are going financially. Company websites can supply many of these documents.

Stories based on company reports need not be dry recitals of statistics. Many companies explain in their reports why profits are small or sales have increased. This kind of information, along with background on the company and its products, can brighten the story and give it depth.

Securities commissions settlements

Allegations made against individuals by staff at Canada's securities commissions are sometimes settled without a formal hearing. These settlements often result in the individual paying a fine or facing other sanctions.

However — and this is where reporters can go wrong — agreeing to a penalty does not mean the individual has admitted the allegations are true or that there has been a finding of culpability. The wording of the settlement is the guide to what can be said about the case. Lawyers for the individual can be expected to take on the media if the characterizations and distinctions they fought to get into the settlement to benefit their client aren't reflected in news stories.

Precise figures

Precise figures are preferred in routine financial items but should be rounded off in business stories.

CALGARY (CP) – Liquidation World Inc., auctioneer and seller of discounted merchandise, says its first-quarter profit fell 31 per cent under pressure from the economic slowdown and pricing competition.

For the 13-week period ended Jan. 6, net profits fell to $1.56 million or 18 cents a share, from $2.28 million or 27 cents a share a year earlier. Sales slipped slightly to $48.7 million from $48.9 million.

Three daily items that need precise figures are: Earnings, Dividends and Trust Distributions.

Earnings
Canadian earnings declared Thursday
(CP) – Canadian earnings declared Thursday:
Amica Mature Lifestyles Inc. (TSX:ACC): Three months ended Feb. 28, 2006, net income $0.10 a share; 2005; net loss $648,000, net loss $0.12 a share. Revenue: 2006, $9,592,000; 2005, $9,685,000.

Dividends
Corporate dividends declared Monday
(CP) – Corporate dividends declared Monday (quarterly unless otherwise indicated):
CHUM Ltd. (TSX:CMH): Non-voting Clas B, $0.01, payable June 1. Record May 12.

Note: If an extra dividend is declared, say so.

Trust-Distributions
Canadian trust distributions declared Wednesday
(CP) – Canadian trust distributions declared Wednesday:
General Donlee Income Fund (TSX:GDI.UN): $0.055 per unit for March, payable April 28. Record April 25.

Foreign currencies

In stories from most parts of the world it is best to convert amounts into Canadian dollars. (The daily item slugged **Tab-Foreign-Exchange** can be used to convert many foreign currencies into Canadian dollars.) Allied agencies usually provide U.S. dollar figures. Convert them and use phrases like **the equivalent of C$500** to avoid giving the impression that people elsewhere use the Canadian currency. The **C$** is usually necessary only on first reference.

Note: When doing conversions it is important to keep the original currency amount in the story, especially in items concerning major takeovers and acquisitions. This makes it easier for editors using the story as background later to determine the exchange rate that was used.

Conversions are not done in the following cases:

1. U.S. dollar figures may be kept in copy with U.S. placelines. Specify the currency on first reference only:

NEW YORK (CP) – Seagram Co. Ltd. said Monday it will spend more than US$10 billion to buy PolyGram, the world's biggest record company. The deal will also mean Seagram will put its juice division up for sale, for about $3 billion.

2. Most of the world's commodities – gold, oil, nickel, lumber and pulp and paper – are traded on world markets in U.S. dollars. In business copy and routine financial items it is acceptable to keep U.S. dollar prices. In broader stories, it may be desirable to include a Canadian dollar equivalent in one or two examples.

Note: In stories where U.S. and Canadian dollars are both used, add an Editors' Note: **EDs: The following figures are in Canadian dollars unless otherwise stated.**

BizFlashes

1. CP moves a BizFlash – a short summary – of every story that moves with a Business designator, in advance of the story, as soon as it is available.

> **TD-Bank-VFC, BizFlash**
> **INDEX: Business, Banks, FinServices, Automotive**
> **SYMBOL:TSX:TD, TSX:VFX**
> **HL:TD Bank wins takeover bid for VFC Inc.**
>   TD Bank (TSX:TD) declares victory in $326-million takeover bid for user-car loan company VFC Inc. (TSX:VFC). About 90 per cent of shares tendererd, rest to be taken up.

2. For more minor news items, there may be no followup story. In those cases, the BizFlash should carry a line noting this:

> **Royal-Bank, BizFlash**
> **EDs: No story planned**

Stock symbols

1. Stock symbols are used by many CP subscribers to search for news on specific companies. All stories moving on the Business and Finance wires should carry the stock symbol in brackets after the first mention of a company.

> TORONTO (CP) – The Royal Bank of Canada (TSX:RY) said Monday it is issuing $300 million in new preferred shares to strengthen its capital ratios.

Note: If two or more companies are mentioned in the lead of a story, put the primary company's stock symbol in the lead and move the other symbols to second reference of the companies.

Note: Stock symbols can be removed from the General wire version of a story if it is being double-filed as a Business item.

2. The story should also carry a slugline that lists the symbols in the story. If no specific companies are mentioned, add the symbols of major companies that may be affected by the news.

SYMBOL:TSX:RY, MFC

3. Stories that mention publicly listed companies that move on wires other than Business and Finance should also include the TSX symbol in a slugline and in the body of the story, but it can be near the bottom of the story.

Elections

Public-opinion polls and clever election strategists have dramatically changed the election process in Canada. So have skeptical and savvy voters.

Fundraising has become an art, candidates' personalities are carefully polished, campaigns are stage-managed for maximum television exposure, news is manipulated. And yet the voters grow ever more wary of elections and intolerant of manipulative politics.

News coverage must adapt to the changes, looking for more effective ways of describing the process and involving the voters.

Stephen Harper and his family celebrate the Conservative Party federal election win in January 2006 in Calgary. Journalists will have opinions and a point of view, but these must not get in the way of balanced reporting.

(CP—Jeff McIntosh)

Some of CP's criteria for an effective news report on an election:

1. **Let the voters, not the politicians, decide what the issues are.**

Campaign coverage that is focused heavily on candidates' travels and statements may be irrelevant to readers. For example, if all the major parties are concentrating on constitutional issues, where does that leave voters worried about their jobs or the air they breathe or the fact that their kids have trouble reading?

Political reporters need to recognize that getting the *tough* one-liner snapped off by a cabinet minister with an eye on the 6 o'clock TV news is often less important than spending 20 minutes talking to voters in the minister's riding.

If reporters listen to what's on the voters' minds, and put those concerns to the candidates, readers may decide the media are worth paying attention to.

The alternative is to allow politicians to decide what's news.

A sound election file can be built by focusing on the party leaders and the apparent issues in the first week or two of the campaign. From then until the final days, the focus should shift to pinpointing what's bothering the voters, explaining the background to the big issues and clarifying the parties' stands on voter concerns.

2. **Be prepared.**

Surprise elections are rare. Supervisors and political reporters aware of an impending election will (a) set up a clear organization for covering the campaign; (b) establish their news priorities; (c) put profiles of the party leaders and other basic backgrounders *in the bank* for use when the election is called.

As the campaign unfolds, measure out special takeouts on the issues dear to the voters' hearts. Some regional issues become important enough to swing whole areas, so they need sensitive explanation. Some unlikely candidates will come on strong and need profiling. Issues like party funding, television ads, all-candidates debates, minor parties and historical trends are often worth looking at.

Election campaigns are also a test of CP's relationship with newspapers and broadcasters. Getting their news supervisors on side ahead of time can mean timely reports on major developments and a consistent supply of spot and feature material from all over a bureau's region.

Being prepared also means recognizing that the general public has lots of other interests besides politics. Campaign coverage shouldn't deprive readers of other news that's important to them.

3. **Don't forget the libel laws.**

Statements are sometimes made in the heat of an election campaign that in other circumstances would be pretty good grounds for a libel suit.

Some basic legal ground rules:

a) A fair and accurate report of public statements made at a meeting that's open to the general public isn't usually risky. But that may not apply if only some members of the public (say, one party's members) are allowed into the meeting. And if a person attacked at the meeting wants to respond, the response must be reported.

b) Potentially libellous statements made in other circumstances — even a radio broadcast — are not safe to publish. Get legal advice.

c) Some provincial and federal laws limit certain forms of campaigning and advertising just before voting day. Check election laws for pitfalls.

4. Provide context, colour, detail.

Reporting on campaign activities means making sense of the political statements. It also means bringing the campaign to life.

Context: What would the promise of a new housing policy mean for house prices? Construction jobs? Increased government debt and taxes? How does the new policy compare with past promises, the other parties' positions? What do outside experts think of it? Not all such questions will be worth answering, but few political statements of any importance should be left to stand alone.

Colour: Most politicians are scarcely known to the public. They often need to be described in action, gesturing and raising their voices to emphasize a point or laughing at the hecklers or making small talk on the street. The towns and crossroads where they campaign should be sketched. The campaign audiences should be shown responding or watching skeptically.

In both context and colour, be specific.

Not: The premier promised to cut government spending.

Instead: For the farm crowd in Ruralia, the premier promised to cut loan guarantees for big business. At the Middleton Rotary Club, she said there would be fewer tax concessions for shopping malls. Back in the capital, she worried about the cost of irrigation projects and secondary roads.

5. For election night, again be prepared.

Smooth, comprehensive coverage of election results depends on thorough advance work. It's too late to look for background information when the voting results are flooding in.

Prepare: profile material on the leaders and any candidates important to the overall coverage; background on the major issues and how the parties stood on them; the range of public-opinion poll results; the best of the campaign anecdotes to lighten up the stories.

Also: statistical histories of which parties have formed the government and when; figures on the size of majorities for past governments; information on minority governments, the defeat of governments and their leaders, the national situation for each major party.

(Most newspapers and broadcasters depend on CP for detailed results, gathered progressively at a single election centre. The results are delivered in ready-to-use formats from a computer programmed to make instantaneous adjustments in vote totals, winners and losers, party votes and other categories. The material is invaluable for those writing lead stories and separates at CP and other media.)

6. **Down with hype.**

The frenzy of election night can be the enemy of clear thinking.

It's common in Canadian elections for one party to win a substantial majority of seats with barely 40 per cent of the votes. That doesn't constitute a **landslide** of popular support. Stories about the result need precise wording.

And sweeping statements about the voters' feelings or intentions are risky. Each voter in a federal or provincial election makes a choice among local candidates, period. Each constituency result is probably influenced by broader issues and the popularity of the party leaders, but they aren't on the ballot.

It's stretching things to write baldly that voters **rejected a spending freeze** or **punished the government for failing to cut unemployment**. The effect of all those individual votes will be a government with some stated commitments. That's the surest way to describe the election result. Informed political observers can help keep the influence of national or provincial factors in perspective.

7. **Don't break the law.**

It is against the law to transmit vote results into an electoral district before all the polling stations there are closed. This means that CP doesn't transmit any federal election results on the Internet until polls close in British Columbia. Results for radio and television services are also moved regionally only, east to west, as polls close.

8. **The cleanup.**

Election campaigns don't end on election night. The days immediately following an election bring some of the most significant stories.

Supervisors need to ensure that fresh staff is available for two or three days after an election to complete reporting on how the results will affect voters.

Working from notes left over by election-night supervisors, the next-day staff should clean up loose ends — late polls, possible recounts, missing ballot boxes.

They can also concentrate on reaching the experts who will help make better sense of the results. They can examine the detailed results more closely for victories and defeats that were overlooked. And CP staff can exploit newspaper material that was neglected in the rush of election night.

9. **Plan for the next one.**

The start of good coverage of the next election begins with a thoughtful file on this one. Before the ink is dry on coverage of any election, a file should be opened that includes:

• Careful notes from supervisors on everything that went well and everything that went wrong — and why.

• Notes from reporters and deskers on how to improve election coverage. Everyone who took part should have something to contribute.

• Examples of the best and the worst stories from the campaign, your own or others'.

• Copies of all the memos, circulars, letters and other paperwork that will be needed as reminders the next time.

A woman casts her vote in the federal election in January 2006. Planning is the best way to ensure good election day coverage.

(CP—David Boily)

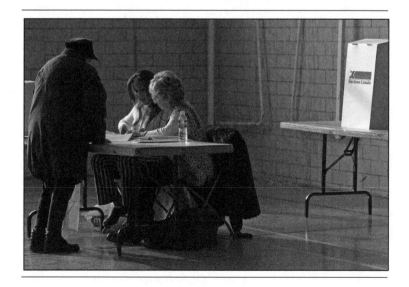

Entertainment

Entertainment is a catch-all title covering a broad range of activities and interests. For so-called popular tastes, there are television and radio, pop music and movies, circuses and standup comedy. For the highbrows, there are books and plays, operas and concerts, museums and balls.

Each of these categories can produce a hard-news story on any given day — everything from a fundraising crisis at the art gallery to the arrest of a prominent actress. On other days, they'll merit a profile or feature.

Or they may be dealt with in a review or column.

News

It's often regarded as soft news, but basic principles of journalism apply to entertainment coverage.

1. **Look for hard news:** Ask the TV actor if and when he plans to move on from his current sitcom. When the tour of a controversial rap group is announced, ask police whether they'll have extra patrols when the musicians hit town. Ask the author of the new bestseller her opinion of sales taxes on books.

2. **Take the high road**: So much entertainment "news" today is actually celebrity gossip. Gossipy items about the lives and loves of celebrities, if properly sourced, are usually harmless. But beware of picking up items from tabloids and celebrity TV shows that are not adequately sourced — their focus is usually on entertaining, not news reporting. Consider the track record of the source. If the news is worthy of pursuit, try to confirm it independently.

3. **Strive for balanced coverage:** If a songwriter complains that music royalties in Canada are tiny, check copyright laws and how royalties compare with those in other countries. When an author trashes a celebrity in a book, get comment from the star or his representatives. In articles about the state of a particular art form in Canada, include representatives from across the country.

4. **Avoid single-source stories:** When the artistic director of a theatre announces a new stage season, some insightful comments may be provided by actors, directors or even academics and drama critics about the choices. In a profile of a sexually provocative singer, talk to others — his parents, perhaps? — about his image.

5. **Inject colour and personality:** Don't say Madonna wore a bathing suit and shoes when she entered the press room. Say The former Material Girl wore very little of it, except for a teeny weeny polka-dot bikini, black spike heels and a gleaming white smile. In reviews of new works, describe the atmosphere in the hall and the reaction of the opening night

audience. If a usually suave young actor trips and falls at your feet when you come to interview him, don't brush it off — include it in your article.

Think pictures and graphics. Nothing sells a story like a good illustration.

For newspapers, keep section deadlines in mind. Deliver a time-sensitive story well in advance of deadline to help editors making up pages. Keep editors advised of late-breaking or short-notice material they can expect soon.

Awards

Industry awards are among the highest profile entertainment events. There are so many of them, the challenge is to determine how much and what type of coverage to give each awards event and how to develop lively, interesting copy from it.

Sarah McLachlan accepts the songwriter of the Year award at the Juno Awards in Edmonton in 2004. Although self-serving, entertainment awards are popular with readers.

(CP—Jeff McIntosh)

Entertainment awards tend to be self-serving. Major events such as the Emmys, Grammys, Oscars, Junos, Geminis and Genies are of interest to the average reader and merit extensive coverage. Lesser-known events may warrant little or no coverage.

A little homework in advance can be valuable. For example, research may turn up that the director of a film on long-distance running suffered polio as a child.

Award ceremonies usually take place in the evening when newspaper deadlines are tight. Whenever possible, ask the organizers for an embargoed list of winners in advance and have the story prepared ahead of time. Colour and quotes can be added in Writethrus after the ceremony begins. Use the special **bargo** coding (See **Advances**, page 404) to ensure the copy isn't sent to other CP clients until the embargo is lifted.

Complete lists of winners are an important companion to stories on the event. The list should give the category first followed by a colon and the name of the winner.

Best songwriter: Arcade Fire

Some category titles may have to be shortened to fit in a single column. **Outstanding Performance by a Lead Actor in a Drama Series** might be changed to **Best Actor – Drama**.

Embargoes and other conditions

Entertainment newsmakers are increasingly demanding embargoes and other restrictions before they will provide information or interviews.

Sometimes the request is reasonable: an embargo on an announcement of a major book prize winner, for instance, seems reasonable in return for getting the information early so a full story can be constructed. It also makes sense to agree to hold a story based on an interview with a singer or the star of a TV show until the singer's album is about to be released or the show is aired.

In other cases the newsmaker's motivation seems more self-serving: a TV network asks for an embargo on news about one of their shows until after they can announce it themselves on their own entertainment news show. Or an over-zealous PR agent might block an interview unless a reporter promises not to ask certain questions.

The news report should not be held hostage by such requests, which need to be considered on a case-by-case basis. Consult a supervisor before agreeing to any conditions.

In all cases, ask yourself if the request is reasonable, given the importance of the news. In many cases, it is not. For instance, if you are asked not to move a story until the release date of the singer's new CD, that is acceptable if it is understood that if the person says something timely, a spot story may move immediately, as well as the longer story later. And it is best to avoid agreeing not to ask about specific subjects, although it makes pragmatic sense to leave such questions until the end of the interview!

Features

Entertainment feature-writing generally allows more freedom to inject colour, personality and imaginative writing.

Colourful metaphors or similes can sometimes paint a vivid mental image. **Rock music on television is a lion in a cage. The BMW on Rodeo Drive glistened like a well-buffed Gucci loafer.**

Summing up a well-known person in a choice phrase can do two things: distil the subject's personality for the reader, plus set a tone for the article. **The artistic film director is a 32-year-old bundle of neuroses.**

While actors may make for identifiable hooks for a story, producers and directors are often more articulate about a project and can provide fresh insight. A good entertainment story often mixes the creative insights with the star quality of a Hollywood figure.

Reviews

In a world teeming with entertainment choices, the thoughtful review is especially important to help readers decide how to spend their leisure time.

Basically, a review gives the reader a synopsis of the work with some commentary on its artistic merit or entertainment value.

Full-time reviewers have more credibility and leeway than part-timers — who would do well to approach the assignment as a news event, describing it and getting audience comment or quoting newspaper reviewers.

Reviewers should avoid cheap shots or gush. While someone like George Bernard Shaw could get away with a demolishing review, readers can be turned off by harshness or apparent unfairness.

Commentary needs to be grounded in specific detail. Saying a rock band's show was atrocious means nothing. Rather: **The lead singer was off-key on three numbers, the lighting failed during another and people at the rear of the hall complained they couldn't hear the lyrics.**

Give readers a signpost: **The band conjures up the driving rhythm of the early Rolling Stones.**

When reviewing drama or books, reveal only as much of the plot as necessary to set the scene for the review. Readers will be annoyed to have the ending revealed by a thoughtless reviewer.

Resist adopting the vocabulary of the industry. Terms such as **genre** and **film noir** smack of trendiness and they're not used by the average reader.

Paula Pizzi in a scene from John Patrick Shankley's Where's My Money, performed at the off-Broadway Manhattan Theatre Club Stage II in 2002. Entertainment reviews need to include specific detail but leave out the cheap shots and gushing.

(AP Photo)

Flashbacks

The key to Flashbacks is to make clear why the events were important when they happened and why they deserve to be remembered now.

Newspapers always seem to have space for a nicely written historical piece on anything from Louis Riel to the October Crisis, especially one sprinkled with human touches and appealing anecdotes.

1. Flashbacks tied to anniversaries should note that connection somewhere in the first two or three paragraphs: **It was 60 years ago this week that** . . .

2. The successful Flashback starts with a strong idea, usually in one of these two categories:

a) Recognizable historical events like Prohibition and the conscription crisis, tied to a specific anniversary, or an event like the Korean War that is tied to a veterans reunion.

b) All-but-forgotten happenings that can be successfully revived for today's reader — events like the Frank landslide of 1903 that killed at least 70 people in the territory that in 1905 became Alberta.

3. Flashbacks on historical figures should usually be tied to a specific anniversary as well (birth, death, special honour, etc.) — the anniversary of Sir John A. Macdonald's first election, for example.

Lesser-known individuals can serve as the focus point for Flashbacks on major events — the security guard who was on duty the night the mine exploded; the woman whose car was lifted during the tornado.

4. Look for topics with some direct effect on people — then or now.

5. Try to find someone who was around at the time. That will be impossible in some cases, of course, so it will mean a trip to an archive or a library — public, university or newspaper — to search for contemporary accounts or comments on the incident being recalled.

6. Opportunities for colour are rife in such stories. Sometimes personal scrapbooks or letters can be helpful. Quoting the flowery language of the day can bring a dusty piece of history to life.

7. If the subject is controversial, check at least three different sources to ensure you're not quoting someone with an axe to grind.

The label **CP Flashback** is intended to be publishable. It goes directly above the writer's byline, separated by a space from photo and other service slugs. See page 41 for a comparable example.

Avian influenza virus studies

Scientists from the U.S. Centers for Disease Control will shortly begin experiments designed to see how likely the avian influenza virus devastating poultry stocks in Southeast Asia is to ignite a human flu pandemic. Some facts about the studies they will undertake:

Co-infecting tissue culture

Human flu virus

H5N1 avian influenza

Tissue culture

Reassortants

The aim: To get a better handle on how easy or hard it is for the virus, H5N1, to mate with human flu viruses and create a hybrid capable of infecting people and spreading easily among them.

Secondary goals: By seeing which gene combinations go together in viable and transmissible viruses, scientists may gain some clues about why H5N1 is so deadly. By testing the viruses in animals, they should get a sense of which combinations are particularly worrisome and require heightened responses should they arise.

Method: There are two ways to produce reassortant viruses, by using a process called reverse genetics or by simultaneously infecting tissue culture with H5N1 and a human flu virus. CDC plans to use both methods.

Reverse genetics: A relatively new technology, this process allows scientists to custom tailor a virus using a predetermined combination of genes from each of the parent viruses. It is quicker and less laborious than the alternative.

Co-infecting tissue culture: The classical way of producing reassortants, this involves adding H5N1 and a human flu virus – either H3N2 or H1N1 – to culture and seeing what grows. It's time-consuming work, but more closely mimics what happens in nature.

Sean Vokey - CP

Lifestyles

Lifestyles coverage should be a mirror on how our society is changing — how we take care of ourselves, how we relate to each other, what we eat, wear, do for fun.

It is a broad field that includes health, fitness, medicine, food, fashion, leisure, human interest, gardening, homes, psychology, social affairs and science.

Lifestyles stories are not fluff. They are often tied to the day's news and can hit page 1.

An inquest into the death of someone following liposuction, for example, calls out for an article outlining the procedure. The closing of a department store chain's fur salons could be accompanied by a story examining trappers who relied on the stores for their livelihoods. A piece on gardening trends could focus on concerns about pesticides.

In short, basic rules of journalism apply in lifestyles coverage: watch for the hard-news angle; keep copy tight; strive for balance; avoid single-source stories.

Aim for QuickQuotes, QuickFacts and graphics that can help an editor lay out a page attractively.

On an ongoing topic, always seek a new angle or twist. A look at the dangers of suntanning may turn up an angle that some sunscreens do little to decrease the dangers of skin cancer.

Remember to include cross-sections of society — both sexes, various age and racial groups, geographical regions and income levels.

Avoid stereotypes. Not all grandmothers are silver-haired matrons in aprons.

Write in simple language. When technical terms must be used, explain them in plain English. Don't talk about **a fractured tibia** when most people are more likely to understand **a broken leg.**

Trends

While readers want to keep abreast of the latest trends, guard against inventing trends by exaggerating their scope. Two or three men seen wearing eye makeup doesn't mark a trend toward men wearing women's cosmetics.

On the other hand, keep an eye out for larger changes in society that narrowly focused writing may overlook. Changes in the family unit, living arrangements, family size and division of work are constant. These changes are worth writing about and should also influence writing on society as a whole.

Use personal observation as a tipoff, then seek out research material and Statistics Canada data to gauge how widespread a trend may be.

Promotion

Guard against promotion. Manufacturers and retailers have an outlet for promoting new goods and services — it's called advertising.

Be wary of the public relations practitioner's sales pitch. Some new products or services are newsworthy. Others are not. Be wary of claims for health treatments, parapsychology, the latest how-to books and so on. The litmus test is: Who will benefit from the story — the source or the reader? Always aim to include comments from outside sources.

Health and medical stories

Fiercely competitive pharmaceutical companies spend millions of dollars on research and development, and are always eager to be mentioned in the news. A positive report about a new drug can have far-reaching implications – it can improve the stock price for the manufacturer, cause patients to request the drug from their doctors and put pressure on provincial health plans to expand their coverage.

Drug manufacturers and health-care lobbyists hire public relations firms to deal with the media. Some of their favourite techniques include polls of Canadians on a particular health issue. A "study" may include the name of a doctor who is actually being paid by the drug manufacturer, and therefore can't be seen as an unbiased expert. The release of a new painkiller may be endorsed by a university or health centre, but did those institutes receive any funding from the firm? Hospitals, in desperate competition for scarce research dollars, may claim breakthroughss and medical firsts. Independent experts should validate those claims.

Reporters and editors who handle health stories should always have their antennae up. Question the source of all material. Be aware of news releases dressed up as something that serves no other purpose than to promote a new health-care product or drug. Find out whether doctors and other health professionals have a pecuniary interest in the story – if they do, let the reader know. Use outside sources to verify or challenge claims.

Some tips:

1. Stories from The Associated Press on drugs being approved or reviewed by the U.S. Food and Drug Administration or pulled from the market by a manufacturer usually require the addition of a line or two about the status of the drug in Canada. This can be obtained by calling Health Canada. If the story is important, send the AP version immediately, then include the Canadian information in a Writethru.

2. When a press release concerns raising awareness of a certain disease, the first question should be "Who is paying to have this release disseminated?" Often, it will turn out to be a manufacturer trying to promote a certain drug or therapy. A story may still be written if the release is deemed to be of interest to readers, but it is essential to include information on who sponsored the release.

3. Reporters should be wary about reporting on a special "week" or "month" dedicated to a certain disease as health news because these are usually linked to fundraising.

4. Medical studies that have been published in a peer-reviewed journal have a stamp of approval in that experts in the field have already assessed the quality of the work and the findings. But often this work is funded by drug companies and interested parties, and their contributions should be noted in the story.

5. Academics and universities that are looking for attention and funding for their work are eager to have their names in the media. Always ask if the work has appeared in a peer-reviewed journal. If it hasn't, and the topic is still worth writing about, then the story should note that the study has not been published in a peer-reviewed journal, and should include comment from outside experts.

6. CP typically does not write about clinical trials before they reach Phase 3, unless a drug or vaccine is considered to be a real breakthrough. For instance, results of a Phase 1 trial on a new statin drug would not be newsworthy since there are many statins on the market already.

7. Websites of reputable organizations can be a useful resource for definitions of various diseases and conditions. The websites for the Public Health Agency of Canada and the Centers for Disease Control and Prevention are considered reliable and official.

8. It is worth remembering that antibiotics are not effective against viruses. When in doubt, check whether a disease is caused by a virus or bacteria.

Obituaries

Readers are attracted to obituaries for many reasons. It may be simple curiosity or wanting to learn the secret of the person's success, happiness or failures, or wanting to know what kind of person society has lost.

Obituaries are stories about life — about recognizing a life for what it was and what it meant.

They should be portraits, with brush strokes provided by friends, family, colleagues or acquaintances who can provide insights into the person's personality and life. Sharp quotes add colour and depth.

But the portraits should be exact, with no attempt to brush out wrinkles and warts. Resist the tendency to canonize the departed; very few are true saints.

Some general guidelines:

1. Report deaths of newsworthy people. Don't limit obits to lawyers, politicians and other automatically prominent members of society. Be on the lookout for the deaths of average folk: the waitress who worked 30 years at the town's most popular diner to put seven foster children through university; the amateur philosopher who operated a downtown newsstand for many decades.

2. Often an obituary item of 100 to 150 words will suffice, but it should include a significant fact or two about the person and his or her life.

3. Unsavoury details may be pertinent as part of a life story but should be kept in perspective.

4. The spot story opens with the simple facts — the name, other identification, notable achievements, cause of death and particularly age — the first questions that a reader wants answered.

Ernie Coombs, friend to generations of Canadians as Mr. Dressup, has died in hospital of a stroke. He was 73.

5. After the lead paragraphs, details of the subject's life are given in inverted-pyramid style rather than chronologically. The early years and schooling are rarely as interesting as later accomplishments. By the same token, details on the death itself, unless it was unusual in some way, should not be the focus of the story.

6. For a next-day story, a featurish top may be the best approach in the absence of worthwhile developments.

The tearful phone calls that poured into the CBC

switchboard are a testament to the enduring bond that Ernie Coombs created with Canadians through his Mr. Dressup character.

7. The length of an obituary depends on the person's newsworthiness. In addition to the lead information, longer obituaries should include biographical facts, the names of survivors and funeral arrangements.

8. For unusually prominent public figures, as well as for people in the news business, include precise details of funeral arrangements.

9. At some point — but preferably not in the lead where it might confuse readers — include the full name of the subject: **Alexander Young Jackson** for the painter usually known as **A.Y. Jackson**.

10. The identifying feature in the first paragraph should be the one that best highlights the subject's life and career. Often it is something that happened years ago.

A.Y. Jackson, a father of modern Canadian painting and last survivor of the original Group of Seven artists, died today in a nursing home at age 91.

11. In reckoning age, take into account the birth month and day. A person born Dec. 27, 1926, who died Jan. 10, 2006, was 79, not 80. To say **She was in her 80th year** is correct but confusing.

12. When the precise age is not available, give some indication of it from the person's activities, such as the year of graduation or the setting up of practice in law.

Cause of death

1. The cause of death should be given, except when the story makes plain that death resulted from the complications of old age. When the cause is not available, say so, and why.

2. Never speculate about the cause. If information doesn't come from someone clearly in a position to know, it is irresponsible to speculate.

3. When the cause is suspected to be suicide or a disease like AIDS, which carries certain connotations, respecting the wishes of the family can normally be justified. However, in the case of someone clearly in public life, the right to privacy in such matters can be outweighed by the public's right to know. If in doubt, consult Head Office.

4. In listing the cause of death, prefer a plain term to medical jargon: **heart attack** and **heart disease** rather than **coronary thrombosis** or **coronary occlusion**.

5. Explain unfamiliar scientific terms: **Hodgkin's disease — an uncommon disorder of the lymph nodes and spleen**.

6. Taste and redundancy often rule out detail when death resulted from violence.

Language

1. Write **die, bury, coffin** and **undertaker** or **funeral director** rather than **pass away, inter** or **laid to rest**. Do not use **resting** for the dead, or other euphemisms.

2. Write **die of**, not **from**, an illness.

3. Use **widow** and **widower**, but **wife** and **husband** until after the funeral. Guard against the redundant **widow of the late**. Write **wife of the late** or **widow of**.

4. Do not describe people as **late** when referring to something they did while alive. Not: **The late doctor fought the epidemic alone**.

5. In general, use **the late** only of a person who died recently. It is not needed, for instance, in **the late John Lennon**.

6. Beware of such common non sequiturs as **Born in Calgary, she was an ardent skier**. The two ideas are not linked by meaning and do not belong in the same sentence. Better: **She was born in Calgary. Six years later, the family moved to Collingwood, Ont., where she soon developed a taste for skiing.**

Prepared obits

1. When an obit shows up in CP's inbox from a newspaper's electronic return news, it is wise to check with the paper by telephone. The story may be one prepared in advance.

2. Each bureau prepares biographical sketches of its most prominent citizens. The Main Desk in Toronto keeps copies on disk. These sketches should be reviewed periodically to make sure they are up to date and complete.

3. As with spot obituaries, prepared obits are made interesting by quotations and anecdotes bringing out the character of the subject.

4. To make an obit stand up for use at any time, avoid past tenses except when tied to a specific date or time. Include religious affiliations or activities if newsworthy.

Funerals

1. Funerals and memorial services are often public events, and arrangements are made for reporters and photographer to attend. In the case of private funerals, journalists should respect the wishes of the family. It is sometimes acceptable to cover the funeral from outside the church or funeral home. At both public and private funerals, do not intrude into the service or approach

the mourners unless it is evident that they are willing to talk to the media.

2. Never misrepresent yourself as a mourner.

3. In coverage, do not sentimentalize the dearly departed. Plain language is best, avoiding any attempt at tear-jerking.

4. Do not suggest that the remains are in any way the person.

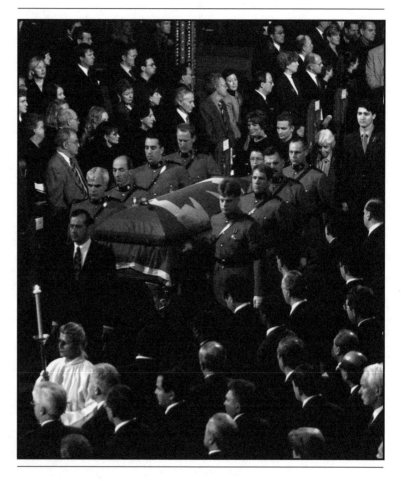

Pierre Trudeau's family follow the coffin of the former prime minister as it is carried into Notre Dame Cathedral in Montreal. Funerals are often of great interest to readers.

(CP—Paul Chiasson)

Polls

Public-opinion polls are like snapshots: it's not always obvious what they're showing. Is that woman on the right smiling or grimacing? Is she the mother of the young girl in the centre with the same blond hair? There are opportunities for misinterpreting the scene — particularly if you try to speculate that the snapshot is typical.

There's another similarity between polls and snapshots: there are too many of them, but no one wants to be the first to give them up. CP limits its coverage to reputable polls dealing with topical issues.

By canvassing the opinions of a relatively small group of people, pollsters are able to calculate how a larger population feels about a topic. But reputable pollsters would never state that the smaller group's views exactly mirror the larger one's, nor that there isn't a possibility of being wildly wrong once in a while.

1. Stories about polls should use verbs like **indicate** and **suggest**, rather than **show** or **report**.

> TORONTO (CP) — Liberal support appeared to be holding stable across Canada in March as measured by the Leger polling organization.
> The Leger poll suggested little change from February for any of the major national parties among voters with an opinion ...

2. An essential qualification is called the *margin of error*. It needs to be spelled out in stories on polls and its significance explained. Where changes in comparative figures are smaller than the margin of error, public opinion cannot be said with any certainty to have moved up or down.

> Leger said the poll was reliable within 2.5 percentage points 19 times out of 20. That means, when applied to the population at large, Liberal support in March could have been as high as 40.5 per cent or as low as 35.5 while Tory strength could range between 29.5 and 34.5 per cent. In one case in 20, the figures could be substantially different.
> Changes from February figures that are smaller than the margin of error have no polling significance. The apparent drop in Liberal support, for instance, is meaningless.

3. A national census is the ultimate poll. An election is a close second: it registers the opinion of all who vote. Comparing a poll on party popularity with the most recent election result is sound practice. When comparing one poll with earlier polls on the same topic, however, don't assume that similar results make the polls more accurate. They don't.

4.   Polls, like snapshots, show a moment in time. By the day after the questions were asked, people have already begun to change their minds. So it's wrong to suggest that a poll result can predict how people will behave — for example, a June political poll that's used to forecast an October election result. And it's wrong to take polling figures from the past and write about them in the present tense as if they are still just as valid.

5.   National poll figures will usually be out by no more than two to four percentage points. But when the national figures are broken down into regions, the risk of error is much greater. The difference needs to be explained.

> By regions, the poll indicated NDP support was at a peak of 38 per cent in Ontario and a low of 12 per cent in Prince Edward Island. However, since the poll's accuracy depends on the number of people surveyed, the Ontario figure might range anywhere from 32 to 44 per cent while the P.E.I. sample was too small to be considered reliable.

6.   There's a big difference between **per cent** and **percentage points**. The poll is accurate within 2.5 percentage points, not per cent. A political party whose support has apparently gone from a level of 16 per cent to 24 per cent has registered an increase of eight percentage points but its support has increased 50 per cent.

7.   Statistical studies produced by Statistics Canada and other reputable organizations are routinely based on a sampling of the general population. They are polls. That means they may not accurately reflect what's happening in the population as a whole; the margin of error needs to be specified and explained, just as in a political poll. And **suggest,** not **show,** is still the verb of choice.

➤ See **Statistics,** page 87.

8.   Some published polls cover a wide range of issues. In reporting on them, it's better to sacrifice polling results on secondary questions than to skip over essential information about the basic poll and its accuracy. Take a narrower focus and do it right. Consider using a Quick-style box to summarize some of the secondary results.

Some other pitfalls

Public-opinion researchers recognize a number of other elements in polling that can affect the accuracy of a poll's results.

1.   The sponsor of a poll may influence the questions asked and other aspects. The story should say if the poll was paid for by a political party, a lobby group or someone else with a vested interest in the outcome. And results from two different polling organizations can't be compared unless they were asking the same questions: for example, about the popularity of **the Liberals** rather than **Paul Martin's Liberals.**

2. The dates a poll was taken can affect the outcome. If there was a significant event before or after the poll that could have coloured the result, say so.

3. A poll that requires members of the public to make a specific effort is likely to attract those who feel strongly about an issue. Specify whether the poll was conducted by personal interview, by phone or by mail. Phone-in or mail-in polls are of dubious value.

4. If the people polled aren't a random selection — that is, with every person having an equal chance of being picked to respond — the results may be skewed. If there were a disproportionate number of middle-class people sampled on the question of income tax rates, the poll might not give a true picture of society's attitudes as a whole. This is why Internet polls, which usually have no guarantees of random selection, are of little value.

5. The question asked can influence the result. Polls suggest most Canadians don't support abortion on demand, but a majority believe a woman whose health is at risk should be able to get an abortion. Depending on the question, poll results can claim to support almost any position in the abortion debate.

6. If 40 per cent of a random selection of people can't be contacted, or refuse to answer a particular question, or don't know the answer, the significance of the remaining responses is reduced. They may not represent society at large. This aspect needs increasingly careful attention since polling organizations report that the growth in answering machines and people's irritation with phone canvassing are leading to more difficulty getting accurate samples.

Partisan polls

Polls are increasingly being used by interest groups to support their causes. The partisan group that pays for the poll gets to frame questions in their language, and may present the issues in an unbalanced or inaccurate way. A poll, for instance, paid for by a group opposed to downloading music from the Internet, could imply that such downloading is illegal in the wording of the questions, when it is not. But such an inference could influence responses and makes the poll's results questionable.

Also be on the alert for news releases on such polls that make conclusions that cannot be supported by the poll results. This is more common than you might expect.

Partisan polls cannot be treated casually, especially when they deal with important public issues. Always weigh whether the results of the poll add anything of value to the reader's knowledge of the subject.

Polls during elections

Polls must be handled with care throughout any election campaign. All such poll stories should be seen by Toronto Main Desk or another senior supervisor.

The Canada Elections Act calls for specific information to be included in election survey stories transmitted in the midst of a federal election campaign. It also restricts when a new poll can be distributed.

When a poll story is transmitted within 24 hours of the poll first being released to the public, it must include: the name of the sponsor of the poll; the name of the polling firm; the date the poll was conducted; the group surveyed (Quebecers, Albertans, women in Ontario, etc.); the sample size; the margin of error; and unless the poll story is being transmitted by broadcast, directions on how to obtain more detail on the survey, including the wording of the question that was asked. These conditions do not apply to stories on polls after the first 24 hours of release.

CP and its broadcast affiliate, Broadcast News, carry polls under the terms of the act on all text and broadcast services with the exception of the headline service, where it is impossible to meet those terms. CP stories should include a mailing address or website address for the polling firm or the poll's sponsor, who by law must make the specific details of the survey available to the public.

Not all stories that touch on new polls will have all the information the act calls for. Roundups, QuickFacts and Graphics may have just a glancing mention of a new poll. However, at least one story should be carried that is focused solely on the poll and includes the required information. Tip publishers by advisory that the more complete story is also available:

EDITORS: Members publishing FedElxn-Roundup on Wednesday may also wish to consider publishing FedElxn-Poll, which carries information required by the Elections Act that is not in the roundup.

The Elections Act also says that any story on an unscientific poll (sometimes called a hamburger poll) should make clear that it is not based on recognized statistical methods if it is being transmitted within 24 hours of first being released to the public.

The act prohibits publication of previously unreleased voter preference polls on election day. This means that stories on polls released the day before the election could present problems, especially for newspapers that would be unable to publish the surveys until voting day. Supervisors should be consulted before a story on such a poll is carried. On election day, publishing exit poll information in regions where polls have not closed is also prohibited.

Profiles and Newsmakers

Profiles and Newsmakers tell people about people. They put human beings into news stories.

Profiles usually deal with people who may not be in the public eye but whose lives, jobs, hobbies or thoughts are interesting and appealing. Newsmakers focus on people in the day's news — the new leader of a national First Nations organization, the provincial cabinet minister whose public statements have caused a furor, the unlikely hero of a Stanley Cup championship game.

Except for the time element — or *peg* — Profiles and Newsmakers have much in common. At their best, they leave the reader with a sense of knowing the subjects as individuals — the next best thing to meeting them in person.

Like all CP stories, the Profile and Newsmaker must be fair and in good taste. They should never be a vehicle for cheap shots, sexist comments, irrelevant detail or clumsy description that can be embarrassing to CP as well as the subject.

These stories should skilfully blend background, colour, personality touches and newsy tidbits about the subject. They should avoid logjams of detail and gratuitous information. Good quotes which convey the mood or personality of the subject are particularly helpful.

Stories such as Profiles and Newsmakers offer a great opportunity to take the reader where the TV camera can rarely go. They also go beyond the canned biography of *Who's Who*.

Look for telling actions that would probably not take place before the cameras: a federal cabinet minister gets upset when he can't get into his hotel room because he's misplaced his key; a notoriously tough football coach spends his days off as a volunteer art instructor for inner city youngsters.

The keen-eyed reporter can also sketch things a TV viewer might miss: the politician's aide always wears red neckties and combs his hair exactly like his mentor; the baseball player warming up for the all-star game keeps a jealous eye on the television camera.

Profiles and Newsmakers should be tight and bright. They should tell readers something about who the subjects are, how they got where they are, a little about what makes them tick. Friends and colleagues can be helpful in providing perceptive insights and anecdotes. So can enemies, but only if they're named.

Did the subject grow up on a farm and save egg money to buy books? Did she run three newspaper routes at the same time to buy a bicycle? Does she read books for blind people at a nursing home?

Let the reader in on your subject's home surroundings, revealing his likes, dislikes and interests.

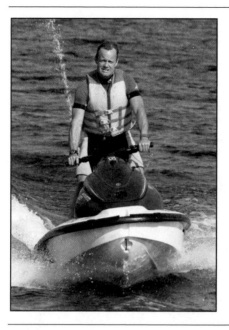

Canadian Alliance Leader Stockwell Day arrives at a news conference on a personal watercraft on Okanagan Lake in Penticton, B.C., in September 2000. Sometimes people in the public eye have interests that can lend colour to a Newsmaker or Profile.

(CP—Adrian Wyld)

Look for the unexpected. Dennis O'Connor, the judge appointed to investigate the tainted water scandal in Walkerton, Ont., went to local hockey games while in the small town conducting hearings. Former Nova Scotia premier John Hamm, a teetotaller, was known for ordering milk with his meals.

Colour and description

1. Description should be fresh, imaginative and relevant. It should help the reader get a sense of the subject's appearance and personality or to feel what it was like to be at the news scene.

2. A string of generalized adjectives is usually less effective than active and specific words.

Not: He laughed heartily as he watched the Three Stooges on TV in his wood-panelled library.

But: His laughter rumbled so forcefully as he watched the Three Stooges on TV that a photograph of his yacht wobbled on the wall of his wood-panelled library.

3. A basic description of physique or character should be provided when it is pertinent to the news event. The lined faces and baggy eyes of the first ministers were worth noting during the endless Meech Lake talks in 1990. But readers do not need to be told that Belinda Stronach has blond hair or that Arnold Schwarzenegger is heavily muscled.

4. Description should always serve a purpose. Too often, the clothing of female newsmakers is carefully described, while that of men is ignored. Inclusion of such details should be driven by relevance, not sex.

5. Watch for chances to use a description that will work better than a bald statement:

Not: **The prime minister was angry.**

But: **The prime minister's face tightened with anger as he spun on his heel and strode quickly off the platform.**

6. It sometimes helps to encourage subjects to talk about themselves. Ask lots of questions about childhood, hobbies, former jobs, dreams and hopes. Many people will be refreshingly open when given the chance.

Sometimes even the well-known public figure will reward the reader with something new and different. For instance, Jerzy Urban, the official spokesman for the former hardline Communist government in Poland, was asked in an interview what the worst day of his life was. He replied it was when his sombre weekly news conferences were cancelled and he ceased being "a TV star."

7. Subjects who are naturally reserved and taciturn are particularly challenging. So is the individual who dislikes media attention. Look for body language from such people. Some of them convey a wealth of information even though their actual answers may be sparse or even gruff.

A media-hating tycoon whose speech is closely clipped can still leave a trail of visual images.

He's big and rough-looking, a yep-and-nope type who seems to shun even those monosyllables if a shrug or nod will do for an answer.

8. Comparisons can be helpful in giving the reader a mental image. *Lincolnesque*, for instance, implies tall and craggy.

Or compare a person's appearance or character to natural objects: **granite-jawed; reed-like; limbs like oak; built along the lines of a water buffalo.**

9. Technical references can even be helpful: **nimble as a Porsche; he was well put together, like a neatly constructed Lego man.**

10. When it comes to effective use of colour and description, one trick is working it in without making it look forced. A paragraph devoted entirely to colour to the exclusion of news, quotes or anything else to inform the reader will seem distracting. Laborious descriptive clauses are also discouraging.

11. Colour should be woven into a story in a natural way:

> The judge who will recommend how much time Albert Walker ought to spend in prison for murdering Ronald Platt denounced the convicted Canadian on Monday as a callous and ruthless man who used people for his own selfish ends.
>
> Walker, 52, blinked twice when the foreman of the eight-woman, four-man jury announced the guilty verdict after two hours of deliberation.
>
> Later, as he was led down the stairs of the dock into the holding cells, the composure Walker maintained throughout the trial appeared on the verge of collapse. His eyes were reddening and his facial muscles seemed ready to give way.

12. But don't fall into the trap of tediously substituting bits of background for the person's identity:

Para 1:   John Simpson said Tuesday . . .

Para 2:   . . . the former Vancouver engineer added.

Para 3:   The lanky, grey-haired bureaucrat insisted . . .

Instead, consider giving readers an early mental image that can stay with them as they read on:

> Simpson, lanky and grey-haired, is a former Vancouver engineer who in 1986 joined the federal Transport Department and rose quickly to the No. 2 spot. In that job he is now insisting that the harbour project be shelved.

Slugs

The word Profile or Newsmaker is included in the first slugline:

> **Sorensen-Profile**
> **Canadian woman faces test Down Under**
> **By Lorrayne Anthony**
> TORONTO (CP) — It's been nearly six solitary months . . .

> **Emerson-Newsmaker, Bgt**
> **Budget**
> **Former Liberal industry minister David Emerson is the surprise member of Tory cabinet**
> **By Bruce Cheadle**
> OTTAWA (CP) — Only a few days ago, David Emerson was part of the Paul Martin team . . .

Sports

General

1.　The standards of good general-news writing apply with equal force to the coverage of sports. People are the focus of reader interest. Bare results are the preserve of the agate page.

2.　The sensitive sports writer should know when a cliché has become threadbare. While athletes still profess to be *taking it one game at a time* and *giving it 110 per cent*, the days of reporting such mundane quotes are over.

3.　When writing game copy, be concise. There's no need to describe every scoring play. Focus on the key play or performer and build the story around it. Pull together the remaining scoring plays into a paragraph or two. Sometimes, one sentence listing the remaining goal-scorers for each team in a hockey game, for example, will suffice. The reader who wants more can find it on the agate page.

Limit game-over stories to 400 words; papers seldom have space for more. If developments warrant, do a Writethru or spin it off into a sidebar. All vital elements of the game must be contained in that initial 400-word story.

4.　Make sure the blinkers are off. Sports is more than what unfolds on the playing field. Capture the mood and size of the crowd and its impact on the game. Were the fans raucous, or sedate? Did they display banners or signs vilifying the visitors?

Watch for the interaction at the bench between players and coach, as well as between teammates. If the coach berates the star defenceman for giving the puck away on the decisive goal, let the reader in on it.

➤　See **More than a game**, page 82.

5.　Be mindful of the competition for sports-page space and write accordingly. Tight writing is particularly needed on weekends when there is a glut of copy for Monday editions. Overwriting hurts a story's chances for publication.

6.　Finally, don't forget something so simple it's often neglected in stories: Was it a good game? Was it well-played? Was it entertaining?

Points to watch

1.　The sport involved must be identified early in every story.

2.　City names used as team names take singular verbs; team titles, even singular ones, usually require plural verbs: **Vancouver is last** . . . but **The Canucks are last. Miami played its first game** . . . but **the Heat played their first game.**

3. Avoid unnecessary possessives. Write **The Canadiens centre stole the puck** not **The Canadiens' centre** . . . However, the possessive is required in the following: **The Canadiens' three straight losses are a season record.** When you are unsure whether the possessive is necessary, mentally substitute the city for the team nickname. By substituting **Montreal** in the examples given, it's quickly apparent which requires the possessive.

4. Avoid nicknames unless they are long-standing. If a person is known to readers by a given name and nickname, put the nickname in parentheses on first reference: **boxer Thomas (Hit Man) Hearns.** Usually, however, when a person is commonly known by a nickname, it is unnecessary to provide the given name as well: **baseball outfielder Chili Davis** and **tennis player Gigi Fernandez,** not **Charles (Chili) Davis** and **Beatrice (Gigi) Fernandez.**

5. Long-established and well-known leagues such as the National Hockey League, the Canadian Football League, the National Football League and the National Basketball Association may be referred to in first reference as **the NHL, the CFL, the NFL** and **the NBA.**

Initials are permissible on second reference for well-known minor leagues such as the American Hockey League **(AHL)**, the International Hockey League **(IHL)** and Canada's three major junior hockey leagues. Otherwise, avoid initials even on second reference.

All leagues named in newspagers and other stories that might end up on non-sports pages should be spelled out in full.

6. Capitalize major events and trophies such as **the Olympic Games, the Olympics, the Pan Am Games, the Commonwealth Games, the Canada Games, the World Series, the Canadian Open, the Grey Cup, the Super Bowl, the Queen's Plate** and **the Vezina Trophy.** On second reference, refer to them simply as **the Games, the Open,** etc.

National and world championships are not capitalized. Write **the Canadian wrestling championships** and **the world hockey championship.**

7. Use the plural of proper nouns advisedly. Write **Boston is a five-time winner of the Stanley Cup** not **Boston has won five Stanley Cups.** Similarly, if referring to baseball's two major leagues, write **The presidents of the American and National leagues** (lowercase *l*) . . .

8. The word *final*, meaning the last round of a competition, is singular. Write **Pittsburgh reached the Stanley Cup final** not **finals.** An exception: **Five swimming finals were scheduled Tuesday.**

9. Don't expect the reader to have a medical dictionary next to the newspaper. What's an *anterior cruciate ligament* and why is it preventing Eric Lindros from playing hockey? Make sure any

medical jargon is explained and the extent of the disability is clear.

Sports . . . More than a game

1. A sports writer who reports only what happens on the field or rink and ignores what takes place off it is being negligent.

2. On many sports pages today, the daily game is often summarized in a few paragraphs or worked into a roundup. Line stories tend to be analyses, backgrounders and profiles, or else they focus on trades, drafts, salaries, racism, substance abuse and legal problems.

3. Certain stories invite a blind eye: substance abuse, racial tension, disciplinary problems. These are not merely personal questions for publicly acclaimed athletes. Writing about these issues may require legal advice, but it should be part of the sports beat.

Wayne Gretzky wipes a tear during a news conference announcing his trade from the Edmonton Oilers to the Los Angeles Kings in 1988. This picture dramatically showed how the business of sports takes a human toll.

(CP—Ray Giguere)

4. Sports pages must reflect the evolution of the multibillion-dollar sports entertainment industry. Every sports writer takes time to interview a team's general manager about a new prospect or a hot trade rumour. But a good sports writer will also get to know a team's business manager to write about attendance, television revenue and taxes.

5. Don't leave the business end of sports out of so-called amateur events. Members of Canada's national teams are no

longer amateurs. Appearance money is now the main criterion for most track meets, so don't ignore it in the story.

6.   As well, Canada's amateur sports federations are part of a substantial bureaucracy and should come under the same journalistic scrutiny as any government department.

7.   The only true amateurs left in sports are people like weekend softball players and neighbourhood joggers. While recreational athletes aren't usually newsworthy, the sports they play are. Keep a close eye on trends in recreational sports. Why are people willing to spend hundreds of dollars on running shoes? How many weekend warriors are seriously injuring themselves on the softball diamond?

Women in sports

1.   Sports pages tend to be filled with stories about male athletes. Despite that, a survey by the National Hockey League found more than 40 per cent of its fans are women. The crowd at any major sports event can show a similar ratio.

2.   Sexist language, stereotypes and references have no more place in sports pages than in any other part of the newspaper.

3.   A few anachronisms survive in sports: **the Ladies Professional Golf Association**. But generally, female athletes are no more *ladies* than males are *gentlemen*.

Beware of sports stereotypes. This picture is proof that hockey – and wrestling – aren't just for men. Gillian Apps of Team Canada is upended by a Team Russia player during a hockey game at the 2006 Winter Olympics in Turin, Italy.

(CP—Ryan Remiorz)

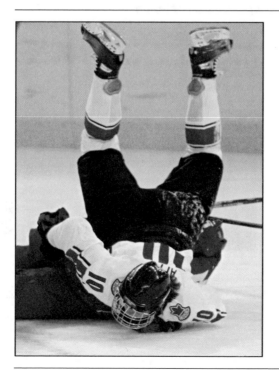

4. There's no justification for always leading with the men's competition in events, such as marathons, where both sexes compete. If separate stories aren't warranted, the most competitive, exciting race deserves the lead — and that's not always the men's event.

5. Be on the lookout for sexism in sports. Female athletes, particularly in golf and tennis, get a disproportionately smaller share of prize money compared with men. If an amateur program seems to be devoting more resources to male athletes, find out why.

6. Physical descriptions of athletes — male and female — are sometimes appropriate, and their personalities and gestures will enliven quotes. But avoid gratuitous descriptions that have sexist undertones. The simple test: Would this type of thing be written about a male athlete?

7. Any sports writer who refers to a female gymnast as a **pixie** or a basketball player as an **amazon** is not relying on a cliche, but is being sexist. Don't patronize. Be thoughtful and tasteful in your use of language.

8. In sports such as women's hockey, sex-specific terms such as **defenceman** and **two-man advantage** are usually preferred over **defencewoman** and **two-woman advantage**, as those in the sport use the traditional terms. But follow personal preference if it is different. Another option is to use a neutral term, such as **defender**.

➤ See **Sexism**, page 22.

Thinking visuals

1. When developing a story, think immediately about illustrations. Discuss the story with a staff photographer or photo editor. Rely on their talents to make your story more complete.

QuickFacts can be used as the basis for an eye-catching graphic.

2. The same holds for graphics. Many sporting events leave writers with more statistics than should be used in a story. The unused stats can make a timely graphic. Sports lends itself to graphics and a good one can sell a story to editors and readers.

3. As well, QuickSketches, QuickFacts and QuickQuotes are welcome complements to sports stories. They can spell out essential background material, leaving more room for colour and personality in the story.

Sponsorship in sport

Sponsorship has crept into every corner of sports, making it difficult to separate the commercial sponsor from the event title.

Avoid unwieldy titles, at least on first reference, but be fair about how sponsorship is handled. It is not fair to write about the **Buick Open** but call it the **Canadian Juniors** for curling when the full title is the **M&M Meat Shops Canadian Juniors**.

Sports are inevitably an advertising vehicle, but the sponsorship should have a legitimate connection to the event in order to rate being mentioned. References to the sponsorship should not be unduly emphasized.

Germany's Michael Schumacher drinks champagne as he embraces his chief engineer Chris Dyer after winning the Canadian Grand Prix in Montreal in 2003. Sponsorship is an inevitable part of sports contests.

(CP—Frank Gunn)

Metric, measurement and numbers

1. CP generally uses metric to measure distances and calculate speeds. However, some sports — baseball, golf, football, horse racing and certain classes of auto racing, for example — are reported in imperial. Use the measurement the sport uses. For

further information, see sections dealing with individual sports.

Remember, however, that a generation of Canadians have been brought up on metric and may be confused by imperial references. Unless precise imperial field demarcations are involved, as in football, or race distances, such as the Indianapolis 500, use metric wherever it's a sensible option.

Note: Many figures, imperial or metric, are rough estimates. When translating imperial to metric, don't use exact conversions unless precision is essential, such as in field events at an athletics meet. Round figures off.

2.   Although some sports use metric for weight classes and the like, personal measurements continue to be imperial. When referring to heights, write **The centre stood six foot three**; as an adjective, it's **the six-foot-three centre**. If it's clear from the context, it's permissible to say **Jones, 6-3, 220 pounds, came to the Blue Bombers . . .**

Don't mix imperial and metric in one sentence: **The six-foot-three forward shot from 10 metres out**. Rephrase it or use separate sentences.

3.   When measurements consist of two or more elements, do not use commas. Write **She stood five foot three** and **She was timed in two hours 15 minutes 35 seconds**.

4.   In times, a colon is used between hours, minutes and seconds; a period before decimal fractions of a second. Write **0:27** (27 seconds), **0:27.7** (27.7 seconds), **2:00.1** (two minutes one-tenth of a second), **3:47:39.67** (three hours 47 minutes 39.67 seconds). Note that times involving only seconds include a zero before the colon.

5.   When not expressing fractions in decimal terms, write **8-100ths of a second** and **3½ minutes**, but **two-thirds of an inning**.

6.   Odds are listed as **20-1**, not **20 to 1** or **20-to-1**.

➤   See **Numbers**, page 219.

Records

When records are established, put them into perspective:

•   Compare a national standard with the world mark.

•   Try to explain why the previous record had been one of long standing or why it has been broken three times in the last year.

Statistics

Statistics can be pillars of the day's news. They are also the devil's playground, luring reporters into errors of interpretation, assumption and fact.

Some of the problems with statistics would diminish if the news media would regularly treat them with the care — and the skepticism — they need. The quote credited to Benjamin Disraeli is deservedly famous: **"There are . . . lies, damned lies and statistics."**

The value of statistics, intelligently used, can hardly be overstated. They help to give substance to stories on hundreds of topics. But there are pitfalls:

1. Some statistical reports rely on actual counts: the number of new cars sold in Vancouver in March, based on sales reports from all dealerships. Some are estimates: the number of unemployed in Canada in August, based on extensive samplings of households. These poll-based statistics are subject to error and reporting on them needs some of the same care applied to writing about public-opinion polls.

➤ See **Polls**, page 73.

2. Some statistical reports are issued on a preliminary basis, subject to adjustments later. The federal government's figures on international trade are one example. Some of the later adjustments can be substantial. That means the figures must always be described as preliminary, and early in the story the importance of the adjustment process needs to be spelled out each time. When the final figures are available, they should be reported and comparisons made with the preliminary figures. Since the preliminary figures are tentative, it doesn't make sense to attribute great significance to the precise numbers. If that makes a story less interesting and less authoritative, so be it.

3. Statistics are usually relevant only for the time period concerned. There can be substantial changes from one year to the next in all sorts of statistics. An obvious example: a poll on the number of homes with high-speed Internet access in 2000 says very little about how many families had jumped on the Net by 2004.

4. Comparisons of statistical studies on the same topic can be useful in detecting trends, such as employment in the manufacturing sector over a few months or even years. However, comparisons between one time period and an earlier one should take account of how the population and other crucial factors have changed in the interim. A 25 per cent increase in auto thefts from 1995 to 2005 might actually represent a decline in the **rate** of thefts, if population and car ownership figures are taken into account. (Rates are more telling when they're available: the

number of murders per 100,000 population.) Similarly, comparisons of value over time must take into account the decline in purchasing power of the dollar.

5. The bases of comparison shouldn't be decided routinely. Comparing January retail sales figures with December's can be meaningless because of the Christmas rush; comparing them with the previous January's is usually best. But when the economy is reaching a peak or a trough, a year-over-year comparison may not be as revealing as month-over-month or some other comparison thoughtfully chosen.

6. The significance of statistics can't be safely stretched. If Canada's overall cost-of-living index goes up mainly because of higher taxes in Ontario, many Canadians will not be affected and a story should make that clear from the start. If a provincial study reports that the number of homeless people in the province has declined eight per cent from a year earlier, that alone can't be taken to suggest declines in other provinces.

7. Similarly, it's risky to assume that American statistical studies are equally valid in Canada. Some academics find it hard to resist using the floods of American studies to buttress arguments about conditions in Canada, adding casually that "there's no reason to think the same figures don't apply in this country." Don't believe it. Check some authorities; there are numerous differences between the two societies.

8. Phrases like **seasonally adjusted**, **gross domestic product** and the like may be understood by specialists, but the ordinary reader can use help. The methods of calculating changes in such basic measurements as the consumer price index or the unemployment index should also be explained from time to time. When available, sample size — 700 of the 2,000 sporting goods stores, for example — should be mentioned. People want to know how reliable these indicators are.

Some terms

Average refers to the result obtained by dividing a sum by the number of quantities added together. The average of 10, 20, 30 and 40 is 100 divided by four, or 25.

Mean usually designates a number in the middle of two extremes.

Median is the middle number of a series arranged in order of size. The median in the group 55, 62, 70, 81 and 95 is 70. The average would be 72.8.

Norm implies a standard of average performance. **The snowfall is below the norm for January in Alberta.**

Travel

Travel stories share many of the requirements of other features: effective use of quotes and people, a lively writing style, a good lead that grabs the reader's interest.

But more than most other features, travel stories must usually convey a sense of place. The writer draws a picture for the reader by selecting vivid detail and using description effectively.

1.   Travel writers need to make their stories interesting — a mere listing of information from travel brochures and government tourist boards won't do.

The airily upbeat style more common in promotional travel literature doesn't work either.

2.   The proper approach is somewhat sharper and reflects the writer's personal observation.

What is it about a particular place that is distinctive, that catches the writer's senses?

What do the city streets look like? What do the people wear? What is striking about the markets, the countryside?

The writer should try to get one or two real people into the story — a street vendor, a passerby, a museum guide. Anyone but the overused taxi driver or hotel desk clerk.

3.   The best travel stories will capture the genuinely interesting aspects of a destination without glossing over harsh reality: poverty, inefficient transportation, anti-tourist sentiment. Experienced travellers expect some discomfort but they also want practical information on what to be prepared for.

At times, the need for plain-speaking will be paramount. When travel is likely to be affected by political developments, earthquakes or floods, terrorist threats or other newspage developments, a travel-page report can hardly ignore it.

4.   Good travel topics include an offbeat site, a new attraction, any interesting destination.

Trends that affect tourists are also worth considering: the modernization of British pubs, the renovation of cathedrals in France.

A narrow focus often provides the best opportunity for colourful writing — for example, a market street in Lima, a festival in Barcelona, a museum on cats in Malaysia. But a large-topic story — travel in eastern Europe, London in summertime, cruising the Caribbean — is also worthwhile.

If the reporter can add some perspective — a sense of familiarity with the country and the people — all the better.

5.   Business people make up a large part of the travelling public.

They want information that can help them travel more efficiently — tips on getting through airports, facts on practical matters like packing, food, ground transportation, foreign customs.

6.   Unlike some magazine material, travel stories for newspapers must be punchy and concise. Interesting historical background can be woven in judiciously.

Facts on accommodation, food, prices and other similar information may be appropriate, especially when organized into an **If you go** sidebar.

7.   The use of the first person is occasionally acceptable when giving a personal account of an unusual adventure, but it should not be overdone.

Top: A view of Quebec City from the ramparts. Below: Tourists visit Tower Bridge over the Thames River in London. Include people in travel shots to liven up structures and landmarks. They also help give a sense of scale. Generally, keep the sun behind you and take lots of pictures.

(CP—Jacques Boissinot, Kevin Frayer)

8.   The most useful length for travel stories is usually 500-800 words. Photos are essential, and a map may be handy to locate offbeat sites.

9.   Travel stories do not need exotic placelines. Many people want ideas on cheaper or shorter holidays within Canada.

Work and the workplace

General

Most people spend more of their waking hours at work than at anything else, including time for friends, family or leisure. They can have strong opinions about work.

That's one of the factors that make reporting on work and the workplace so demanding. There are many other complications that increase the need for care in maintaining accuracy and fairness.

For instance, relations between employee and employer, between labour and management, tend to be complex and sensitive.

Despite its reputation, work isn't always something people perform numbingly. For many, work is how they define themselves. For others, it's something they regularly discuss with friends and family and continually contemplate.

Workers go through periods of great ambition and satisfaction and swings of unproductiveness and discontent. They are often part of a business or profession that can boom one year and go bust the next.

And they are an increasingly transient and adapting force. Where a generation ago someone had a lifelong career, today workers can expect to have two or more different careers, sometimes at the same time.

That means workers, and people seeking work, must be thoughtfully portrayed. Stories about work need to reflect that work is a focal point for many and a diversion for others. Stories need to vividly represent work's role in society and examine the many aspects of the work environment.

The workforce

1. Although contract disputes provide the most drama, coverage of work needs to go far beyond the union-shop floor. A majority of the workforce is not unionized.

2. Two-income families are the norm, not the exception.

3. An increasing number of skilled workers and skill-seeking businesses are looking for ways to alter the employee-employer relationship. With initiatives like *flex time*, more people would work from home, more would have flexible or reduced work hours, more would share jobs, more would take leaves of absence for retraining and professional development. Workplaces increasingly offer such benefits as on-site child care or fitness centres.

4. There has been steady growth in the number of term contract employees — people hired for a specific function for a specific period of time. They are often paid a lump sum in lieu of benefits or pensions.

5. Whether it's the effects of contract work or the legacy of the "downsizing" phenomenon of the past two decades, today's employees are less likely to stay with the same employers for their entire careers.

The workplace

1. If the nature of labour is changing, so is the nature of management. Experts say more duties are being delegated, more decisions are being made by workers and more ideas are working their way up to the boardroom from the office or factory floor.

2. Consultation between workers and managers is becoming more common. The *us-against-them* approach is slowly breaking down, and partnerships among business, labour and governments in industrial and professional risk-taking have begun to appear.

3. These changes in turn produce other changes in traditional practice. Workers make concessions on salaries in exchange for bonuses tied to performance. Managers make concessions on professional leaves even if that creates short-term expertise problems.

Coverage of news about work and the workplace has to reflect such changes.

But even when covering more traditional union-management situations, the goal should be perspectives that are tied to human beings: how someone is making ends meet during a strike; how a local merchant is coping with a lockout; what prompted someone to become active in the labour movement.

Conditions of work

The basic document governing conditions for employees and workers in unionized plants and offices is the contract. Non-unionized workers generally live under more casual arrangements. Complicated economic times bring complex work arrangements that require careful, clear explanations.

Some general guides:

1. **Wages:** In contracts, always compare the previous basic or average wage with the new rate, using a recognizable job (a bricklayer in the construction industry, a production line employee in an auto plant, a senior reporter at a newspaper). When wage changes vary according to the job category, the range should be specified.

When using percentage changes in wage stories, always use

actual examples of change. And compare like elements: report a $50 weekly increase in a $700 weekly salary, not a 50-cent hourly increase in an $800 weekly salary. Beware of baldly totalling percentage increases. An increase of 10 per cent now and 10 per cent next year is not a 20 per cent increase; compounded, it is 21 per cent. Don't make readers do math.

2. **Dates:** In contract stories, spell out the starting date to indicate how much retroactivity is involved in a contract settlement. Spell out the dates of further changes in the contract during its identified full term. Don't say a new contract gives workers $4 an hour more, when in fact it gives $2 now and $2 in two years' time.

3. **Inflation protection:** Mention when wage arrangements provide for additional increases if inflation is a specified rate, commonly called **indexation** or a **cola (cost-of-living-allowance) clause**, terms to be avoided except in quotes and to be explained no matter what.

4. **Job protection:** Summarize measures that shield workers from unemployment, including advance notice of layoffs or plant closings, guaranteed payments for those laid off, retraining programs, pension protection and offers of corporate transfers to other communities.

5. **Worker concessions:** In contract stories, summarize changes that might limit strikes or other activities to protest work conditions, or agreements to limit salary increases in order to protect jobs or increase the workforce.

6. **Non-monetary issues:** Contracts are often fought over conditions of work, including the flexibility of work hours, the ability of workers to curtail their work hours or to share jobs, the amount of continual worker training a company will provide, or health and safety issues.

These should be highlighted as interesting elements for readers with similar or contracted jobs. When estimates of the value of these benefits are carried, the source of the estimate must be given: **The company says the new child-care provisions are worth $100 a week per employee.**

When neither workers nor companies mention these aspects of a contract, try to get the information independently.

Labour organizations and affiliations

Unions are grouped in national and regional groups but have a large measure of autonomy within them.

The largest federation in Canada is the **Canadian Labour Congress**, with more than three million members. A majority of the national and international unions in the country belong to the congress. Affiliated secondary bodies include all provincial and territorial federations and 137 district labour councils. CLC headquarters is in Ottawa.

People are members of the CLC only through their affiliated unions. In most provinces, such unions are grouped in provincial federations — the Saskatchewan Federation of Labour, for example. CLC unions also maintain district labour councils in most urban areas.

Large unions in Canada, especially those spread over a wide area, are usually broken down into locals. The biggest unions include the *Canadian Union of Public Employees*, the *National Union of Public and General Employees*, the *National Automobile, Aerospace, Transportation and General Workers Union of Canada* (formal name for *Canadian Auto Workers*), the *United Food and Commercial Workers International Union* and the *United Steelworkers of America*.

Note: When writing about a union that has a French name only, avoid using the French name unless the story requires it. Paraphrase the nature of the membership — a **Quebec civil servants union** — rather than invent a capitalized English name.

Union membership

Specific terms describe the various forms of union membership.

Closed shop: an employer may only hire people who are members of the union.

Union shop: an employer may select employees but all are obliged to join the union within a specified time.

Maintenance of membership: employees must retain membership for the duration of the contract.

Open shop: employees are free to join or not join a union. Workers who don't join are commonly called **free riders**, a term to avoid.

Rand formula: named after Justice Ivan Rand, who arbitrated a 1945 Ford strike. It requires all members of a bargaining unit to pay union dues but makes membership in the unit voluntary.

Checkoff: The employer acts as a collecting agent for a union by deducting dues from the employee's pay.

Laws and courts

Labour relations in Canada are divided into federal and provincial jurisdictions, each governed by a labour code.

The Canada Labour Code covers employees of federally chartered companies like banks, Crown corporations and those in such regulated businesses as transportation and communications that have interprovincial dealings. Provincial codes cover all others.

The federal code is enforced by the Canada Industrial Relations

Board, a quasi-judicial body that investigates and rules on union accreditations and violations of the code, such as illegal strikes and lockouts, unfair labour practices and inter-union membership raids.

Similar bodies exist in the provinces. Such functions in Quebec are filled by a labour court.

Federal civil servants are governed by the Public Service Staff Relations Board and disputes are regulated by a special act.

Conciliation

When the federal government intervenes in a dispute, there are several stages:

Stage 1: A conciliator is appointed who tries to get the sides talking.

Stage 2: A conciliation commission, often the original conciliator, is next appointed. The commission studies the issues and, unless it is felt the sides are too far apart for agreement, writes suggestions for a settlement.

Stage 3: A mediator goes back and forth to the parties and tries to craft a report for a vote by management and union membership.

Stage 4: An arbitrator can be brought in to devise a binding settlement. Arbitrators are also used in grievance procedures and, on occasion, for contract negotiations.

Provincial governments intervene in different ways, and a reporter covering a dispute under provincial jurisdiction should be aware of specific procedures that apply.

Strikes and lockouts

Strikes are the cessation of work to press the workers' position. **Lockouts** are the closure of all or part of an establishment to counter a work slowdown, to gain concessions from workers or to resist their position. Always distinguish between the two.

The reasons for a dispute must always be at the top of a story. Every story should say how long the strike or lockout has been in effect and the number of employees involved. Specify the average or base wage before the dispute — preferably the average.

As with any labour story, reporters should seek out the human elements when strikes or lockouts occur. There are economic consequences from a prolonged dispute for both the workers and their industry, and occasionally there are moments of violence and high drama. Less well explored are the psychological impacts for healthy workers to be away from their jobs and for managers to be in open conflict with employees.

Vocabulary

Labour-management reporting is loaded with euphemisms and pejoratives, so tread warily.

1. People are not **terminated** and workforces are not **downsized** or **consolidated**. People are **laid off** or **fired** and workforces are **cut**. (Avoid the term **cutbacks**. It's simply **cuts**.) Always say whether layoffs are temporary or permanent.

2. Employees are not **engaged in study sessions** or **job actions**. They have **stopped work** or **slowed work**.

3. **Scab**, a term used since 1777 for a worker who refuses to join a strike or who takes over the work of strikers, is permissible only in direct quotes; even so, use with discretion. **Strikebreaker** is a vague, rarely accurate term — a strike is seldom broken by the hiring of people to replace striking workers. A more accurate term — even though it doesn't reflect the hostility of strikers that can accompany such hiring — is **replacement worker**. In Quebec, companies are forbidden to hire outside workers to do the jobs of strikers.

4. Avoid **company offer** and **union demand**. **Proposal** and **counter-proposal** are neutral terms.

5. A **picket**, borrowed from the military term for a small body of soldiers on guard duty, is a force of workers stationed outside an establishment to dissuade customers or workers from going in. A **sympathy picket** involves people outside the bargaining unit joining in. A **demonstration picket** is a temporary form of protest by workers about employment conditions or bargaining talks. An **electronic picket** involves a striking union tying up all incoming lines to an establishment relying on telephones for business.

Avoid the term **honour a picket line**. It implies some legal obligation which may not exist. Report that someone or some group **refused** or **declined to cross a picket line**. Similarly, do not write that pickets **barred access** to a struck establishment unless someone was actually prevented from entering.

6. Avoid the term **union bosses**. Union leaders in some cases may not legally order members to walk off the job. Strike decisions and executive appointments in unions depend by law on a majority vote of union members or of members present and voting at a union meeting.

7. A **wildcat strike** is a strike for which union leaders disclaim responsibility. It is not an **illegal strike**, which comes when workers leave their jobs when under contract, strike when they are legally prevented from doing so, or continue a strike when they have been ordered back to work by a court.

8. A number of specialist terms deal with workforce reduction. **Attrition** involves reduction through normal retirement, leaves of absence and resignation. A **buyout** involves a company offer to pay special compensation — improved pension, generous severance or the like — to employees who will retire early or quit. In some cases, if attrition or a buyout doesn't achieve the desired workforce reduction, **layoffs** would be the next step. But a buyout is not a layoff.

World news

Canadians play an active role in world affairs: as soldiers in trouble spots, diplomats advancing Canada's objectives abroad, business people getting a share of the global market. CP gives the Canadian angle due attention in the flow of international news.

A young boy gives a Canadian soldier the thumb's up during a patrol in Kabul, Afghanistan, in 2003. CP photographers and writers travelling abroad can bring home stories that are of particular interest to Canadians.

(CP—Tom Hanson)

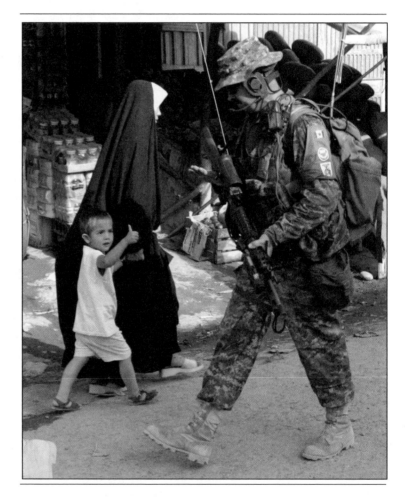

CP has a network of staff and freelance correspondents to report on international stories with significance for Canadian readers. Reporter/editors with the CP World Desk in Toronto and bureaus across Canada actively pursue the Canadian connection in foreign stories by phone, e-mail and Internet searches, or travel outside the country to cover such news.

These efforts by CP personnel add a Canadian dimension to the world report provided mainly by The Associated Press. AP offers a comprehensive report on developments around the world but its stories are not written with a Canadian readership in mind.

CP's goal is to make world news relevant to Canadians, who have their own perspective. Canadian reporters abroad and their editors back in Canada are more likely to notice parallels of interest to Canadian readers. They can make foreign developments understandable in Canadian terms.

CP makes sure that the Canadian perspective is at the core of a rich menu of international news — extending beyond politics and disasters into business, entertainment, medical, scientific, lifestyles and human interest issues. International news is not only the doings of world leaders along with riots and civil wars. It is also ordinary people doing extraordinary things anywhere in the world. It is the small triumphs and defeats of the human spirit. It is social and cultural trends that can reach across continents. Sometimes, Canadians are in the middle of these developments and deserve coverage.

At the same time, CP ensures that Canada's influence on the international stage is seen in the proper context. For example, the activities of the Canadian delegation at a major international conference are certainly worth reporting in detail, but a balanced story should contain the most important overall developments spearheaded by other countries at the conference. A complete world report includes stories on how other nations try to solve issues that Canadians also face. A report on how problems such as health care, pollution and taxation are handled abroad can provide Canadians with fresh alternatives to ponder. And in the same way that Canada isn't just Mounties and snow, other countries are more than the stereotypes for which they are known. CP aims to provide a world report that goes beyond clichés, shedding light on the fascinating complexities of different societies.

Chasing world news

The CP World Desk relies on stringers, correspondents and allied news services to cover international events. But the phone is also a prime tool in tracking down news involving Canadians abroad. Some tips:

1. Make calls early in a breaking story. Interview subjects are usually talkative within the first few hours of major news. After that window of opportunity, many clam up on their own or are instructed by head office to decline interviews.

2. Remember when calling abroad that almost anyone you reach is likely to know more about the country and its information sources than you do. Ask them who they would call if they were trying to get the information you need. And always ask the person you've managed to contact for the names and numbers of anyone else who might also be able to help.

3. The Internet and e-mail are invaluable tools to communicate with newsmakers and correspondents abroad and overcome time-zone barriers. Electronic messages, however, should be kept clear and concise to avoid misunderstandings arising from unintended distortions in the meaning of the written word.

Editing world news

1. Keep in mind the changing complexion of Canada's population. Most newcomers now come from countries outside the traditional European sources of immigrants. Slang once commonly understood among people from the British Isles, for example, may be indecipherable to new immigrants from another part of the world.

2. Stories from abroad can refer to local currency figures if it serves a purpose, such as to add colour or a regional flavour to copy. The U.S. dollar is widely used in international transactions and most Canadians know roughly how much it is worth. There is no need to uniformly convert all U.S. dollar references into their Canadian equivalent — do the conversion only when it is needed to enhance understanding of the story.

➤ See **Foreign currencies**, page 51.

3. Keeping the news report free of legal problems presents special challenges for editors. U.S. libel laws, for example, permit the reporting of statements that would be dangerous in Canada. Check with a supervisor or legal counsel before releasing doubtful material. Kill any story found to be dangerous. Withhold any story that has given rise to legal questions. See Legal, page 101.

➤ See **Legal,** page 103.

Legal

Legal

Although this section provides general information on journalism and the law, it is written for CP editors and reporters and reflects the news agency's needs. The guidelines and policies in this section do not represent an agreed professional standard; nor do they represent the practices of all newspapers. Its main focus is to alert CP staff to situations that may require advice from legal counsel. It is not a substitute for such advice and should not be used in that way.

Engraved in the memory of every reporter and editor should be:

1. Carelessness and bad judgment on legal questions can ruin people's lives. Every journalist must weigh this responsibility when working.

2. It is dangerous to publish statements that damage a person's reputation or livelihood unless the statements are provably true or unless the law clearly provides a special exemption.

3. It is particularly dangerous to suggest criminal conduct unless it has been proved in the courts.

4. Every person charged and before the courts is entitled to be presumed innocent and to receive a fair trial. It is forbidden to publish anything that passes judgment on an accused or that could hinder a fair trial unless it has been admitted in court as evidence. (Of course, the court's judgment is publishable.)

5. Juveniles involved with the law — accused, witnesses or victims — must not be identified, even indirectly, without legal advice.

6. In cases where legal action is a possibility, or could involve a dispute over what was said, reporters should keep notes, audio tapes and related documents for three months. It's expected that notification of any legal action would be given by that time. Reporters should also note that during examination for discovery they may be required to make available to the court all material related to the story in question – including such things as e-mails to sources or other versions of the story.

Follow these rules:

1. Check legal authority before writing anything legally doubtful

2. Cut out anything that looks legally questionable until it can be cleared for use.

3. If legal doubts arise after a story has been distributed, order the story killed or withheld immediately until the doubts can be resolved.

Crime

Reporting on crime

No area of reporting requires greater care than crime.

People's reputations and livelihoods are at stake. Concepts of fairness that are at the core of Canadian democracy come regularly into play.

On the other hand, a justice system that deals effectively with criminals is a legitimate goal of every democracy. And one of the bases of an effective justice system is public scrutiny: the public must see justice being done, if not in person then through the media.

Courtrooms are natural theatres of human drama and good court reporting takes the reader to the heart of the drama – but always with fairness and objectivity in the recording of testimony and the description of witnesses.

Reporters and editors should make themselves familiar with the entire legal section of the *CP Stylebook* in a general fashion. The subsections are set out in such a way that those working on a specific step in the legal process can refer to the portion dealing with that step. The worst pitfalls are highlighted at the start of each subsection.

However, the law is complex. A stylebook is no substitute for legal counsel on doubtful issues.

Criminal cases

Some general rules:

1. Court reporting must be fair and accurate to be legally protected. Otherwise, the protection is lost. That means straightforward coverage of testimony, even-handed descriptions of accused or witnesses, balance between Crown and defence cases, no plain or implied taking of sides.

2. Coverage must also be contemporaneous. It is risky to report well after the fact on a criminal proceeding, particularly if the accused was acquitted. It can seem like an attempt to blacken the accused's name needlessly. Consult counsel before reporting on an old proceeding.

3. Give the exact charge in a criminal case, not a generality. If the charge is sexual assault, don't write **attack**.

4. Don't refer casually to a defendant's religion, race, political party, profession or other qualification unless it's directly relevant. Beware of categorizing an accused in a way that could reflect on an entire group of people.

5. Identifying alleged victims or other witnesses in sexual assault cases and some other sensitive areas may be banned by the court. Even if not banned, it is usually wrong to identify alleged victims of sexual assault without their active consent. Always consult a supervisor if an exception is being considered.

6. In important cases, provide the possible penalty, but also mention that the maximum penalty is rarely imposed and prison terms are rarely served in full.

7. When substantial prison terms have been imposed, specify promptly how much time must be served before parole can be considered.

8. Don't total concurrent sentences (**sentenced to a total of 120 years**). Report the individual sentences on various charges and the actual maximum prison term.

9. Don't attempt to pull together two or more court cases into one story unless they were linked in court. Such natural linkages are rare anyway, but on days when a number of parallel cases are going on in different courts — say, concerted disturbances by activists — publishing a roundup can risk influencing a sitting jury or potential jurors.

Some general background:

1. Criminal offences are generally of two types, **summary conviction** (less serious) and **indictable** (more serious). Some offences such as theft under $1,000 may be prosecuted either summarily or by indictment, at the discretion of the Crown.

2. Summary conviction offences are dealt with in a streamlined procedure under which the accused goes directly to trial without a preliminary hearing. Examples include causing a disturbance, indecent exhibition in a public place or being found in what are called **common gaming-houses** or **bawdy-houses**.

3. Summary conviction offences are tried by a justice of the peace or by the lowest of a province's courts. There are no jury trials at this level.

4. Indictable offences generally involve a choice of courts, at the discretion of the Crown, and sometimes a choice of trial with or without jury, at the discretion of the accused.

5. For many indictable offences — including armed robbery, breaking and entering, forgery and arson — the options are:

   a) Trial by provincially appointed judge (lower courts) without jury and without first undergoing a preliminary inquiry.

   b) Trial by federally appointed judge in a provincial superior court without jury but with a preliminary inquiry.

   c) Trial by a federally appointed judge with jury in a provincial superior court. Such courts have a variety of names in different provinces: Court of Queen's Bench, Supreme Court, Superior Court.

6. For the most serious indictable offences, such as murder or treason, there is no option. They must be tried in a superior court. And they must be heard by a jury unless the accused and the provincial attorney general both agree otherwise.

7. Appeals of convictions for indictable offences are heard by provincial courts of appeal. Appeals for summary conviction offences are heard by a variety of courts depending on the province.

8. The Supreme Court of Canada hears criminal appeals only if a point of law is involved and if leave to appeal is granted by a panel of three justices or by a provincial appeal court. Leave to appeal is not necessary if a provincial appeal court has reversed an acquittal won in the trial court; if at least one justice has dissented in the appeal court's decision; or if a co-accused, having been tried jointly, has had an acquittal sustained on appeal.

Before charges are laid

Dangers:

1. Naming a person before formally charged.
2. Providing past criminal record.
3. Linking a suspect to a crime.

Police take an interest in many people. Often nothing comes of it. But to write that someone **is under investigation** for a criminal offence can cast a cloud over the person's life. The courts consider a false allegation of criminal conduct among the worst forms of libel.

Therefore, special care must be taken with any story identifying a person being investigated but who has not been charged or has not appeared in court to answer a charge.

CP does not normally name individuals until they face formal charges. There may be exceptions depending on particular legal circumstances and news value, but the exceptions are rare.

Always check supervisors or seek legal advice before using doubtful information. With that caution, following are some general comments and examples:

1. Contempt of court – appearing to influence a court proceeding – becomes more of a risk as a trial nears. The most sensitive time is when a jury is about to be chosen.

2. Even if not contemptuous, a report that police are **investigating** a specific person, or **considering charges** against a specific person, can be libellous in some cases.

3. Depending on the circumstances, it may be permissible to

report that **an investigation is under way** or **searches have been carried out**.

4. It is proper to publish the fact that a warrant has been issued for the arrest of a named person, or that he or she has in fact been arrested, or has received a summons to appear in court, or has signed a promise to appear.

5. The exact nature of the charge can be stated if the person has appeared before a judge, or if the charge is outlined in a warrant, summons or other document. It is probably dangerous to go into further detail without documentary evidence or testimony in open court.

6. Occasionally, the criminal record or other background of the accused is virtually inseparable from the description of the crime. A breakout or a riot at a prison or detention centre, for example, is committed by people who either have a criminal record or are held without bail for trial.

7. Trickier is the case of a murder committed by someone on parole. If the suspect's previous conviction was also for murder, a strong editorial case could be made for reporting that fact on grounds of public interest, although legally the information would be totally prejudicial. If the previous crime was petty theft, the record is irrelevant.

8. Under these and other circumstances, it may be OK to refer to the criminal record of an accused at the time of arrest. But Toronto Main Desk, which can consult counsel in tricky cases, must check all stories that make such references. Contempt is a real risk. The references need to be relevant and in the public interest, and the information must be presented concisely and fairly. Unless there are special circumstances, such references to a past record should be dropped after the first few stories done at the time of arrest and shortly after. Don't continue to carry such information later in the legal process without getting the approval of counsel.

9. Even when it's permissible to mention the background, a story must never imply that the suspect's record means he or she is guilty of the new offence.

10. Occasionally, a criminal comes before the courts who's so notorious that virtually anything may safely be written about the person's past and character until trial is imminent. Resist the temptation to abuse this liberty. If the criminal is truly notorious, the public doesn't need constant reminders of the reasons. And such stories can send the wrong signal about the media's concern for fair play.

11. On rare occasions — a hostage-taker who surrenders, a bank robber wounded in the act — the suspect's identity may be obvious even before being charged. In such cases, write only that a named person has been arrested or is in custody, without going into detail.

12. A suspect must be kept separate from the crime. For example, it may be all right to say: **A robbery was committed. John Doe is being held.** It is never all right to say: **John Doe committed a robbery.** Similarly, it is not acceptable to write: **A drug ring was broken today with the announcement of charges against three people.**

13. Witnesses can be interviewed when a crime is committed, but their statements should not be used to link a specific suspect to actions that could be disputed later in court. Witnesses must not be interviewed once a suspect has come before the courts.

14. Reporting police statements carries no immunity from the risk of libel or contempt. Such statements have to be weighed as carefully as any other information and checked for accuracy when possible. Whether a particular police force can be depended upon for fairness and accuracy is a matter of past experience. It is no defence against a libel or contempt charge to say the police were thought to be trustworthy.

Inquests

Dangers:

1. Publication bans.
2. Later use of incriminating evidence.

1. Coroner's inquests — sometimes called **fatality inquiries** — are held to investigate the cause of a violent death and make recommendations designed to avoid future deaths. They are presided over by a judge or coroner, depending on provincial law.

2. Inquests are usually open to media and public. The general rule holds that public hearings may be reported fairly and accurately.

3. However, the person presiding may order the inquiry closed, temporarily or permanently, because of possible prejudice to a potential accused, national security, public safety or intimate testimony, depending on provincial law. In such cases, whether evidence from the inquiry becomes public later is a matter for the presiding officer and/or provincial law.

4. An inquest may hear evidence that would be inadmissible at a later court proceeding, such as a confession. It may be reported at the time, unless the presiding officer directs otherwise, but it should not be repeated without legal advice once the case is before the courts.

5. Inquest juries are usually forbidden to make any finding of civil or legal responsibility. However, their investigations can

sometimes lead to questions of who might have committed a crime, in a way not normally open to the courts, and that could lead to criminal charges. It's unwise to speculate about such possibilities without legal advice, however.

6. Inquest juries, like those at criminal trials, are forbidden by law from disclosing any information about their deliberations.

7. In Quebec, among things the law forbids:

a) Publishing a photograph of the dead body without consent.

b) Publishing any identifying information about a witness under 18 years of age implicated in the events.

c) Publishing autopsy reports.

Arraignment and bail hearing

Dangers:
1. Violating publication ban.
2. Reporting confession or criminal record.

---

1. Arraignment is normally the first step in a criminal court proceeding. It usually involves just an appearance by the accused before a judge, reading of the charge, making a plea and selecting a trial option. It's not essential that the accused enter a plea; the court may record a plea of **not guilty** if no plea is entered.

2. The court may hear evidence from a psychiatrist or other qualified person and order a psychiatric examination to test the accused's fitness to stand trial. The judge usually orders a ban on publication of such evidence; if not, it may be reported. There are normally no other restrictions on reporting arraignments.

3. A decision on bail may be made at arraignment, or at a separate bail (or **interim release**) hearing. If the accused requests a ban on publicity, the judge must grant it. It is then forbidden to publish testimony or the judge's reasons for granting or denying bail. The fact of whether bail was granted, and any conditions for release, may be reported.

4. Even without a publication ban, no confession offered in evidence by police or other witnesses may be reported at this stage without legal advice. There should be no mention of a criminal record without approval from a supervisor or counsel.

Change of venue

Danger:

1.   Reporting court decision.

1.   When a criminal case becomes so notorious in a community that it would be almost impossible to find jury members who could be impartial, a change of location (**venue**) can be ordered by the court to ensure a fair jury trial for the defendant. The change is usually to a community well removed from the scene of the crime.

2.   Since the point of changing location is to find untainted jury members, the court may order severe limitations on what can be published about the case.

3.   On occasion, the court may ban publication of anything about the change of location — including the fact that a change of venue has been requested or granted.

4.   When the trial begins in the new location, the court can order a ban on reporting that a change of venue has taken place. The ban remains in effect until a verdict has been handed down or the trial otherwise ends.

Preliminary inquiry

Dangers:

1.   Violating a publication ban.
2.   Reporting a confession.

1.   A preliminary inquiry is held to determine if there's enough evidence to warrant a trial. The accused usually asks for a ban on publicity. The judge is required to grant it on request, and no evidence may then be reported.

2.   What may be reported:

a)   Whether the accused is sent to trial.

b)   The exact charge on which the accused was brought to preliminary hearing and, if appropriate, on which he or she was sent to trial.

c)   The number of witnesses heard.

d)   Any comment by the lawyers, or the accused, or any part of the judge's decision not referring to the evidence heard.

3. Even without a publication ban, the Criminal Code prohibits reporting any confession — by the accused at the hearing (rare) or mentioned in evidence by police or other third parties at this stage — at risk of a fine, time in jail, or both.

4. A confession in this context can mean a literal admission of guilt or any statement or action implying guilt. For example, if police testify that the accused led them to the body in a murder case, it should be avoided as an implied admission of guilt.

5. Any publication ban remains in effect until the conclusion of any subsequent trial, defined as the point at which a verdict is reached, regardless of intention to appeal. At that point, testimony at the preliminary hearing becomes publishable.

6. If the accused is discharged at the end of a preliminary hearing for lack of sufficient evidence, the banned testimony becomes publishable. An exception is a confession offered as evidence by police but not admitted by the judge; in such cases, consult a supervisor or counsel.

Trial

Dangers:

1. Reporting what the jury hasn't heard.

2. Evidence of criminal record.

1. The general rule is that any evidence admitted by the judge at a public trial can be reported. This includes confessions and other evidence that may have been excluded at previous stages, if the evidence is presented again in open court.

2. It is dangerous to resurrect any other previous submissions made at a preliminary inquiry until the trial ends.

3. Evidence or arguments presented with the jury absent should not be reported, except in the rare cases where the jury has been sequestered. For example, no reference should be made to evidence at a hearing (**voir dire**) held to determine whether certain evidence, such as confessions or wiretaps, may be legally presented to the jury.

4. If such evidence is admitted by the judge, it can be reported when presented to the jury. If not admitted, it may not be reported until after the trial, and then only with consent of supervisors or counsel.

5. Statements ordered struck from the record by the judge may still be reported. The judge's ruling has the effect of erasing the statements only from the trial record.

6. Any reporter who starts to cover a trial part way through

must confirm that there is no voir dire or other restriction on what may be reported.

7. Evidence of previous convictions is usually not admitted at trial. If an accused presents evidence intended to show good character, he or she may then be asked about any prior criminal record.

8. On rare occasions, the public is excluded from all or part of a trial:

a) Trials of young people under the federal act dealing with youth crime.

b) Trials in which there is risk of disclosing information affecting national security or defence, international relations or the public interest.

c) Cases where the judge orders a trial closed in the interests of maintaining order or the proper administration of justice. No testimony may then be reported, but the verdict can be.

9. If the public is excluded to maintain order but the media are allowed to remain, the proceedings may be reported unless the judge directs otherwise.

10. Immediately after a verdict in a criminal trial has been rendered — and even if one of the parties plans to appeal — it is permissible to report fair and accurate comments by editorial writers, columnists and legal experts on the facts of the case, the parties, their lawyers, the judge's conduct and the administration of justice.

11. There is increasing leeway now to criticize the administration of justice, including the conduct of judges and the validity of their judgments. But to suggest unworthy motives by a judge is courting a contempt citation.

Undercover police in court

Danger:

1. Identifying and endangering undercover police officer.

1. When an undercover police officer testifies at a trial, courts often order bans on publication of any information, including images, that could serve to identify the officer or other undercover officers mentioned in testimony.

2. Such a ban is very broad and reporters should assume that it includes any reference made in court to a first name used by the officer. This may seem unusual since a first name may not normally amount to identifying an individual. However, it is not unusual for an undercover officer to be identified on the street

by first name only. Such officers regularly use their real first names and could be in serious danger if they are discovered to be undercover officers.

3. Reporters should never use the first name or any identifying information of the undercover officer when reporting on the matter without specifically checking with the Crown attorney for bans. Even if there are no bans, reporters should strive to ensure that their report does not imperil the safety of undercover officers.

Appeals

Danger:

1. Suggesting bias.

1. Normally, anything and everything said at an open appeal court hearing can be reported.

2. Appeal court judges are generally considered to be above being prejudiced by the publication of comment or opinion about a case being heard on appeal.

3. Nonetheless, to suggest bias or prejudgment on the part of a judge — appeal court or otherwise — is tempting fate.

4. And of course the normal rules of court reporting — fair and balanced coverage — apply to appeal court hearings.

Retrials

Dangers:

1. Recalling previous verdict.
2. Recalling previous evidence.

1. When a trial ends in a hung jury, or when a conviction or acquittal has been overturned on appeal, a new trial may be ordered. That means that for the accused, the slate has in effect been wiped clean. It is as if the first trial did not take place.

2. The appeal court's decision may be reported at the time with full background. But well before a new trial begins there must be the same restraint in reporting on evidence or testimony as would have applied before the first trial, especially if a jury trial is possible.

3. Unless specifically banned, it is permissible to report that a previous trial ended in a hung jury, or that the verdict of the

previous trial was overturned on appeal. When retrial is imminent, it is not normally permitted to report what the previous verdict was, or that there was a hung jury, since that could influence the new jury.

Young persons

The Youth Criminal Justice Act, which covers people from their 12th to their 18th birthdays, replaced the Young Offenders Act in April 2003. It is significantly different from its predecessor.

1. All trials of people aged 12 to 18 take place in youth courts. No one is transferred to adult court.

2. The act bans publishing the name or other identifying characteristics of the accused through at least until sentencing.

3. After sentencing, some young offenders can be identified, but only those who have committed certain crimes or have been sentenced under specific circumstances. Youth who can be identified include:

a) those given adult sentences;

b) those sentenced for murder, manslaughter, attempted murder or aggravated sexual assault;

c) those for whom the Crown sought an adult sentence for a violent offence where there were at least two previous convictions for violent offences, provided there are no publication bans specifically issued by the court.

4. Once persons turn 18, they can consent to be identified as having been prosecuted under the act, as long as they are not still incarcerated for the crime.

5. The act bans publishing the names and other identifying characteristics of juvenile victims of youth crimes, including deceased victims. It also bans identifying young people as persons who have appeared as witnesses at youth court hearings. Exceptions to both restrictions involve permission from the court, parents, and – in the case of witnesses or victims who have turned 18 – the young people themselves. When dealing with possible exceptions to the ban, make sure there are no court orders affecting identification; and ensure identifying the witness or victim will not also identify another young person whose identity is protected.

6. If police ask, the court can allow the identification of young people they are trying to arrest. Such a court order can last five days.

7. The prohibitions against identification of some young people include carrying information that could identify them, such as where they live, where they go to school, sports teams they belong to, the names of members of their families, and the institution where they are held.

8. When a young person is suspected in a crime involving family members, no story may include both the victim's name and her or his relationship to the suspect, since this could identify the young person. When the first news of such a crime becomes available:

a) Do not name the victims or describe their relationship with the suspect until it is clear where the chief news interest will lie: in the relationship or in the stature of the family.

b) Try to develop a consensus with other media on what to publicize – the names or the relationship.

c) Once a decision is made on which element to publicize, do not switch tracks without consulting counsel. Anyone putting together the names from one story and the relationship from the other can identify the suspect.

Child protection laws

Care must be taken when handling stories that deal with proceedings under provincial laws on child custody and guardianship. These acts restrict reporting in order to shield children from harmful publicity.

The rules vary from province to province, so check before running a story that identifies children in custody cases.

In British Columbia, for instance, it is up to the courts to decide if the children can be identified. In Ontario, the Child and Family Services Act prohibits the identification of children involved in proceedings or hearings. It also prohibits identifying the child's parents, foster parents or other family members. It is OK to identify a couple in court on drug trafficking charges, and to say they have a daughter. But it contravenes the act to include that the daughter was taken into protective custody by the Children's Aid Society. A proceeding under the Child and Family Services Act begins as soon as a child protection worker intervenes to take a child to a place of safety. No court need be involved.

Sensitive cases

1. In cases involving sexual offences, extortion or usury, a judge must ban publication of the identity of victims or a juvenile witness if asked to do so by either the victim, the witness or the Crown.

2. In such cases, it is forbidden not only to name the victim or witness but also to provide any information that could disclose their identity.

3. Among information that could reveal their identity would be a family relationship, address, place of employment or other characteristic that could allow some members of the community to make an identification.

4. Even where no ban is in effect, it is usually wrong to identify

alleged victims of sexual assault without their active consent. CP does not name minors who are victims of sexual assault, even with the consent of their parents.

5. In rare cases, a victim's name somehow becomes widely known in the community and publication of the name is not banned. Nevertheless, editors should still weigh whether using the name will send a signal to readers that the media are indifferent to the problems of sexual assault victims in general. Any story that does contain the name of an alleged sex assault victim should include a reference explaining why the person is being identified.

6. Reporting on divorce and annulment proceedings is subject by law to restraints. Generally, only a bare identification of those involved, the main issues and the judgment can safely be reported.

7. Generally, provincial legislation that requires the reporting of communicable diseases also provides for strict confidentiality. It is therefore risky to breach the anonymity of those with a sexually transmitted disease, AIDS or other reportable infection without their consent.

8. Certain offences are regarded by the law as relatively minor, subject to small fines at most. But publicly naming those accused of communicating with a prostitute, indecent exposure or similar offences can have ruinous consequences. It should be done rarely.

9. The law, not just ethics, can determine what gruesome or indecent details to publish in court cases. The law forbids reporting on indecent matters or indecent medical details that could injure public morals — phrases that are vague enough to require legal advice when in doubt.

Amber Alerts

When a child is reported missing, police can issue an Amber Alert — a warning to the public to be on the lookout for a child. The warning gets to the public via broadcasters and digital highway signs and other media.

The declaration of the alert confers no special rights on media and it doesn't trump statutory publishing bans such as child welfare laws. However, if the police are giving information to the media that is truly pertinent to the recovery of a child, it is almost certainly going to be legally defensible. There are strong defences for carrying information as it becomes available from police on where the child was taken from, who is believed to have taken the child and the nature of any threat from the suspect — information important to the recovery of a child. There may be reasons to consult legal counsel on some facts that come to light related to the Amber Alert, but the core information released by police to help in recovery of the child should make its way to wire quickly.

However, if the child has been found alive, consult with counsel for guidance on whether it is wise to continue to publish these facts, given that the reason it was OK to do so earlier — to help find the child — is no longer applicable.

Civil cases

While criminal cases involve society's attempt to control wrongdoing or protect the public good, civil cases involve disputes between private individuals or corporations. Society provides the court structure and a set of laws designed to make the settlement of grievances an orderly process.

Civil cases require the same care and dispassion of reporters as criminal cases do.

Vocabulary:

1. In civil cases, there is no **prosecutor**. Nobody is said to be **charged**. At the end of a court hearing, no one is **convicted** or **acquitted**, nor found **guilty** or **not guilty**.

2. The person initiating a civil case is the **plaintiff** or **petitioner**. The process involves **bringing suit** or **taking action** or **seeking damages**. The other party is the **defendant** or **respondent**.

Claims

1. Small claims are heard in a variety of lower courts depending on the province. The upper limit for the amount claimed in such cases also varies with the province.

2. Small claims are usually heard directly by a judge, without lawyers acting for the contesting parties.

3. Intermediate claims are heard at lower or intermediate court levels, with lawyers representing the parties. Jury trials are rare.

4. The largest civil claims are heard in provincial superior courts, by judge alone or with jury.

5. Jury trials are no longer provided for in Quebec for civil suits.

Other civil cases

1. Surrogate or probate courts exist in some provinces to deal with wills and estates. In other provinces, such cases are heard by the courts that handle other civil actions.

2. The Federal Court of Canada has jurisdiction over citizenship, taxation, immigration, copyright, trademark and patent cases, judicial review of federal administrative tribunals, and claims brought against the government of Canada.

Appeals

1. Appeals in civil cases are heard by the appeal division of a provincial superior court or court of appeal. Leave to appeal must almost always be sought from the higher court.

2. The appeal division of Federal Court hears appeals from decisions of that court.

3. The Supreme Court of Canada hears appeals on civil cases if there is a matter of public importance or an important point of law at issue.

Examination for discovery

1. Before trial of a civil suit, a process called examination for discovery is normally held. It allows the parties to examine each other's case and to clarify the issues to be resolved at trial.

2. Although the testimony is recorded and those testifying are under oath, the evidence at examination for discovery is not subject to all the normal safeguards of a courtroom.

3. Such examinations are not considered public hearings and cannot be covered by reporters. The transcripts are not public documents and are not normally accessible to the media. Publication of such evidence should not be considered without legal advice.

Damage suits

Dangers:

1. Quoting from one-sided documents.

2. Referring to amount claimed.

1. When one party files suit for damages against another, a writ or statement of claim is issued. A fair and accurate account of what is in the writ normally may be carried, but the story should strive for balance by:

a) including comment from principals named in the writ;

b) making clear the writ consists of allegations that are still to be tested in court.

A report on a statement of claim could present a libel risk if the above conditions are not met. In cases where a writ contains extremely defamatory information, it is prudent to seek counsel's advice before filing a story.

2. When a jury is hearing a civil suit for damages, it is not supposed to be informed about the amount of damages sought, for fear it will be misled. There is no real limit to the damages a person can claim and the amount may be ridiculous. As a working (but not infallible) rule, don't report the amount of damages sought during a jury trial or for a month before such a trial. Once a case has been decided, there is no such restriction.

3. The restriction does not apply to cases heard by a judge alone, nor to civil cases in Quebec where there are no longer jury trials in civil suits.

Contempt of court

Every journalist must be on guard against contempt of court in reporting on crimes, investigations and court cases.

Contempt of court doesn't mean despising a judge or the justice system. It's an old usage of the word **contempt**, meaning to **interfere** with the administration of justice or **disobey** the courts.

Controlling contempt is intended to protect a person's right to a fair trial, a cornerstone of democracy.

General guidelines

Dangers:

1. Defendant's confession.
2. Previous convictions.
3. Speculation.
4. Ignoring publication bans.

---

1. When a story is known to be in contempt, kill it at once. If contempt is suspected, withhold the story from publication, check it with counsel and keep editors advised.

➤ See **Libel**, page 123.

2. It is a basic rule that nothing must be published that interferes with the proper course of justice. That particularly includes anything that impairs an accused person's right to a fair trial.

3. Even if a statement is true and not libellous, it may be in contempt of court if it hurts a person's right to a fair trial.

4. A statement made in a legislature, court or other place of privilege is not protected from contempt. If an MP makes a statement in the Commons that could be prejudicial, it should not be published without consulting counsel.

5. There is a particular risk of prejudice in reporting on a defendant's confession unless it has been accepted as evidence in open court.

6. Check counsel before referring to previous convictions unless they are mentioned in open court. Such information is not necessarily admissible at trial.

7. The publication or repetition of a statement in contempt of court is itself contempt. The source of the statement or its accuracy doesn't matter.

8. Guilt or innocence should not be imputed to any party in a court case. It is also dangerous to speculate on possible motive for a crime, the credibility of witnesses or the likely outcome in a jury trial.

9. Do not report testimony or other material from previous stages of a criminal proceeding — preliminary hearing, death inquiry or the like — unless it is introduced again in open court.

10. At a jury trial, it is a crime to report evidence heard by a judge at a *voir dire,* a hearing held to determine whether certain evidence will be presented to the jury. Such hearings are always held with the jury excluded. However, publication of voir dire evidence may be allowed when it involves a case being tried by judge alone or in those rare cases where a jury is being sequestered. If in doubt, check counsel.

11. Any restriction imposed by a court on publication remains in effect until the court sets it aside.

12. It is a crime in Canada for jurors to disclose any information on their deliberations. While there's no law forbidding reporters to interview jurors, the reporter could be charged with inducing a juror to break the law by encouraging the juror to reveal protected information.

13. Once a case has ended, it is usually permissible to report criticism of the administration of justice or the conduct of a judge. It is risky to suggest the judge had improper motives. In some provinces, a statement may also be in contempt if it vilifies a court or judge. Check counsel when in doubt.

Foreign cases

1. Exercise care on any story from abroad that includes out-of-court statements by police or others about Canadian individuals or businesses if a subsequent trial is likely to take place in Canada.

2. In particular, beware of assuming that U.S. laws and legal procedures apply in this country. Statements about an accused person from police and other authorities of a kind that are routine in the United States can be considered contempt in Canada.

Libel

Remember:

1. Statements damaging to reputation must never be published unless there is a clear legal basis for doing so.

2. Anyone who repeats a libel is fully responsible for the libel, no matter what its source.

3. A libel can cause great damage to a person's life.

4. Individual reporters and editors can be sued along with their employers for libels they permit to be published.

Libel is the publication of a false and damaging statement. It is part of the broader legal category known as **defamation**, covering **slander** (ordinary conversation) and **libel** (published or broadcast).

Defamation is a statement that tends to lower a person in the opinion of others, or exposes the person to hatred, contempt or ridicule. Defamation is also a statement that injures another's reputation in a way that affects that person's livelihood — work, trade or profession — or financial credit.

When a story is known to be libellous, **kill** it at once.

BULLETIN
   EDITORS: Kill Moncton Accusation. No charge laid yet. Story is possibly dangerous. Will be no sub.
   CP Halifax

When even a slight doubt exists, **withhold** the story from publication immediately while a check is made.

URGENT
   EDITORS: Withhold Brandon Wheat from publication. Contains possibly dangerous quotes. CP is checking with counsel.
   CP Winnipeg

Then either kill it or release it promptly. If a kill is needed, advise whether a sub will be sent. If the story is approved as sent, release it urgently in an advisory.

Don't blame libel or libellous material for a kill or withhold. It might weaken CP's defence against a subsequent suit.

Note: The CP-BN newswires provide instant publication of every word filed. As soon as stories are sent to wire, they immediately reach a lot of people. Aside from quickly being posted on websites or read by TV and radio news presenters, many stories, as well as advisories and budget lines, are automatically routed to clients of the Command News database. This means all words – slugs, headlines, update notes – have the same potential to be legal risks. If a story about alleged transgressions of a public figure were cavalierly slugged **Nailed-the-Stinker,** for instance, this could be used in court to suggest the subject of the story was not given fair treatment.

General information

Key points:

1. Truth difficult to prove.
2. Public interest must be weighed.

1. Libel has serious potential to harm not only CP and its employees, but any newspaper or broadcaster using the material. A plaintiff can sue everyone, or pick and choose arbitrarily — even to the point of aiming at the weakest links, those with the smallest resources who are most likely to pay to settle a libel suit without contest.

2. Libel involves an untrue report. Truth is a **complete defence** against a libel suit. A true statement of fact is not vulnerable even if it is damaging. But the one who publishes a damaging statement is responsible for proving the truth of the statement, and that is often extremely difficult. In some cases it may be impossible. It's not up to the plaintiff to prove the statement is false.

3. In Quebec, in addition to truth, the Civil Code requires that publication be in the **public interest** and **without malice.**

4. **Public interest** and **lack of malice** are not specified by law elsewhere in Canada. However, professional ethics dictate that before publishing a truthful but damaging statement, the press will weigh carefully whether the public interest is served by publication. And absence of malice must be a foregone conclusion in the publication of any news report.

5. The Canadian Press and other media whose reports reach an audience within Quebec must take into account Quebec's legal requirements when considering publication of potentially libellous material from elsewhere in Canada, particularly if the report concerns a Quebec resident.

6. Consent can be used as a defence in a libel suit, but it requires proof that:

a) the person defamed has been informed defamatory information will be published, and

b) the person knows what he or she is consenting to, and

c) the person consents to publication.

If consent is to be used as a defence, the proof of it will have to meet certain standards that stand up in court. A signed formal statement or an audio tape of an interview may be called for. Consult with counsel beforehand to work out details.

7. Except in Quebec, it is virtually impossible to libel the dead. And a libel suit launched by someone who subsequently dies is normally dropped. However, it could be dangerous to defame a dead person in a way that affects the living: for example, suggesting a man sexually abused his children before he died.

Privilege

Key points:

1. Fair, accurate, no malice.
2. Right to rebuttal.

1. Privilege means **protection from legal action**, even when defamatory material has been published. Privilege is based on two traditional assumptions:

a) It would be in the public interest for every citizen to attend certain events or read certain reports. Failing that, all citizens should have access to fair and accurate reports of such events.

b) In some cases, the public good is better served through unrestrained debate and the free communication of information than it is through a normal concern about accuracy or defamation.

2. Privilege is never absolute. At its most fundamental, it still requires that any report be **fair, accurate** and **without malice:**

a) **Fairness** means lack of bias, not taking statements out of context.

b) **Accuracy** means reporting the facts correctly. A report need not be textual or complete; it can be a fair synopsis.

c) **Lack of malice** means there is no dishonest or hidden motive nor reckless disregard for the truth.

3. The protection of privilege is also lost as a defence in a libel action if there has been a refusal to publish a reasonable

statement of explanation or contradiction despite a request from the person defamed to do so.

4. Privilege does not extend to matters of contempt. Statements that could interfere with a person's right to a fair trial risk contempt even if made by an elected representative during an open session of a legislature. A fair and accurate account of a court case could be in contempt as well if it prejudices another case.

5. A statement of claim filed in court as part of a libel action is a privileged document and often provides the legal basis needed for reporting the alleged libel. Any story on the libel action should be fair, accurate, without malice and contemporaneous to the action in order to preserve the privilege. This means including views from both sides in the case. Source the material to the statement of claim, and consult Main Desk before moving the story on the wire.

What's protected

Key points:

1. Legislative bodies, courts.
2. Quasi-judicial bodies.
3. Meetings, reports.
4. Public proceedings.
5. Notices to the public.

---

1. The common law — that is, traditional rights recognized by the courts — and the Civil Code in Quebec provide general principles for the protection known as privilege.

2. In addition, all provinces have specific statutes dealing with libel and privilege. The statutes vary; in tricky cases, get legal advice. However, the following may be considered privileged:

a) Debates and committee meetings of the House of Commons, the Senate and provincial legislatures, as well as public reports and documents issued by these bodies.

Note: The privilege doesn't extend to statements made outside of a chamber or committee hearing, such as in a scrum.

b) Proceedings heard in public before any court exercising judicial authority, and reports issued by courts. The privilege doesn't extend to hearings from which public and press are excluded, nor to any matter on which the court has banned publication. If a report is not contemporaneous, consult counsel.

c) Death inquiries or coroner's inquests, royal commissions and other commissions of inquiry are not strictly courts but their proceedings and reports or documents are generally privileged.

d) Hearings of federal and provincial regulatory agencies and administrative tribunals, such as labour relations boards and human rights tribunals, and their reports or documents.

e) Meetings and reports of local government bodies and their agencies, such as municipal councils, municipal planning boards, school boards, boards of health.

f) Public meetings. This broad category can be tricky. It is usually defined as a meeting open to the general public, lawfully convened, to discuss a matter of public interest. It probably doesn't cover a news conference, nor a political meeting to which only supporters of one party have been invited. When in doubt, check counsel.

g) Any bulletin, report, notice or other document issued for the information of the public from any government office or department, medical officer of health or local board of health. This would include, for example, a warning that a particular product is dangerous to health.

h) Any notice or report issued by any government or municipal official, commissioner of police or chief constable for the information of the public, and published at that person's request. The most common example is a police appeal for public help in locating a fugitive or missing person.

Provincial statutes

Key points:

1. Professional, business, sports bodies.
2. Right of rebuttal.
3. Retraction, apology.

1. Each province in Canada has some form of libel legislation, dealing with issues of defamation and protection from legal action under certain conditions.

2. In addition to the categories of privilege listed previously, most provincial laws extend privilege to the findings and proceedings of professional, business and sports organizations that are formed in Canada. Included would be the disciplinary proceedings of law societies, medical associations, trade and business associations and sports leagues.

3. However, provincial law states that refusal to carry a reasonable statement of explanation or contradiction from the complainant, if asked to do so, will wipe out the privilege.

4. The law also specifies that a full and fair retraction for a defamatory story, if published with equal prominence to the original story and within *three days* of receiving legal notice, will reduce damages. The provision doesn't apply to a story that suggests a criminal offence was committed.

5. Damages may also be reduced if a full apology is published either before legal action was started or promptly afterwards.

6. The Quebec Press Act, in addition to most of the above, also extends privilege to the reports of the provincial ombudsman when tabled in the legislature, and to reports by the government or an authorized person about the financial solvency of companies or the value of certain stock and bond issues.

7. The Quebec law provides for reduced damages by apology, but that doesn't apply when a criminal offence is suggested. Nor does it apply when the defamation involves a candidate for Parliament, the national assembly or municipal office and when it is published in the period extending from three days before nomination day until election day.

Special concerns

1. People in certain areas of society make outrageous statements as a matter of course. Politics and sports are prime examples.

2. Public statements from people in these fields are routinely harsh, overstated and malicious. If such statements were made by others under different circumstances, the courts would be much busier.

3. The fact that political or sports comments rarely result in libel claims does not mean there is no need for caution in reporting them. Libel is libel. Check counsel before taking chances.

4. A separate concern involves non-Canadians who have business or other interests in Canada. Such people can sue for libel in this country if news from abroad is published in Canada which affects their reputation or livelihood in Canada. Thus, for example, a report from somewhere in the United States that alleges drug-taking by a football player now in the Canadian Football League — or even with CFL prospects — would be dangerous. So would a report from abroad that damages the reputation of a Hong Kong businessman with Canadian business interests.

Good faith

1. If a statement is false, it is no defence to claim that it was thought to be true at time of publication.

2. However, the damages awarded in a libel suit may be reduced because of absence of malice and evidence of good faith:

a) if there were reasonable grounds for believing the defamatory statement was true, and

b) if an apology was published when the statement was discovered to be false.

Fair comment

Key points:

1. Honest opinion.

2. Based on provable fact.

3. Public interest.

1. Commentary involves questions of opinion and interpretation. A different test is applied to commentary than to factual reporting. Comment or opinion (**the government's program is ruining the economy**) need not be proved true in the sense that an objective fact (**the government has increased the sales tax**) is true.

2. The defence of fair comment has often been applied to editorials and to artistic criticism such as book, film or theatre reviews. But it isn't limited to such material. It can be used to defend any story that mixes factual material with interpretation and analysis.

3. To be defensible, comment must meet these criteria:

a) It must express an opinion honestly held. It can't be presented maliciously or out of a hidden motive.

b) Most important, it must be based on facts *presented in the story* that can be proved to be true. An honest opinion based on false information cannot be defended.

c) It must relate to a matter of public interest, not a purely private matter.

4. Public interest is roughly parallel to news value. But publication in one province on the grounds of public interest could be libellous in another province.

5. The basic rule holds: When in doubt, get legal advice.

Copyright

Dangers:

1. Substantial quotes without OK.
2. Permission not in writing.

---

1. Copyright is what gives the creator of an original work the exclusive right to benefit from it.

2. Copyright covers such creations as books, films, songs, articles and essays, letters, diaries, pictures or anything else that's original and in some permanent form. It can even extend to distinctive titles.

3. The copyright owner controls the right to reproduce the work, in whole or in substantial part.

4. For the press, this means there can be no substantial quotations from copyrighted material without written permission of the copyright owner. Giving a mere credit to the copyright owner isn't sufficient.

5. *Substantial* has different meanings for different works. A complete stanza from a short pop song could be substantial. Generally, copying the heart of a work would be against copyright law. Check counsel when in doubt.

6. An exception is made for quotations used in a review or critique, but it must be a bona fide review and the quotes should be no more than needed to make a critical point.

7. Generally, government documents, speeches and most other material used in daily journalism are not copyright.

8. Over time, copyright protection is lost and the work falls into the public domain. In Canada, literary and artistic copyright expires 50 years after the author's death. Copyright on photographs expires 50 years after the negative has been processed.

9. Information cannot be copyrighted, only the form in which it is presented. Although newspapers frequently identify a story as being copyright, the actual news in the story cannot be protected. Someone else using an original method of expression may reproduce the information. Making a few changes in expression is not sufficient; the presentation must be substantially original.

10. The Canadian Press has first right to use staff-written local news from newspapers that are part of the co-operative news agency, whether or not the newspaper declares it to be copyright.

11. However, worked-up exclusives or news from beyond the newspaper's normal coverage area cannot legally be distributed in their original form by CP without permission from the managing editor or other senior officer at the paper. Giving credit to the paper is not a substitute for getting permission if there are to be substantial quotes or reproductions from the original. Permission can be assumed if the paper has transmitted the story to CP electronically

12. Like anyone else, in the absence of permission, CP may distribute a report based on the information in the copyright story. It must use substantially different words and it should be brief — no longer than needed to report the substance of the story. Direct quotes of more than a sentence or two are not allowed.

13. CP may also not normally use a published feature created by a freelance, even if it involves local news. Freelance work is usually identified by a different credit line (e.g., **Special to the Mirror**) than staff work. Ignoring the copyright owned by a freelance can be costly.

14. The copyright in a Letter to the Editor is held by the letter writer, who automatically gives a right of publication to the newspaper that receives the letter. To reproduce all or part of the letter elsewhere would require written permission from the copyright holder, in strict legal terms. But in practical terms, verbal permission from the newspaper will do. (Few letter writers are likely to sue because their views have been given a wider audience, and if they won a suit the damages would likely be minimal.)

15. Freelance photographers hired by CP negotiate in advance the ownership and resale rights for their film. The work of newspapers' regular freelance photographers is available to CP. In most instances of spontaneous photography — the bystander's shots of a hot news event — the freelance is told by the paper to negotiate directly with CP.

➤ See **Pictures**, page 367.

16. News distributed on the Internet has no special status in terms of copyright law. A story published in an Internet edition of a newspaper or any other website is subject to the law just as it would be if it were in a print edition. Permission must be given by the copyright holder before it is reproduced in substantially the same form.

➤ See **Writing for and about the Internet,** page 180.

Privacy, wiretaps

Dangers:

1. Disclosing others' communications.
2. Broadcasting private conversations.

---

1. Anyone may record their own conversations, without the permission of the other party, whether in person or on the telephone or other circumstance.

2. However, it's illegal to intercept or record conversations or private communications of other people without the consent of one of the other parties.

3. It's also illegal to broadcast on radio (but, oddly, not on TV) any part of one's own conversation with someone else without the consent of the other person. An exception is when the other person has phoned in to participate in the broadcast.

4. And it's illegal to use or disclose anything about others' private communications without the consent of one of the parties.

Media and police

Police in Canada have shown a disturbing tendency to turn to the print and broadcast media for information and evidence in recent years. They have demanded the use of photographs and film to document charges against possible rioters and others involved in public disturbances, and have made other demands on news people to support police work.

The media have generally resisted. If people come to view the media as an arm of the justice system, they will lose confidence in the media as an intermediary between ordinary citizens and authorities.

Following are normal guidelines for dealings with police:

Public notices

1. The media normally co-operate when police ask for publicity about the hunt for suspects or lost persons. Accuracy in identification is essential. Racial description and other characteristics — not usually part of a news report — are a normal part of such published identification material.

2. Do not casually refer to a person as dangerous. The description would be prejudicial if referring to someone whose jury trial is imminent. It should be based on a *written* release from police intended for the public.

Co-operation with police

1. There is normally no objection to providing police with copies of stories or photographs that have already been published, or other routine material of a non-confidential nature, as a matter of courtesy.

2. However, reporters' notes, unpublished film, background files, electronic mail and other material dealing with ongoing stories or anything of a private or confidential nature should not be provided to police unless they produce a search warrant.

3. Material gathered by reporters and other employees in the course of their work is the property of the employer. No employee has the right to turn over such material to police without permission from a senior supervisor.

Newsroom searches

1. Police will sometimes provide advance notice that they intend to present a search warrant. In any case, police arriving in a newsroom with a search warrant — with or without notice — must not be delayed, obstructed or resisted. They are not obliged to wait until legal counsel is on the scene.

2. However, police should be referred immediately to a senior

supervisor, and legal counsel should be informed immediately by phone.

3. The warrant should be inspected closely to ensure that

a) all factual references (address, name of company or person, date) are accurate;

b) a suspected offence is specified;

c) it is properly signed by a justice of the peace.

4. If there are errors, the police should be asked to leave. If there aren't, the supervisor can watch any search being conducted. Others on staff can observe and, if necessary later, serve as witnesses about the way the search was conducted, but only the supervisor should talk to police.

5. While not obliged to assist searchers, the supervisor may decide it is best to direct them to a specific desk or area and otherwise help them if the alternative is a wide sweep that could uncover unrelated confidential material elsewhere in the newsroom.

6. The supervisor should ask permission to photocopy any material that is to be seized. If the request is refused, legal counsel should be consulted immediately.

7. If the searchers intend to take confidential material relating to sources, or unpublished material, the supervisor should insist that it be placed in a sealed envelope until the question of privilege can be decided in court.

8. Legal counsel should be consulted promptly about any question that arises as a result of being served with a search warrant.

Legal vocabulary

The language of courts and lawyers is extremely precise, but it can be distant from plain speech. Latin terms and jargon abound. Legal language may find its way into a story legitimately for effect or precision, but in most cases a plain substitute or clear explanation is best.

Some standard legal terms:

affidavit: sworn written statement to be used as evidence.

arraign: charge before the courts.

bawdy-house: archaic term still used in Criminal Code for brothel.

common law: unwritten law based on ancient custom and judicial precedent.

> **common-law marriage**: relationship based on living together without legal recognition. **Note:** It is not usually necessary to specify if a relationship is common-law.

concurrent: at the same time; of a number of jail sentences, to be served simultaneously (as opposed to consecutively).

contempt (of court): not disdain for the judge, but interference with justice or disobedience of court order.

copyright: protection of exclusive use of original work.

ex parte (Latin for *from one party*): one-sided; submission by one party in legal dispute without contest from other side.

habeas corpus (Latin for *You have the body*): writ requiring person be brought before court, usually to test whether person's detention is legal.

house arrest: detention in one's own home instead of prison.

in camera (Latin for *in a room*): private(ly); hearing with public excluded.

indeterminate sentence: of no fixed term, dependent on prisoner's conduct.

indict, indictment: formally accuse of crime; formal accusation or charge.

> **indictable offence**: more serious level of criminal charge (less serious is called summary offence).

interim release: term increasingly used instead of **release on bail**.

leave: permission, as in **leave to appeal**.

open custody: assignment of offender to group home or other lightly supervised environment, usually for juveniles.

plaintiff: person who brings complaint to court in civil case.

plead no contest: in the United States, the name of a plea in a criminal action that has the same effect as a guilty plea.

pré-enquête (*pre-inquiry*): rare form of private hearing by judge or justice of peace to decide whether charge should be laid.

privilege: immunity granted under certain conditions to speak without fear, or to report such speech.

remand (from Latin for *commit*): return to custody or the order doing so.

stayed charges: a direction of the court that charges not be acted on at least until some other step is taken.

sub judice (Latin for *under a judge*): before the courts; for the court alone to decide.

subpoena (Latin for *under penalty*): writ commanding presence in court.

surety (from Latin for *security*): person who takes responsibility for another's performance, such as appearing in court; also the money given as a guarantee.

suspended sentence: unenforced sentence that is subject to good behaviour.

venue (change of): location; move trial to another community to avoid prejudice against accused.

voir dire (Old French for *say the truth*): hearing within a trial, with jury excluded, to test admissibility of confession or other evidence.

writ: court order requiring specified act or giving authority to someone to have act done.

> **writ of certiorari** (from Latin for *inform*): demand from higher court for records from lower court.

> **writ of mandamus** (Latin for *We command*): command to inferior court, or to person to perform legal duty.

young person: in law, male or female between 12th and 18th birthdays.

> **child**: person under 12.

Canadian courts

Each province has different names for its courts. Here is a list, including federal courts, with upper courts listed first . Capitalization is in CP style, which is lowercase for lower courts in keeping with general capitalization rules. This is not the style used by the courts:

Federal:
Supreme Court
Federal Court of Appeal
Federal Court
Tax Court

Alberta, New Brunswick, Manitoba:
Court of Appeal
Court of Queen's Bench
provincial court

British Columbia:
Court of Appeal
Supreme Court
provincial court

Newfoundland:
Supreme Court (Court of
   Appeal and trial division)
unified family court
provincial court

Northwest Territories, Yukon:
Court of Appeal
Supreme Court
territorial court

Nova Scotia:
Court of Appeal
Supreme Court
provincial court
family court

Nunavut:
Court of Justice

Ontario:
Court of Appeal
Superior Court of Justice
Ontario court of justice

Prince Edward Island:
Supreme Court (appeal
   division and trial division)
provincial court

Quebec:
Court of Appeal
Superior Court
Quebec court (provincial)

Saskatchewan:
Court of Appeal
Court of Queen's Bench
unified family court
provincial court

The working journalist

Freedom of information laws

The federal government and all provinces currently have laws that give Canadian citizens, corporations and others the right to acquire government-controlled information.

The federal law, in effect since 1983, is called the Access to Information Act. Provinces generally use the phrase "freedom of information" in their statutes. The laws are intended to foster open, transparent and accountable government and are used primarily by businesses, lawyers and individual citizens.

Freedom of information laws can be effective tools for journalists looking for the story behind the headlines. The process can also be lengthy, frustrating and costly, depending on the jurisdiction and the nature of the request.

Delays are common. Media requests for sensitive material normally take far longer than the 30-day deadline imposed by the federal law, for example, which also gives departments the right to claim time extensions. Even so, dated material can shed new light on key issues and developments and provide an opportunity to revisit important stories. Other information on issues never before in the public arena can still play as news, even though the audit, report or study may be months or years old. Typically, the released material has the added attraction of being exclusive to a reporter or newsroom.

Freedom of information requests are a supplement to, not a substitute for, informal requests for government information. A formal request has the advantage of clear rules and a system of appeals. But a reporter working a source effectively can often get more timely information. Consider using both approaches simultaneously when chasing a story.

The laws are generally inexpensive to use, despite horror stories about million-dollar fees for searching and photocopying. Most jurisdictions charge a fee for making an application, $5 under the federal law. A certain amount of free search time and photocopying is usually available, but costs can rise steeply after these thresholds are crossed.

Some tips

1. A well-focused request can avoid additional charges. Limit the time period covered; cite specific subject areas or issues; exclude newspaper clippings; ask for executive summaries only; break down large requests into smaller individual requests; ask for title pages, indices or lists of documents, then file second requests for specific documents.

2. Photocopy charges can be avoided by asking to view the records in a local office of the government department. Some departments will provide records in digital formats, such as on a CD or in electronic files that can be e-mailed, thereby cutting costs for the requester.

3. Some categories of records are relatively fruitful sources of information: briefing notes, audits, program reviews, polls, expense claims, contracts, minutes, and accident investigation reports. Ask for draft versions if the final version is not yet complete.

4. Many governments routinely post some material on their websites. Do a thorough web search before making a request, but consider that governments may suppress controversial material by posting only abbreviated versions.

5. Requests for information can usually be sent by letter, though pre-printed forms are faster. Some departments and agencies accept requests electronically, with fees paid by credit card.

6. Use the word "record" when asking for federal material, as this term includes a broad range of formats, from photographs, audio tapes, videotapes and computer disks to printed reports, letters and memorandums. Governments are not required to create records in response to a request, only to release existing records.

7. Requests are sent directly to the person designated by a department, agency or ministry to handle freedom of information inquiries. This person can often be a good source of confidential advice about how to narrow requests. Always diligently follow up requests by telephone, e-mail or letter to ensure deadlines and commitments are met. Busy freedom-of-information units tend to provide better service to those who demand it.

Some examples (federal law):

"All briefing notes provided to the defence minister since Jan. 1, 2006, on Hercules aircraft."

"Minutes of, records of decisions, agendas and materials distributed at or for the most recent meeting of the senior management committee of the Health Department, including any draft or interim versions if final versions not yet complete."

"Executive summary of the internal program review of the RCMP's aboriginal policing initiative."

Limitations

The statutes give governments the right to refuse disclosure of certain kinds of information. Cabinet confidences, police investigation records, material related to inter-government relations, legal advice, national security records, records impinging on the privacy of a person or business, can all be withheld legally. Crown corporations such as Canada Post are sometimes exempt altogether, as are some quasi-public bodies, such as Nav Canada. The laws are also typically restricted to governments rather than Parliament or legislative assemblies. The federal auditor general, for example, is not covered by the Access to Information Act because that office answers to Parliament rather than to the federal government.

Complaints about delays or exemptions can be made to public officials whose job is to investigate alleged breaches of the law. At the federal level, the office of the Information Commissioner of Canada can take complaints to court at taxpayer's expense on behalf of a requester if moral suasion does not resolve disputes. Requesters can themselves take matters directly to court. Such cases can further delay release of material but may also heighten public interest. Requesters should attempt to resolve the dispute directly with the offending department, however, before making a formal complaint.

Keep trying

Freedom of information laws can be an exercise in frustration, but for tenacious reporters they can also unlock vital information about government operations and public policy. Despite their weaknesses, the laws remain effective tools for enterprising journalists. Freedom of information stories have become an important addition to investigative journalism as practised in Canada, providing readers and viewers with fresh perspectives on the actions, intentions and foibles of governments.

The future

The Access to Information Act has been reviewed numerous times, though no fundamental changes have been made since it was passed in 1983. Federal court decisions over the last two decades have generally broadened the scope and strengthened the provisions. The scope of provincial laws has also generally broadened, often to include municipal, hospital and university records, though fees have increased sharply in some jurisdictions. Governments have also become more cautious about releasing any information touching on security. User groups can be a source for information and advice, including the Canadian Access and Privacy Association. The Canadian Association of Journalists also regularly conducts FOI seminars at its annual conventions.

Websites

The federal government's main Access to Information Act website:

http://www.tbs-sct.gc.ca/gos-sog/atip-aiprp/index_e.asp

Information Commissioner of Canada website:

http://www.infocom.gc.ca/menu-e.asp

Breaking news

The fast-breaking story goes to the very heart of CP. The Canadian news industry — print, online, radio and TV — fixes its eyes on the CP wire when major news erupts. CP faces a potential deadline every minute. It must deliver at breakneck speed. But absolute accuracy and precise attribution rank ahead of speed in handling breaking news.

Getting organized

There is no textbook on handling the spot news break. Circumstances in any two breaks are never the same.

There may be official sources, such as police, to help. But there may not be — at least in the early stages.

Improvisation and resourcefulness are the standards. So are clear-cut organization, precise assignments, steady direction and cool heads.

Confusion at the scene of a plane crash, prison riot or tornado is the norm. Expect it but don't get caught up in it. Officialdom may be in a dither. The official version of what has happened may change in minutes. And then change again. Damage estimates and death tolls can swing wildly.

But disorder has no place in a newsroom when a big story is breaking.

Some basic guidelines:

1. Respond immediately to a tip of a major break. Assign someone to concentrate on getting it confirmed or denied. Notify Main Desk and a bureau supervisor so planning can begin immediately on staff assignments: on-site staff, main lead writer, other writers, chasers, editors; and on logistics like rental cars and chartered aircraft (see *Equipment* below). Main Desk will tip other desks responsible for specific services, including BN, CP Pictures and CP Online. If a report cannot be confirmed immediately, send an advisory to all services that advises CP-BN is checking an unconfirmed *(repeat, unconfirmed)* report or angle, and include the gist of what is involved. If the report is confirmed, send a publishable item first and work on the advisory next. The advisory should say as precisely as possible when copy is expected. Then deliver it on time. Or, in rare cases, send another note saying why it has been delayed. Never leave editors or news directors hanging.

➤ See **Advisories**, page 380.

2. Never move a story on a major break that isn't nailed directly to an identified source. That can be anyone from the prime minister announcing a declaration of war to a tow-truck driver at the scene of a multi-vehicle pileup. Move a NewsAlert and-or a

QuickHit as soon as the report is confirmed. Get the attribution in the first paragraph. Every detail must be secure. Hold back if there is even the slightest doubt about a new development. But don't sit on a hot angle or wait for official sources to return calls. Move immediately to get it confirmed or denied. Nail down all sources. Ask them to spell their names — twice if there is any possibility of error. Ask for precise ranks or titles. This takes only seconds. Corrections take minutes and disfigure the report. Hold on to audio or original notes of who said what and when.

➤ See **Slugs and Coding**, page 428.

For most urgent breaking news, a NewsAlert is the first item that moves. (The most major news should move as a Bulletin or even a Flash.)

NB-Plane-Crash-Report, NewsAlert
PENNFIELD, N.B. (CP) – Witnesses tell local radio station that a large plane has crashed in flames in southwestern New Brunswick.

---

3. Then a QuickHit takes over as the fastest way to provide details to broadcasters, websites and newspapers at once during the first hectic minutes.

URGENT-NB-Plane-Crash-Report

Witnesses report seeing a large plane go down in water in southeast New Brunswick
PENNFIELD, N.B. (CP) — Eyewitnesses have told a local radio station that a plane has crashed in flames in southeastern New Brunswick.
The plane, described by some as a four-engine aircraft, apparently went down in water near Pocologan in New Brunswick.
RCMP have not confirmed the reports.
Transport Canada says it has no reports of any missing civilian aircraft.
Capt. John Pulchny, a military spokesman, told The Canadian Press that all military aircraft are accounted for.
He said a Hercules cargo aircraft was in the area on a training mission but the control tower at its home base in Nova Scotia has been in contact.

QuickHits are primarily written in a conversational style that serves the needs of broadcasters who may "rip and read" the copy on air, online clients who want a few details as quickly as possible, and newspapers that need information but not a publishable story.

QuickHits work best before 6 p.m. ET. After that time, the emphasis should be on newspaper-ready copy as deadlines approach.

Sometimes a series of QuickHits can serve a purpose, especially if it is early in the day, the story is continuing to change, and bureau or desk resources are limited. At other times, it makes more sense to hive separate reports off for each service to reflect their specific needs after the initial QuickHit. There are still other times when it is best to split a story into print and broadcast versions from the get-go. Consult with supervisors or Main Desk about what makes the most sense.

4.   After the initial details of the story are on the wire, move a coverage advisory as soon as plans are firm:

Ferry-Aground, Advisory
   Editors: Reporter Terri Theodore and photographer Chuck Stoody are en route to West Vancouver, where a B.C. ferry has crashed into a marina near the Horseshoe Bay terminal. Information from the scene is expected by 2 p.m PT.
   CP Vancouver

---

5.   Quickly pin down the location, including the nearest town if the site is remote. Tip Graphics so a newsmap can get rolling. Keep the location high in all subsequent leads.

6.   Don't wait for local authorities to get back from the scene. Chasers should not stop pressing while waiting for a promised call-back from an official source.

Each bureau should have current telephone listings for every community in its region. CD-ROM or Internet phone listings can be a great help. Scour listings for likely unofficial sources — a local service station or coffee shop. If there is nothing obvious, take a stab at random listed numbers. Chances are most people in the area will know something. Or know someone who does.

Note: Long before authorities were saying anything for the record, an eyewitness to the 1989 University of Montreal massacre told a CP reporter that a man carrying a gun had burst into a classroom.

"Someone asked him if it was a joke and the guy started firing," the eyewitness said.

Another said: "It was a human hunt and we were the quarry."

Caution: Don't say witnesses or sources when only one person is being quoted.

7.   Aim to move a 1st Writethru within 20 minutes of moving a QuickHit. Alerts can and should interrupt the flow of Writethrus any time there is an official confirmation or significant story development. If newspaper deadlines are approaching yet the story is still being handled as an all-points QuickHit, a Writethru specifically intended for print should be moved as quickly as possible.

8. Don't bury the news when new — but less important — information becomes available. Survivors found staggering from the scene or casualties on the ground belong at the top. But don't leapfrog the real news with secondary information such as an RCMP announcement of a news conference on the plane crash. That sort of information is vital for the news media — but not the reader.

9. Try for fresh information for the top of Writethrus, but it must be pertinent to the main news. If necessary, stay with the original lead and keep later secondary information lower.

Here is an example of a lead that keeps essentials at the top:

By Greg Bonnell

TORONTO (CP) – Air France said none of the 309 people aboard an Air France passenger jet perished Tuesday when it skidded off the runway, slammed into a stand of trees and burst into flames during a fierce thunderstorm at Pearson International Airport.

Injured passengers and crew members aboard Air France Flight 358 from Paris, including one of the co-pilots, staggered a short distance from the wreckage to flag down commuters along Highway 401, Canada's busiest highway, in the moments after the crash, said Peel police Sgt. Glyn Griffiths.

``We located the co-pilot on Highway 401,'' Griffiths said.

Not all breaking news comes as a surprise and a writer can benefit from advance preparation:

By Greg Bonnell and Les Perreaux

STE-ANNE-DES-PLAINES, Que. (CP) – Karla Homolka was quietly spirited away from a Quebec prison Monday to face a daunting and uncertain future she fears will be fraught with peril after 12 years behind bars for her role in the sordid sex slayings of two Ontario schoolgirls.

Homolka, the notorious ex-wife of convicted serial rapist and killer Paul Bernardo, was whisked out of the Ste-Anne-des-Plaines prison north of Montreal where she was transferred four weeks ago.

Tim Danson, lawyer for the victims' families, said Homolka had been released but could not provide details.

``I just know that she's been released but I've still got one more family member to speak to,'' Danson said.

Homolka's hopes of evading the glare of the national media spotlight appeared largely intact as she slipped past a gauntlet of reporters and photographers, apparently inside one of a pair of red minivans that drove away from the facility at the same time.

10. Give a wide berth to generalized and vaguely attributed statements, especially related to death tolls and damage estimates:

Not: Witnesses at the scene estimated about 20 people were killed and 40 or more injured.

But: "I counted 20 or 21 bodies and there must have been twice that many people who were showing some sign of life," said Jackie Lo, one of the first to reach the scene.

If figures prove badly out of line, it was Lo who was wrong — not those reporting her words:

The official toll — 11 dead and 46 injured — was provided by RMCP Sgt. Laura Bridges and coroner Luis Alvarez. Earlier, one of the first volunteer rescuers to reach the area said she had counted 20 or 21 bodies.

10. Although initial QuickHits can be in the present tense because they are not intended to be published in newspapers, guard against slipping into the present tense in later Writethrus for newspapers, especially when picking up material from radio or TV. Writing in the past tense has two advantages: the story can be quickly led without having to change the tensing of the original; and the story stands up even if the situation changes after a paper has gone to press.

Off-hours news breaks

Major news breaks at any hour of the day. A solo staffer who gets word on such a break should:

1. Brief Main Desk.

2. Move a Bulletin, NewsAlert or QuickHit, as appropriate.

3. Alert local supervisors who can call in reinforcements and start making plans for getting staff to the scene.

4. Send an advisory on coverage plans, even if it has to be tentative.

Organizing chaos

As noted, no two big news breaks are alike. But there are some tried and proven procedures to follow:

1. Get a strong lead writer in place immediately and let that person stick with the job. (Ask Main Desk for help if no one can be freed up locally.) The writer knows what information has been placed where in the story, where figures are first reported and where sources are first named, where new information can be smoothly blended in and where pickups should naturally occur.

2. The lead writer should be assigned an editor who can work directly with the writer, checking content, smoothing the flow and setting up slugging, coding and headers. The editor keeps an eye

on the clock to ensure updates are moving at reasonable intervals — she knows that last-minute detail or appealing touch of colour can go in the next Writethru rather than holding up the current one. The editor ensures the writer knows about any major changes being made in the story.

3.   The writer and editor should not be involved in any other news while handling the big break. Their undivided attention is needed.

4.   A bureau supervisor decides how much other copy is to be handled. Depending on available staff, or if the story is big enough, everything else may have to be put on hold. Often, though, the best course is to free one reporter-editor to handle all unrelated copy, likely in bare-bones form.

5.   A supervisor, consulting with the writer and editor, decides what angles need chasing, who should go where and what information is needed for the next main lead or sidebars. If others are providing quotes or other details for the main story, remember this from the Old Lead Writer's Creed: Don't tell me — write it.

6.   One supervisor or senior staff member should be the bureau funnel, dealing with Main Desk, photo and BN supervisors at Head Office and other media to ensure the bureau is gleaning all it can from local newspapers, radio and TV stations. The lead writer and editor should not be answering phones and worrying about logistics and other details.

7.   An editorial assistant or Head Office librarian may be able to help the lead writer by chasing down a piece of background, checking a map for spelling or digging into electronic archives or library files. This staffer may also help Pictures and Graphics if a file photo needs to be transmitted or information is needed for a locator map or cutline.

Equipment

Proper equipment and fast action on logistics like transportation are critical when big stories break. Editorial and Communications supervisors should ensure:

1.   That cellphones, minidiscs and laptop computers are in top shape, fully charged and ready for action at all times. Company credit cards should be available for staff on short notice. There also should be some system in place for supplying cash in off-hours.

2.   That each bureau has at hand the after-hours phone numbers for at least two charter plane companies. Phone immediately and get a quick estimate of cost and availability. Competition for charter aircraft can become intense when a big story breaks. It is often wise to make a tentative booking. Check other local media quickly about possible cost-sharing.

3.   That reporters and photographers have current passports. The United States is considering passports for Canadians entering the country. St-Pierre-Miquelon lie just off Newfoundland but belong to France.

Common faults

The most common faults in news writing are lack of imagination, muted curiosity, and a deaf ear and closed eye for the reader's interests.

These faults lead straight to news stories that are predictable, unfocused and boring.

By turn or together, they may confuse readers with conflicting information, leave them gasping for missing facts or infuriated at what they know is misinformation.

Such stories can puzzle readers with fog and bafflegab, and have them wondering what the news means to them and their everyday lives.

Bluntly put, they turn readers off.

Unanswered questions

Never leave basic questions unanswered.

Not: The price of two litres of milk is going up five cents in New Brunswick today.

But: The price of two litres of milk in New Brunswick is going up today by five cents to $3.10 a carton or two-bag plastic pack. It is the second five-cent increase in just over seven months.

Not: She was sentenced to life in prison.

But: She was sentenced to life in prison with no chance of parole for 17 years.

Not: A police officer was shot Friday as two men sped away from the scene of a bank holdup in downtown Brandon.

But: A police officer was shot in the chest and seriously wounded as two men sped away ...

Not: Canadian shoe manufacturers say a federal government plan to lift import quotas on leather footwear will deliver a severe blow to the industry.

But: Canadian shoe manufacturers say a federal government plan to lift import quotas on leather footwear will ultimately lead to higher shoe prices for Canadians, especially women. It will also mean hundreds of Canadians will lose their jobs in shoe factories, they said.

Dig for treasure

Search a story for hidden angles that would snatch a reader's attention if even a hint of the buried treasure were woven into the lead.

Not: A local man faces three counts of attempted murder and four counts of assault with a weapon causing bodily harm after a hotel brawl at a wedding reception sent seven men to hospital, six with knife wounds, early Saturday morning.

But: A brawl at a wedding reception between friends of the bride and friends of the groom left seven men hurt and a country lodge with a heap of shattered furniture, antiques and chandeliers early Saturday.

Sentences and paragraphs

Readability has never been more important. People are busier and have less time than ever to read news. They will quickly bail out from a story that is heavy and dull.

One key factor in readability is sentence length.

A sentence is more likely to be clear if it is short and conveys one idea:

People with near-death experiences agree about details to a remarkable extent.

A longer sentence which closely connects several ideas also works:

Many of them say they float out of their bodies, encounter God or a spirit figure, meet deceased relatives, review their past lives, feel great peacefulness and finally return to their bodies.

That sentence runs to 32 words, but its meaning never falters because everything relates to the same subject and the language is simple.

Try to begin sentences with words that have punch and power. Avoid starting with phrases, longer clauses or attribution.

Keep paragraphs short and active. Paragraphs of two or three tight sentences are inviting. Long, grey blobs of print are not.

Active vs. passive

Think of active verbs as power words — words that drive your sentences, keep the reader's attention and move her briskly along.

Not: The economy experienced a quick revival.

But: The economy revived quickly.

Not: At first light there was no sign of the ship.

But: The ship vanished in the night.

Use the passive when a switch in emphasis is helpful, for

instance, to put the news ahead of the source:

Not: A grievance board has ordered the reinstatement of a counsellor fired for kicking a patient.

But: A counsellor fired for kicking a patient has been ordered reinstated by a grievance board.

And the passive may lighten a sentence by removing secondary information that can wait: **A banker wanted for questioning in the disappearance of $1 million is believed to have flown to Mexico, police said today.** (But be sure a later paragraph gives reasons for the belief.)

More than words

Tell the reader what has happened, certainly. But also help the reader understand why and how it has happened in terms that strike home:

Not: The hurricane caused widespread damage to buildings, farm equipment, trees and hydro lines.

But: The hurricane's winds lifted roofs off houses and barns and flipped over cars, tractors and even lumbering dump trucks used to carry grain. Almost every fruit and shade tree in the region was knocked over, and linemen said about 3,000 hydro poles had been snapped off.

Trippers

Be alert for words, phrasing and sentences that will cause a reader to stumble:

Not: Manness said he met with trucking industry officials earlier this year who said they were concerned about taxes.

But: Manness said he met earlier this year with trucking industry officials who said they were concerned about taxes.

Not: After dining on hundreds of pet cats and dogs, the provincial Environment Ministry has decided to round up coyotes and ship them to remote parts of the province.

But: Coyotes have killed dozens of pet cats and dogs, so the provincial Environment Ministry has decided to round up the predators and ship them to remote parts of the province.

Not: The bears were destroyed when they would not leave a tree in which they were munching leaves.

But: The bears were shot when they could not be coaxed out of a playground tree where they were munching leaves.

Front-end loading

Avoid it like the plague.

Not: United States envoy Herman Cohen said in London after meeting government and rebel representatives at peace talks that the two sides had agreed to a ceasefire.

But: The two sides have agreed to a ceasefire, United States envoy Herman Cohen said after ...

Not: In an e-mail to Prime Minister Stephen Harper urging that the offices Canada Post plans to eliminate be retained, the union said it was appalled by the proposed measures.

But: The union said it was "appalled" by Canada Post's plans to close the offices. It urged in an e-mail to Prime Minister Stephen Harper that all the post offices be retained.

Not: An official of the Nova Scotia Environment Department, who was at the scene on the Annapolis River near the small community of Paradise about 170 kilometres west of Halifax, said both tractor-trailer units were spilling chemicals into the river.

But: Both tractor-trailer units were spilling chemicals into the Annapolis River near the small community of Paradise, a Nova Scotia Environment Department official said from the scene, about 170 kilometres west of Halifax.

Not: British Columbia and Yukon Birders Association executive director Anne-Marie Sheehey will be the featured speaker.

But: Executive director Anne-Marie Sheehey of the British Columbia and Yukon Birders Association will be the featured speaker.

Overloads

The overloaded lead is sure to turn the reader off:

Not: The family and friends of William John Fortune have raised enough money to rescue the stranded Canadian tourist and, with the help of volunteers from the Barbados police department, will send an airplane on Tuesday to lift him and his two daughters, Louise and Samantha, from a tiny sandspit north of the Caribbean island, longtime friend Lorne Pulsifer said Tuesday.

But: An airplane will head for a tiny Caribbean sandspit north of Barbados on Tuesday to rescue a stranded Canadian tourist and his two daughters, a family friend said Tuesday.

The overblown statement is another turnoff:

Not: Once the wind was at his back, the hometown quarterback wreaked as much havoc on the defence as Hurricane Katrina did in New Orleans.

But: The hometown quarterback, with the wind now at his back, threw touchdown passes on three consecutive drives.

Overwriting weakens stories and repels readers:

Not: The legislation was greeted with howls of protest.

But: One opposition member after another criticized the legislation, calling it ill-conceived and dangerous.

The facts are best presented in plain conversational style with deft phrasing, touches of human interest, significant details and strong quotes.

Avoid overcharged words: **blast, charged, chastise, flail, flay, lambaste, enraged, lash** and **slam**.

Simply report in an even tone what was said:

Not: Labour leader Buzz Hargrove launched a bitter attack on the company offer.

But: "It is the most preposterous company offer I've seen in the last 15 years," said labour leader Buzz Hargrove.

The formula lead

Avoid the formula approach, where every story sounds the same.

Not: BARRIE, Ont. (CP) — Three men suffered minor injuries when their light plane crashed into a field after striking hydro lines Friday.

But: BARRIE, Ont. (CP) — A light plane hit power lines while taking off in a rainstorm Friday, flipped and crashed upside down in a farmer's potato field. The three men aboard escaped with minor injuries.

Everyday words

Treat the reader to words and phrases that are short and familiar.

About, not **approximately**

Met, not **held a meeting**

Approve, not **authorize**

Improve, never **ameliorate**

Plan or **program**, not **initiative** or **strategy**

Lazy words

Cast an inquisitive eye on words like **colourful, controversial** and **zany**. An editor who asks why Mayor Horsefall is **colourful** may learn Horsefall once ate his hat on the town hall steps when he lost a hockey bet with the mayor of a rival town. Tell the reader.

Say and variants

Early CP stylebooks described **say** and **said** as honest and inconspicuous. They are also not to be toyed with.

Say and **said** should be attached to words and ideas that exactly mirror the speaker's, not an interpretation or extension. Words like **indicate** or **suggest** may be appropriate where **said** is not and are mandatory in stories on opinion polls.

Not: The poll shows fewer than 10 per cent of Canadians believe . . .

But: The poll suggests fewer than 10 per cent . . .

Many substitutes for **say** and **said** are risky or, at best, vague:

Admit implies confession, **affirm** states a fact, **assert** declares strongly, **claim** and **maintain** hint of doubt, **confide** implies a confidence, **declare** states explicitly, **disclose** and **reveal** presume earlier concealment.

Be especially wary of **explain, point out, claim** and **note**. They all imply that what is being said is fact. **According to** and **said she believes** may question the speaker's credibility.

Words like **recalled** and **predicted** can be tricky. Make sure they fit the circumstances.

Attribution

Avoid the hackneyed **told reporters**. That the speaker said something after her speech, or after her statement in the Commons, or after a news release was issued is always sufficient.

Told The Canadian Press, The Canadian Press has learned or **said in an interview with The Canadian Press** should be used sparingly, such as when:

•   The same person has said different things to different media and it seems appropriate to spell out the differing versions.

•   CP has an exclusive interview with the prime minister or some other high official, or with a newsmaker on a significant story.

•   An interview is obtained from an unusually distant or hard-to-reach point such as a submerged submarine or the tip of Mount Everest.

•   Exclusive material has been gained through the Access to

Information Act or similar legislation.

- CP has broken a story on the basis of sourced material.

The mention that CP has obtained an exclusive report is usually best played in the second or third paragraph, not in the lead. When other media catch up on the story, a Writethru may be required that reflects CP is no longer the only organization to "learn" the news.

Headlines should also occasionally reflect that CP is the source of a story. Either CP reports or Canadian Press reports is acceptable in a headline. As in the story, this credit should be removed when the story is no longer exclusive.

Arithmetic

Writers should mind their math when dealing with statistical percentages and other figures. Never make the reader do the arithmetic.

Reporting that the number of flagpole-sitters in Canada has increased 100 per cent in the last year is meaningless without the base figure. An increase from five flagpole-sitters to 10 is 100 per cent but the percentage figure alone suggests a population explosion.

Take care as well in phrasing changes in percentage statistics. A poll that suggests a drop in government support to 25 from 50 per cent does not mean a 25 per cent drop. It's a change of 25 percentage points.

Headline language

Keep headline language out of news copy.

Not: Joseph inked a six-year contract.

But: Joseph signed a six-year contract.

Not: The commission will launch a three-pronged probe into the fire.

But: The commission will investigate the fire in three ways.

Short general-purpose words may fit in a headline, but not in a story.

Avoid words like:

Ban, beef up, bid, boost, cop, ink, ire, laud, lash, pact, probe, quiz, rap, shun, vow

The headline-writer's practice of dropping **a, the, of** and the like to save space leads to lumpy sentences in the body of a story.

Not: He was intrigued by Canadian Imperial Bank of Commerce chairman John Hunkin's defence of Dome Petroleum's rescue.

But: He was intrigued by the defence of Dome Petroleum's rescue offered by John Hunkin, chairman of the Canadian Imperial Bank of Commerce.

Verbs ending in -ize

Verbs ending in *-ize* strike many readers as ungainly, although some have gained acceptance.

Accessorize, capsulize, decimalize, definitize, hospitalize, therapize

Accept them when there is no satisfactory alternative.

Time element

Put the time element where it falls naturally in speech, usually right after the verb or at the end of the sentence.

Not: Veterans Affairs Minister Greg Thompson Thursday said the new policy . . .

But: Veterans Affairs Minister Greg Thompson said Thursday the new policy . . .

Try to put the time element at the end if putting it directly between the verb and its object is awkward:

Not: Finance Minister James Flaherty announced Wednesday a $2-billion job program.

But: Finance Minister James Flaherty announced a $2-billion job program Wednesday.

There are situations where the time element is at home either in the middle or at the end.

Dawn Coe-Jones came out of the pack Saturday to score a five-shot victory in the Canadian women's golf championship (Saturday).

That

Dropping **that** often makes for smoother reading, especially in shorter sentences.

She said (that) **she wanted to be alone.**

But retain it to avoid misleading the reader even momentarily.

Carr said that **on May 1 he was in Halifax; Justice Minister Vic Toews warned** that **the government would step in.**

That should also be retained and repeated with two or more clauses.

He promised that **the singer would appear and** that **the evening would be a success.**

That-which

When it comes to introducing a clause in the middle of a sentence, there's sometimes confusion about whether **that** or **which** is correct. **Which** sounds grammatical somehow, so it ends up being used too often.

That is generally used when the clause is essential to the noun it defines or narrows the topic: **The movie** that **opened at the Roxy last week.** (It's not just any movie, it's the one that opened last week at a specific theatre.)

Which clauses give a reason or add a new element: **The movie,** which **cost $4 million to make, has done landslide business.** (The assumption here is that the reader already knows which movie is being discussed, and its cost is an added bit of information.)

A helpful distinction: **which** clauses generally need commas, **that** clauses don't. Read the clause over in your mind. If it makes sense using **that** instead of **which**, chances are **that** is the right word to use.

Who and whom

Correct usage of these two eluders can be determined by dividing a sentence in two. Use **who** when it stands for **he, she** or **they**. Use **whom** when it stands for **him, her** or **them**.

The police issued a public alert for a man who they said was armed and dangerous. (They said **he** was armed and dangerous so **who** is correct.)

She took refuge with her next-door neighbour whom she had trusted in the past. (She trusted **her** so **whom** is correct.)

Clichés

Tired expressions are indeed tiresome. No one needs to read about a **hurler** who **toed the slab** or the **red-faced** MP who got a **tongue-lashing** from the opposition.

But use a cliché if it expresses your meaning exactly and if it will spare the reader some cumbersome second choice. It would be hard to improve on such gems as **sour grapes, cry wolf** or **tip of the iceberg** which sum up complex ideas in a few words.

Avoid the automatic or lazy cliché:

Grind to a halt, unveil, in the wake of, launch, seriously consider, shock waves

And the fad term:

Downsize, peer group, quantify, underachievers, wannabe, yuppie

And the fossil that no longer raises the faintest image:

Moot point, short shrift, at loggerheads, by the same token

Word order

Words out of order can create chaos.

Not: After falling from the ceiling for years, the Hamilton-Wentworth school board will remove tiles containing asbestos this summer from an area high school.

But: After falling from the ceiling for years, tiles containing asbestos will finally be removed from a Hamilton-Wentworth high school this summer.

Not: She has a six-figure income as a model, a horse and a Jaguar.

But: Modelling has given her a six-figure income, a horse and a Jaguar.

Mind-reading

Reporters and editors should not consider themselves mind-readers who can somehow measure others' true feelings.

Not: Genereux believes the government is corrupt.

But: Genereux said he believes the government is corrupt.

Not: Iroshima is furious about the layoffs.

But: "We're not taking this lying down," Iroshima said, shaking with anger and smashing his clenched fist into the factory fence.

Splits and prepositions

The normal position for an adverb that modifies a compound verb (**is missing, was reached**) is between the parts of the verb: **The plane is still missing. Agreement was soon reached.**

Split an infinitive (**to satisfy, to keep**) rather than create a confusing or unnatural sentence: **The discovery is expected to more than satisfy investors. Godfrey told him to kindly keep his opinion to himself.** But don't split infinitives unnecessarily: **The parents asked the babysitter to quietly leave by the back door.**

If a preposition falls naturally at the end of the sentence, leave it there: **Reuben wants to know which team he'll be on.**

A graphic can help a reader quickly understand where the story is taking place.

B.C. ferry sinks: A look at what happened

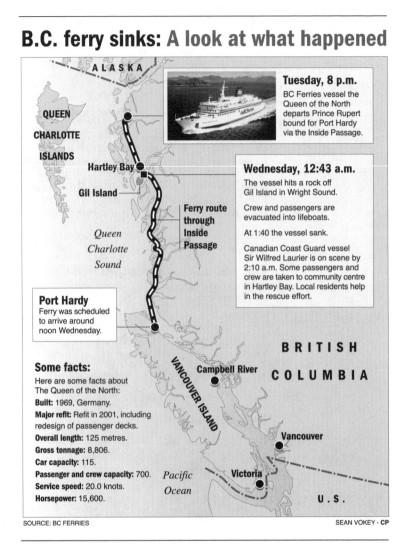

Tuesday, 8 p.m.
BC Ferries vessel the Queen of the North departs Prince Rupert bound for Port Hardy via the Inside Passage.

Wednesday, 12:43 a.m.
The vessel hits a rock off Gil Island in Wright Sound.

Crew and passengers are evacuated into lifeboats.

At 1:40 the vessel sank.

Canadian Coast Guard vessel Sir Wilfred Laurier is on scene by 2:10 a.m. Some passengers and crew are taken to community centre in Hartley Bay. Local residents help in the rescue effort.

ALASKA

QUEEN CHARLOTTE ISLANDS

Hartley Bay

Gil Island

Queen Charlotte Sound

Ferry route through Inside Passage

Port Hardy
Ferry was scheduled to arrive around noon Wednesday.

Some facts:
Here are some facts about The Queen of the North:
Built: 1969, Germany.
Major refit: Refit in 2001, including redesign of passenger decks.
Overall length: 125 metres.
Gross tonnage: 8,806.
Car capacity: 115.
Passenger and crew capacity: 700.
Service speed: 20.0 knots.
Horsepower: 15,600.

VANCOUVER ISLAND

Campbell River

B R I T I S H

C O L U M B I A

Vancouver

Victoria

Pacific Ocean

U . S .

SOURCE: BC FERRIES

SEAN VOKEY - CP

Locating the news

1. Today's reader is more interested than ever in knowing exactly where the news is happening, both in Canada and abroad. Few Canadians live their full lives in the area in which they were born and brought up. Career moves take them from one part of the country to another and sometimes to still another. And, of course, thousands of Canadians have come here from other parts of the world.

2. Name well-known streets or areas in stories about major fires and the like. In Halifax it might be: **a block from Barrington Street in the restored Historic Properties district of the waterfront beneath Citadel Hill.** In Hong Kong: **in the heart of the Central District within sight of the Bank of China Tower and just three blocks from the Star Ferry Pier.**

3. Readers interested in entertainment and celebrities want to know where events are held. In a review of a show or coverage of an event involving a big-name star, try to set the scene for the reader: **the cast met for an after-show dinner at the Bayshore Inn, on Burrard Inlet facing the mountains of West Vancouver.**

4. But keep in mind as well those readers who are unfamiliar with even the biggest cities. Pause early in the story to set the scene: **highrises on the Toronto harbourfront with a view over boat-dotted Lake Ontario and out to the greenery of the Toronto Islands; the shooting at the University of Montreal, whose Art Deco administration tower atop Mount Royal can be seen from all over the city.**

5. Don't assume readers know precisely where familiar mid-size cities are. Give places like Moncton, Kitchener, Prince Albert and Kelowna a physical presence and geographical location when that would help readers picture an event.

6. Pinpoint the location of news in remote areas, as well: **The two tankers collided at the tiny community of Purple Springs on Alberta Highway 3 just east of Taber and about a 40-minute drive from Lethbridge; The power station is near Gillam in a rugged area of northeastern Manitoba inland from Hudson Bay and about 14 hours by road from Winnipeg.**

7. Sometimes referring back to the story's placeline helps: (Glenwood, N.L.) — **this central Newfoundland logging town about 300 kilometres west of St. John's;** (Mahim, India) — **this seaside town just outside Mumbai.**

Flight 358: The investigation

Transportation Safety Board lead investigator Real Levasseur says information from the flight data recorder showed no signs of anything wrong with the systems that help to slow the Airbus A-340 once its wheels are on the ground. Air France Flight 358 was attempting to land during a fierce thunderstorm Aug. 2 when it skidded off the end of the runway and crashed into a ravine before bursting into flames.

Some key events:

Derry Rd.
Airport Rd.

1 Plane crosses 24L runway threshold
Altitude: 15-30 metres
Speed: 270-285 km/h
409

TERMINAL 3
TERMINAL 1   TERMINAL 2

Lester B. Pearson International Airport

2 Plane lands about 1.2 km down 2.7-km runway
Speed: About 247 km/h
427

RUNWAY 24L

Etobicoke Creek

401

Dixie Rd.

3 Plane crosses end of runway
Speed: Just under 150 km/h

4 Plane crashes into Etobicoke Creek ravine
All 309 people escape with 43 suffering minor injuries

Sean Vokey - CP

8.   Don't assume the placeline is going to give the reader a clear geographic sense of where the news has happened. For example, a story from Edmonton that says a force of specially trained police officers has been set up to give immediate emotional support to battered women must make clear where the force will function. In Edmonton alone? In all major Alberta centres? Or throughout Alberta? Watch phrases like *city police* and *the provincial department* which may be adequate for local newspapers but rarely for CP. Usually it is better to name the city and province in first references.

Writing

The first page of one of the early CP stylebooks had this to say about writing news:

"Every story worth printing can be written for The Canadian Press."

That remains the case, although much about writing news has changed.

No longer is the role of the news writer merely to inform. Readers (call them news consumers, if you will) are bombarded with information.

But what many modern-day messengers fail to provide, whether they are delivering the news over the Internet, on a traditional newsprint page or in a broadcast report, are context, background, balance and the sights, smells and sounds of the news. Things that tell readers why this is important and what it means, in terms that strike home.

Newspapers are fighting to attract new readers and hold the ones they have. Readability has always been an issue in the newspaper business, but never more than in today's reality: Fewer people are reading newspapers. Those who are reading papers spend less time at it.

If they haven't tuned news out completely, many people are choosing to get their news from a website or perhaps their phone or BlackBerry. But this format must also compete with many distractions that lure the reader elsewhere. To help, reporters and editors must present news stories that are uniformly appealing.

Readability is often tied to sentence length. Sure signs of trouble: too many ideas, too many subordinate clauses.

It's possible to write brightly and clearly in sentences that run to 30 words and more. Possible — but not probable.

Be human

Stories must be human, specific, clear, concise, imaginative and factual.

1. Write about people. Personal words like **father, pilot, nurse, welder** put life into news stories:

> An ice fisherman trudging along the edge of an isolated lake found the wreckage.

> A power failure crippled most of Quebec's electricity network Tuesday afternoon. It left about six million people without heat and light in freezing temperatures.

A five-year-old girl lies with her teddy bear as she is airlifted to a hospital from Walkerton, Ont. She was one of the victims of the tainted water tragedy in the town in 2000. The photo brings a huge news story down to a human scale.

(CP—Kevin Frayer)

Look for the human angle in every story: the sheet-metal worker replaced by a robot, the single parent whose rent has doubled, the teller robbed by a gunman with a shaking hand. A roundup on unemployment could open this way:

> Like anyone buying insurance, Donald Good hoped he wouldn't need it. He insured himself last March against being laid off. As it turned out, he did need it.

Put things in real-people terms:

Not: An Alberta provincial court judge has thrown out charges against two men, ruling that the six days they spent in a Camrose jail constituted cruel and unusual punishment.

But: Two young Alberta farmhands were freed from jail after telling a judge their cell had a broken window and was so cold the water pipes to the sink and toilet froze for days on end.

2.   Relate the news to the reader's life whenever possible, which is often:

> Airfare negotiations between Canada and the United States broke down Wednesday, dashing the hopes of thousands of travellers for bargain flights over the Labour Day weekend.

> Scientists believe they have detected the deadly chemical dioxin in the lake, but they say the levels appear too low to harm cottagers who drink its water or swim in it.

> The ruling means the plant workers will be eligible to apply for unemployment benefits within a week.

3. Enliven the story with quotes that set the scene, capture the flavour of the news or provide insight:

> "He burst through the swinging door and ran straight to the checkout counter," she said. "He waved this baseball bat he was carrying over his head and kept saying: `Give me the money — all the money.'"

> "I've dealt with the Raineys ever since I've been a cop," said Ephraim H. Branton, the affable deputy sheriff of the Lake County police and a 24-year veteran.
> "A lot of 'em came from ol' river rats. I've dealt with 'em on everything from runnin' moonshine to huntin' gators illegal."

4. Perk up stories that are devoid of anything human, except perhaps some unnamed *spokesman* or *official*. Season them with examples that bear directly on readers' lives:

> Just when you thought you had finally caught up with the Joneses, along came Statistics Canada on Tuesday announcing that 1.2 million households have more than one plasma-screen television.

Be specific

1. Give the reader specific details. Ask yourself: How does this look? sound? feel?

> ASTOR, Fla. (CP) — Inland from the shimmering beaches and swaying palm trees featured on garish postcards is where many locals say you will find the real Florida.
> Swampy bogs and inky rivers are stealthily patrolled by alligators. Snakes slither across the sun-baked asphalt greased by constant humidity. And every kind of criminal has come here to either ply their trade or escape from the law.

2.   Get interesting human nuggets into the lead:

> A prison guard killed in the Archambault Penitentiary last July "was looking at pictures of his family and crying like a baby" when convicts burst in on him, a murder trial was told Tuesday.

> Carolyn Kay shakes her gnarled, 91-year-old fingers, still bloody from the caribou she's been butchering, as she emphasizes the message she wants taken to hearings on a northern gas pipeline.

> This morning they were young offenders, breathing the stale air of jail.
> This afternoon they are hunters, zooming over the snowy tundra in snowmobiles and sleds.

3.   Paint word pictures:

Not: The accused were overjoyed.

But: The accused kissed and hugged each other.

Not: Candidates often encounter strange things while campaigning for the election.

But: In at least one riding, voter nudity overshadows ferocious dogs, slippery walks or long-winded residents as the greatest test of a candidate's composure.

Not: The MPs showed disgust at a rape scene in one of the censored films.

But: The MPs winced as the Confederate soldiers grabbed and raped a black slave in one of the censored films.

Be clear

1.   Always organize the story in your mind before you start writing.

Decide what the news is and put that in your lead. Stories with leads like these stand a good chance of flowing smoothly:

> A convicted 50-year-old rapist whose record for violent crimes stretches back to 1975 was sent to jail for at least 35 years Monday. The judge said he was so "sickened" by the case that he would ignore sentencing guidelines.

> American daredevil Maxie Anderson has decided to give up trying to fly around the world in a balloon after his third attempt came to an abrupt end Monday in the trees of a southern Ontario peach grove.

2.   But there are other ways to a reader's heart as well:

> The old Tory tune played in Alberta again on Thursday, but a lot fewer people got up to dance.

> Liberal party policy seems a lot like Scottish weather. If you don't like it, wait a few minutes — it's bound to change.

> Lotteries. Those spine-tingling, dream-inducing, pot-of-gold-at-the-end-of-the-rainbow lotteries are everywhere.

3.   Use plain words, but always the right words. Make it **wicked**, not **nefarious**; **remaining**, not **residual**; **tone down**, not **modulate**.

4.   Use specific words when details are useful. Write **hamburger and french fries**, not **food**; **shouting and laughing**, not **making a noise**; **a man of 87**, not **an elderly man**.

Be direct

1.   Don't write **a number of cars** if you can say **five cars**; **a six-figure income** if you can say **an income of $415,000**; **a long dry spell** if you can say **37 days without rain**.

2.   Don't use lazy terms for unknown quantities: **fairly**, **really**, **pretty**, **few**, **quite**, **very**.

3.   Translate pompous phrases.

Not: A poor public response.

But: Only a quarter of the tickets were sold.

Not: There is a doctor availability problem in the health delivery system.

But: There are not enough doctors in hospitals and private practice.

4.   Avoid putting more than one thought in a sentence. In general, the contents and structure rather than length itself make sentences hard to understand.

Not: Union leader John Dickerson declared, "I have no regrets and would do the same again" as he entered prison today to begin serving a three-month sentence imposed last week for defying the legislature and refusing to call off a strike of civil servants angered by wage rollbacks.

But: Union leader John Dickerson said he had "no regrets and would do the same again" as he entered prison today to begin serving a three-month term.

Dickerson was sentenced last week for defying the legislature and refusing to call off a strike of civil servants angered by wage rollbacks.

5. Beware of too many dependent clauses, especially in mid-sentence where they break the flow. Each clause adds more ideas to the sentence, making it harder and harder to grasp.

Not: The U.S. vice-president flew into Berlin from Bonn, along with the German chancellor, with whom he held talks Monday on disarmament strategy on the first stop of a seven-country tour.

But: The U.S. vice-president flew into Berlin from Bonn on the second stop during his seven-country tour. With him was the German chancellor, with whom he held talks Monday on disarmament.

6. Keep introductory phrases and clauses short and simple.

Not: Noting spirited and repeated suggestions from the floor that the group should press Ottawa for a higher salmon quota for British Columbia fishermen who have complained bitterly about competition from foreign fishing fleets, especially the Japanese and American, but to some extent the Russians, association vice-president Hedley Evansson said ...

But: As for higher salmon quotas, Evansson said ...

7. Sentence length can grow comfortably when the sentence is simply a list of closely linked ideas referring to the same subject:

The Blue Jays pulled off the first triple play of the major league season when shortstop Russ Adams stabbed what looked like a sure hit to left field by Oakland's Jeremy Brown, stepped quickly on second base to double off Mark Ellis and then drilled the ball to third baseman Troy Glaus, catching Jay Payton as he tried to get back to the bag.

Be concise

Keep your story tight in content as well as phrasing. Stick with the truly significant angles. A *full* report can often mean a dull report.

Be aware that a 1,000-word story in standard newspaper print would cover the back of a corn flakes box. Ask if the story would really hold a reader through an entire bowl of cereal.

If a story threatens to run long, consider whether some of the material could be broken out as highlights, a chronology or a point summary.

Clutter chokes meaning. Simplify:

1. Ditch the long word that says no more than the short:

attempt (try), **approximately** (about), **preponderance** (most), **consequently** (so), **substantiate** (prove), **initiative** (plan).

2. Ditch the laborious phrase: **despite the fact that** (although), **at this point in time** (now), **in the event that** (if), **ahead of schedule** (early), **in the majority of cases** (usually).

3. Ditch ponderous euphemisms and gobbledygook: **correctional facility** (prison), **job action** (strike, slowdown), **depressed socio-economic area** (slum), **in a classroom setting** (in a classroom), **resource centre** (library or lab), **lower rates of infant mortality** (fewer baby deaths).

4. Ditch words that aren't doing any work: **He said** (that) **the cut**(back)**s in** (the) **health care** (field) **have put hospitals in a crisis** (situation).

Next-day stories

Newspapers are increasingly turning to more analytical approaches on stories, especially staged news events, as a way to attract readers who are likely to have already heard the facts from last night's TV newscast, a 24-hour news channel or a brief radio report. Copy for papers must keep alive a story that may have already been reported for more than 24 hours. Try to avoid past-tense wording as much as possible: **Canada can no longer export goods to Spain**, rather than, **The government imposed export restrictions Tuesday.**

Don't place undue emphasis on minor developments to freshen a story. But do look for a different perspective. For example, on a provincial budget: Were human-interest angles neglected? How will the budget influence the next election? On a disaster, was there an eyewitness who can provide a lively account of what it is like to be caught in such a situation? Could it have been prevented? What are the implications?

The essential details of the news must be covered so it is understandable to readers who may be hearing about it for the first time. If these details are lengthy or complex, they can sometimes be handled in a Quick so they don't burden down a lead that is taking a new approach.

A writing checklist

1. Is the lead right? Does it capture only the most significant angles? Is there secondary information getting in the way of the main points? Is there an appealing human touch or quotation deep in the story that would fit in the first paragraph? Is the time element placed where it falls naturally in speech?

2. Does the writing appeal to a reader's senses? Are there gobs of *officialese*, jargon or abstractions? If so, can they be translated into direct language? The language people use when they're discussing events of the day over dinner?

3. Would a point summary help the reader? With the main news angle covered in the lead, should readers be given a capsule taste of other interesting angles awaiting them lower in the story?

4. Does the story give the reader any sense of where the news happened and how it happened, how people in the immediate area reacted? Did some of the audience start to leave before the speech was over? Did the speaker seem to notice?

5. Is there another side to the story? Is one side buried, throwing the story off balance? If someone whose viewpoint is obviously part of the story was unavailable, does the story say so? When pertinent, does it spell out what efforts were made to reach the unavailable source?

6. Have legally questionable elements in the story been cleared by a lawyer?

7. Is there overattribution? Are all those *he said*s necessary? Does every direct quote need attribution tacked on?

8. How about sentences? Is each sentence limited to one thought or a closely connected range of thoughts? Can a subordinate clause be changed into a sentence to give the reader a clearer path? Are the sentences active? Are inactive verbs adding fat to sentences? Is there an idea that needs explaining? If so, find a way to explain it better. Or could the problem sentence be cut without loss?

9. How about quotes? Could the story be brightened with stronger human voices? In cutting quotes, have the strongest been saved and the weaker sacrificed? Can some quotes be cut because they aren't controversial and don't give any character to the speaker? Is the story sprinkled with fragmented quotes? Is it necessary to say, **He said he was "out of touch"**?

10. Have words been wasted? Can single words replace phrases: **placed under arrest** (arrested), **in the vicinity of** (near), **charged in connection with** (charged), **in the shooting incident** (shooting)?

11. Can shorter or more familiar words be used: **They attempted** (tried) **to expedite** (speed up) **what they perceived** (saw) **as a viable** (workable) **plan**?

12. Has bafflegab been translated? Have **accommodation units** been turned into **houses and apartments**; methods of **intercity transportation** into **planes, trains, buses and cars; disadvantaged** into **poor; upwardly mobile** into **ambitious**?

13. Does the writing read like normal English? Is any of it unlike anything you would ever say: **the six-foot-eight 290-pound University of Manitoba product; Paramount vice-president of corporate communications Deborah Rosen**?

14. Are there stale expressions? Is the story dulled by clichés: **court was told; 14-hour marathon session; grim-faced delegates**?

15. Do the transitions lead the reader smoothly from one idea to the next? Could a bump between two sentences be removed with an **and, but, meanwhile** or some other transition? Would it help to repeat a key word or phrase from the preceding sentence or paragraph? **This new strategy** . . . ?

16. Is the tone right? Is the writing too formal, slangy or trendy? Has sexist, racist or other tasteless language slipped in?

Editing

Few people grow up longing to edit someone else's writing. It's not glamorous work; it is invisible at best and resented at worst.

But some people who love the written language develop a passion for perfecting its use on the page. The best publications rely on such editors for success. The best editors strive for excellence in every story they handle.

Pride comes from turning around a mediocre or erroneous story. The trick is to do more than just catch mistakes but less than rewrite.

As the last ones to touch copy before it gets into the reader's hands, editors have a vital role. They are the watchdogs over clarity, good taste, balance and accuracy.

Editors should be the reader's best friend. They add background and perspective. They make a story relevant and fun. They don't challenge readers to get through a story — they dare them not to.

Principles

1. When time allows, read a story three times: once for content, once to edit and once to clean up.

2. If you don't understand the story, the reader certainly won't. When something is unclear, either get it explained or chop it.

3. Generalities blur the picture; demand specifics for your readers. Make sure the story is animated by human beings.

4. Suggest improvements to the writer: revealing quotes, touches of colour, specific details, an example or anecdote.

5. Watch for holes and fill them. Ask the writer. Check reference works. Consult a supervisor.

6. Shorten the story — but not at the expense of human interest, significant detail, daubs of colour or meaty quotations.

7. Avoid overediting, which can reduce good writing to mediocrity or headline language.

8. Change copy if you have a good, explainable reason — not just because it's not the way you would have written it yourself. Leave extensive rewriting to the writer whenever possible.

How to do it

Look at the lead. The first sentence is supposed to lead the reader into the story. If it isn't interesting, why would the reader go any further? If readers aren't enticed by the first sentence or two, they're not going to stick around to be informed or educated or provoked.

1. Replace vague or complicated words with simple, specific ones.

2. Brighten the lead with descriptive verbs and the active voice.

Not: Two men are dead following an avalanche Tuesday on a popular ski slope in the Rocky Mountains.

Better: An avalanche thundered down Mount Norquay on Tuesday, crushing two men who had been learning to ski at the Rocky Mountain resort.

3. Take a scalpel to long leads. Aim for fewer than 30 words. Cut unwieldy phrases. Remove secondary information or unnecessary attribution from the lead and place it lower.

Not: Human Resources Minister Diane Finley announced Monday that after six months of study and $3 million in funding, the government has come up with new educational and job training guidelines that she predicts will make the Canadian labour force the most skilled in the world.

Better: After spending $3 million and six months studying education and job training, the federal government has a plan it predicts will make Canadians the most skilled labour force in the world.

4. Never assume the reader knows the subject as intimately as the writer does.

Not: Joy Medinski was found Thursday in Bienfait, apparently unharmed.

Better: A five-year-old girl who vanished from a family campsite in southeastern Saskatchewan last week was found two kilometres away on Monday, apparently unharmed.

5. Beware of the double-barrelled lead.

Not: Thousands of seniors angry over federal pension changes marched on Parliament Hill on Monday while their national spokesman condemned the Conservative government as the worst threat to seniors in Canadian history.

Pick the most interesting or important element, the seniors or the spokesman, and make that the lead. Put the other one in the second paragraph.

Tighten the story

1. Keep paragraphs short, usually no more than two or three sentences for newspaper copy. Don't assault the reader's eyes with massive blocks of grey.

2. Tighten sentences to clarify, inject life and save space. Be ruthless in cutting wordiness and secondary detail.

3. Replace cumbersome words with short, everyday words that convey the same meaning.

Not: The correctional facility workers voted in favour of a prolonged work stoppage.

But: The jail guards voted to strike.

4.   Cut vague modifiers and qualifiers: **fairly, really, pretty, quite, very.**

5.   Cut overattribution. Are all those *he said*s necessary?

Brighten the story

1.   Prefer one or two interesting angles fully developed to a dull, bare-bones account that touches all bases regardless of merit.

2.   Change passive voice to active where appropriate. **Police took no action** is better than **No action was taken by police.**

3.   Change boring expressions to lively ones. Watch for participles ending in *-ing* or nouns ending in *-ion* — they may signal that a sentence can be punched up. Watch for the weak verb *to be*. Can it be replaced by an active verb?

Not: **The government is planning to implement a program aiming for a reduction in the number of alcohol-related deaths this year.**

Better: **The government aims to cut alcohol-related deaths this year through a new program.**

Best: **Police will be able to seize the cars of drinking drivers on the spot under a government plan to cut alcohol-related deaths this year.**

4.   Translate or cut journalistic hype and jargon, the kind of language you would never use in ordinary speech. Prefer the specific to the general.

Not: **Residents of this farming community were reeling in shock Thursday in the wake of the slaying of two respected schoolteachers.**

Better: **Flags flew at half-mast outside the Shoal Lake elementary school Thursday in tribute to two teachers killed in an apparently unprovoked attack.**

Not: **A twofold habitat mitigation program is in full swing at the Oldman River dam site.**

Better: **The provincial government is spending $2 million to preserve the environment for wildlife around the Oldman River dam and create new protected areas to replace those destroyed by the dam.**

Best: **Ducks will swim in new ponds and deer will munch on their favourite grasses under a $2-million program to preserve wildlife around the Oldman dam.**

Check accuracy

1.   Check proper names and unusual spellings. Make sure unusual surnames are spelled the same way throughout. Never

guess at capitalization. Think of your reader again — few things are as annoying as misspelled names.

2.   Check math. Make sure percentages are right. If portions of a total number are used, make sure they add up.

3.   Check days and dates for obvious errors.

4.   Watch closely for mistakes in the use of *not* in court cases and important judgments: *not guilty, not responsible.*

Check style

1.   Strive to retain the writer's tone and choice of phrasing.

2.   Fix errors in grammar, style and structure. Watch for mistakes in word order that mislead the reader.

Not: A Winnipeg police officer who shot a man with a toy gun has been cleared of any wrongdoing.

Better: A Winnipeg police officer who shot a man pointing a toy gun has been cleared of any wrongdoing.

3.   Check that plural subjects are followed by plural verbs and pronouns, singular by singular. **The government announced its** (not **their**) **long-awaited social reform package Tuesday.**

4.   Does punctuation mislead the reader? Fix it.

Not: She said the company is run by men, who have no ethics.

But: She said the company is run by men who have no ethics.

Make it clear

1.   Lighten overloaded sentences by putting some of the facts into another sentence.

Not: The U.S. economy slid into recession in March but consumer spending has managed to hold up relatively well during the slump, due to low interest rates, free-financing offers, extra cash coming from a refinancing boom in home mortgages, heavily discounted merchandise and improved consumer confidence.

Better: The U.S. economy slid into recession in March but consumer spending has managed to hold up relatively well during the slump. Low interest rates, free-financing offers, extra cash coming from a refinancing boom in home mortgages and merchandise sales have induced people to spend. Consumer confidence also has improved.

2.   Answer all pertinent questions. Make sure all unusual and technical terms are explained.

Wealthy Britons often buy private health insurance, just as they send their children to "public" schools, which in Britain means fee-paying, private and elite.

3. Move sentences or paragraphs to improve flow or strengthen emphasis.

Make it fair

1. Put both sides of a controversial issue high in the story.

2. Tone down or play up material wrongly treated by the writer. Guard against partial quotes that may create the wrong impression.

The woman was hired for her "talent," the premier said.

3. Watch for unintentional editorializing.

Not: The Opposition blamed the government for ruining the economy.

Better: The Opposition accused the government of ruining the economy.

4. Remove material that is potentially libellous or in bad taste.

Handle with care

1. When source material is sensitive or confidential, lock it safely away while the reporter works from a copy.

2. Make sure a supervisor is fully aware of the source material's contents and the source's reliability.

3. Before an investigative report is published, make every effort to give everyone who may be criticized an opportunity to reply.

4. Counsel must approve the final wording of any possibly dangerous material.

➤ See **Principles**, page 13.

Writing for and about the Internet

General

A great many people are turning to the Internet to get news and information. Readership is increasing all the time. Yet many readers have reached the limit of their "human bandwidth." They can't handle any more information. Online editors and webmasters have to help them or they'll go away.

Many of these people are Canadians seeking out stories written and produced by CP. The words, audio and pictures are seen several million times a day. The multimedia combination of stories, pictures and audio along with CP Interactive Graphics makes for ideal information packages. People come to our stories because we have something they need to know. Our credibility makes them come back.

For all editors working in the online world, it is important to understand that writing for a reader with a browser is different than writing for a reader with a paper document. The online reading experience is comparable to this:

It's the morning before your final history exam. You have loads of notes to go through but they're nicely organized, with lots of highlighting and margin notes. You can skim over each section and stop to dig deeper whenever you feel it's necessary. All of the information is there, but without the highlighting and subheads you'd be lost in a block of text.

Online readers are impatient and critical. Some read the entire item. However, research suggests that almost 80 per cent of them scan the page first. They pick out parts of interest to them. Although they may read it all, they don't necessarily read the item the way it is laid out.

A study has indicated that reading from a computer screen is 25 per cent slower than from paper. When readers are presented with a large scrolling block of text with little structure, they'll read the first paragraph or two and then start skipping around. If they can't find what they are looking for almost immediately, 70 per cent will move on to the next website. That's why a good online editor knows to add subheads, boldface and other tools that help readers navigate the site. Layers, story links, images, audio, video, interactive elements, maps, source sites, links to subheads or complementary articles can all be added.

Keep in mind that people reading news online are not doing it as a leisure activity. They are not sprawled on the couch with a newspaper or a big-screen television in front of them. The technical limitations of their hardware – a small screen (especially for wireless users), for instance – severely limit their appreciation of stories that beat around the bush. Get to the point. Quickly.

Online writing

The traditional rules of newspaper writing – pyramid style, tight leads, strong quotes – also apply to online writing, as long as long passages are broken into chunks. A story that sums up its main elements in a paragraph or two at the top is effective, while one with a circle-back ending – a teaser in the first paragraph and the answer in the last paragraph – doesn't work as well.

Other techniques to try:

1. Readers eat up quotes. Use them in stories and around stories as supporting material or to break up copy.

2. Highlight key words with boldface or colour to help the reader navigate through the material. But don't go overboard. Too much of this makes copy harder to read.

3. Text is not as easy to read on screen as on paper, so short, clear headings help. Use bullets with subheads to organize key points. Bullets should be constructed in a consistent fashion. But don't turn your entire story into a list. The point is to break up copy, not turn copy into a repetitive list of bullets.

4. Your biggest hook is the headline, even bigger than a picture. Sometimes the simple, direct headline works well, yet most of the time you need to draw the reader into the story. For information on what makes a good headline, see **Headlines**, page 398.

5. Keep a light tone. The web is an informal setting, so there is lots of room for levity.

6. Don't put every story in pyramid style. Readers will quickly tire of such a formulaic approach. There is always room for a story with a beginning, middle and end if you engage readers' interest throughout and help them through the piece with some of the other devices mentioned here. Profiles or histories can often be best told chronologically, with signposts highlighting turning points or key developments.

7. Some writers forgo brevity unless it is forced upon them by the demands of their medium. With the web, any length fits. This can lead to overwriting of the worst sort. But from a user's perspective, the computer screen is more limiting than a newspaper page. Readers shouldn't have to scroll to get to the point. Edit ruthlessly. Use simpler words. Watch run-on sentences. Don't repeat yourself – say it once, well.

8. Proof, proof and re-proof your copy. This shows your reader your site is credible.

➤ For further tips, see **Writing**, page 163.

Keep it current

1. Don't sit on developments. The web can update stories over and over again.

2. Remove old content regularly. Clearly date material so readers can judge whether it is still relevant to them.

3. Consider whether the headline also needs to be updated to reflect the new developments.

Not just words

Sound can be a huge plus online, especially in web journalism. Audio that explains the basic facts of a story has some value but the really crucial clip reveals mood and emotions. Especially strong are the voices of the newsmakers themselves – the figure skater tearfully thanking the crowd after she wins the gold medal; the Queen speaking for the first time publicly on the death of the Princess of Wales. A short clip works best.

Pictures help sell a story online just as well as they do in print. Pictures make the item more pleasing to the eye. Online adds the additional opportunity for interactive graphics, which can both entertain and help a reader through a story.

➤ For more details, see **Graphics,** page 370.

Hyperlinks

1. Following a reference to another page can be cumbersome with paper – think of footnotes – but natural on a screen. Hyperlinks are useful for expanded material that is relevant but not essential, such as definitions, deeper background and sources.

2. Hyperlinks can also sidetrack a reader to move off the story, so don't overdo them. Don't use a link just because it exists; make sure it will take the reader somewhere worthwhile that is directly related to the subject at hand. Readers should not be surprised by where they end up. Test links regularly to make sure they still work. If it doesn't work, readers will be annoyed.

3. Only link once to the same site, not every time the subject is mentioned.

4. Keep writing about your subject. Don't switch to giving the reader instructions just because you have added a hyperlink:

Not: Go to <u>Anne Murray's home page</u> for a full biography

Or: Click <u>here</u> to visit Anne Murray's home page.

But: <u>Anne Murray</u> is one of Canada's most recognized singers.

6. Ensure that links are not to websites that are obscene, racist or otherwise offensive. In stories about such websites, it is not usually necessary to provide the address.

Source it

Avoid anonymity – the web is already anonymous enough. Be clear about where material comes from. Readers want to see a byline. On CP copy, our logo tells readers the material has our credibility behind it.

Copyright

News distributed on the Internet has no special status in terms of copyright law. A story published in an Internet edition of a newspaper is subject to the law just as it would be if it were in a newsprint edition. The same holds true for a CP story, or any material, available on a website that pays for or produces the content. Others must seek permission before reproducing or using those stories in substantially the same form.

Correcting mistakes

It is just as important to fix errors in online stories as it is in stories published in print. The good news is the web offers the advantage of being able to go back and clean stories up. But this presents its own issues – is it responsible to fix an error without acknowledging that a mistake was made?

Newspapers traditionally run a correction to a story in the same spot in the newspaper each day, which allows readers to easily find it. Alternatively, they run the correction in the same page or section of the paper where the original story ran, hoping to catch the readers who saw the earlier piece. But how do we catch an Internet reader? Say she plugs into a website every day at 6 a.m. to read the CP news. One day there is a mistake in a story, which is fixed after our reader logs off. She isn't going to go back and read that same story again the next time she logs in – unless we give her a heads up to do so.

If the mistake is a minor factual one, or a spelling or grammatical problem, it should be fixed as soon as it is noted. But for more serious errors and changes, correct the story and put an **Update Note** on the top to alert readers that this story has changed. On the CP Online service, Update notes can be used as headlines. This means if readers are scrolling through a list of stories, they will know from the Update note that a change has been made and they should have another look at the item.

➤ For style on **Update** notes, see page 433.

For the most serious errors that may involve a legal challenge, a **CP Corrective** is also posted on the site that carried the original item. The Corrective appears for the same length of time as the original appeared. Seriously wrong stories are also removed from databases that are accessible by CP clients, and the corrected versions, complete with any Correctives that were moved, are filed in the database.

Writing about computer technology

Too much of what is written about technology and the online world is filled with buzzwords and obscure abbreviations. A good writer knows when to mix the jargon with the everyday. Some tech talk works if set against a familiar backdrop that makes it understandable:

> If you're feeling a little guilty about the hundreds of MP3s you've downloaded but still don't feel like shelling out for a CD, Fairtunes.com believes it can help.
> The Winnipeg-based web service allows fans to make financial contributions to a musical artist – any artist. It's kind of like an Internet tip jar with a pay-what-you-like philosophy, and its designers hope it will help musicians get their just desserts in the digital domain.

In general, however, forgo the buzzwords. Although it is almost impossible to write about technology without using acronyms or abbreviations, go easy – clusters of them make sentences virtually impenetrable. Stick to well-known ones. It is usually safer to use the longer form (**instant message**, not **IM**) or a generic description (**high-speed link** instead of **T-1**). That way you can be confident that both insiders and outsiders will understand. Remember: you are trying to attract readers, not give them a reason to tune out.

➤ See **Abbreviations and acronyms**, page 191.

Style specifics

1. If providing an actual web address (URL), follow upper and lowercase exactly: **www.cp.org**. The **http://** does not need to be included because it is the most common start of an address and almost all web software supplies it. Some addresses begin with other expressions (**ftp://**, for instance), and these must be included. Long web addresses should be allowed to wrap.

Note: Web addresses don't always belong in news stories. They have to work their way in as a piece of information the reader is likely to find helpful. For instance, a story on the Bank of Montreal does not need to include the bank's website, any more than it needs to include the address of its head office. Stories on interest groups or commercial products do not require routine mention of a website as it amounts to free advertising. But if the site provides relevant, reliable and current material about the subject at hand, then including the URL will help readers obtain further information. For instance, a story on cancer survivors could include the URL of a site for such people. Apply the same standards of relevance, balance and reliability that are applied to any piece of information in a story.

2. If a company uses a variation of its Internet address as its corporate name, capitalize the first letter: **Amazon.com**. Also capitalize the first letter when the reference is not to the URL, but to the domain name:

"The search engines I use the most are Google.com and Yahoo.com," he said.

3. E-mail addresses must be written the way they appear, which is usually all lowercase. CP does not put them in angle brackets or parentheses.

4. Use **disc** for CDs (compact discs), CD-ROMs (compact disc-read-only memory) and laserdiscs, all of which are generally round and made of metal. Use **disk** for the square plastic disks often called floppy disks (even though they are no longer floppy) or diskettes, and hard disks (found on a hard drive).

5. Filenames, including extensions, are case sensitive and should be written the way they appear.

➤ See also **Capitalization**, page 214.

Television text news

Up-to-the-minute news, weather and sports are available in households and offices across the country on the cable news service, displayed in text form on television screens.

Cable news goes directly to the public, and CP editors face the challenge of informing viewers of breaking news before others can get on the air or in print.

With the exception of story size, filing the cable service is similar to handling other news services — get it to the reader quickly and accurately.

The cable editor is faced with a very tight format. This is tough. Keep the emphasis on short, punchy words and simple sentence structure.

Some cable formats can handle nothing more than a three-line item. Others can take two or three paragraphs. Both must inform the reader without leaving out essential information.

Tight writing is crucial, and editors employ a variety of tricks to keep stories short:

• Avoid generalities — screen space is at a premium. All sentences need substance. Don't tell the reader that the federal government brought down a budget today. Go right to the contents of the budget.

• Cable writing must be conversational. It's a hybrid between news written for the eye (newspaper) and news written for the ear (radio and television). Try reading it as though you were telling a story to another person. Lengthy attributions at the end of a sentence don't work. A chain of clauses is too ponderous for the reader/viewer.

• Stories work best if they can be summed up in one screen — so a viewer can see the entire story at once. Top or exceptional news stories can run more than one screen if the particular format allows it, but the names of anyone being quoted should be repeated in the second screen. The cable reader may have missed the first screen, where the person's name first appeared, or have forgotten it.

• Although quotes are permitted in cable reports, they can eat up a lot of space without providing much information. Paraphrase or keep them pithy.

• Brevity allows for some casualness in style, but try to be consistent. If abbreviations must be used, keep to familiar ones. Don't interchange **Tto**, **Tor** and **T.O.** for **Toronto**; use **T.O.**

• Numbers below 10 don't need to be written out. **First** becomes **1st**, and so on.

• Some cable formats are all-caps and this adds a further wrinkle. Acronyms and short forms such as UN take periods (U.N.).

Writing for broadcast

It's radio — it's the way we speak.

Writing for radio is writing that's meant to be spoken and heard. It requires special style and form.

(CP Photo)

1. Write tight opening sentences that grab the listener's attention.

The first sentence should make listeners want to hear more but not confuse them with too many details.

In other words, it serves as a headline.

Never write lead lines on broadcast copy that are over 15 words long. A long lead line can throw an announcer's breathing off for the entire newscast.

2. Write in the present tense or active voice.

It's the way people speak.

Avoid the passive voice: verb forms like **was hit, have grabbed**, etc.

Broadcast copy, written in the active voice, should place the verb as close to the subject as possible.

Not: A Hamilton man has been arrested by police.

But: Police arrested a Hamilton man.

3. Limit sentences to a single idea or closely connected range of thoughts.

Not: Alex Hickman, chief justice of the trial division of the Supreme Court of Newfoundland, has been cleared of any wrongdoing by the Canadian Judicial Council after a review of his financial dealings.

But: The chief justice of the Newfoundland Supreme Court has been cleared of any financial wrongdoing. The Canadian Judicial Council cleared Alex Hickman after a review of the judge's financial dealings.

4. Simplify complex and wordy sentences.

Not: The minister of employment, Jasper Brown, has established a study group within his department to conduct a review of the principles and objectives of the unemployment insurance program. He told the Commons today he expects to table the findings this fall for further discussion.

But: Employment Minister Jasper Brown has ordered a review of the unemployment insurance program. Brown told the Commons he expects to table the findings in the fall.

5. Use the subject-verb-object approach to tell the story in as straight a line as possible.

Not: The gunman was shot by the police.

But: Police shot the gunman.

6. Place the time element, if needed, after the verb.

Don't use **yesterday, last night**, etc. in a lead sentence.

Don't use **continues** in a lead sentence.

Don't start a broadcast story with **as expected.**

7. For ease of understanding, put a person's identification ahead of the name.

Former dentist Barney Clark has become the first person to live with an artificial heart implant.

Twenty-five-year-old Beverly Amies of Toronto was killed.

8. Prefer plain words to fancy ones.

Prefer **end** to **terminate, build** to **construct, confuse** to **obfuscate, poor** to **disadvantaged, shops** to **retail outlets.**

9. Use specific words, not general ones.

Write **rain, snow, fog,** not **bad weather.** Write **one million dollars,** not **financial aid.** Write **She smiled,** not **She looked pleased.**

10. Keep sentences lean. Excess words clutter the facts.

Write **failed,** not **was unsuccessful.** Write **won,** not **chalked up a victory.** Write **lives at,** not **makes her home at.** Write **burned,** not **was devoured by flames.** Write **presided,** not **acted as chairman.**

Eliminate unnecessary and long titles. Would **a union spokesman** serve just as well as **Jean Talon, secretary-treasurer of Local 136?**

11. Write incomplete sentences occasionally. Like this. To make an idea easier to absorb. For a change of pace.

12. Put the source at the beginning of the sentence rather than at the end.

Not: A new wave of violence is showing up, the movie critic added.

But: The movie critic says a new wave of violence is showing up.

13. Use contractions occasionally, as the ear dictates.

I don't know whether he'll come has the sound of everyday English. The formal **I do not know whether he will come** would be starchy in shirtsleeve contexts.

Use **she won't, it couldn't** and other common contractions. Avoid forced contractions like **would've, it'd.**

14. To reflect spoken usage, hyphenate abbreviations that the news reader should pronounce letter by letter.

Write **C-B-C, M-P, N-D-P, R-C-M-P, U-N, U-S** but **NATO, MiG, Sidbec, Stelco.**

Note: BN practice is to hyphenate network abbreviations, **C-B-S, C-T-V,** but to write station call letters solid, **CIHI Fredericton, CKLH-FM Hamilton, CJON-TV St. John's.**

15. Guard against a string of *s*'s and other repeated letters.

Sources at city hall say might cause the news reader to stumble or slow down.

16. Round off large numbers to make them digestible and spell out the dollar sign.

The robber got away with more than 13 hundred dollars is easier on the listener — and the news reader — than **$1,335.** For ease of reading, spell out and hyphenate dollars and cents: **The increase will add one-dollar-and-25-cents to the average monthly electricity bill.**

17. For economy and directness, prefer paraphrased speech to direct quotation. But use a quotation if it is unusually forceful.

The judge explained why he had ruled in favour of the 20-year-old cerebral palsy victim. He said: "We have recognized a gentle, trusting, believing spirit who has a part to play in our compassionate, independent society."

18. Repeat key points in major news breaks.

In an airliner crash, for example, give the location a second time for listeners who missed it. Don't hesitate to add a throw-away sentence at the end summarizing the story.

To recap: An airliner has crashed at the Edmonton airport and at least a dozen people are dead.

For a full treatment of writing for broadcasting, see *BN NewsTalk*, also available from The Canadian Press.

Bloc Québécois Leader Gilles Duceppe is scrummed as he votes in the January 2006 election. Audio clips add drama and interest to broadcast news stories.

(CP–Kevin Frayer)

Tools and technical guides

Abbreviations and acronyms

General

1. Text studded with abbreviations is hard to read and unsightly. Avoid when an option exists.

2. Use only abbreviations and acronyms (abbreviations pronounced as words) that are familiar to ordinary readers.

CN, CTV, MP; Stelco, NATO, radar

3. An abbreviation is sometimes acceptable to avoid an unwieldy lead: **a PLO rocket attack**. But in general, provide the full name later: **Palestine Liberation Organization.**

4. Abbreviations that have become household terms are acceptable in all references. That is, they need not be spelled out, though the full word or phrase may make for more graceful reading.

CBC, MP, NATO, NDP, PoW, RCMP

Note: As to familiarity, it is impossible to set lasting rules. The once-familiar **RAF** (Royal Air Force), for instance, no longer commands widespread recognition, whereas **BBC** does. When in doubt, spell out.

5. In general, do not put a bracketed abbreviation after the name of an organization: Transportation Safety Board (**TSB**), World Health Organization (**WHO**).

Abbreviations that need this device to be clear should rarely be used.

6. For ease of reading or variety, a general term is often preferable to an abbreviation.

the industrial relations board, mad cow disease, the union, the autoworkers, the company, the association instead of **CIRB, BSE, CAW** and the like.

7. Do not spell out common abbreviations if the full term is not in general use or is hard to pronounce: **TNT** (for **trinitrotoluene**), DNA (**deoxyribonucleic acid**).

Where necessary, include a brief description to help the reader: **DNA, the carrier of genetic information.**

8. Abbreviations suitable in one context may be unsuitable in another. **MLA**, for instance, might puzzle readers in Newfoundland, Quebec and Ontario, and should be spelled out for general service: **member of the legislative assembly,** or **member of the legislature. IPO** (for **initial public offering**) might work in a business story but not in a general story.

Similarly: **MHA** — member of the (Newfoundland) house of assembly; **MNA** — member of the (Quebec) national assembly; **MPP** — member of the (Ontario) provincial parliament.

9. Non-English abbreviations that may be unfamiliar to English-speaking readers should be explained at some point.

the terrorist group ETA, the acronym for the Basque name meaning Basque Land and Liberty; the French union federation CGT, short for Confédération générale du travail; the Quebec steel company Sidbec; Soquip, which stands for a French name meaning Quebec Petroleum Development Corp.

Style for abbreviations

1. Omit periods in all-capital abbreviations unless the abbreviation is geographical or refers to a person.

AD, CST, IPO, UBC, UFO, VIP, URL; B.C., P.E.I., N.W.T., U.S., T.O., L.A.; J. R. Ewing, J.R., E.T., good ol' J.B.

Note 1: Some public figures become known by initials without periods.

FDR (Franklin Delano Roosevelt), **JFK** (John Fitzgerald Kennedy), **PET** (Pierre Elliott Trudeau), **GBS** (George Bernard Shaw)

Note 2: Compound abbreviations are written without spaces.

M.Sc., P.Eng.

Note 4: Omit periods from currency abbreviations.

US$500, C$800

2. Most lowercase and mixed abbreviations take periods.

f.o.b., Jr., lb., Mrs., No., m.p.h., B.Comm.

Note: Metric symbols are not abbreviations and take periods only at the end of a sentence.

m, l, km/h

3. Mixed abbreviations that begin and end with a capital letter do not take periods.

PhD, PoW, MiG, U of T

4. Single-letter abbreviations are followed by a period.

36 King St. E. (for East)

But **brand X, the letter E**

Style for acronyms

1. Acronyms formed from only the first letter of each word are all capitals.

NATO (North Atlantic Treaty Organization), a CT (computerized tomography) scan, AIDS (acquired immune deficiency syndrome), CD-ROM (compact disc read-only memory)

2. Acronyms formed from initial and other letters are in caps and lowercase.

Dofasco (Dominion Foundries and Steel Corp.), Nabisco (National Biscuit Company), Vanoc (Vancouver Organizing Committee for the 2010 Olympic and Paralympic Winter Games)

3. Acronyms that have become common words are not capitalized.

radar (radio detection and ranging), scuba (self-contained underwater breathing apparatus), snafu (situation normal, all fouled up), laser (light amplification by stimulated emission of radiation), zip (zoning improvement plan)

Academic degrees and honours

1. In general, avoid the abbreviation and use a phrase instead: John Woo, who has a doctorate in chemistry.

2. If it would be cumbersome to follow No. 1, or if the degree is well-known, the abbreviation can be used.

The teen actor earned his BA while working on his first movie. Pauline Regan, MA, and Ann Bullock, B.Sc., spoke to the homeless about educational programs.

3. Follow usual style for abbreviations, as spelled out on page 190: B.Sc., BA, M.Sc., MA, B.Comm., PhD, OBE, VC, P.Eng.

Dates and times

1. For months used with a specific date, abbreviate only Jan., Feb., Aug., Sept., Oct., Nov. and Dec. Spell out standing alone or with a year alone.

Oct. 1, 1999, was a Friday. January 2006 was wet.

Note: Do not abbreviate a month spelled out in the name of an organization: the November 17 terrorist group.

2. In tabular matter, use these forms without periods:

Jan, Feb, Mar, Apr, May, Jun, Jul, Aug, Sep, Oct, Nov, Dec

3. Days of the week are abbreviated only in tabular matter and without periods.

Sun, Mon, Tue, Wed, Thu, Fri, Sat

4. **AD** is acceptable in all references for **anno Domini** (Latin for *in the year of the Lord*) and **BC** for **before Christ**. AD precedes the year; BC follows it.

AD 410, 55 BC

But write **12th century AD.**

5. Write **10 a.m., 3:30 p.m., EDT, AST**

➤ See **Time**, page 318.

Measurements

1. In general, spell out such terms as **kilogram, metre** and **minute**.

A five-kilogram packet costs $2.

2. A few common terms — **km/h, mm, m.p.h., c.c.** — are acceptable on second reference when used with figures.

70 km/h, 105-mm cannon, the old 30-m.p.h. limit, 2,000-c.c. engine

3. Terms may be abbreviated in tabular matter and if used repeatedly.

kg, l, cwt., min.

4. Use this style for imperial abbreviations, both singular and plural, in tabulations:

in., ft., yd., mi.; oz., lb., cwt.; sq. ft.

Similarly: **sec., min., hr.**

5. Use this style for metric symbols, both singular and plural, in tabulations:

mm, cm, m, KB, km, kg, g, t, ml, l, ha, kPa

➤ See **Metric**, page 245; **Numbers**, page 263.

Organizations

1. Use **Bros., Co., Corp., Inc.** and **Ltd.** with corporate names and without commas.

General Motors Acceptance Corp., Canadian Pacific Ltd., Texaco Inc.

Note: Spell out **company**, etc., in the names of entertainment groups unless the group name includes an abbreviation.

Canadian Opera Company, Smothers Brothers

2. Do not abbreviate other terms — **association, department, division, organization** and so on — in corporate and government names.

Reader's Digest Association, Justice Department

3. An ampersand is acceptable in corporate names if the organization uses it: **AT&T, A&P, S&P.**

4. Spell out **United Nations** as a noun, but the abbreviation **UN** may be used as an adjective with well-known organizations.

The United Nations will meet. The UN Security Council voted no.

Places

1. For Canadian provinces and territories, use these abbreviations after the name of a community:

Alta.	N.B.	N.S.	Que.
B.C.	N.L.	Ont.	Sask.
Man.	N.W.T.	P.E.I.	

Note 1: After the name of a community, use **Yukon** rather than Y.T. When standing alone, make it **the Yukon.**
Note 2: An abbreviation has not yet been established for Nunavut, so it should be written out in all references.

2. For American states, use these abbreviations after the name of a community.

Ala.	Kan.	Nev.	S.C.
Ariz.	Ky.	N.H.	S.D.
Ark.	La.	N.J.	Tenn.
Calif.	Md.	N.M.	Vt.
Colo.	Mass.	N.Y.	Va.
Conn.	Mich.	N.C.	Wash.
Del.	Minn.	N.D.	W.Va.
Fla.	Miss.	Okla.	Wis.
Ga.	Mo.	Ore.	Wyo.
Ill.	Mont.	Pa	
Ind.	Neb.	R.I.	

Note: Do not abbreviate Alaska, Hawaii, Idaho, Iowa, Maine, Ohio, Texas, Utah; or Puerto Rico, Virgin Islands.

➤ See **Placelines**, page 275; **Place names**, page 280; and **People, places**, page 282.

3. Generally do not abbreviate the names of countries, provinces or states when standing alone or used adjectivally.

The United States (not U.S.) declared war. The Nova Scotia (not N.S.) cabinet met. The United Kingdom (not U.K.) consists of Britain and Northern Ireland.

Note: The abbreviations U.K., U.S., B.C. and P.E.I. may be used adjectivally to reflect spoken usage.

the B.C. legislature, a U.K. bank holiday, rival U.S. teams

4. In numbered addresses, write **Ave., Blvd., Cir., Cres., Dr., Hwy., Pky., Rd., Rte., Sq., St., Ter.**

36 King St. E., 111 Sutherland Dr., 9 Binkley Ter.

Note 1: Spell out general locations.

on King Street, down Portage Avenue, the Yonge Street subway

Note 2: Spell out these official residences:

24 Sussex Drive, 10 Downing Street.

5. In general, abbreviate Saint and Sainte in place names.

St. John's, N.L., Sault Ste. Marie

But **Saint John, N.B.**

Note: Use a hyphen instead of a period after **St** and **Ste** in Quebec place names.

Ste-Agathe, St-Eustache

➤ See **French**, page 238.

6. Do not abbreviate **county, fort, mount, point** and **port** as part of a proper name.

Fort McMurray, Mount Everest, Port Stanley, Ont.

Titles

1. Abbreviate **Gov. Gen.** and **Lt.-Gov.** before names on first reference.

Gov. Gen. Pamela King, Lt.-Govs. Joan Pappas and Alan Bucyk.

Note: Lowercase former governor general (not former Gov. Gen.), former governors general Georges Vanier and Adrienne Clarkson, the late lieutenant-governor Pat Filippo, the then-president John Redway (but prefer a more graceful construction: **John Redway, who was president at the time**).

2. Do not abbreviate **attorney general, auditor general, district attorney, postmaster general, representative, secretary, secretary general, senator** or **treasurer.**

3. Abbreviate **Dr., Msgr., Prof., Rev., Sgt.** and the like before full names on first reference.

Dr. Pamela Gucci, Msgr. Brian Doyle, Profs. Eva Oberast and John Green, Rev. Freda Cernetig

Miscellaneous usages

1. Use this style for bracketed political affiliations in parliamentary and legislature copy:

Tom Arlee (NDP-Edmonton East), Senator Mary Atkins (Con-Man.), Myron Martin (Lib-Snowy River), Representative John Whyte (R-Pa.), Senator Obie Black (Ind-Va.), state Senator Darleen Healey (D-Queens)

Note: In general, prefer a descriptive phrase to the bracketed style.

➤ See **Government**, page 240.

2. Abbreviate ship and plane designations.

HMCS Restigouche, USS Johnson, SST (but spell out on first reference: **supersonic transport**)

Note: The is not required before HMCS or HMS, since HM stands for Her Majesty.

➤ See **Ships,** page 201.

3. Do not abbreviate books of the Bible.

Genesis, Leviticus

4. In general, spell out serial terms, but **article (Art.), number (No.), page (p.), section (Sec.)** and **volume (Vol.)** may be abbreviated before a number.

Block 1, Chapter 2, page 3, p. 3, Vol. 9

➤ See **Numbers**, page 263.

5. Do not use periods with clipped forms that have become accepted as complete words.

ad, disco, exam, gym, hi-tech, lab, math, polio, porn

6. Do not use periods with shortened forms of first names if they are pronounced as spelled.

Al, Alex, Barb, Ben, Ed, Fred, Marj, Pat, Sam, Will

But **Danl., Geo., Thos.** when such terms appear in textual matter.

7. Do not use periods when letters designate persons or things.

the spy chief Z, exhibit A, the mysterious Madame X

But use a period if the letter is an abbreviation.

Mrs. G., (shortened from **Gamp**), **T.O.** (**Toronto**)

8. In general, do not use such shortenings as **Penetang** (for **Penetanguishene**), **Peterboro** (for **Peterborough**), **Soo** (for Sault Ste. Marie) and **Xmas** (for **Christmas**).

Note: Write **Soo Greyhounds,** the official name of the Ontario Hockey League team.

Abbreviations can be used in graphics where space is at a premium.

Prime rib perfection

Follow these three easy steps:

1. Place roast, bone side down, on rack in roasting pan.

2. Season roast. Insert meat thermometer into centre of roast, avoiding fat or bone.

3. Cook uncovered, in 160°C (325°F) oven to desired doneness (see chart). Remove roast from oven; tent with foil 10-15 minutes to allow temperature to rise an additional 3°C (5°F). Remove twine and carve across the grain.

| | ESTIMATED ROASTING TIME | | INTERNAL TEMPERATURE | |
DONENESS	Minutes per kg	Minutes per lb	When removed from oven	After standing 10-15 minutes
Med-rare	44	22	60°C (140°F)	63°C (145°F)
Medium	50	25	68°C (155°F)	71°C (160°F)
Well	60	30	74°C (165°F)	77°C (170°F)

NOTE: Temperature estimates are based on a minimum roast weight of 2 kg (4 lb). For accurate measure of doneness, use a food thermometer to determine the meats' internal temperature. All times estimated.

SOURCE: Beef Information Centre

CP

Aboriginal Peoples

First Nations, Métis, Inuit

Canada's Aboriginal Peoples comprise three distinct groups: First Nations (sometimes called Indians), Inuit and Métis. Their numbers are estimated at about one million. In the 2000 census they made up 3.3 per cent of the Canadian population. This group is younger than the general Canadian population and is growing at twice the rate.

It is a common misconception that most Aboriginal Peoples live on reserves. In fact, Inuit and Métis generally do not, and 53 per cent of those who identified themselves in the census as North American Indians lived off reserves, many of them in large urban centres.

Three subgroups apply to First Nations in Canada. **Status Indians**, of which there are about 700,000, qualify as Indians under the Indian Act and can take advantage of certain rights reserved for them. **Non-status Indians** are those who have never registered or are not eligible to register under the terms of the act. **Treaty Indians** are those who are registered with a treaty band and are descended from Indians who signed treaties with the Crown.

By agreeing to treaties most Canadian Indians exchanged some interests in their ancestral lands in return for various payments and promises from Crown officials.

There are 614 First Nation bands in Canada. A **band** is a First Nation community for whom lands have been set apart and for whom money is held in trust by the Crown.

Writing about Aboriginal Peoples

1. Canada's Aboriginal Peoples are not a homogeneous group with a standard set of interests and grievances. An effort should be made to reflect their diversity in stories specifically dealing with aboriginal groups.

Saying someone is **an Alberta native** is unhelpful. Try to identify the tribal affiliation or the reserve.

Milton Born With a Tooth, an Alberta Peigan; Barbara Harris of the Six Nations of the Grand River Territory; Neil Sterritt, hereditary chief of the Gitxsan-Wet'suwet'en Nation in British Columbia; Angie Wahienhawi Barnes, grand chief of the Mohawk council at Akwesasne Territory near Cornwall, Ont.

2. If a language other than English or French is spoken, include it in the body of the story: **John Mark, who addressed the forum in Cree.**

3. Use the style and spelling preferred by aboriginals for the names of their communities: **Nickel Palm Reserve, Grassy Narrows First Nation**. A good resource is the Indian and Northern Affairs Department's website, which lists the names of most aboriginal communities.

Identities

1. The term **First Nation** or **Nations** is widely used by status and non-status Indians. It does not have a legal definition. Others still prefer to be called **Indian**. When known, use the preference of the group or individual.

First Nation, rather than **reserve**, is also used by many bands in the name of their community: **Gameti First Nation**.

2. Originally, the word **Métis** was applied to descendants of French traders and trappers and Indian women in the Canadian northwest. Now it is usually taken to mean anyone of mixed Indian and European ancestry. Many Canadians have this mixed ancestry but not all describe themselves as Métis. Even Métis organizations have different definitions of who is Métis.

3. There are about 56,000 **Inuit** (never Eskimo) in Canada. They live in about 50 small settlements above the treeline from Labrador to Alaska. The Inuit population is growing rapidly. Inuit make up 85 per cent of the population of the territory of Nunavut.

The singular of Inuit is **Inuk**. Their language is **Inuktitut**.

The Inuit of the western Arctic call themselves **Inuvialuit**.

Note: Do not confuse the **Inuit** and the **Innu**, a First Nations people who live in Labrador and northeastern Quebec.

Languages

There are many different aboriginal languages spoken in Canada. **Cree** is the most common, followed by **Inuktitut** and **Ojibwa**. Many of the other languages are spoken by only a couple of thousand people.

Iroquois languages are spoken by such groups as the Six Nations, including the Mohawk and Oneidas.

Northern aboriginal people speak **Athapaskan** languages, while those in British Columbia speak languages from several families, the most common being **Salishan**.

Aircraft, ships, guns

Style for names

1. For the names of aircraft, guns, tanks, rockets and the like, use a hyphen when a figure follows a letter.

a DC-10 jetliner, a CF-18 fighter, an M-16 rifle, an M-60 tank, a Russian SSN-8 rocket

Note: Satellite names do not take a hyphen: **Anik F1, Anik F2.**

2. Do not use a hyphen when a letter follows a figure.

an FA-18A fighter, a 727-100C cargo plane, the JT-15D fan-jet engine

3. Do not put a hyphen between a spelled-out name and a number.

a Dash 8-300, an F-4 Phantom 2 fighter, a Leopard 2 tank, a Polaris A-3 rocket

4. Form plurals by adding *s* without an apostrophe.

two Dash 7s, a shipment of AK-47s, 15 M-60s

Aircraft

1. Refer to an aircraft with or without the name of the maker or designer.

Lockheed L-1011 TriStar, Lockheed L-1011, L-1011, TriStar

2. North American military aircraft carry a prefixed letter to indicate the basic function: *A* for *attack,* *B* for *bomber,* *C* for *cargo* or transport, *F* for *fighter,* *H* for *helicopter,* *S* for *anti-submarine,* *T* for *trainer.*

Note: Do not confuse the prefix *C* for *Canadian* (a CF-18 fighter) with the *C* for *cargo* (a CC-130 Hercules).

3. Russian aircraft carry a prefix that is an abbreviation of the maker's or designer's name: *Il* for *Ilyushin,* *M* for *Myasishchev,* *MiG* for *Mikoyan and Gurevich,* *Su* for *Sukhoi,* *Tu* for *Tupolev,* *Yak* for *Yakovlev.*

4. The NATO name for a Russian plane may be used or omitted as desired.

Tu-144 Charger, MiG-25 Foxbat, M-4 Bison, Il-76 Candid

5. A jumbo jet is any very large jet aircraft, such as a *DC-10, Boeing 747, L-1011* or *Airbus.*

Ships

1. The terms **ship** and **boat** are less than precise. A good general rule is to use **boat** for smaller inshore or lake craft, **ship** for larger ocean-going craft. **Vessel** is a handy catch-all for anything bigger than a rowboat. Deepsea freighters, tankers, bulk carriers, container ships, ocean-going passenger liners and most naval ships should never be called boats. (Naval exceptions: motor torpedo boats and submarines.)

2. Words to describe boats and ships vary from region to region. **Laker** is a common term for Great Lakes vessels but may be unfamiliar to readers in some areas of the country. **Fish boat** is an everyday term on the West Coast but unheard of on the East Coast, where such craft are called **fishing boats**.

3. Avoid *nauticalese* that is indecipherable to the average reader — or be prepared to translate it: **fo'c's'le** (forward part of a ship where crew live); **bottom** (a freighter or tanker); **hawser** (cable or heavy rope used to secure a ship to a wharf); **dead-reckoning** (fixing a ship's position by instruments when observation of stars is not possible); **"She's going down by the head."** (A ship is sinking bow-first.)

4. For numbers in ships' names, use the vessel's own style: **Queen Elizabeth 2, Bluenose II**.

5. The familiar abbreviations **HMCS, USS** or **HMS** may be used before the name of a military ship: **HMCS Terra Nova, USS Coral Sea**, etc.

Note: Do not put *the* in front of HMCS or HMS for reasons that are obvious when the abbreviation is written out: *(the)* **Her Majesty's Canadian Ship Halifax**, etc. Naval tradition also drops *the* on second reference to military ships: **The damaged tanker was escorted by Terra Nova into port at Vancouver.** But use the article *the* before names of non-military ships: **The Titanic sank off Cape Race, N.l.**.

6. Avoid or spell out less familiar, cumbersome or archaic abbreviations: **MV** (for motor vessel) **Lollipop**; **CCGS** (for Canadian Coast Guard Ship) **Louis S. St. Laurent**; **RMS** (for Royal Mail Ship) **Titanic**, etc.

7. Avoid terms like **seamen** and **fishermen** unless the sex is important and known to be male. **Crew members** and **crew** are always serviceable.

8. Ships have been referred to in the feminine form — **she** and **her** — for generations. But some readers find it objectionable, especially if the statement being made is sexist (**she's temperamental**). Use **it**, except in direct quotes.

9. Ships' tonnage is measured and expressed in several ways, all of them complex. In general, the tonnage of warships reflects

their weight, while the tonnage of other ships reflects their capacity. If tonnage must be noted, use the **gross register tonnage** as listed in large boldface type in column No. 3 of each ship's entry in *Lloyd's Register of Shipping*. Never write that a ship **weighs** such-and-such. Better to check Lloyd's for such dimensions as length and try to express these in everyday terms to provide a sense of size: **The tanker is about as long as 40 typical transit buses parked bumper to bumper.**

10. A ship's country and port of registration may have nothing to do with the vessel's ownership or the nationality of its crew. Many ships sail under what is known as a **flag of convenience**, meaning they are registered in countries with lower registry charges and wage rates than the owners would pay in their home countries. Hence, a ship identified as **Panamanian-registered** may in fact be owned in a country halfway around the world from Panama. Check Lloyd's for the name and nationality of the ship's owners. Shipping agents may be able to help with such details as the nationality of the crew, the nature of the cargo, last port of call, etc.

11. Some marine measures:

nautical mile	1.853 kilometres (6,080 feet)
knot	one nautical mile an hour
fathom	six feet (slightly under two metres)

Graphics can be particularly useful in presenting technical details to the reader.

A look at HMCS Halifax

Stir Fire control radar — Harpoon anti-ship missiles — Sea Sparrow launchers — Sea Giraffe search radar — Stir Fire control radar — Bofors 57-mm gun

Helicopter deck

330

Towed array sonar — Torpedo tubes — SPS-49 long-range air surveillance radar

		Typical weapon fit
Length	134 m	57-mm Bofors gun; 6 x
Draft	5.00 m	12.7-mm machine-guns;
Displacement, full	4,750 t	24 VLS Sea Sparrow
Speed, maximum	30+ knots	SAMs; phalanx 20-mm
Speed, cruise	18 knots	CIWS; 8 harpoon SSMs;
Range at cruise speed	6,000 nautical miles	and 4 Mark 32 torpedo
Power	2 x 17,000 kW gas turbines	launchers (twin tubes) with
	1 x 6,470 kW diesel	Mark 46 torpedoes.
Complement	235 officers and ratings	

Source: Saint John Shipbuilding   CP

Guns

1. A **rifle** has a grooved bore and fires bullets from cartridges. A **shotgun** has a smooth bore, may be double-barrelled and fires shot from shells. A **pistol** may be a revolver, which holds cartridges in a revolving cylinder, or an automatic, which holds cartridges in a magazine. A **cartridge** is a case consisting of an explosive charge and a bullet or shot. Shotgun **shells** are filled with powder and shot made of lead or steel.

2. When reporting crime stories, avoid the casual use of the term **hunting rifle**, which wildlife and hunting organizations argue is accurate only when used in context with a hunter legally pursuing game. Try to get a precise description of weapons from police and other authorities.

3. Rifles, pistols, revolvers and other small arms are usually described in **calibre**, which is a measurement of the diameter of the inside of the barrel and is expressed in decimal fractions of an inch or in metric. The word calibre is not used in metric measurements. Write **a .22-calibre rifle, a 9-mm pistol**.

4. More precise description of calibre is expressed by an added set of figures (after a hyphen) to designate load, speed of bullet or year of adoption: **.30-30, .250-3000, .30-06**. Often such precision is necessary to differentiate among .30-calibre guns.

5. Shotguns are measured in **gauge**. Gauge refers to the number of balls, with a diameter the size of the inside of the barrel, that can be made from a pound of lead. For a shotgun with a barrel 0.729 inches in diameter, for instance, a pound of lead yields 12 balls, so the gun is called a **12 gauge**. The .410 is a calibre but is commonly called a gauge. Other gauges have no decimal point.

6. **Gun** is an acceptable term for any firearm; it may also be used to describe larger weapons, such as artillery pieces.

7. Large naval and artillery guns fire **shells**; mortars fire **bombs**. A **round** is one shot, whether from a handgun, a rifle or a cannon.

8. The **magazine** of a firearm simply refers to the reservoir or device holding extra rounds of ammunition to be fed into the chamber through spring, bolt or some other action. The magazine can take various forms, such as the **rotary** (as found on the Thompson machine-gun or **tommy-gun**), **tubular** (in some bolt action, semi-automatic, lever and pump-action rifles), **belt** (which feeds ammunition into rapid-fire automatic weapons) or **box** (either a fixed or detachable compartment).

The term **clip** describes a detachable magazine used with bolt-action, semi-automatic and automatic rifles, as well as some shotguns and handguns (usually semi-automatic or fully automatic) holding a varying number of cartridges, from two up. Note that a magazine is not always a clip.

9.   A **semi-automatic** reloads itself after each shot and fires once each time the trigger is depressed. An **automatic** weapon fires continuously as long as the trigger is depressed and there are rounds in the magazine.

10.   The production and use of anti-personnel **landmines** are banned by an international treaty, although a number of countries, notably the United States, are not signatories. The treaty bans only anti-personnel mines. Anti-tank mines and weapons such as Claymore mines are legal. The former only go off under the weight of a heavy vehicle. The latter are command-detonated, that is they must be manually triggered.

➤   See **Military**, page 253.

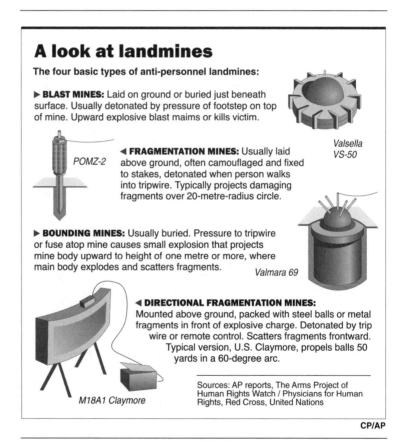

A look at landmines

The four basic types of anti-personnel landmines:

▶ **BLAST MINES:** Laid on ground or buried just beneath surface. Usually detonated by pressure of footstep on top of mine. Upward explosive blast maims or kills victim.

Valsella VS-50

◀ **FRAGMENTATION MINES:** Usually laid above ground, often camouflaged and fixed to stakes, detonated when person walks into tripwire. Typically projects damaging fragments over 20-metre-radius circle.

POMZ-2

▶ **BOUNDING MINES:** Usually buried. Pressure to tripwire or fuse atop mine causes small explosion that projects mine body upward to height of one metre or more, where main body explodes and scatters fragments.

Valmara 69

◀ **DIRECTIONAL FRAGMENTATION MINES:** Mounted above ground, packed with steel balls or metal fragments in front of explosive charge. Detonated by trip wire or remote control. Scatters fragments frontward. Typical version, U.S. Claymore, propels balls 50 yards in a 60-degree arc.

M18A1 Claymore

Sources: AP reports, The Arms Project of Human Rights Watch / Physicians for Human Rights, Red Cross, United Nations

CP/AP

Capitalization

General

1. The Canadian Press follows a modified down style. That is, where a reasonable choice exists, CP uses lowercase. This is the basic rule:

Capitalize all proper names, trade names, government departments and agencies of government, names of associations, companies, clubs, religions, languages, nations, races, places, addresses. Otherwise lowercase is favoured where a reasonable option exists.

Here are some guidelines:

2. Capitalize common nouns — base, drive, ocean, church, department — when they are part of a formal name: **Canadian Forces Base Trenton, Sussex Drive, Atlantic Ocean, Catholic Church, Fisheries Department.** Generally, lowercase them when standing alone in subsequent references: **the Canadian Forces base, the drive, the ocean, the church, the department.**

Note: In sports references the words **Games** (as in **Olympic** or **Commonwealth Games**), **Plate** (as in **Queen's Plate**), **Series** (as in **World Series**) and so on are capitalized when standing alone in subsequent references. This is to avoid confusion with the generic use of the words (as in **a series of rained-out games**). Also, it is three **Cups,** in second references for such awards as Stanley Cups.

3. Lowercase the common-noun elements of names in plural uses: **the Atlantic and Pacific oceans, prime ministers Marie Leclair and James Dunn.** But retain capitalization for the plurals of abbreviations: **Lt.-Govs. Michael O'Hara and Robert Bernard, Drs. (Revs., Profs., Sgts.) Fraser Douglas and Berthe Lucas.**

4. Capitalize formal titles directly preceding a name: **Energy Minister Marc Edmond.** Lowercase them when standing alone or set off from the name with commas: **the energy minister; the energy minister, Marc Edmond; Marc Edmond, the minister of energy.**

5. As a rule of thumb, formal titles are those that could be used with the surname alone: **Bishop Vardy.** These embrace government titles (**Prime Minister Brown, Ald. Chester**), professional titles (**Dr. Masse, Prof. Seguin**), military and paramilitary titles (**Pte. Kirkup, Insp. Low**) and religious titles (**Rabbi Dubuc, Brother Agnew**).

6. Lowercase occupational titles and job descriptions: **GM president Andre Lefort, general manager Sid James, news editor Agathe Simard, author Susan Sontag, nurse Tom Atfield.**

➤ See **Titles**, page 321.

7. The instruction *capitalize* refers only to the first letter of a word. If other letters are to be capitalized, *all-caps* or other specific instructions are given.

8. In sections dealing with the capitalization of book, film, music and other such titles, the term *principal words* means nouns, pronouns, adjectives, adverbs, verbs, the first and last word of the title, as well as prepositions and conjunctions of four letters or more.

9. In The Canadian Press and many other organizations, internal documents capitalize staff titles (even when standing alone), department names and the like.

the President; Editor-in-Chief, Head Office; Personnel

Alliances

1. Capitalize alliances and similar groupings.

Confederation, the British Empire, Commonwealth, NATO allies, Warsaw Pact, East and West (ideological groupings), Allies (in world wars), Group of Seven (industrial countries)

2. Write western allies, imperial ambitions, the coalition against Iraq.

Animals and birds

1. Generally lowercase the names of animals, birds, fish and so on.

collie, dachshund, pit bull, grizzly bear, palomino, pinto, quarter-horse, shorthorn, blue jay, herring gull, mallard, phoebe, robin, snowy owl, eastern cottontail rabbit, brown trout, snapping turtle, western rattlesnake, red admiral, hawk moth, dragonfly

2. Capitalize names derived from proper nouns except where usage has established the lowercase.

angora (cat, goat, rabbit), Angus cattle, Baltimore oriole, Canada goose, Clydesdale horse, Dalmatian, German shepherd, Great Dane, Guernsey cow, Holstein-Friesian, Irish terrier, Kodiak bear, mandarin duck, Newfoundland dog, Percheron, Rottweiler, St. Bernard, Shetland pony, Siamese cat, spaniel

Note: Unless the sex has been established, refer to an animal as *it*.

The dog wolfed its dinner. Toby, who was famished, wolfed his dinner. A bull gored his tormentor. The doe licked her leg.

3. In scientific names, capitalize only the first word.

Orcinus orca (killer whale), **Ovis canadensis** (Rocky Mountain bighorn sheep), **Ursus arctos horribilis** (grizzly bear), **Branta canadensis** (Canada goose), **Cyanocitta cristata** (blue jay), **Grus americana** (whooping crane)

Awards

1. Capitalize awards, honours and decorations.

Order of Canada, Order of Merit, Knight Commander of the Bath, Governor General's Awards, National Newspaper Awards, Nobel Peace Prize, Nobel Prize for chemistry, a Nobel Prize winner, Pulitzer Prize for international reporting, a Pulitzer Prize-winning writer, Victoria Cross, Bronze Star.

Note: French awards follow French style: **Croix de guerre.**

2. Lowercase common-noun references standing alone.

the order, the awards, the prize, the cross

Buildings

1. Capitalize the proper names of well-known buildings, bridges, canals, parks, roads, rooms and other manufactured features.

Parliament Buildings, East Block, White House, Oval Office, Buckingham Palace, U.S. Capitol, Archambault Penitentiary, Calgary City Hall, Lions Gate Bridge, St. Lawrence Seaway, Welland Canal, Laurentian Autoroute, Vancouver International Airport, Union Station, War Memorial, CN Tower, Montreal Neurological Institute, Toronto Hospital, Square of Heavenly Peace, Hall of Mirrors, Sistine Chapel, Fundy National Park, French Embassy

2. Lowercase general terms standing alone, in plurals or in descriptive uses.

the palace, the international airport, the capitol, the city hall, the hospital, the Panama and Suez canals, a St. Lawrence bridge, Banff and Jasper national parks

Compositions

1. Capitalize the principal words in the titles of books, broadcast programs, films, plays, poems, songs, speeches, works of art and other compositions. For a definition of principal words, see page 207, No. 8.

The Watch That Ends the Night, CBC's World at Six, Gone With the Wind, The Taming of the Shrew, In Flanders Fields, Gettysburg Address, The Da Vinci Code

Note: Composition titles, except for the Bible, are written in italics to differentiate them from regular copy, when technically possible, or enclosed in quotation marks when italics are not an option.

2. Do not capitalize *the* at the start of names of almanacs, the Bible, dictionaries, directories, encyclopedias, gazetteers, handbooks and the like.

the *Canadian Almanac*, the *Canadian Oxford Dictionary*, the *Encyclopaedia Britannica*, the *Canadian Press Stylebook*

3. Volume, chapter, section, act, scene, etc., are capitalized when they precede a number. But **page, paragraph, verse** and **line** are lowercase in keeping with widespread practice: **page 20, line 7**.

➤ See **Numbers** below.

4. Use this style for references:

Act 1, Scene 2; 1 Kings 15:5-7 (i.e. First Book of Kings, Chapter 15, verses 5-7); Henry IV, Part 2 or 2 Henry IV

5. Lowercase art styles, schools and movements unless the word is derived from a proper noun or can be confused with a common word:

art deco, art nouveau, baroque, cubism, **impressionism**, neoclassical

But Dada, Gothic, Renaissance, Romanesque, the Bloomsbury Group

➤ See **Music** below.

Courts

1. Capitalize superior, including appeal, courts.

Privy Council, Supreme Court, Federal Court, Court of Queen's Bench, Superior Court (Quebec, Ontario), Appeal Court, International Court of Justice (the World Court), European Court of Justice, High Court of Justice (the High Court), U.S. Tax Court, U.S. Court of Military Appeals, U.S. Court of Appeals

Lowercase divisions.

the appeal division (or trial division) of the Supreme Court

2.   Lowercase lower courts.

family court, youth court, U.S. customs court, U.S. district court

➤   For a full list of Canadian courts see page 137.

3.   Capitalize **Crown** when referring to the supreme governing power.

The Crown dropped the charge. The matter was in the hands of the Crown attorney.

CP, PC, AP, AFP

1.   Capitalize **The Canadian Press** and **The Associated Press** when the full names are used. On second reference, write **CP** and **AP** or **the AP** (lowercase *the*).

Note: Where the use is possessive, *The* is capitalized: **The Canadian Press's membership, The Associated Press's reporter**. But where the use is adjectival rather than possessive, the article is lowercased and the apostrophe omitted: **the Canadian Press membership, the Associated Press reporter.**

2.   The name of CP's French-language operation is **La Presse Canadienne**. The abbreviation **PC** is acceptable in second reference.

3.   **Agence France-Presse** is so spelled. **AFP** is acceptable in second reference.

➤   See **Newspapers and magazines** below.

Derivatives

1.   Lowercase proper names that have acquired independent meaning.

arabic numerals, bohemian, brussels sprouts, cardigan, chinese red, draconian, duffel coat, dutch oven, french fries, mackintosh, manhattan, manila paper, morocco leather, oxford cloth, plaster of paris, portland cement, roman type, sandwich, scotch whisky, spartan, venetian blind, watt

2.   Medical terms tend to retain the capital longer than commoner words.

Achilles tendon, Fallopian tube, Pap smear, Freudian slip

But **caesarean section**

Note: When in doubt, capitalize.

Food and drink

1. Brand names of foods and drinks are capitalized.

Alphabits   Skor bar
Timbits   Pepsi-Cola

2. In food names, there is no consistency in the capitalization of proper nouns. Some are capped: **oysters Rockefeller, McIntosh apple, Bing cherries**. Others are not: **baked alaska, cheddar cheese, caesar salad**. Follow the *Canadian Oxford Dictionary* unless *(CP) Caps and Spelling* shows otherwise.

3. The names of drinks are generally lowercased: **brandy, manhattan, champagne, scotch**. But wines named after grape varieties are likely to be capitalized: **Zinfandel, Pinot Noir, Sauterne**. Follow Oxford unless *Caps and Spelling* shows otherwise.

4. At the start of a recipe list, capitalize the name of the dish being made:

Apple Oatmeal Squares
250 ml (1 cup) all-purpose flour
250 ml (1 cup) quick-cooking rolled oats, etc.

➤ See **Metric**, page 251, for more on recipes.

Foreign personal names

Such particles as **de, des, di, du, le, la, lo, van** and **von** are usually lowercase except when they begin a sentence.

Charles de Gaulle. De Gaulle said no. Manfred von Richthofen was nicknamed the Red Baron. Von Richthofen was a flying ace.

Note 1: Observe personal preferences.

Pierre De Bane, S. S. Van Dine, Martin Van Buren, Jean de La Fontaine

Note 2: Particles are sometimes dropped on second reference.

Ludwig van Beethoven, Beethoven; Guy de Maupassant, Maupassant; Jean de La Fontaine, La Fontaine; Joachim von Ribbentrop, Ribbentrop; Lorenzo de Medici, the Medici

Geography

1. Capitalize geographic and widely recognized descriptive regions.

the North (Canada), **Far North, Northern Canada, High Arctic, Western Canada, Central Canada, East Coast** (region, not shoreline), **Maritime provinces, Prairies, Barrens, the Front, Niagara Peninsula, Nile Delta, Alaska Panhandle, Downtown Eastside** (Vancouver), **Lower Manhattan** (New York City), **West End** (London), **Upstate New York, Southern California, Far East, Orient, North Atlantic, Central Africa, Central Asia, Western Hemisphere, North Pole, the Pole, Tropic of Cancer**

Note 1: Write **eastern Quebec, southern Ontario, northern Ontario.**

Note 2: The **Atlantic provinces** are New Brunswick, Newfoundland, Nova Scotia and Prince Edward Island. The **Maritimes** consist of New Brunswick, Nova Scotia and Prince Edward Island.

Note 3: Write **English Canada** and **French Canada** but **English-Canadian** and **French-Canadian.**

➤ See **Political divisions** below.

2. Capitalize specific natural features.

Canadian Shield, Gulf Stream, Rocky Mountains, Mackenzie River, Yellowhead Pass, Niagara Escarpment, Lake Winnipeg, Great Lakes

3. Capitalize fanciful or imaginative terms.

Rust Belt, Deep South, Down Under, Bible Belt, Ho Chi Minh Trail, Promised Land, Eternal City, Silicon Valley

4. Lowercase points of the compass, mere direction and location, and descriptive regions not widely recognized as such.

north, to the west of Newfoundland, rain sweeping south, east coast (shoreline, not region), **southern Saskatchewan, northwestern Ontario, eastern Newfoundland, downtown Calgary, north-end Toronto**

5. Lowercase **northern, southern, eastern** and **western** in terms derived from regions.

a northern custom, southern hospitality, southern Californians, an easterner, eastern provinces, a western Canadian, a westerner, western armies, far eastern peoples

Note: In **Western Canada,** Ontario people are referred to as **easterners.** In Ontario, Maritimers are referred to as **easterners.** Don't use **Eastern Canada** unless the meaning is clear.

6. Lowercase **parallel** and the like.

48th parallel, international date line, equator

7. Lowercase generic terms standing alone except when they are conventionally used as a short form of the proper noun.

Lake Erie, the lake; Rocky Mountains, the mountains; Grand Canyon, the canyon

But the Interior (for instance, British Columbia), **the Island** (for instance, Prince Edward Island), **the States** (the United States), **the Continent** (Europe), **the Channel** (English Channel), **the Lakes** (Great Lakes)

8. Lowercase the common-noun element in plurals.

lakes Superior and Erie, Red and Assiniboine rivers, the Northern and Southern hemispheres, King and Front streets

9. Lowercase **province** and **state** used in a geographic sense.

Quebec province, New York state

But capitalize as part of the corporate name.

Province of Quebec bonds, New York State vs. Smith

➤ See **Political divisions** below.

Government departments

1. Capitalize specific international, national, provincial and state government departments, ministries, agencies, boards, etc., including short forms of the proper name.

World Health Organization, United Nations Children's Fund, Department of Agriculture, Agriculture Department, Canada Post Corp., Canada Post, St. Lawrence Seaway Authority, National Parole Service, Library of Parliament, Canada Industrial Relations Board, Pensions Appeal Board, Census Bureau (U.S.), Vietnam Health Ministry, Ukrainian Embassy, Italian Consulate, Secret Service, Office of the Commissioner of Official Languages, Ontario Ministry of Labour, Ontario Labour Ministry, B.C. Highways Ministry, Georgia Department of Human Resources

2. Capitalize cabinet portfolios only as part of a title directly preceding a name: **Finance Minister June Atkins.** But **June Atkins, minister of finance.**

3. Capitalize proper-name elements of a department or ministry when they stand alone and are being used as a noun to represent the ministry.

The cuts will affect Justice and Communications. In those 25 years, she worked in Housing and Natural Resources.

But not Ellen Howe, a former Justice minister

4.   Lowercase common-noun elements standing alone and in plurals.

the department, a ministry spokeswoman, board figures, the authority, the service's record, departments of Justice and Defence

5.   Lowercase local government councils, departments, boards, etc.

Peel regional council, Edmonton city council, Saskatoon board of education, Moncton development department

Historical terms

Capitalize the names of historic periods and events.

Stone Age, Dark Ages, Middle Ages, Crusades, Norman Conquest, Reformation, Industrial Revolution, the Depression or the Great Depression, Dirty '30s, Cultural Revolution, Creation, Exodus, the Flood, Civil War (American), Battle of the Plains of Abraham, War of 1812, Reign of Terror, Riel Rebellion, First World War, Prohibition, Holocaust, Battle of Britain, Vietnam War, Quiet Revolution, October Crisis, Winnipeg General Strike, Montreal Massacre

But medieval, a reformation, a renaissance in painting, 19th century, ice age (no single period)

Note: Capitalize **Confederation** in references to Canada: Fathers of Confederation.

Holidays

Capitalize holidays, religious feasts and all special times.

New Year's Eve (but in the new year), Ash Wednesday, April Fool's Day, Mother's Day, Canada Day, St-Jean-Baptiste Day, July Fourth, Fourth of July, Halloween, Christmas Day, Hanukkah, Yom Kippur, Passover, Ramadan, D-Day, Education Week, Weedless Wednesday

Note: Write election day.

Internet terms

1.   Capitalize specific proper names.

World Wide Web, Internet, the Net, Adobe Acrobat, Windows Explorer

2.   Lowercase descriptive or generic terms.

chat room, cyberspace, domain name, e-mail, home

page, intranet, web, web browser, webcam, webcast, webmaster, website

3. Use all-caps for such abbreviations and acronyms as:

HTML (Hypertext Markup Language); CD-ROM (compact disc read-only memory); RAM (random access memory); URL (universal resource locator)

➤ See **Writing for and about the Internet,** page 177.

Laws and documents

1. Capitalize proclaimed laws, treaties, important legal codes and historic documents.

British North America Act, Constitution (Canada), **Charter of Rights, Colombo Plan, UN Charter, Criminal Code, Declaration of Independence, Magna Carta**

Note: Constitution is capitalized in all references when the Canadian Constitution is meant. Otherwise it is capitalized only when preceded by a name: **the U.S. Constitution, the constitution.** Also lowercase **constitutional: the constitutional crisis.**

2. Lowercase proposed and defeated legislation, general references and plurals.

the proposed charter of rights, the Charlottetown accord, a disarmament treaty, the code, the BNA and human rights acts

3. Lowercase **speech from the throne, royal assent, third reading, the president's state of the union message, white paper, green paper.**

Legislative bodies

1. Capitalize international and national legislative bodies and their equivalents, including some short forms.

UN Security Council (Security Council), UN General Assembly (General Assembly), Parliament (national), **House of Commons, the House, the Commons, the Senate, House of Lords (the Lords), House of Representatives (the House), Chamber of Deputies (the Chamber), Bundestag, Cortes, Diet, Knesset, National Assembly** (French)

Note: Generic uses of parliament are lowercase: **the Knesset, Israel's parliament; the Sejm (Polish parliament).**

2. Lowercase general terms, informal terms (except short forms listed above), plurals and derivatives.

the administration, the council, an assembly motion, government, cabinet, lower house, the Canadian and British

parliaments, parliamentary, senatorial

But the Commons motion

3.   Lowercase provincial, state and regional legislatures and local councils.

Quebec national assembly, Ontario legislature, Ontario provincial parliament (but avoid), **Newfoundland and Labrador house of assembly**, New South Wales parliament, the Virginia senate, the Northwest Territories council, Peel regional council, Victoria city council

4.   Lowercase committees and subcommittees.

the committee on communications and culture

5.   Capitalize the full name of royal commissions. But lowercase more informal references to commissions of inquiry.

the Royal Commission on Corporate Concentration, the Royal Commission on Bilingualism and Biculturalism, the Gomery inquiry

But the royal commission, the bilingualism commission

➤   See **Laws and documents** above.

Military

1.   Capitalize **Canadian Forces, the Forces** (Canada only).

2.   Capitalize **Canadian Army, (Royal) Canadian Navy** and **(Royal) Canadian Air Force** in references to pre-unification forces (before 1968).

3.   The general terms **army, navy** and **air force**, written lowercase, may be used of the appropriate branches of the unified Canadian Forces: **a Canadian navy boat.**

4.   For foreign forces, lowercase **army, navy** and **air force** when they are preceded by the name of a country.

Lebanese army, U.S. air force, Russian navy

Note: This style is intended for consistency. Many countries do not use **army, navy** or **air force** as the proper name.

5.   Otherwise capitalize full, specific names of formations, both military and paramilitary.

Royal Navy, U.S. 8th Air Force, the 27th Army, French Foreign Legion, Royal Marines, Canadian Coast Guard, U.S. National Guard

But the army, the navy, the air force, the legion, the

marines, a marine, the coast guard, a coast guard plane, the national guard, a national guardsman

6. Capitalize specific bases, commands, schools and ships.

Canadian Forces Headquarters, Canadian Forces Base Comox, the Citadel (Quebec City), Joint Chiefs of Staff, French General Staff, 6th Fleet, Royal Military College, HMCS Restigouche, HMS Antelope, USS Iowa

But a Canadian Forces base

➤ See **Aircraft, ships, guns**, page 201.

7. Capitalize official names of units.

Royal 22nd Regiment, 3rd Battalion, B Company, 3rd Infantry Division, 126 Squadron

8. Capitalize nicknames of units.

Van Doo, Desert Rats, Green Berets

9. Capitalize major armed conflicts and rebellions.

Battle of Marathon, Wars of the Roses, French Revolution, U.S. Civil War, Boxer Rebellion, Bolshevik Revolution, Battle of Britain, Battle of the Bulge, Six-Day War, Cultural Revolution

10. Capitalize fronts and important positions.

Western Front, Maginot Line

➤ See **Abbreviations**, page 191; **Military**, page 253.

Music

1. In general, capitalize the principal words in the English titles of musical compositions.

Tchaikovsky's *Symphony No. 4 in F minor,* Tchaikovsky's *Fourth Symphony, Light My Fire* by the Doors, Avril Lavigne's *Complicated*

Note: The words **major, minor, sharp** and **flat** are written lowercase in keeping with widespread practice.

2. When the opus number is given, set it off with a comma.

Handel's *Concerti Grossi Nos. 4-6, op. 6*; Mozart's *Exultate, Jubilate, K. 165*; Bach's *St. Matthew Passion, BWV 244*

3. Translate a foreign title into English unless the work is commonly known by its foreign name.

La Bohème, L'Après-midi d'un faune, Eine kleine Nachtmusik

4. For non-English titles the style varies.

In French titles, capitalize the first word, and the second word too when the first word is an article, and proper nouns: *Mon rêve, Le Rêve passé.*

In Italian, capitalize the first word and proper nouns: *La donna e mobile, La clemenza di Tito.*

In German, capitalize the first word and every noun: *Du bist mein ganzes Sehnen.*

In Latin, capitalize each word: *Te Deum.*

Names

1. For all-caps corporate and promotional names, capitalize only the first letters of words.

Amtrak (not AMTRAK), Band-Aid (not BAND-AID), Oxfam (not OXFAM), Scrabble (not SCRABBLE), Via Rail (not VIA Rail), Visa (not VISA), Gap (not GAP)

Note: Initials are capitalized: IBM, CTV, EMI.

2. For names consisting of two or more words written solid, or for names with other internal capitalization, follow the organization's capitalization unless it hampers readability.

WestJet, PepsiCo, MuchMusic, TransCanada Pipelines

3. For names of people or performing groups, follow their preference, as long as it doesn't hamper readability.

k.d. lang (not K.D. Lang); KISS (not Kiss); e.e. cummings (not E.E. Cummings)

Note: Do capitalize at the start of a sentence.

But for other names, follow normal style and always uppercase the first letter:

Adidas (not adidas); EBay (not eBay); Citytv (not citytv)

Nationalities and race

1. Capitalize the proper names of nationalities, peoples, races, tribes and the like.

Aboriginal Peoples, Arab, Arabic, African, African-American, Asian, Caucasian, Chipewyan, Chinese, English-Canadian, Gypsy, Hispanic, Indian, Inuk, Inuit, Jew, Jewish, Latin, Negro, Nordic, Pygmy

2. Write **aboriginal** (but **Aborigine** for the Australian race), **black, brown, white.**

Newspapers and magazines

1. Lowercase **the** in names of newspapers.

the Toronto Star, the Star; the New York Times, the Times

2. For French-language papers, write **Montreal La Presse** rather than **the Montreal La Presse** in first reference. In subsequent references avoid sentence constructions that juxtapose **the** and **le** or **la**: **the La Presse editorial.** Alternatives include **La Presse's editorial, an editorial in La Presse, La Presse said in an editorial.**

3. CP includes qualifiers like **daily, evening** and **Sunday** if the paper prefers them: **Halifax Daily News; New York Daily News.**

4. Capitalize **magazine** only when it is part of the title.

Maclean's magazine, Harper's Magazine

➤ See **CP, PC, AP, AFP** above.

Nicknames

Capitalize fanciful names and nicknames.

Iron Curtain, Third World, Boat People, Red Power, Little Italy, Golden Horseshoe, Old Guard, Big Three, Grits, Grand Old Party (GOP, but avoid), Tiger Williams, Herman (Babe) Ruth, Mack the Knife, Ethelred the Unready, Coeur de Lion, the Sun King

➤ See also **Names, nicknames, initials**, page 260.

Note: Father, Mother, Mom, Uncle and the like are capitalized when used as a name: **The doctor told Father that Aunt Jane is worse.** After a personal pronoun, they are lowercased: **The doctor told my father that my aunt Jane is worse.**

Numbers

1. In general, capitalize a noun followed by a number denoting place in a numbered series.

Act 1, Article 29, Book 3, Channel 2, Chapter 10, Cloud 9, Cosmos 150, Figure 13, Grade 3, Part 2, Pershing 2, Phase 1,

Room 125, Square 1, Volume 12, Ward 7

Note: Avoid roman numerals except in personal sequences and in proper names where specified. **Henry Ford III, Bluenose II, Rocky IV**

2. Lowercase such words in plural use.

acts 3 and 5, chapters 1-3, grades 9 through 11

3. Lowercase **page, paragraph, sentence, size, verse, line.**

page 36, paragraph 2, line 3

Organizations

1. Capitalize the full names of organizations and institutions, but lowercase general references, with the exceptions noted below.

American Airlines, the B'nai Brith, the National Organization for Women, Queen's University, the airline, the autoworkers, the organization, the university

Note 1: Company, Limited, Incorporated, Brothers and similar words are abbreviated as part of a name, **Inco Ltd.,** except in cultural references: **Canadian Opera Company, Good Brothers.**

Note 2: For consistency, lowercase **the** in the names of organizations, except for those noted in *(CP) Caps and Spelling.*

➤ See **The** below.

2. Capitalize the names of major subdivisions of an organization.

the General Council of the United Church of Canada, the Chevrolet Division of General Motors

3. Lowercase ordinary internal elements of an organization.

the United Church's division of mission, the board of directors of General Motors, the fire management centre of the Ministry of Natural Resources

4. Retain capitalization when the short form of a name is a household word. But use lowercase when referring to members of an organization.

Scouts Canada, the Scouts but **two boy scouts; International Brotherhood of Teamsters, Chauffeurs, Warehousemen and Helpers of America, Teamsters union, the Teamsters; Ku Klux Klan, the Klan, a klansman; Odd Fellows** and an **Odd Fellow** (capped to avoid ambiguity); **Knights of Columbus, the Knights.**

5. Retain capitalization when popular usage has reversed a name and eliminated **of, of the** and the like.

Department of Justice, Justice Department; Ministry of the Interior, Interior Ministry

➤ See **Abbreviations and acronyms**, page 191.

Plants

1. In plant names, capitalize proper nouns and adjectives derived from proper nouns.

Scotch pine, Kentucky blue grass, Douglas fir, white Dutch clover

2. In botanical names, capitalize the first word, lowercase others.

Primula japonica (Japanese primrose), **Taraxacum officinale** (dandelion), **Acer rubrum** (red maple), **Cornus florida** (dogwood)

3. Capitalize the names of fruit and vegetable varieties.

McIntosh, Delicious (apples); Yukon Gold (potatoes)

4. Capitalize wheat varieties generally except where usage has established the lowercase.

Selkirk, durum

➤ See **Technical terms**, page 314.

Political divisions

1. Capitalize specific political and administrative divisions.

British Empire, Dominion (Canada), United Kingdom, French Republic, Greater Vancouver Regional District, Montreal Urban Community, Ward 2, 11th Congressional District, Precinct 2, Muskoka District, McGillivray Township, Niagara Region.

But **Niagara region, Muskoka district** when referring to the geographical area.

2. Lowercase such words as **city, county, province** and **state** except when they are part of the incorporated name.

in the city of Halifax, the City of Halifax's credit rating; in Quebec province, the Province of Quebec vs. Smithers; the California state capital, the State of California's damage suit; Quebec City, New York City, Kansas City, Greenwich Village

Politics

1.   Capitalize the full names of political parties and movements, but lowercase **party** in short forms.

Liberal Party of Canada, Liberal party, Conservative Party of Canada, Conservative party, Green party, Christian Heritage party, Communist party, Young Liberals, National Liberation Front

But **New Democratic Party, Bloc Québécois, Parti Québécois**

2.   Capitalize **Communist, Conservative, Democrat, Fascist, Liberal, Nazi, New Democrat, Socialist** and the like when they refer to a specific party or its members.

3.   Lowercase these words when they refer to a political philosophy, except when they are derived from a proper name.

communism, democracy, fascism, socialism, separatism, democratic rights, conservative principles, independent nations, republican system, the left, right-wing group, liberals, communists, social democrats

But **Marxism, Marxists, Nazism, Nazis**

4.   Capitalize fanciful names and nicknames.

Grits, Tories, Grand Old Party (GOP, but avoid), **Old Guard, Young Turks, Black Power, Greens**

5.   Capitalize **Leader, Chairman** or **Secretary** when used with the name of a party and directly preceding a name, but lowercase as the title for others.

New Democrat Leader Jack Layton (but party leader Jack Layton); Communist party General Secretary Do Muoi (but prefer Do Muoi, the Communist party general secretary)

But **Libyan leader Moammar Gadhafi, PLO leader Yasser Arafat, NDP chairman Roy Brown, party secretary Ann Rogers**

6.   Capitalize **Politburo** and **Central Committee,** but lowercase other principal political bodies as well as political conventions.

the government, the administration, the cabinet, Liberal leadership convention, Republican platform committee

➤   See **Legislative bodies** above.

Quotations

1. Capitalize the first word of a complete quotation.

Pickets yelling "Scab!" deterred 200 men from entering.

McCabe replied to the lawyer's "Ah, Mr. McCabe" with an "Oh, hello, Mr. Trout."

Poirier asked, "Did you expect to hear shouts of 'Well done' and 'Good luck'?"

2. Do not capitalize a word or phrase that is quoted merely for discussion or because it is controversial or used ironically or oddly.

What does "gating" mean?

One of the words used was "scab."

The "gift" cost $10.

➤ See **Punctuation**, page 289.

Religion

1. Capitalize sacred names.

Adonai	Lord of Lords
Allah	the Madonna
the Almighty	the Messiah
the Angel Gabriel	Mother Mary
the Apostle Paul,	the Omnipotent
Paul the Apostle	the One Great Spirit
the Baptist	our Lady
Blessed Virgin	Prince of Peace
Buddha	the Prophet (Muhammad)
the Child Jesus	the Saviour
Divine Providence	Siva
Father	the Son
God	the Son of Man
the Godhead	the Twelve Apostles
the Guru	the Virgin
the Holy Family	Vishnu
the Holy Spirit	the Word
Jehovah	Yahweh
King of Kings	

Note: Lowercase fatherhood, providence (in a general sense), messianic, a saviour (in a non-religious sense), the angel, an apostle, holy father (for the Pope).

2. Capitalize personal pronouns referring to God: He, Him, His, Me, My, Mine, Thou, Thee, Thine and so on. Lowercase relative pronouns: who, whom, whose.

3. Capitalize the proper names and nicknames of the devil.

Satan, Lucifer, Father of Lies, Old Nick, the Antichrist

Note: Lowercase **satanic**, capitalize **Satanism**.

4. Lowercase **god** and **goddess** in references to pagan gods but capitalize their proper names.

the sun god, the gods of Olympus, the goddess Venus, the god Thor

5. Capitalize the names of religions, faiths, their current heads and their adherents.

the Baha'i faith	Islam	Parsee
Buddhist	Jain	the Pope
Christianity	Jew	Shintoist
the Dalai Lama	Muslim	the Sikh religion
Hinduism	Neo-Confucianism	Zen-Buddhism

Note: Lowercase **pagan, atheist, agnostic** (in a general sense), **gentile, spiritualist, theosophist**.

6. Capitalize the names of religious denominations, movements, orders and their adherents.

an Anglican	New Age
Baptist	Oxford Movement
Catholicism	Papists
Christian Science, a Scientist	Pharisees
	Protestantism
Church of Jesus Christ of Latter-day Saints, a Mormon, Mormonism	Reform Jews
	Salvation Army, the Army
Eastern Orthodoxy	Sephardism
Franciscans	Seventh-day Adventist, an Adventist
Grey Nuns	
High, Low Church	Sons of Freedom, a Freedomite
Jehovah's Witness, a Witness	

7. Capitalize sacred writings and their parts.

the Bible	Lord's Prayer	Scripture
Book of Genesis	New, Old Testament	Shariah
the Epistles	the Qur'an	the Talmud
Laws of Manu	Romans	the Vedas

Note: Lowercase **fisherman's bible, biblical, the gospel truth, a parable, an epistle, apocryphal, talmudic, vedic**.

8. Capitalize such familar references as the following.

Garden of Eden	Holy Week	the Shroud of Turin
the Chosen People	Good Friday	Diet of Worms
Tower of Babel	the Crucifixion	the Hegira
Noah's Ark	the Resurrection	(Muhammad's)
Ten Commandments	the Prodigal Son	Ramadan
City of David	Three Wise Men	Festival of Sacrifice
Day of Atonement	Good Samaritan	Sabbath
the Second Coming	Yom Kippur	Council of Trent
the Last Day		

Note: Lowercase heaven, hell, paradise, purgatory, nirvana.

9. Lowercase sacraments, rituals, meetings and the like.

aqiqa	evensong	shiva
baptism	high mass	stations of the
bar mitzvah	holy communion	cross
christening	kaddish	synod
confession	mass	way of the cross
eucharist	seder	

10. Capitalize **church** as part of the name of a building, a congregation or a denomination.

St. Paul's United Church, the Anglican Church

Note: Write an Anglican church, the Roman Catholic and Anglican churches, church and state.

11. Capitalize major subdivisions or sections within a church, but lowercase ordinary internal elements.

the General Council of the United Church, the Anglican Communion, the church's division of mission, the church's revitalization committee.

➤ See **Capitalization**, pages 220 and **Titles**, page 323.

Schools

1. Capitalize universities and colleges but not their departments.

Simon Fraser University, Macdonald College, McGill medical school, department of dentistry, English department, faculty of education

2. Uppercase the proper name of schools. Otherwise, lowercase.

York Collegiate Institute, Banff High School, St. John's Catholic School, London School of Economics, Harvard Graduate School of Business, University of Toronto Schools (proper names); York high school, Rolph Road elementary school, St. John's separate school (not proper names).

3. Lowercase the names of courses and programs.

political studies program, world history course

Slogans, headlines, greetings

1. Capitalize the principal words of written slogans and newspaper headlines when quoted in the body of a story, but do not use quotation marks.

On one placard was written Restraint — Practise What You Preach. Another sign read Help the Economy.

The editorial appeared under the heading Show Some Leadership.

➤ See **No. 8**, page 207, for a definition of principal words.

➤ For rules on **Headlines**, see page 406.

2. Capitalize common specific greetings such as **Merry Christmas**, **Happy New Year** and **Happy Birthday**. Lowercase season's greetings.

Space

1. Capitalize the proper names of asteroids, comets, constellations, planets, satellites, stars and other unique celestial objects, and nouns and adjectives derived from proper names.

Ceres, Andromeda, Great Bear, Ursa Major, Charles's Wain, Big Dipper, Milky Way, Anik E1, Martian, Jovian, Venusian

2. In general, lowercase the common-noun element of the names of celestial objects.

Ceres asteroids, the constellation of Andromeda, Halley's comet, Crab nebula, Barnard's star

But the North Star (Polaris)

3. Lowercase **earth** except when referred to as a planet. Lowercase **sun** and **moon** in all instances.

down to earth, move heaven and earth, returned to Earth from Mars, Earth's atmosphere, the new moon

4. Lowercase the names of meteorological phenomena.

northern lights, aurora borealis

Sports

1. Capitalize major sports events and trophies.

Olympic Games, Winter Olympics, World Series, World Cup, Canadian Open, Canada Cup, Grey Cup, Queen's Plate, Stanley Cup playoffs, Super Bowl, Vezina Trophy

2. In second references, capitalize **Games, Series, Cup, Open, Plate, Stakes** and the like: **the Series' leading batter, the Plate also-rans.** This is an exception to the rule that common nouns standing alone are lowercased.

➤ See **Sports**, page 80.

The

1. The word **the** (or its non-English equivalent) is capitalized at the start of titles of books, magazines, movies, TV programs, songs, paintings and other compositions, as well as specialty TV channels when **the** is part of the name.

The Last Spike, The New Yorker, L'Amour masqué, The Journal, The Holly and the Ivy, The Artist and His Model, The Sports Network

2. **The** is not capitalized at the start of the names of such works as almanacs, the Bible, directories, encyclopedias, gazetteers and handbooks.

the *Canadian Almanac*, the *Reader's Encyclopedia*, the *Concise Oxford Dictionary*, the *Canadian Press Stylebook*

3. When **the** is capitalized in a geographical name, retain the capitalization.

The Pas, The Hague, El Salvador

But the **Yukon, the Netherlands, the Congo, the City** (London financial district), **the Front** (sealing ground off Labrador), **the Barrens**

4. In rare instances, **the** can be capitalized when it is used to give a singular meaning to an ordinary word.

The Change (menopause), **The Show** (baseball's major leagues)

5. For consistency, lowercase **the** in all other names: companies, associations, institutions, newspapers, awards, ships, trains, nicknames, rock groups and so on.

the **Bay, the Royal Canadian Legion, the House of Commons, the Foreign Affairs Department, the Anglican Church, the Gazette, the Juno Awards, the Queen Elizabeth, the Transcontinental, the Royal York Hotel, Mack the Knife, the Beatles, the Prince of Wales**

Note: Capitalize the definite article in the names of French-language newspapers in accordance with French style: **Le Droit**.

➤ See **Newspapers and magazines** above.

Times and seasons

Lowercase the seasons and spelled-out references to time.

spring, winter
mountain standard time, eastern daylight time,
Atlantic daylight time

But MST, EDT, ADT

Titles

1. Capitalize formal titles — those that are almost an integral part of a person's identity — when they directly precede the name.

Pope Benedict, Queen Elizabeth, Prime Minister Tony Blair, Dr. Hans Selye, Prof. Harold Smith, Sgt. Ann Rutherford, Brother Marcus, Mayor David Miller

Note: With few exceptions, a title more than two words long should be set off from the name with commas: **Arnold Schaur, trade and commerce minister, . . .**

2. A title set off from a name by commas is lowercased. **The prime minister, Tony Blair, will represent Britain at the talks.**

3. Lowercase occupational titles and descriptions. Titles of officials of companies, unions, political organizations and the like are also lowercased.

Widget president Barbara Sansom, CAW secretary Margaret Wilson, defenceman Ted Green, general manager Art Simpson, commissioner Bert Nobby, coach Guy Lebrun, contralto Maureen Forrester, astronaut John Young, school principal Paul Chambers

Note 1: Avoid the inelegant practice of invariably affixing the description to a person's name as a false title: **rock star Bill Glass, bus driver Mary Owens, Niagara Falls businessman Mario Gucci.** Offer occasional relief by using a **the** phrase: **the contralto Maureen Forrester, the English historian Arnold Toynbee.** Or use a comma construction: **Violet Haynes, a Liberal member, disagreed. The spokesman, Tom Jameson, refused to comment. Ford's president, Alain Batty; a truck driver, Mary Owens.**

Note 2: Avoid such pileups as **public relations director John O'Connor's department; best-selling Canadian mystery writer Eric Wright.**

4. Capitalize all references to the current Pope, Canada's reigning monarch and the current Canadian Governor General. But lowercase most formal titles standing alone.

the Pope's visit, the Queen's family, wrote to the Governor General

But the king of Denmark, the prime minister, the president, the Communist party chairman

Note: Lowercase pontiff.

5. Capitalize **Royal Family** when referring to the British Royal Family. Also **Queen Mother, Her** or **His Majesty** and **Her** or **His Royal Highness**, whether standing alone or with names. For former and future British monarchs, capitalize the title: **the former King.** With foreign royalty, capitalize all current titles used with a proper name and lowercase others: **Queen Astrid, former king Farouk.**

6. **Royal** — as in **royal visit, royal assent** — is lowercase.

7. **Crown** is capitalized when it refers to the state.

the Crown corporation, the Crown alleged, the Crown jewels; but the Queen's crown

8. Capitalize titles of nobility, religion and such that are commonly used instead of the personal name. Lowercase on subsequent references.

the Prince of Wales, the prince; the Earl of Snowden, the earl; the Archbishop of Canterbury, the archbishop; the Bishop of Toronto, the bishop

9. Capitalize terms of honour, nobility and respect.

His Excellency, His Honour, Your Honour, Hon. John Jones, Her Worship, His Grace, My Lord

Note: Use such terms only when they appear in direct quotations.

10. To avoid ambiguity, all references to legislative **Speakers** are capped.

11. Lowercase titles preceded by **former, acting** and so on.

prime minister-designate Mary Brown, acting prime minister John Burgess, president-elect Tony Leech, the onetime president Gerald Ford, former mayor Joanne Lesniak

But Deputy Prime Minister Oskar Arendt

Note 1: Abbreviated titles are capped: **the late Dr. Jean Savard**.

Note 2: In references to past events, titles are capped when words like **former** and **the late** are dropped:

The official opening of the St. Lawrence Seaway — on June 26, 1959 — was attended by Prime Minister John Diefenbaker and U.S. President Dwight Eisenhower.

12. Lowercase plural uses of titles.

premiers Jean Martineau and Gerry Germain, popes John Paul II and John XXIII

Note: Capitalize the plural use of abbreviations: **Profs. Giuseppe Gucci and Helen Bruno.**

13. Lowercase derivatives.

presidential, papal, ministerial, senatorial, mayoral

14. Variations on the titles of cabinet ministers are not capitalized.

junior finance minister Robert Jack; acting health minister Kim Shen

Note: Titles of government officials below cabinet rank are lowercased: **deputy minister Eva Swartz**, House leader Ian Loy (federal), **house leader Ian Loy** (provincial).

15. Following titles are in CP style:

Prime Minister Stephen Harper
Deputy Prime Minister Tony Soprano
the prime minister, Stephen Harper
former prime minister John Turner
junior finance minister Jean Fortin
deputy trade minister Aldo Conti
Liberal Leader Bill Graham
the Speaker
the Governor General
Gov. Gen. Michaelle Jean
lieutenant-governor
Lt.-Gov. James Bartleman
Senator Marjory LeBreton

➤ See **Government**, page 240; **Titles**, page 321. Also, **Government departments**, **Military** and **Religion** above. For composition titles, see **Compositions** and **Music** above.

Trade names

1. Capitalize all trade names but use them only when they give point, colour or impact to a story.

The doctor refused to prescribe Tamiflu.
She blew the inheritance on a Mercedes.
Jim Jones gave Kool-Aid laced with poison to 900 members of the People's Temple.

2. A generic term can often be used instead.

headache pill (Aspirin); adhesive bandage (Band-Aid); cola (Coca-Cola); fibreglass or glass fibre (Fiberglas); jelly dessert (Jell-O); tissues or paper handkerchiefs (Kleenex); hardboard (Masonite); heat-resistant glass (Pyrex); cotton swabs (Q-Tips); sticky tape (Scotch Tape); plastic foam (Styrofoam); petroleum jelly (Vaseline); photocopier (Xerox)

Note: Trade names subject to protection in Canada are normally listed in the *Canadian Trade Index*. Do not follow the capitalization in the *Canadian Oxford Dictionary*.

➤ See **Trade names**, page 327.

Compound words

General

1. In the absence of widely agreed rules, writers and editors sometimes have to decide whether a compound word should be written open (**knuckle ball**), hyphenated (**knuckle-ball**) or solid (**knuckleball**).

2. In practice, a new compound is normally written at first as two or more words (**on line**), becomes increasingly hyphenated (**on-line**) and is then combined into a single word (**online**).

3. In North America, the tendency is to drop the hyphen as soon as a new compound becomes familiar.

4. For compound nouns, follow the *Canadian Oxford Dictionary* unless *(CP) Caps and Spelling* differs. If neither offers help, write it as separate words.

Note: Compound nouns are not necessarily created from nouns but may be combinations of verbs, adverbs and so on.

teeter-totter, know-how, the down-at-heel, letdown

Guidelines

1. Hyphens are used to unravel meaning.

an old-book collector, an old book-collector; a white-slave racket, a white slave-racket; a light-blue coat; a dry-ice machine

2. Compound adjectives are often hyphenated before the noun they modify.

a world-class athlete, up-to-the-minute fashion, a 12-year-old child

3. When the words forming a compound adjective stand alone in a sentence, they are usually not hyphenated.

an athlete of world class, fashion that's up to the minute, the child is 12 years old

Note: In the sentence **The 12-year-old is from Vancouver**, 12-year-old is properly hyphenated as a noun. Similarly: **a race for three-year-olds.**

5. Compound verbs are usually either hyphenated or written as one word.

hand-picked, babysit, whitewash, deep-six

6. Compound verbs ending in an adverb or a preposition are not hyphenated.

break away, hold up, shoot out, run in, lean to, clip on

Note: The same two words used as nouns or adjectives are written solid. But if the solid form would be hard to grasp, use a hyphen.

breakaway, holdup, shootout
But **run-in** (not **runin**), **lean-to** (not **leanto**), a **clip-on** lid (not **clipon**), **log-on** (not **logon**)

➤ See **Punctuation**, page 299-301.

French

The Canadian Press delivers its news report in English for an audience that is not necessarily bilingual. Stories peppered with French break the flow and make reading difficult. At the same time, it is not always possible to avoid the use of French in the names of organizations or movie and book titles. In that case, a translation that remains as faithful as possible to the French should be provided. If a precise translation is impossible, an explanation or description can be used.

The aim is always ease of understanding without sacrificing the meaning of the French text.

Names of organizations

1.   Prefer the English form for the names of organizations.

Quebec Liquor Corp. (not Société des alcools du Québec); **University of Montreal** (not Université de Montréal); the **Montreal campus of the University of Quebec** (not Université du Québec à Montréal or University of Quebec in Montreal); **Montreal Transit Corp.** (not Société de transport de la communauté urbaine de Montréal); **Quebec Federation of Labour** (not Fédération des travailleurs du Québec); **Quebec provincial police** (not Sûreté du Québec); **Museum of Fine Arts** (not Musée des beaux-arts); **Great Whale hydro project** (not the Grande baleine project)

2.   The names of some organizations cannot readily be translated. Others become familiar in their French version, or have no official English version. In such cases, the French name should be accompanied by an explanation.

Conseil du patronat, the largest employers group in Quebec; **Centrale des syndicats du Québec,** the teachers federation; **Société pour vaincre la pollution,** an environmental group; **Union des producteurs agricoles,** the farmers union; **Ecole polytechnique,** the engineering school affiliated with the University of Montreal

Note: Be careful with the following agencies set up in conjunction with Quebec's French-language law *(Law 101)*.

Office de la langue française, the agency that administers the provisions of the provincial language law; **Conseil de la langue française,** a research and advisory body on language issues.

3. For some organizations, known even to English speakers in Quebec by their initials, prefer a substitute rather than the full name or initials.

CEGEP (Collège d'enseignement général et professionel): junior college; CLSC (Centre local de services communautaires): community health centre

4. Some Quebec titles have equivalents in other provinces. Prefer a similar form for the Quebec version even if that means the translation is not identical to the French.

Corporation professionnelle des médecins du Québec: Quebec College of Physicians rather than the **Professional Corporation of Quebec Doctors; Directeur général des élections: chief electoral officer**

5. A few organizations, titles and the like are commonly known by their French names and need not be followed by a translation.

Le Droit, Société St-Jean-Baptiste, Notre Dame

Books, movies, etc.

1. Prefer the English form for the titles of books, movies and the like if the English name is widely known.

Remembrance of Things Past (not *A la recherche du temps perdu*); *Jesus of Montreal* (not *Jésus de Montréal*); *The Decline of the American Empire* (not Le *Declin de l'empire américain*)

2. When a French name or title is used in a quotation, a list of awards or a review, it should be followed by the official translation, if available, in parentheses.

Le Malade imaginaire (The Imaginary Invalid); Le Matou (The Alley Cat); Dans l'oeil de l'aigle (In the Eye of the Eagle); Dans le ventre du dragon (In the Belly of the Dragon)

3. When there is no official translation — for example, if the movie or book has not been issued in English — provide a translation in parentheses that accurately conveys the meaning of the French title.

Au revoir, les enfants (Goodbye Children); Les Belles-soeurs (The Sisters-in-Law)

4. When there is no official or simple English title of a novel, TV program, movie or the like, or when the English translation conveys a different meaning from the French, an explanation is in order.

Les Fous de Bassan, the novel by Anne Hebert which was issued in English as *In the Shadow of the Wind*. Fous de Bassan refers to gannets, a type of seabird.

Bonheur d'occasion by Gabrielle Roy, which translates as Second-Hand Happiness but was issued in English as *The Tin Flute*

Un Train d'enfer, a movie whose title translates as A Train From Hell, but which also carries the meaning of breakneck speed

René Lévesque's *Memoirs,* whose original title, *Attendez que je me rappelle*, had a typically offhand suggestion of Hang On, It'll Come to Me — with a hint of Quebec's official motto

Accents

1. When technically possible, use accents on French proper names, including place names, and on the rare instances when French common words are not translated into English.

Jean Chrétien, L'Actualité, Trois Rivières, Fête nationale, raison d'être

Note: Accents are not used on **Quebec** and **Montreal**, which have long-established English versions, unless they are part of a proper name: **Le Journal de Montréal**

2. Follow Oxford for English words.

cliché, resumé, café, debut

Capitalization

1. For most names in French, capitalize the first word, the second word too when the first is an article, and proper nouns.

This applies to:

a) Titles of books, songs, movies and the like.

De la terre à la lune, Sur le pont d'Avignon, Les Liaisons dangereuses

b) Names of newspapers and magazines.

Le Journal de Montréal, L'Actualité, Le Courrier du peuple, L'Acadie nouvelle, La Voix de l'Est (l'Est, meaning the East, is capitalized as the name of a region)

Note: When referring to a French newspaper, avoid repetition of the article. **La Presse reported today** (not **the La Presse report said today**).

c) A variety of other kinds of names.

Fête nationale (a holiday), **L'Auberge bonne nuit** (a hotel), **La Petite marmite** (a restaurant), **L'Académie canadienne-française** (an association), **Place d'armes** (a city square), **Conseil du patronat** (employers' organization), **Office de la langue française** (government agency)

2. For names of corporate organizations, CP uses the English article preceding the name. Otherwise, capitalize the first word and proper nouns, lowercase other words.

the Service de perception, Emballages St-Laurent ltée, the Caisse de dépôt et placement

3. The main exception to the basic rule is for place names, which follow normal CP capitalization.

La Tuque, Pointe-aux-Trembles, St-Basile-le-Grand

4. **Franco-Albertan** and **Anglo-Quebecer** take capital letters; **francophone** and **anglophone** do not. Generally, prefer **French-speaking** and **English-speaking**. The word **allophone** is also entering the vocabulary to describe someone who is neither French- nor English-speaking, but it should be avoided.

5. **Fleur-de-lis** is capitalized when it refers to Quebec's flag.

Hyphens in place names

1. Most multiple-word place names in Quebec and other French-speaking areas of the world are hyphenated.

Trois-Rivières, St-Georges-de-Beauce, Stanstead-Est, Que.; Petit-Rocher, N.B.; Val-d'Isère, France

Note: In names preceded by the definite article, do not put a hyphen after the article.

La Malbaie, La Pocatière

2. Hyphens are omitted from purely English place names.

Stanstead Plain, East Broughton, Otterburn Park

3. Hyphens are omitted in the names of natural features such as lakes and mountains.

Lac Barrière, Baie des Chaleurs, Rivière des Prairies

Note: A natural feature can be part of the name of some municipalities. They are hyphenated: **Baie-Comeau, Lac-Beauport, Mont-Laurier.**

4. Street names take hyphens.

Ste-Catherine Street, 136 René-Lévesque Blvd.

Saint

1. Family and place names that include *saint* or a variant are tricky, needing the same care in checking as *Mac* and *Mc* names.

2. In Quebec place names, *saint* and *sainte* are abbreviated to *St* and *Ste* (no periods) and joined to the next word by a hyphen. Elsewhere in Canada, practice varies.

St-Jean-Port-Joli, Que; Ste-Anne-des-Monts, Que.

But **St. Boniface, Man.; Sault Ste. Marie, Ont.; Saint John, N.B.; St. John's, N.L.; St. Brieux, Sask.; Saint-Antoine, N.B.; St. Jacques, N.L.**

Note: It is not always obvious that a name is feminine or masculine (e.g. **St-Hyacinthe**); check if in doubt.

3. Quebec family names may be written either with **saint** and **sainte** spelled out (**Louise Saint-Pierre, Marcel Sainte-Marie**) or in abbreviated form (**Chantal St-Amour** or **Pierre Ste-Croix**). Check with the person for a preferred spelling; if that is not possible, prefer the long form.

4. For the names of saints, follow normal English practice and use St. for female as well as male saints and do not hyphenate.

St. Jean de Brébeuf, St. Marguerite Bourgeoys

5. For institutions, follow their preference.

Saint Mary's University, Auberge Saint-Antoine

Translation

1. CP avoids double translation. The risk of error is compounded when a quotation moves from one language into another and then back again. Paraphrasing a quotation reduces the risk.

2. When translating from an interview or from a French text, avoid awkward literal translations. Translate to convey the meaning of the quote or French text while remaining as true as possible to the original. If that requires too many contortions, paraphrase.

"Il a réussi à sauver les meubles": not "He managed to save the furniture" but "He was able to salvage the essentials."

3. Be alert to words that look alike in French and English but have different meanings.

amateur (in sports, fan); bulletin d'information (news report); circulation (traffic); commission parlementaire (legislature committee); déception (disappointment), déçu (disappointed); éditeur (publisher), rédacteur-en-chef (editor); exploiter (operate); formation (training, education); ignorer (be unaware of, not know); impliquer (involve); militant (member of a political party); nomination (appointment); populaire (popular, but more often of or for the people); sécurité (safety); sensibiliser (educate), sensible (sensitive to)

4. **Business terminology:** The business world uses some terms that present translation problems.

actif (assets); action (share); administrateur (director); bénéfice net (profit); chef de l'exploitation (chief operating officer); chiffres d'affaires (income); membre de la direction (officer); obligation (bond, debenture); passif (liabilities); président-directeur-général — pdg (president and chief executive officer — CEO); président du conseil (chairman of the board); société (company or corporation); société fermée (private company); société ouverte (public company)

5. **Legal terminology:**

effraction (break and enter); homicide involontaire (manslaughter); mandat de perquisition (search warrant); outrage au tribunal (contempt of court); voies de fait (assault)

Note: In Quebec, the Civil Code based on the French Napoleonic Code is used in civil litigation. The Canadian Criminal Code applies in criminal cases.

As a result, many procedures differ from elsewhere in Canada.

➤ See **Legal** section, page 103.

Government

Introduction

Question period shouting matches and hallway scrums offer only a small glimpse of what government does. Good reporting goes further. It humanizes statistics, puts issues into perspective, illustrates the effects of new regulations and penetrates the silent bureaucracies that shape the lives of Canadians.

Most people connect with government through taxes, schools, police, hospitals, highways, jobs and the price of beer. These are tangible elements. They should appear in stories. That means putting real people looking for jobs in a report on unemployment statistics. It means showing how car owners and trout anglers will be affected by new environmental laws.

Corruption and waste are pursued, where they exist, but reporters must not become another official Opposition, looking only for something — *anything* — to criticize. The best reporting is concerned with more than quick hits from mock-indignant politicians. Time is better spent exploring how little-known regulatory agencies affect everyday concerns like food quality, aircraft safety or personal privacy.

The relationship between issues raised in the political arena and the concerns of the reader at home is often obscure. The reporter works to make that connection clear.

Capitalization

➤ For questions of capitalization on government, parliaments, laws, royalty, etc., see the chapter **Capitalization**, starting page 204.

National and provincial legislatures

1. Ministers with more than one portfolio should be referred to by the title most appropriate to the story. **Intergovernmental Affairs Minister Michael Chong** becomes **Sport Minister Michael Chong** in stories about the Olympics.

2. The **official Opposition** is the opposition party with most seats: **the Opposition Liberals, the two opposition parties**.

3. **MP** is always acceptable for member of Parliament. Don't use an abbreviation for members of provincial legislatures, since the title varies from province to province.

4. Write **Senate, Senator Nate Nurgitz, a senator, former senator Robert de Cotret**.

5. Make it **Parliament Hill, the Hill, Parliament Buildings, East Block, Peace Tower, lower chamber, upper chamber,**

lower house, upper house.

6. The official residence of the Canadian prime minister is **24 Sussex Drive**; that of the Opposition leader is **Stornoway**.

7. Write **prime minister-designate** Stephen Harper, not **prime minister-elect** Stephen Harper, because the Canadian electorate does not vote for a prime minister or premier as such. But **president-elect** George W. Bush is correct in U.S. contexts.

8. Federally, it is the **Conservative Party of Canada,** formed by the merger of the Canadian Alliance and the federal Progressive Conservative party. **Conservative** is also acceptable. The form **Progressive Conservative** is still in use for provincial parties.

Political affiliations and designations

1. The political affiliation of elected members and the names of their constituencies are specified when they are relevant. For members of Parliament and provincial legislatures, give the party and constituency; for senators, party and province.

2. Streamlined abbreviations for party designations are fine in routine parliamentary and legislature copy, or in stories where many members are named. They are also used in election results. They are avoided otherwise, except for **NDP** and **PQ**.

Abbreviations for some of the better-known parties are: **ADQ** (L'Action democratique), **BQ** (Bloc Québécois), **CHP** (Christian Heritage Party), **Con** (Conservative), **EP** (Equality Party), **GRN** (Green Party), **Ind** (Independent), **Lib** (Liberal), **NDP** (New Democratic Party), **PC** (Progressive Conservative), **PQ** (Parti Québécois), **SP** (Saskatchewan Party), **SC** (Social Credit).

Style is **(Lib-Winnipeg North Centre)**. The abbreviation is separated from the constituency by a hyphen with no spaces on either side.

Usually, a descriptive phrase reads better than a streamlined style: **George Baker, the longtime Liberal member for Gander-Grand Falls**. Sometimes a fuller description is desirable. For example, in a debate about federal transfer payments to Newfoundland: **George Baker, Liberal member for Gander-Grand Falls, is a politically well-connected Newfoundlander whose brother, Winston, is the province's deputy premier and finance minister.**

3. In the bracketed style, the names of federal constituencies not easily identified are followed by the name of the province: **(Lib-Egmont, P.E.I.)**.

4. The names of cities are given when they have more than one seat: **Toronto Broadview-Greenwood** (city first). Similarly, the name of a subdivided constituency precedes that of the subdivision: **York West**.

First minister

Where the choice is between **prime minister** and **premier**, use **prime minister** for the heads of national governments in general but **premier** for the heads of government in France and its former colonies, Canadian provinces and Australian states. Some West Indies governments also have premiers; follow individual preferences.

Monarchy

The Queen and members of the Royal Family deserve normal respect for their constitutional role in Canada, but coverage of their visits to this country and other activities is governed by basic news standards.

In particular, that means stories should not gush (**looking radiant**). Nor should they pretend the visitor's casual asides are profound or witty, nor quote meaningless exclamations from bystanders (**"It's the most thrilling day of my life,"** said 11-year-old Melanie Simpson), nor be littered with royal this's and that's (the **royal breakfast**, the **royal limousine**, etc.).

It is no more acceptable to write condescendingly about ordinary people's responses to a royal tour. The fact that someone puts on hat and gloves to watch royalty pass, or belongs to the Monarchist League, is a matter of personal choice, not an occasion for fun.

The best stories tend to focus on one or two events in the visitor's day, stressing human elements that are genuinely newsworthy and describing them fully and frankly. The organization is also worth a story at times: in Halifax, they once used green paint on a bald stretch of the common as part of their spruce-up.

Such coverage excludes the kind of social-page filler that lists every hand shaken, royal guard inspected, memorial book inscribed and ribbon cut.

1. The Queen is Canada's **head of state**; the prime minister is **head of government**. Officially, the **Governor General** acts as head of state when the Queen isn't in Canada, but avoid referring to the Governor General in such terms.

2. Unless there are problems with identification — for instance, in a story dealing with a number of monarchs — the preferred term for Queen Elizabeth is **the Queen**, rather than **Queen Elizabeth**. Use **Queen of Canada**, not **Queen of England**. Prince Charles is not **heir to the British throne**; he is **heir to the throne**.

3. Camilla, wife of Prince Charles, uses the title **the Duchess of Cornwall**.

3. Don't refer to the late Princess of Wales as **Princess Diana**, since she wasn't a princess by birth.

> See **Titles**, page 321.

Succession

Order of succession to the throne:

1. Prince Charles, Prince of Wales (Queen's eldest son)
2. Prince William (elder son of Charles)
3. Prince Henry (second son of Charles)
4. Prince Andrew (second son of the Queen)
5. Princess Beatrice (elder daughter of Andrew)
6. Princess Eugenie (second daughter of Andrew)
7. Prince Edward (third son of the Queen)
8. Princess Anne (only daughter of the Queen)
9. Peter Phillips (only son of Anne)
10. Zara Phillips (only daughter of Anne)

Ceremonies

1. The Queen and other members of the Royal Family receive a **royal salute** — the playing of *God Save the Queen* by a royal guard.

2. The Governor General and lieutenant-governors are accorded a **vice-regal salute** — part *God Save the Queen,* part *O Canada.*

3. The prime minister, visiting heads of state and political leaders, etc., are greeted with a **general salute** — a few bars of music other than *God Save the Queen* or *O Canada.*

➤ See **Military**, page 253.

First lady

The Americanism **first lady** refers to the wife of a U.S. president and is capitalized as a fanciful term. CP prefers **Laura Bush** and the like. Do not apply the term to the Queen or to the wives of Canadian governors general, lieutenant-governors or prime ministers.

Nationhood

Nation means the people of a country; **country** is the territory of a nation. Hence avoid **nationwide** when used in a geographical sense, **the nation's capital** (for Ottawa), etc.

Canada

1. The national flag is the Maple Leaf.

2. The national anthem is *O Canada;* the royal anthem, *God Save the Queen.* The patriotic song *The Maple Leaf Forever* enjoys semi-anthem status outside Quebec.

3. The national emblem is the maple leaf. The beaver is a semi-official emblem.

4. Canada's coat of arms bears the inscription *A Mari Usque Ad Mare* (From Sea Even Unto Sea).

5. Canada's patron saint is St. Joseph (March 19).

Government jargon

1. Avoid using the jargon that often flows so freely from government news releases or officials' mouths. Jargon fails to convey information to those unfamiliar with the term and can even mislead.

2. Some words or phrases may be used sparingly. For example, **committee** can usually be substituted for **task force**. But **the Task Force on National Unity** may be referred to as **the task force**, because it is part of the official name.

3. Steer clear of pompous or awkward phrasing. Not **government initiative**. Initiative means **personal drive**. Use **government program** or **plan**. Not **referenced** (use **refer to**), not **impact on** (use **affect**), not **negatively impact on** (use **hurt**).

4. Government budgets are rife with specialized terms. Keep it simple. A **negative growth in revenues** means government took in less money. A **surplus on the ordinary account** should not find its way into copy. Explain it instead: **The government showed a modest $10-million surplus on day-to-day operations, but once money spent on capital projects was taken into account — such as road repairs and a new court building — it ran a deficit of $500 million for the year.**

Many institutional stories, such as annual budget coverage, can be illustrated with graphics that help a reader navigate through numbers and other material that is easier to understand in a visual format.

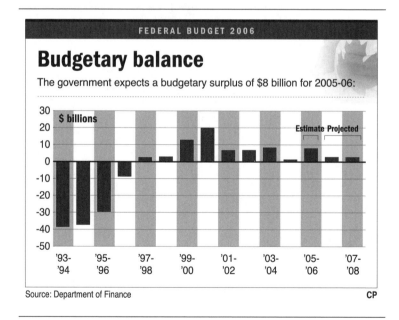

FEDERAL BUDGET 2006

Budgetary balance

The government expects a budgetary surplus of $8 billion for 2005-06:

$ billions

Estimate Projected

'93-'94   '95-'96   '97-'98   '99-'00   '01-'02   '03-'04   '05-'06   '07-'08

Source: Department of Finance

CP

Metric

General

CP uses metric for most measurements. As with any measurement, the most important instruction is: **Be clear**. Specific descriptions are often needed, but comparative examples from everyday life can be even more helpful: **big as a truck, small as a thimble, knee-deep snow** and the like.

When metric?

1. Among the lingering exceptions to metric are cases where some other measurement remains conventional — personal weights and heights, precious metals in troy ounces, two-by-fours, quarter-inch screws and the like.

2. The number of exceptions is limited. Many farmers in Canada may still think in acres and grocery shoppers in pounds, but CP uses metric when figures are needed and descriptions when they're not (**a dusty patch of Saskatchewan grain field, a bag full of turnips**).

3. Metric measurements are not put into the mouths of those who speak in the inch-pound system, either in direct quotes or in indirect speech. Rephrasing can be used to limit such occasions.

4. In most other cases when imperial must be used, it should be accompanied by a metric equivalent. For example, Canada's 200-nautical-mile (**370-kilometre**) fishing limit, or the number of litres in a 35-gallon barrel of oil (**about 159**).

5. But when repeated use of bracketed equivalents may slow down or annoy the reader, consider a separate line or paragraph giving the metric equivalent. Thereafter let the specialists speak in their own tongue.

6. Speed and distances are expressed in metric, including very great distances such as the number of kilometres between planets in the solar system. Certain astronomical distances, such as those between stars or galaxies, are often measured in light-years — the distance light travels in one year moving at almost 300,000 kilometres a second, or about 9.46 trillion kilometres.

7. The altitude of airplanes and the height of mountains are expressed in metres, not feet, and distances at sea are expressed in kilometres, not miles or nautical miles. Measure speeds in kilometres an hour, not knots.

8. The size of animals is expressed in kilograms and metres (centimetres and the like for extremely small animals). Meat on the store shelf is in kilograms.

Let logic be your guide

1.   In handling material from U.S. sources, it is usually possible to make a straight conversion from imperial. **The plane crashed about 90 metres from a home for the elderly.** (The source material reads **100 yards.**)

2.   But tend to use round figures. Most of the world uses metric and material routed through the United States from abroad has possibly gone through one conversion already.

3.   In converting to metric, do not use figures that imply greater accuracy than justified by the original data. For instance, using 2.54 centimetres to the inch, convert 35 inches to 89 or even 90 centimetres, not 88.9.

4.   Don't needlessly mix imperial and metric in comparisons in the same sentence. Make it **the 60-pound boy was attacked by a dog almost twice his weight.** Save the exact weight of the dog (50 kilograms in this case) for another sentence.

5.   People often talk in imperial. Again, try to avoid juxtaposing a quote containing imperial with metric.

6.   And, of course, it's axiomatic that a writer doesn't meddle with the idiomatic: **The crowd inched forward.**

Sports

1.   Most Olympic and many non-Olympic sports are contested and reported in metric. But others, such as golf, horse racing and North American football, continue to use imperial.

2.   Where figures are appropriate in descriptions of imperial-measure sports, CP increasingly uses metric: **a 10-metre slapshot, a 120-metre homer to left field.** And use of imperial is kept to essentials in stories and results. Often a descriptive phrase will do instead: **won by three car lengths.**

3.   Different types of motor racing use different measures. Grand Prix racing is in metric, but motorcycle, U.S. stock car and Indy-type racing are in imperial.

4.   A race for 12-metre yachts should be described as such. But include an explanatory note that the vessels themselves are about 20 metres long and that the classification of 12 metres is determined through a complicated formula involving length, sail area and displacement.

➤   For details, see **Sports**, page 80.

Odds and ends

1.   The names of metric units are usually spelled out: **a 20-kilogram sack**, not **a 20-kg sack**; **covering 50 hectares**, not **covering 50 ha**; **ran 10 kilometres**, not **ran 10 km.**

2.   There are no abbreviations in metric, only symbols. These

symbols take periods only at the end of a sentence, never take *s* in the plural and are separated from a number by a space. In adjectival uses, the space is replaced by a hyphen.

3.   **C** (for Celsius) can be used on first reference. Other common symbols such as **km/h, mm** and **KB** should be written out in first reference but may be used on second reference when preceded by a number: **at 70 km/h, a 105-mm cannon, a 112-KB file.**

4.   A number less than one has a zero before the decimal: **0.25 ha,** not **.25 ha**; but prefer **a quarter hectare** and the like when common fractions are involved.

5.   Treat the names of metric units as singular when the number preceding them is less than one: **0.25 litre** but **2.5 litres.**

6.   For temperatures less than 0 C do not write **below zero**; use a minus sign as in **-5 C.** The minus sign is a dash preceding a number with no space between.

7.   The clipped form **kilo** is not acceptable for **kilogram** or **kilometre** since kilo simply means a thousand and is not a specific unit.

8.   Superior numbers are not available on many keyboards for the preferred symbols for square metres (m^2), cubic centimetres (cm^3) and such. Instead write **sq. m, cu. cm,** etc. The symbol for degree (°) is unavailable; for **15°C** write **15 C,** or **15 degrees C.**

9.   Symbols may be used in tabular matter and certain sports and financial routine.

10. Metric units named after people have capitalized symbols (**A** for Andrew Marie **A**mpere, **C** for Anders **C**elsius, **Pa** for Blaise **Pa**scal and **W** for James **W**att); but when the name of a unit is written in full, only Celsius is capitalized. Otherwise write ampere, pascal, watt, etc.

11. A few symbols for metric prefixes are capped, including **M** for **mega** (one million) and **G** for **giga** (one billion); for example, **MPa** (megapascal), **GJ** (gigajoule). But avoid prefixes denoting extremely large multiples and such small fractions as **pico** (one-trillionth), **nano** (one-billionth), **micro** (one-millionth).

➤   See **Abbreviations and acronyms,** page 191.

Metric conversion table

Into metric

If you know	multiply by	to get
Length		
inches	25.4	millimetres
inches	2.54	centimetres
inches	0.0254	metres
feet	0.3	metres
yards	0.91	metres
miles	1.61	kilometres
Area		
sq. inches	6.45	sq. centimetres
sq. feet	0.09	sq. metres
sq. yards	0.84	sq. metres
sq. miles	2.59	sq. kilometres
acres	0.4	hectares
Mass (weight)		
ounces	28.35	grams
pounds	0.45	kilograms
tons (short)	0.907	tonnes/metric tons
Volume		
Imp. — not U.S.		
fluid ounces	28.41	millilitres (cu. cm)
pints	0.57	litres
quarts	1.13	litres
gallons	4.54	litres
cubic inches	16.39	cubic centimetres
cubic feet	0.03	cubic metres
cubic yards	0.76	cubic metres
Temperature		
Fahrenheit	Subtract 32, then multiply by 5/9ths	Celsius
Temperature variations		
Fahrenheit	.555	Celsius

Out of metric

If you know	multiply by	to get

Length

millimetres	0.04	inches
centimetres	0.39	inches
metres	3.28	feet
metres	1.09	yards
kilometres	0.62	miles

Area

sq. centimetres	0.15	sq. inches
sq. metres	10.76	sq. feet
sq. metres	1.19	sq. yards
sq. kilometres	0.4	sq. miles
hectares	2.47	acres

Mass (weight)

grams	0.035	ounces
kilograms	2.2	pounds
tonnes/metric tons	1.1	tons (short)

Volume

		Imp. — not U.S.
millilitres (cu. cm)	0.03	fluid ounces
litres	1.76	pints
litres	0.88	quarts
litres	0.22	gallons
cubic centimetres	0.06	cubic inches
cubic metres	35.31	cubic feet
cubic metres	1.31	cubic yards

Temperature

Celsius	Multiply by 9/5ths, then add 32	Fahrenheit

Temperature variations

Celsius	1.8	Fahrenheit

Common metric units

	CP style for symbol		CP style for symbol
Length			
millimetre	mm	metre	m
centimetre	cm	kilometre	km
Area			
square millimetre	sq. mm	hectare (10,000 sq. m)	ha
square centimetre	sq. cm	square kilometre	sq. km
square metre	sq. m		

Note: To convert hectares to square kilometres, divide by 100.

Volume			
millilitre	ml		
litre	l		
cubic centimetre	cu. cm		
cubic metre	cu. m		

Mass (weight)			
milligram	mg	kilogram	kg
gram	g	tonne/metric ton (1,000 kg)	t

Electricity			
volt	V	ohm	ohm
ampere	A	hertz	Hz

Energy		**Power**	
joule	J	watt	W
kilojoule	kJ	kilowatt	kW
megajoule	MJ	megawatt	MW
kilowatt hour	kW-h		

Pressure		**Temperature**	
pascal	Pa	Celsius	C
kilopascal	kPa		
megapascal	MPa		

Speed		**Memory**	
metres a second	m/s	kilobyte	KB
kilometres an hour	km/h		

Different strokes

1. In much of the world, spaces are used to separate long numbers into blocks of three digits (**25 353 425**) and a comma is used as a decimal mark (**245,3**). CP style is to separate figures with commas rather than spaces (**25,353,425**) and to use a period rather than a comma in decimals (**245.3**).

2. In Quebec, French-language media have adopted the international style: a space instead of a comma in long numbers, a comma instead of a decimal point and a currency symbol after an amount instead of before. Thus **12,24$** is used for **$12.24**.

Converting

1. Fuel consumption of automobiles is given in number of litres per hundred kilometres, written **l per 100 km**. The lower the figure, the lower the rate of consumption. To convert miles per U.S. gallon into litres per 100 kilometres, divide 234.2146 by the number of miles. To convert miles per Canadian gallon into litres per 100 kilometres, divide 282.48 by the number of miles.

2. To change Fahrenheit to Celsius, subtract 32, then multiply by five and divide by nine. To convert Celsius to Fahrenheit, multiply by nine, divide by five, then add 32.

3. Convert large numbers of hectares into square kilometres. To do so, divide the number of hectares by 100.

4. In Canada the results of cholesterol tests are given in millimoles per litre (mmol/l). In the United States, the results are in milligrams per decilitre (mg/dl). To determine the Canadian equivalent of an American cholesterol reading, multiply by .0259. For example, 140 mg/dl is about 3.6 mmol/l.

Recipes

Follow this style for recipes, where imperial continues to be in wide use:

Apple Oatmeal Squares

250 ml (1 cup) all-purpose flour
250 ml (1 cup) quick-cooking rolled oats
125 ml (1/2 cup) firmly packed brown sugar
5 ml (1 tsp) nutmeg
2 ml (1/2 tsp) salt
175 ml (3/4 cup) butter
6 medium cooking apples
50 ml (1/4 cup) sunflower seeds

In a bowl, combine flour, oats, sugar, nutmeg and salt. Cut in butter until mixture is crumbly. Measure out 125 ml (1/2 cup) and set aside for topping. Press remaining mixture evenly in bottom of greased 23-cm (9-inch) square pan.

Peel and core apples, cut in halves lengthwise. Place cut side down on oatmeal base. Add sunflower seeds to reserved crumb mixture and sprinkle over top. Bake at 190 C (375 F) for 40 to 45 minutes. Cut into squares and serve warm or cooled.

Makes 12 squares.

Note: To save space, punctuation in abbreviations (tsp, tbsp) can be eliminated and numbers below 10 don't need to be written out.

Military

General

1. All Canadian servicemen and servicewomen are members of the **Canadian Forces**, often shortened to the **Forces**.

Note: Uppercase **Forces** applies only to Canadian forces; all others are down.

2. The Canadian Forces are headed by the **chief of the defence staff**, responsible to the minister of defence.

3. There are five commands: **Maritime; Air; Land Forces; Canadian Forces Recruiting, Education and Training;** and **Canadian Forces North Area.**

4. Units making up land, sea and air formations go by a variety of names. The main field units are **division, brigade, regiment, battalion, squadron, company, troop** and **platoon**; naval units are **fleet, squadron** and **ship**; air units are **division, group, wing, squadron** and **flight.**

5. One rank structure, based on army grades, is used for army and air force personnel, another for navy personnel.

➤ See **Ranks**, page 254.

6. The terms **army, navy** and **air force** are acceptable, and personnel may be referred to as **soldiers, sailors** and **airmen** or **airwomen.**

Bases

1. National Defence Headquarters in Ottawa is the headquarters of the Canadian Forces and the Defence Department.

2. Major service establishments include **Canadian Forces bases: Canadian Forces Base Comox, B.C.**, or **CFB Comox** in second reference. There are smaller establishments called **Canadian Forces stations** and specialist installations such as **Canadian Forces ammunition depots.**

3. Canada's three **rescue co-ordination centres** — at Halifax, Trenton, Ont., and Victoria — are jointly staffed by the Canadian Forces and the Canadian Coast Guard. The Forces co-ordinate air searches and the Coast Guard co-ordinates marine searches. The Forces contribute most of the aircraft used in searches while the Coast Guard contributes most of the marine vessels.

4. Avoid the abbreviations **CFS, CFAD** and **RCC** as being unfamiliar to readers.

Units

1. To help readers evaluate a military action, put the numbers and types of troops and their support high in the story. Because **battalion, brigade, army** and other formations vary in size and makeup from country to country, the terms mean little unless qualified.

2. These are some Canadian land units and their approximate sizes: **section**, 10 soldiers; **platoon**, three sections totalling 35; **company**, three platoons totalling 125-150; **battalion**, three or four companies totalling 375-600. A **brigade** consists of three battalions. A **battle group** numbers about 1,000 to 1,800 and includes representatives from various branches of the military such as infantry and armour.

Note: The figures do not add up because, in addition to fighting personnel, each unit includes a varying number of commanders, signallers, etc.

3. A **regiment** is a unit with a proper name. Canada's Armed Forces has three infantry regiments (each with three battalions), three armoured regiments and three artillery regiments, in addition to dozens of reserve units.

The infantry regiments (in order of seniority): **Royal Canadian Regiment, Princess Patricia's Canadian Light Infantry, Royal 22nd Regiment.**

Armour: **Royal Canadian Dragoons, Lord Strathcona's Horse (Royal Canadians), 12me regiment blinde du Canada.**

Artillery: **1 Royal Canadian Horse Artillery, 2 Canadian Horse Artillery, 5 regiment d'artillerie legere du Canada.**

Capitalization

➤ See chapter **Capitalization**, page 216.

Ranks

1. The Canadian Forces modify British tradition in the use of ranks and appointment titles, particularly for land forces. In an artillery regiment, for example, a private is a gunner, and a corporal is a bombardier. In an engineer regiment, a private is a sapper; in an armoured unit, a trooper; in a communications unit, a signalman; in a guards regiment, a guardsman; in a rifle regiment, a rifleman.

2. Plurals of military ranks and appointments add *s* to the principal rank category, not to the qualifying word: **major-generals, lieutenant-colonels, sergeants major.**

3. A person with at least four years of service who has achieved certain technical qualifications holds the rank of **corporal**. In effect, it is equivalent to a senior private rather than a rank indicating leadership responsibility. The first level requiring leadership and special qualifications is the rank of **master corporal**.

4. Sometimes **commissioned** and **non-commissioned** officers are confused. Non-commissioned officers — master corporals, sergeants and warrant officers — have leadership functions, but do not hold formal commissions; the documents signed by the Queen that formally "commission" officers (from 2nd lieutenant to general) to do their jobs. **Warrant officers** actually have a "warrant" — a sort of lesser-grade commission.

Titles

The Canadian Forces use such titles as guardsman and master seaman for both males and females. Following are listed by descending order of rank.

Note: For clarity for a non-military audience CP does not use abbreviations used by the Forces.

Use these titles for army and air force personnel:

Rank	Before a name
general	Gen.
lieutenant-general	Lt.-Gen.
major-general	Maj.-Gen.
brigadier-general	Brig.-Gen.
colonel	Col.
lieutenant-colonel	Lt.-Col.
major	Maj.
captain	Capt.
lieutenant	Lt.
second lieutenant	2nd Lt.
officer cadet	Officer Cadet
chief warrant officer	Chief Warrant Officer
master warrant officer	Master Warrant Officer
warrant officer	Warrant Officer
sergeant	Sgt.
master corporal	Master Cpl.
corporal	Cpl.
bombardier	Bombardier
private	Pte.
guardsman	Guardsman
gunner	Gunner
rifleman	Rifleman
sapper	Sapper
signalman	Signalman
trooper	Trooper

Use these titles for navy personnel:

Rank	Before a name
admiral	Admiral
vice-admiral	Vice-Admiral
rear admiral	Rear Admiral
commodore	Commodore
captain	navy Capt.*
commander	Cmdr.
lieutenant-commander	Lt.-Cmdr.

lieutenant	navy Lt.*
sub-lieutenant	Sub-Lt.
acting sub-lieutenant	Acting Sub-Lt.
chief petty officer	Chief Petty Officer
first class, second class	1st Class, 2nd Class
master seaman	Master Seaman
leading seaman	Leading Seaman
able seaman	Able Seaman
ordinary seaman	Ordinary Seaman

* The word **navy,** lowercase, should be used before these titles to differentiate them from the army and air force titles of captain and lieutenant, which are ranked lower.

Usage for some foreign ranks and old Canadian ranks that may appear in copy periodically. They are listed alphabetically, not by descending order of rank:

Rank	**Before a name**
air commodore	Air Commodore
aircraftman first class	Aircraftman 1st Class
airman	Airman
airman first class	Airman 1st Class
air marshal	Air Marshal
air vice-marshal	Air Vice-Marshal
chief master sergeant	Chief Master Sgt.
commissioned warrant officer	Commissioned Warrant Officer
craftman	Craftman
ensign	Ensign
field marshal	Field Marshal
first lieutenant	1st Lt.
first sergeant	1st Sgt.
flying officer	Flying Officer
fusilier	Fusilier
group captain	Group Capt.
gunnery sergeant	Gunnery Sgt.
lance-corporal	Lance-Cpl.
leading aircraftman	Leading Aircraftman
master chief petty officer	Master Chief Petty Officer
master gunnery sergeant	Master Gunnery Sgt.
master sergeant	Master Sgt.
midshipman	Midshipman
pilot officer	Pilot Officer
platoon sergeant	Platoon Sgt.
private first class	Pte. 1st Class
regimental sergeant major	Regimental Sgt. Maj.
seaman apprentice	Seaman Apprentice
seaman recruit	Seaman Recruit
senior chief petty officer	Senior Chief Petty Officer
sergeant first class	Sgt. 1st Class
sergeant major of the army	Army Sgt. Maj.
technical sergeant	Tech. Sgt.
wing commander	Wing Cmdr.

Retired officers

1. In certain circumstances, a military rank may be used in first reference before the name of an officer who has retired. Do not use the abbreviation **Ret.** but put **retired** before the lowercase rank: **retired brigadier Pat Turner**.

2. In stories involving military activities, former majors, lieutenant-commanders, squadron leaders and other high officers may be referred to by their old rank.

3. Even in stories involving purely civilian matters, brigadiers and higher may be referred to by rank, if the officers prefer.

4. When rank is used, decorations may at times be added. In civilian stories, decorations need not be mentioned except for the Victoria Cross, Cross of Valour or other outstanding awards normally pertinent to the story.

Courts martial

1. Military courts martial are properly open to the media, though in many instances the media are not advised they are in progress. Their decisions are privileged.

2. A court martial's decision may be overruled by the federal cabinet or the Court Martial Appeal Court upon the person aggrieved presenting a petition. In either case the further ruling merits equal prominence.

Ceremonies

1. **Guards**

a) A **royal guard** is paraded for visiting royalty, governors general and lieutenant-governors. It consists of 100 men and women with arms, a band and colours (regimental flags). A **guard of honour** is turned out for any other dignitary: 50 troops with arms and usually a band. A **mounted escort** accompanies the dignitary's vehicle, the riders armed, often with lances, and drawn from the RCMP or a regiment.

b) In Canada, a dignitary **inspects** the guard by walking up and down the ranks. In the United States, a dignitary **reviews** it.

2. **Colours**

a) In Canada, the colours are carried by a **colour party**, an officer bearer escorted by non-commissioned officers. The American equivalent is called a **colour guard**.

b) Regimental colours are dipped only to the sovereign or a member of the Royal Family. In the ceremony of **trooping the colour** — carrying the regimental flag along ranks of soldiers — only one colour is trooped, hence the name.

c) Flags are always raised to the top of the mast or pole. Then, if required, they are **lowered to half-mast**. If tangled with the rope, they are **fouled**.

3. **Military funerals**

a) A **gun carriage** consists of a towed gun, with a platform fixed above the barrel, on which the coffin is fastened. The six who carry the coffin are the **bearer party**; the 12 who fire volleys at the graveside are the **firing party**.

b) Wreaths are **laid** or **placed**, trumpets **sounded** and bugles **blown** or **sounded**.

Miscellaneous

1. Write **promoted major-general**, not **promoted to major-general**. But **promoted to the rank of major-general** is correct.

2. Distinguish between **rank** (position within the military hierarchy) and **appointment** (specific duty). A person with the **rank** of master warrant officer may be given the **duties** of regimental quartermaster sergeant, a non-commissioned officer in charge of a regiment's quarters, supplies, etc.

Master Warrant Officer Pat Smith has been named regimental quartermaster sergeant.

Regimental Quartermaster Sergeant John Smith holds the rank of master warrant officer.

3. When locating a Canadian regiment, be sure to use the *official* home town or towns.

4. Do not refer to the Princess Patricia's Canadian Light Infantry as **the Pats**, a term disliked by its members. But **the Patricias** (no apostrophe) is acceptable for the unit or a group of individuals.

5. The nickname of Quebec's Royal 22nd Regiment is **the Van Doo** (from vingt-deux). Personnel of the regiment may be referred to as **the Van Doos** and one of them as **a Van Doo**.

6. The term **Snowbirds** is officially used to designate the Canadian Forces aerobatic team. The full complement including support personnel is designated 431 Air Demonstration Squadron.

7. The **Skyhawks** parachuting performers are formally known as the Canadian Forces Parachute Team.

8. **CF-18** is the designation for the Canadian version of the U.S. fighter aircraft F-18.

9. Avoid Americanisms. Canadian usage is **Last Post, guard of honour** and **AWL** (absent without leave). American usage is **Taps, honour guard** and **AWOL**. Canadians take **basic military training**; they do not attend **boot camp**. And they fly flags at **half-mast**, not **half-staff**.

10. Do not refer to the Royal Military College at Kingston, Ont., as the **West Point of Canada** or **Canada's Sandhurst** in stories for Canadian consumption.

11. A **volley** is one shot from each of several weapons fired simultaneously; a **fusillade** is several shots fired from one weapon sequentially. One gunman can fire a fusillade but not a volley. Artillery fires in **salvos**.

12. A **sniper** fires shots from hiding, usually at long range, into the enemy's camp or at individuals.

13. In flying, a **sortie** is one mission by one plane.

14. While the term **troops** can be used to refer to a body of soldiers — **100 troops advanced** — it should not be used in the singular as a substitute for **soldier**. A troop is a military unit.

➤ See **Aircraft, ships, guns**, page 201.

Three Canadian snipers watch over Canadian troops in a valley in Afghanistan in March 2002. To help readers evaluate a military action, put the numbers and types of troops high in a story.

(CP—Stephen Thorne)

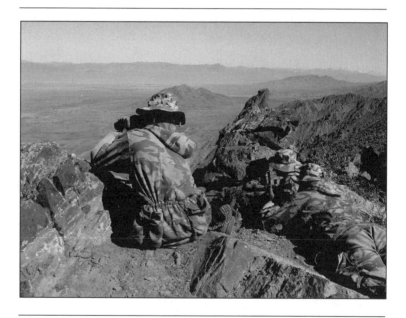

Names, nicknames, initials

1. In general, the names of people should be given in the spelling and form they normally use: **Ed Schreyer**, not **Edward Schreyer**; **Joe Clark**; **Kenneth Thomson**, not **Lord Thomson**; **John F. Kennedy** or **J.F. Kennedy**; **P.G. Wodehouse**.

2. Follow personal preference for lowercased names: **k.d. lang** (not **K.D. Lang**), **bp Nichol** (not **B.P. Nichol**) except at the start of a sentence.

➤ For the names of organizations, see **Capitalization**, page 220.

3. In obituaries, try to spell out initials at some point but not in the lead where the unfamiliar name might confuse readers: **Pelham Grenville Wodehouse**.

4. A given name reads better than a single initial: **Robin Hood**, not **R. Hood**.

5. First and middle initials are used if that is a person's preference: **W.O. Mitchell**, **George W. Bush**. And they are important in identifying a person charged with a crime and in listing accident victims.

6. Occasionally a public figure becomes known by initials without periods: **GBS**, **PET**. But most of the time, use periods after initials.

7. Use **Sr.** and **Jr.** only with the full name and do not set them off with commas: **John Smith Jr.** But **John Smith Jr., PhD, B.Comm.**, was the name on the card.

Note: In general, reserve **Sr.** and **Jr.** for cases where father and son are alive and known and there is possibility for confusion: **Edgar Bronfman Jr.**

8. Retain the designation **II** or **2nd** and the like if it is a person's preference: **Henry Ford III**, **Eric Van Husen 2nd**.

9. When necessary to distinguish between father and son in second reference, write **the elder** or **the younger Talbot**.

10. If confusion with another person is possible, include clarifying information: **O'Brien is not related to the businessman of the same name.**

11. When common names like **Mary Smith** and **Jean Dupont** get into the news, ages and occupations are needed to ensure proper identification, especially in police stories and if middle initials are not known.

12. People with first names applicable to either sex — **Beverley, Chris, Jean, Lee, Leslie, Terry, Tony** — should be identified as man or woman. Not **the accused, Pat O'Brien**, but **the woman accused, Pat O'Brien**. Often a pronoun introduced quickly — **he** or **she**, **him** or **her** — suffices.

13. A nickname is essential if it helps identify the subject: **Joseph (Joey) Smallwood**. Use a nickname instead of a given name only when a person is best known by the nickname: **Magic Johnson** (given name Earvin).

➤ See **Sports**, page 80.

14. To enclose nicknames, use parentheses, not quotation marks: **Mike (Pinball) Clemons**, not **Mike "Pinball" Clemons**.

15. In non-English names, **de, di, la, ter, van, von** and the like are usually lowercase except at the start of a sentence: **Charles de Gaulle, the de Gaulle era**. But: **She said, "De Gaulle lived to retire."** And respect an individual's preference: **Bill Vander Zalm**. If a building or some other memorial is named after the person, capitalize it: **Van Gogh Museum**.

16. In transliterating a Russian name, use the English phonetic equivalent where one exists: **Alexander Solzhenitsyn**, not **Aleksandr**. Prefer -ov and -ev endings: **Khrushchev**, not **Khrushchyov**. But with Russian émigré names, follow the individual's preference: **Ignatieff, Rachmaninoff**.

17. In Chinese, Korean and many other Asian names, the family name comes first: **Roh in Roh Tae-Woo**. But westernized people often put the given name first: **Morris Lee**.

18. For Spanish and Portuguese names, the only safe guide is the way the individuals use them.

19. For Arabic names, use an English spelling that approximates the way a name sounds in Arabic. If an individual has a preferred spelling in English, use it. If usage has established a particular spelling, use it. (Many inconsistencies in the transliteration of Arabic names are the result of pronunciations that vary from region to region.) Arabs are usually known by two or three names, with the final name being used on second reference. The articles **al-** or **el-** may be dropped or not depending on the person's preference. The Arabic word for son (**ibn** or **bin**) is sometimes part of a name: **Osama bin Laden** (**bin Laden** on second reference). Some Arabs are known only by title and a given name on first reference: **King Hussein**. Others use both the title and their full name (**Sheik Sabah Salem Sabah**). Follow common usage on first reference. On second reference, use the last name in the sequence (**Hussein, Sabah**).

20. After first reference, it is often useful to include in important stories the pronunciation of unfamiliar, difficult names of people and places breaking into the news, especially if the item is also moving on broadcast services: **Former Supreme Court justice Frank Iacobucci (yak-a-BOOCH-ee)**. Check Broadcast News as a source.

21. If a person goes by one name only, mention this so the reader doesn't think part of the name is missing: **Abdullah, who goes by one name.**

22. First names may be used on second reference for children and youths under 18, except in sports stories; they may also be used for adults for deliberate informality.

23. Plurals of proper names are usually formed by adding *s* or *es:* **Alexes, Burnses, Charleses, Henrys, Joneses, Marys, Perrys, Rubys.** But **Tommies, Johnnies.**

➤ See **Capitalization**, page 204; **Government**, page 240; **Plurals of nouns**, page 283; and **Titles**, page 321.

Canadian singer k.d. lang performs in New York's Rockefeller Center. Follow the preference of the person on the capitalization of their name.

(AP Photo)

Numbers

General

1. In general, spell out whole numbers below 10 and use figures for 10 and above.

three batters, the fifth inning, nine minutes, 10 guests, the 16th hole, the 22nd day, the sixth Earl of Hodderston

2. In a series there will often be a mixture.

There are 27 trees: two beeches, 10 chestnuts, three elms and 12 maples. The dealer sold 10 four-cylinder cars, three sixes and 12 eights.

3. For numbers in official names, follow the organization's spelling style even when it is at odds with CP practice.

7Up, the film 7 Fathers, 360networks Inc.

4. Use arabic numerals unless roman numerals are specified below.

5. Do not use commas with dimensions, measurements and weights consisting of two or more elements.

a woman five feet 11 inches tall; the baby weighs seven pounds six ounces; a trip of six months three weeks two days; in two hours 21 minutes 45 seconds (but the six-foot-three, 250-pound tackle)

6. To avoid ambiguity, write **increased to 15 per cent from 10** (not **increased from 10 to 15 per cent**).

7. To be meaningful, a percentage loss or gain should normally be accompanied by a dollar or some other amount.

Sales fell 10 per cent to $10,000. Sophie Dukakis, a hairdresser, said she now had 10 customers, a 20 per cent increase.

When to use figures

1. In addresses:

2 Newgate St., 3A Western Ave.

Note: Spell out **First** through **Ninth** as street names.

37 Fifth Ave., 23 59th St.

2. In ages standing alone after a name:

Melanie, 2, has two brothers, eight and nine. Tim, two months old, had typhoid.

Note: When the context does not require **years** or **years old**, the reader presumes the number is years: **He was 21. One girl is five.**

3. In dates and years:

3 BC, AD 5; Dec. 8, 8th of December; 1983, '83; the 1920s, the '20s; the Dirty '30s; the mid-1940s, the mid-'40s; he's in his late 50s.

Note: Write **the second century, the 20th century, the fifth century BC.**

4. In decimals, and in numbers larger than 1 with fractions, and in uncommon fractions:

0.15 of a percentage point, 0.25 centimetre, a .30-calibre rifle, pressures of 0.45 and 3.25, 2½ days, 15/16ths, 99 44/100ths, 3½-year-old

But two-fifths, two-thirds finished

Note 1: Unless precision is essential, keep decimals to two places: **12.25 metres** (not **12.254 metres**).

Note 2: If there is no unit before a decimal point, use a cipher: **0.25.** But write **.30 calibre** and the like in keeping with common practice.

5. In decisions, rulings, scores, votes and odds:

The court ruled 6-3, a 6-3 ruling. Montreal beat Vancouver 3-1 (but a two-goal margin). The bill was passed by a vote of 35-6, with one abstention; or a 35-6 vote. Of the 35 ballots, two were spoiled. It was a majority of nine.

odds of 5-2, a 10-1 longshot

6. In heights expressed informally:

He stands 6-11.

7. In highlights at the start of an item:

— 156 tanks and armoured personnel carriers.

— $1.8 billion for new aircraft engines.

8. In military and paramilitary terms:

2nd Lt. Esther White (but White is a second lieutenant), U.S. Petty Officer 3rd Class Mike Kenny (but prefer Mike Kenny, a U.S. petty officer third class), a 6-pounder, 8 mm, M-16 rifle, 8th Army, 6th Fleet, 1st Canadian Division

9. In monetary units preceded by a symbol:

$2 (not $2.00), two dollars; two francs, 2.5 francs; $1 million (but one million people); $2 billion, the $2-billion project; but the two-million-member federation and the 2.2-million-member CLC

10. In designations of aircraft, ships, spacecraft and vehicles:

Dash 7, A-4 Skyhawk, the liner Queen Elizabeth 2, QE2, the yachts Australia II and Canada 1, Apollo 8, Alouette 2

Note: Use a hyphen before the numeral but not after it: DC-8B.

11. In sequential designations:

Act 1 (but the first act), Article 3, Channel 2, Chapter 9, Grade 7, Highway 6, in No. 2 position, Room 4, RR 2, Section 5, back to Square 1

Note: The common nouns line, page, paragraph and size followed by figures are not capitalized: page 3, line 9, size 8 shoes.

12. In temperatures:

5 C, -6 C (use a hyphen)

But when Celsius or Fahrenheit is not specified spell out: five degrees.

13. In times:

1 a.m. (not 1:00 a.m.), 9 at night, 2 o'clock, 10:15 p.m., a 2:09 run, 3:20:15 but a time of three hours 20 minutes 15 seconds

14. In lists of figures that include both whole numbers and ones with decimals:

The interest rates are 7.35 per cent for six years, 7.25 per cent for five years and 7.00 per cent for four years.

15. For latitude and longitude:

59 degrees 30 minutes north

When to spell out

1. At the start of a sentence, if you must start with a number:

Twenty to 30 escaped unharmed, as well as 10 horses.

Note 1: Do not spell out the year at the start, but avoid: **1972 was a leap year.**

Note 2: Do not spell out a street address at the start: **221 had a** discreet sign: Oceano Palms.

Note 3: When numbers from 21 through 99 must be written out, use a hyphen: **Thirty-five or 36 may have died.**

2. In informal or casual usage:

Letters poured in by hundreds and thousands. Damage was in the millions. a thousand and one delights

3. In figures of speech and the like:

Twelve Apostles, Ten Commandments, Big Ten, wouldn't touch it with a ten-foot pole, a ten-gallon hat

Note: Write the **Dirty '30s, the Roaring '20s, the No. 1** or **number 1 choice.**

4. In common fractions below 1 standing alone:

one-half, one-quarter inch, five-eighths

Note: In casual use, write **a half, half a loaf, a quarter share.**

Roman numerals

Use roman numerals to indicate sequence for people and animals and in proper names where that is the widely accepted style. Otherwise avoid them as hard to grasp.

Queen Elizabeth II (rarely needed); **Pope John XXIII; Henry Ford III; Nijinsky II; Bluenose II** (but **Canada 1**); **The Godfather, Part II; Superman III.**

In particular, paraphrase large numbers: **the 36th Super Bowl,** not Superbowl XXXVI.

Note 1: For the ship, write **Queen Elizabeth 2** or **QE2.**

Note 2: Write **SALT II, Vatican II** and the like to conform to widespread practice.

Large numbers

1. Round numbers in the thousands are usually given in figures.

They took 2,000 prisoners. $3,500, 375,000 francs

Note: Spell out for casual usage: **There were thousands of mosquitoes.**

2. Express large numbers in millions and billions instead of the less familiar **trillion, quadrillion** and the like.

a million billion (instead of **quadrillion**), **a billion billion** (instead of **quintillion**)

Note: In Canada and the United States, a billion is a thousand million; in the United Kingdom and some other places, it is a million million.

3. Except for monetary units preceded by a symbol, round numbers in the millions and billions generally follow the rule of spelling out below 10.

two million bushels, 2.5 million bushels, 10 billion cubic metres, five billion marks, $1 billion

Note: Spell out for casual usage: **What's a billion? I've told you a million times. a billion and a half**

4. In expressing a range, repeat **million** or **billion**.

25 million to 30 million

Note: The adjectival form may be written **a $2- to $3-million loss,** but prefer **a loss of $2 million to $3 million.**

5. Hyphenate adjectival forms before nouns.

a two-million-bushel crop, a $10-billion gap, the 2.2-million-member CLC

6. Use commas to set off numbers of four or more figures except house, telephone, page, year and other serial numbers.

2,500; 100,000 billion; 1265 Yonge St.; 1-800-268-9237; p. 1025; 2000 (year)

7. Use figures for numbers up to 999,999. Above that, switch to words if absolute precision is not required.

a loss of $100,000, a $1.2-million project

People, places

(Numbers refer to notes at end, page 274.)

Country/ Region	Noun	Adjective	Capital	Currency
Afghanistan	Afghan(s)	Afghan	Kabul	afghani
Albania	Albanian(s)	Albanian	Tirana	lek
Algeria	Algerian(s)	Algerian	Algiers	dinar
American Samoa	American Samoan(s)	American Samoan	Pago Pago	dollar
Andorra	Andorran(s)	Andorran	Andorra La Vella	euro
Angola	Angolan(s)	Angolan	Luanda	kwanza
Antigua	Antiguan(s)	Antiguan	St. John's	dollar
Argentina	Argentine(s)	Argentine	Buenos Aires	peso
Armenia	Armenian(s)	Armenian	Yerevan	dram
Aruba	Aruban(s)	Aruban	Oranjestad	guilder
Australia	Australian(s)	Australian	Canberra	dollar
Austria	Austrian(s)	Austrian	Vienna	euro
Azerbaijan	Azerbaijani(s)	Azerbaijani	Baku	manat
Azores	Azorean(s)	Azorean	Ponta Delgada	escudo
Bahamas	Bahamian(s)	Bahamian	Nassau	dollar
Bahrain	Bahraini(s)	Bahraini	Manama	dinar
Bangladesh	Bangladeshi(s)	Bangladesh	Dhaka	taka
Barbados	Barbadian(s)	Barbadian	Bridgetown	dollar
Belarus	Belarusian(s)	Belarus	Minsk	ruble
Belgium	Belgian(s)	Belgian	Brussels	euro
Belize	Belizean(s)	Belizean	Belmopan	dollar
Benin	Beninese (sing., pl.)	Beninese	Porto-Novo	franc
Bermuda	Bermudian(s)	Bermudian	Hamilton	dollar
Bhutan	Bhutanese (sing., pl.)	Bhutanese	Thimphu	ngultrum/ rupee
Bolivia	Bolivian(s)	Bolivian	La Paz	boliviano
Bosnia- Herzegovina	Bosnian(s)	Bosnian	Sarajevo	marka
Botswana	Motswana (sing.) Batswana (pl.)	Botswana	Gaborone	pula
Brazil	Brazilian(s)	Brazilian	Brasilia	real
Brunei	Bruneian(s)	Bruneian	Bandar Seri Begawan	dollar
Bulgaria	Bulgarian(s)	Bulgarian	Sofia	lev
Burkina Faso	Burkinabe (sing., pl.)	Burkina Fasan	Ouagadougou	franc

Country/ Region	Noun	Adjective	Capital	Currency
Burundi	Burundian(s)	Burundi	Bujumbura	franc
Cambodia	Cambodian(s)	Cambodian	Phnom Penh	riel
Cameroon	Cameroonian(s)	Cameroonian	Yaounde	franc
Canary Islands	Canary Islander(s)	Canary Island	Las Palmas	peseta
Cape Verde	Cape Verdean(s)	Cape Verdean	Praia	escudo
Cayman Islands	Cayman Islander(s)	Cayman	Georgetown	dollar
Central African Republic	Central African(s)	Central African	Bangui	franc
Chad	Chadian(s)	Chadian	N'djamena	franc
Chile	Chilean(s)	Chilean	Santiago	peso
China	Chinese (sing., pl.)	Chinese	Beijing	renminbi/ yuan
Colombia	Colombian(s)	Colombian	Bogota	peso
Comoros	Comoran(s)	Comoran	Moroni	franc
Congo, Democratic Republic of❶ (formerly Zaire)	Congolese (sing., pl.)	Congolese	Kinshasa	franc
Congo, Republic of❶	Congolese (sing., pl.)	Congolese	Brazzaville	franc
Cook Islands	Cook Islander(s)	Cook Islands	Avarua	dollar
Costa Rica	Costa Rican(s)	Costa Rican	San Jose	colon
Croatia	Croat(s)	Croatian	Zagreb	kuna
Cuba	Cuban(s)	Cuban	Havana	peso
Cyprus	Cypriot(s)	Cypriot	Nicosia	pound/lira
Czech Republic	Czech(s)	Czech	Prague	koruna
Denmark	Dane(s)	Danish	Copenhagen	krone
Djibouti	Djiboutian(s)	Afar, Issa	Djibouti	franc
Dominica	Dominican(s)	Dominican	Roseau	dollar
Dominican Republic	Dominican(s)	Dominican	Santo Domingo	peso
East Timor	Timorese	Timorese	Dili	U.S. dollar
Ecuador	Ecuadorian(s)	Ecuadorian	Quito	U.S. dollar
Egypt	Egyptian(s)	Egyptian	Cairo	pound
El Salvador	Salvadoran(s)	Salvadoran	San Salvador	colon
Equatorial Guinea	Equatorial Guinean(s)	Equatorial Guinean	Malabo	franc
Eritrea	Eritrean(s)	Eritrean	Asmara	nakfa
Estonia	Estonian(s)	Estonian	Tallinn	kroon
Ethiopia	Ethiopian(s)	Ethiopian	Addis Ababa	birr
Falkland Islands	Falkland Islander(s)	Falkland	Stanley Island	pound
Faroe Islands	Faroe Islander(s)	Faroe Islands	Thorshavn	krone
Fiji	Fijian(s)	Fijian	Suva	dollar
Finland	Finn(s)	Finnish	Helsinki	euro
France	French(wo)man	French	Paris	euro
French Guiana	French Guianese (sing., pl.)	French Guianese	Cayenne	euro

Country/ Region	Noun	Adjective	Capital	Currency
French Polynesia	French Polynesian(s)	French Polynesian	Papeete	franc
Gabon	Gabonese (sing., pl.)	Gabonese	Libreville	franc
Gambia	Gambian(s)	Gambian	Banjul	dalasi
Georgia	Georgian(s)	Georgian	Tbilisi	lari
Germany	German(s)	German	Berlin	euro
Ghana	Ghanaian(s)	Ghanaian	Accra	cedi
Gibraltar	Gibraltan(s)	Gibraltan	Gibraltar	pound
Greece	Greek(s)	Greek	Athens	euro
Greenland	Greenlander(s)	Greenlandic	Godthab	krone
Grenada	Grenadian(s)	Grenadian	St. George's	dollar
Guadeloupe	Guadeloupian(s)	Guadeloupe	Basse-Terre	euro
Guam	Guamanian(s)	Guamanian	Agana	dollar
Guatemala	Guatemalan(s)	Guatemalan	Guatemala	quetzal
Guinea	Guinean(s)	Guinea	Conakry	franc
Guinea-Bissau	Guinean(s)	Guinean	Bissau	franc
Guyana	Guyanese (sing., pl.)	Guyanese	Georgetown	dollar
Haiti	Haitian(s)	Haitian	Port-au-Prince	gourde
Honduras	Honduran(s)	Honduran	Tegucigalpa	lempira
Hong Kong		Hong Kong	(part of China)	dollar
Hungary	Hungarian(s)	Hungarian	Budapest	forint
Iceland	Icelander(s)	Icelandic	Reykjavik	krona
India	Indian(s)	Indian	New Delhi	rupee
Indonesia	Indonesian(s)	Indonesian	Jakarta	rupiah
Iran	Iranian(s)	Iranian	Tehran	rial
Iraq	Iraqi(s)	Iraqi	Baghdad	dinar
Ireland	Irish(wo)man	Irish	Dublin	euro
Israel	Israeli(s)	Israeli	Jerusalem[2]	shekel
Italy	Italian(s)	Italian	Rome	euro
Ivory Coast	Ivorian(s)	Ivorian	Abidjan	franc
Jamaica	Jamaican(s)	Jamaican	Kingston	dollar
Japan	Japanese (sing., pl.)	Japanese	Tokyo	yen
Jordan	Jordanian(s)	Jordanian	Amman	dinar
Kazakhstan	Kazakhstani(s)	Kazakhstani	Astana	tenge
Kenya	Kenyan(s)	Kenyan	Nairobi	shilling
Kiribati	Kiribatan(s)	Kiribatan	Tarawa	dollar
Kuwait	Kuwaiti(s)	Kuwaiti	Kuwait	dinar
Kyrgyzstan	Kyrgstani(s)	Kyrgstani	Bishkek	som
Laos	Laotian(s)	Laotian	Vientiane	kip
Latvia	Latvian(s)	Latvian	Riga	lat
Lebanon	Lebanese (sing., pl.)	Lebanese	Beirut	pound
Lesotho	Masotho (sing.) Basotho (pl.)	Basotho	Maseru	maloti
Liberia	Liberian(s)	Liberian	Monrovia	dollar
Libya	Libyan(s)	Libyan	Tripoli	dinar
Liechtenstein	Liechtensteiner(s)	Liechtenstein	Vaduz	franc

Country/ Region	Noun	Adjective	Capital	Currency
Lithuania	Lithuanian(s)	Lithuanian	Vilnius	litas
Luxembourg	Luxembourger(s)	Luxembourg	Luxembourg	euro
Macedonia	Macedonian(s)	Macedonian	Skopje	dinar
Madagascar	Malagasy (sing., pl.)	Malagasy	Antananarivo	franc
Malawi	Malawian(s)	Malawian	Lilongwe	kwacha
Malaysia	Malaysian(s)	Malaysian	Kuala Lumpur	ringgit
Maldives	Maldivian(s)	Maldivian	Male	rufiyaa
Mali	Malian(s)	Malian	Bamako	franc
Malta	Maltese (sing., pl.)	Maltese	Valletta	lira
Martinique	Martinican(s)	Martinican	Fort-de-France	euro
Mauritania	Mauritanian(s)	Mauritanian	Nouakchott	ouguiya
Mauritius	Mauritian(s)	Mauritian	Port Louis	rupee
Mexico	Mexican(s)	Mexican	Mexico City	peso
Micronesia, Federated States of	Micronesian(s)	Micronesian	Palikir	dollar
Moldova	Moldovan(s)	Moldovan	Chisinau	leu
Monaco	Monegasque	Monegasque	Monaco	euro
Mongolia	Mongolian(s)	Mongolian	Ulan Bator	tugrik
Montserrat	Montserratan(s)	Montserratan	Plymouth	dollar
Morocco	Moroccan(s)	Moroccan	Rabat	dirham
Mozambique	Mozambican(s)	Mozambican	Maputo	metical
Myanmar	Myanmarese	Myanmar	Yangon	kyat
Namibia	Namibian(s)	Namibian	Windhoek	dollar
Nauru	Nauruan(s)	Nauruan	Yaren	dollar
Nepal	Nepalese (sing., pl.)	Nepalese	Kathmandu	rupee
Netherlands❸	Netherlander(s)/ Dutch(wo)man	Netherlander/ Dutch	Amsterdam❹	euro
Netherlands Antilles	Netherlands Antillean(s)	Netherlands Antillean	Willemstad	guilder
New Caledonia	New Caledonian(s)	New Caledonian	Noumea	franc
New Zealand	New Zealander(s)	New Zealand	Wellington	dollar
Nicaragua	Nicaraguan(s)	Nicaraguan	Managua	cordoba
Niger	Nigerois (sing., pl.)	Niger	Niamey	franc
Nigeria	Nigerian(s)	Nigerian	Abuja	naira
Niue	Niuean(s)	Niuean	Alofi	dollar
Norfolk Island	Norfolk Islander(s)	Norfolk Island	Kingston	dollar
North Korea	North Korean(s)	North Korean	Pyongyang	won
Norway	Norwegian(s)	Norwegian	Oslo	krone
Oman	Omani(s)	Omani	Muscat	rial
Pakistan	Pakistani(s)	Pakistani	Islamabad	rupee
Panama	Panamanian(s)	Panamanian	Panama City	balboa

Country/ Region	Noun	Adjective	Capital	Currency
Papua New Guinea	Papua New Guinean(s)	Papua New Guinean	Port Moresby	kina
Paraguay	Paraguayan(s)	Paraguayan	Asuncion	guarani
Peru	Peruvian(s)	Peruvian	Lima	sol
Philippines	Filipino(s) (male) Filipina(s) (female)	Philippine	Manila	peso
Pitcairn Island	Pitcairn Islander(s)	Pitcairn Island	Adamstown	dollar
Poland	Pole(s)	Polish	Warsaw	zloty
Portugal	Portuguese (sing., pl.)	Portuguese	Lisbon	euro
Puerto Rico	Puerto Rican(s)	Puerto Rican	San Juan	dollar
Qatar	Qatari(s)	Qatari	Doha	rial
Reunion	Reunionese (sing., pl.)	Reunionese	Saint-Denis	euro
Romania	Romanian(s)	Romanian	Bucharest	leu
Russia	Russian(s)	Russian	Moscow	ruble
Rwanda	Rwandan(s)	Rwandan	Kigali	franc
St. Helena	St. Helenan(s)	St. Helenan	Jamestown	pound
St. Kitts-Nevis	Kittsian(s), Nevisian(s)	Kittsian, Nevisian	Basseterre	dollar
St. Lucia	St. Lucian(s)	St. Lucian	Castries	dollar
St-Pierre-Miquelon	St-Pierrais (sing., pl.)	St-Pierrais	St-Pierre	euro
St. Vincent, Grenadines	Vincentian(s), Grenadinian(s)	St. Vincentian, Grenadinian	Kingstown	dollar
Samoa	Samoan(s)	Samoan	Apia	tala
San Marino	San Marinese (sing., pl.)	San Marinese	San Marino	euro
Sao Tome and Principe	Sao Tomean(s), Principian(s)	Sao Tomean, Principian	Sao Tome	dobra
Saudi Arabia	Saudi(s)	Saudi Arabian, Saudi	Riyadh	riyal
Senegal	Senegalese (sing., pl.)	Senegalese	Dakar	franc
Serbia and Montenegro	Serb, Montenegrin	Serbian, Montenegrin	Belgrade	dinar
Seychelles	Seychellois (sing., pl.)	Seychellois	Victoria	rupee
Sierra Leone	Sierra Leonean(s)	Sierra Leonean	Freetown	leone
Sikkim	Sikkimese (sing., pl.)	Sikkimese	Gangtok	rupee
Singapore	Singaporean(s)	Singaporean	Singapore	dollar
Slovakia	Slovak(s)	Slovak	Bratislava	koruna
Slovenia	Slovene(s)	Slovenian	Ljubljana	tolar
Solomon Islands	Solomon Islander(s)	Solomon Island	Honiara	dollar
Somalia	Somali(s)	Somalian	Mogadishu	shilling
South Africa	South African(s)	South African	Pretoria❺	rand

Country/ Region	Noun	Adjective	Capital	Currency
South Korea	South Korean(s)	South Korean	Seoul	won
Spain	Spaniard(s)	Spanish	Madrid	euro
Sri Lanka	Sri Lankan(s)	Sri Lankan	Colombo	rupee
Sudan	Sudanese (sing., pl.)	Sudanese	Khartoum	dinar
Suriname	Surinamer(s)	Surinamese	Paramaribo	dollar
Swaziland	Swazi(s)	Swazi	Mbabane	lilageni (emalangeni, pl.)
Sweden	Swede(s)	Swedish	Stockholm	krona
Switzerland	Swiss (sing., pl.)	Swiss	Bern	franc
Syria	Syrian(s)	Syrian	Damascus	pound
Taiwan	Taiwanese (sing., pl.)	Taiwanese	Taipei	dollar
Tajikistan	Tajik(s)	Tajik	Dushanbe	ruble
Tanzania	Tanzanian(s)	Tanzanian	Dar es Salaam	shilling
Thailand	Thai(s)	Thai	Bangkok	baht
Togo	Togolese (sing., pl.)	Togolese	Lome	franc
Tokelau Islands	Tokelau Islander(s)	Tokelau Islands	Fakaofo	dollar
Tonga	Tongan(s)	Tongan	Nuku'alofa	pa'anga
Trinidad and Tobago	Trinidadian(s), Tobagan(s)	Trinidadian, Tobagan	Port-of-Spain	dollar
Tunisia	Tunisian(s)	Tunisian	Tunis	dinar
Turkey	Turk(s)	Turkish	Ankara	lira
Turkmenistan	Turkmen (sing., pl.)	Turkmen	Ashkhabad	manat
Turks and Caicos Is.	Turks/Caicos Islander(s)	Turks/Caicos Islands	Grand Turk	dollar
Tuvalu	Tuvaluan(s)	Tuvaluan	Funafuti⑥	dollar
Uganda	Ugandan(s)	Ugandan	Kampala	shilling
Ukraine (not the)	Ukrainian(s)	Ukrainian	Kyiv	hryvnya
United Arab Emirates	Emirati(s)	Emirati	Abu Dhabi	dirham
United Kingdom	Briton(s)	British	London	pound
United States	American(s)	American/U.S.	Washington	dollar
Uruguay	Uruguayan(s)	Uruguayan	Montevideo	peso
Uzbekistan	Uzbek(s)	Uzbek	Tashkent	soum
Vanuatu	Vanuatuan(s)	Vanuatuan	Port Vila	vatu
Vatican City		Vatican	Vatican City	lira
Venezuela	Venezuelan(s)	Venezuelan	Caracas	bolivar
Vietnam	Vietnamese (sing., pl.)	Vietnamese	Hanoi	dong
Virgin Islands (Br.)	Virgin Islander(s)	Virgin Island	Road Town	dollar

Country/Region	Noun	Adjective	Capital	Currency
Virgin Islands (U.S.)	Virgin Islander(s)	Virgin Island	Charlotte Amalie	dollar
Yemen	Yemeni(s)	Yemeni	Sanaa	rial
Zambia	Zambian(s)	Zambian	Lusaka	kwacha
Zimbabwe	Zimbabwean(s)	Zimbabwean	Harare	dollar

❶ Congo can be used in second reference for both countries unless confusion is likely.

❷ Recognition withheld by many countries over the Palestinian question. Tel Aviv is the administrative capital.

❸ Holland may be used in casual contexts.

❹ The seat of government is The Hague.

❺ Pretoria is the executive capital, site of the president's office and of foreign embassies. The legislature sits in Cape Town.

❻ Funafuti is capital, but administrative officees are on Fongafale island.

U.S. state descriptive terms

Alabamian	Louisianian	Ohioan
Alaskan	Mainer	Oklahoman
Arizonan	Marylander	Oregonian
Arkansan	Massachusettsan	Pennsylvanian
Californian	Michiganite	Rhode Islander
Coloradan	Minnesotan	South Carolinian
Connecticuter	Mississippian	South Dakotan
Delawarean	Missourian	Tennessean
Floridian	Montanan	Texan
Georgian	Nebraskan	Utahn (Utahan, adj.)
Hawaiian	Nevadan	Vermonter
Idahoan	New Hampshirite	Virginian
Illinoisan	New Jerseyite	Washingtonian
Indianian	New Mexican	West Virginian
Iowan	New Yorker	Wisconsinite
Kansan	North Carolinian	Wyomingite
Kentuckian	North Dakotan	

Provincial descriptive terms

Albertan	Nova Scotian
British Columbian	Ontarian
Manitoban	Prince Edward Islander, Islander
New Brunswicker	Quebecer
Newfoundlander, Labradorian	Saskatchewanian (rare; prefer *a resident of Saskatchewan*)

Placelines

General

1. Most stories carry a placeline as their first piece of information. The placeline tells a reader where most of the story took place. Whenever possible, place stories where the main event occurred. The community is written in lightface capitals and any other designation (country, province, state) is in upper and lower. On news agency copy, the agency logo and a heavy dash follow.

Avoid **here** in copy, since it may force the reader to check the placeline a second time. Do the reader a favour by repeating the name of the community at appropriate times in the story (**the mayor of Ste. Agathe, south of Winnipeg**).

2. Although the placeline normally tells the reader where the event occurred, there are exceptions. On an exclusive picked up from a newspaper, the placeline is usually the city where the paper is based, even if the event took place elsewhere. Such pickups are usually under 300 words and the fact that the exclusive is being reported is as much a part of the story as the news itself.

> **WINNIPEG (CP)** — The Conservatives plan a leadership convention in March, the Winnipeg Free Press said today in a report from Ottawa.

But use the placeline given by a newspaper to a story when the material is not exclusive or is readily available, and the newspaper has granted permission for it to be used.

> **MONTREAL (CP)** — As much as 20 per cent of Canada's 10 million tonnes of annual newsprint capacity could disappear over the next two years as producers close aging and unproductive mills.
> "It's a disaster out there," consultant Jim Rowland told the Globe and Mail in an interview.

Note: It is often necessary to obtain permission from the newspaper to pick up a story from outside the paper's Return News district. If the story is voluntarily filed to CP, that implies permission for it to be picked up.

3. A story that rounds up events or developments in several centres does not have a placeline, but instead is slugged **Roundup**.

> **FedBudget-Rxn-Rdp, Bgt**
> **Roundup Budget**
> **Taxpayers across Canada angered by increase in GST**
>
> **By Bruce Cheadle**
> **The Canadian Press**

Note: Many member papers prefer a placeline on all stories, so use one whenever possible. The **Roundup** slug should be reserved for those stories that are true roundups, not stories with most of the elements from one centre and a couple of elements from another. In that case, placeline the story in the first centre and specify in the body of the story where the secondary material came from.

4. Other items that don't carry a placeline include stories and Quicks that don't have or need a geographic focus, and columns for sports, entertainment or other inside sections. These types of stories do not need an UNDATED slug.

Video-Views
Capt. Corelli's Mandolin, new on video, is war romance with awkward accents

By John McKay
The Canadian Press

Use an UNDATED slug on an exceptional story from a specific community where the reporter deserves a byline, but was not in the community. This will alert editors not to put a placeline on the story if they are using the byline.

5. A byline is used on a placelined story only when the reporter has been in the community to collect information. In a story obtained by phone but carrying the placeline of the event, it is sometimes worth explaining how the information was gathered.

The masked gunman disrupted the meeting just as city council was to vote on the Sunday shopping proposal, Mayor Shirley Millson said in a phone interview.

➤ See **Bylines**, page 416.

6. For stories from websites, use the placeline where the website originates if the story is an exclusive. For member stories that CP has been granted permission to carry, use the placeline where the story occurred or was written.

7. Stories from conference calls or teleconferences should be placelined where those holding the conference are located. However, if the reporter has added major elements to the story, it can be placelined from the location of the reporter and a byline added.

8. Stories based on news releases in Canada reporting incidents abroad should be placelined where the release is issued.

9. Avoid contrived novelty placelines, for example: **IN THE CAB OF A SEMI-TRAILER TRUCK SOMEWHERE ON HIGHWAY 97.** Unconventional placelines are occasionally legitimate when copy is written and filed from that point, for example: **HMCS ATHABASKAN** (not **ON BOARD HMCS ATHABASKAN**). Ensure the approximate position of the ship is described early in the text.

10. Stories that take place on Canadian Forces bases can carry the short form CFB – for example, **CFB TRENTON, Ont**. Or they can be placelined in a nearby civilian community – for example, **HALIFAX** – with an explanation in the body of the story that the event took place on a Forces base.

11. Prefer placelines that would fit in one line of body type in a newspaper column. Most domestic and foreign news is reported from capitals or major cities; those listed in this chapter under Canadian, U.S. and foreign placelines require no other identification in the placeline.

12. It saves readers the trouble of guessing if stories from lesser-known placelines outside Canada and the United States name the country in the placeline or the first paragraph.

13. Placelines are always written all-capped with the province, state or country, if necessary, in upper and lowercase: FORT MCMURRAY, Alta.; LAC LA BICHE, Alta., TURIN, Italy.

Canadian placelines

1. The community is followed by the province or territory with the exceptions of these well-known cities:

CALGARY	MONTREAL	VANCOUVER
CHARLOTTETOWN	OTTAWA	VICTORIA
EDMONTON	QUEBEC	WHITEHORSE
FREDERICTON	REGINA	WINNIPEG
HALIFAX	SASKATOON	YELLOWKNIFE
HAMILTON	TORONTO	

Note 1: WHITEHORSE and YELLOWKNIFE stand alone as placelines, but *the Northwest Territories* or *the Yukon* should be mentioned in the opening paragraph.

Note 2: QUEBEC stands alone as a placeline; use *Quebec City* in the body of a story.

Note 3: Write **ST. JOHN'S, N.L.**, and **SAINT JOHN, N.B.**, to avoid confusion.

2. A short form for the territory of Nunavut has not yet been established so the name should be written out in all placelines, including stories from its capital: **IQALUIT, Nunavut**.

3. The former municipalities of *Scarborough, Etobicoke, York, East York* and *North York* are all part of Toronto and should be identified as such in placelines and copy. All other Greater Toronto Area communities carry their own placelines.

The 28 municipalities on the Island of Montreal are part of the Montreal Urban Community and carry a MONTREAL placeline. Communities off the island carry their own placelines.

Vancouver does not have a regional government, so communities such as *West Vancouver* and *North Vancouver* carry their own placelines.

4. For reserves and First Nations communities, use the name favoured by the community: **GRASSY NARROW FIRST NATION, Ont.**

U.S. placelines

1. The community is followed by the state abbreviation with these exceptions:

ATLANTA	INDIANAPOLIS	PHOENIX
BALTIMORE	LAS VEGAS	PITTSBURGH
BOSTON	LOS ANGELES	ST. LOUIS
CHICAGO	MIAMI	SALT LAKE CITY
CINCINNATI	MILWAUKEE	SAN ANTONIO
CLEVELAND	MINNEAPOLIS	SAN DIEGO
DALLAS	NASHVILLE	SAN FRANCISCO
DENVER	NEW ORLEANS	SEATTLE
DETROIT	NEW YORK	WASHINGTON
HONOLULU	OKLAHOMA CITY	
HOUSTON	PHILADELPHIA	

➤ For state abbreviations, see **Abbreviations**, page 195.

2. Use the commonly accepted **United States**, not United States of America.

Other foreign placelines

1. The community is followed by the country in the placeline with these exceptions:

ATHENS	HONG KONG	MOSCOW
BAGHDAD	JERUSALEM	NEW DELHI
BEIJING	KUWAIT CITY	PANAMA CITY
BEIRUT	LONDON	PARIS
BERLIN	LUXEMBOURG	ROME
DJIBOUTI	MEXICO CITY	SINGAPORE
GENEVA	MONACO	TOKYO
GUATEMALA CITY	MONTE CARLO	VATICAN CITY

Note: Write HAMILTON, Bermuda, SYDNEY, Australia and ST. PETERSBURG, Russia, to avoid confusion with the Canadian cities and St. Petersburg, Fla. MONTE CARLO is used for racing stories; MONACO for all others.

2. Use the commonly accepted short version of a country's or region's name.

Argentina, not Republic of Argentina
Bahamas, not Commonwealth of the Bahamas
China, not People's Republic of China
Hong Kong, not Special Administrative Region of Hong Kong

Kuwait, not State of Kuwait
Sikkim, not Kingdom of Sikkim
Taiwan, not Republic of China

3.   Do not use *The* with the name of a country in placelines.

Bahamas   Gambia   Philippines
Congo   Netherlands

Note: It is always **Ukraine**, never the Ukraine.

Note: Do use El Salvador.

4.   Use **UNITED NATIONS** alone in placelines.

Canadian Formula One driver Jacques Villeneuve in practice for the Monaco Grand Prix in Monte Carlo. The placeline MONTE CARLO is used for auto racing stories, but use MONACO for all other stories.

(AP Photo)

Place names

General

1. The style authority for Canadian place names is the *Canadian Oxford Dictionary*, with some exceptions. Those exceptions are listed in *Caps and Spelling*. If the place name is not in Oxford, editors should turn to the Secretariat of the Canadian Permanent Committee on Geographical Names (http://geonames.nrcan.gc.ca/). So check Caps first, then Oxford, then the Web site.

2. In Quebec place names, retain hyphens and shorten *saint* and *sainte* to *St* and *Ste* (no periods): **Ste-Anne-des-Monts**. When technically possible, retain accents except in the case of **Montreal** and **Quebec**, which have long-standing English versions of their names. Do not hyphenate English place names in Quebec: **East Broughton, Otterburn Park**. Names preceded by the definite article do not need a hyphen after the article: **La Malbaie**.

➤ See **French**, page 237.

3. Use the full name of Canada's easternmost province, **Newfoundland and Labrador**, whenever space permits. **Newfoundland**, alone, can be used in more casual references or when the island only is being described.

4. *The National Geographic Atlas of the World* is CP's authority for place names outside Canada with exceptions listed below.

5. The umlaut in German names is indicated by placing the letter *e* after the vowel affected. *Düsseldorf* becomes *Duesseldorf.*

6. Use the Ukrainian, not the Russian, transliteration for Ukrainian place names. This means it is **Kyiv** (not Kiev) and **Chornobyl** (not Chernobyl). Other Ukrainian transliterations: **Kharkiv, Lviv, Odesa** (cities); **Crimea** (southern region of Ukraine); and **Carpathy** and **Zacarpatia** (mountains).

Exceptions

The following are exceptions to *National Geographic Society* spellings:

Algiers	Copenhagen	Genoa
Antwerp	Corfu	Havana
Athens	Corinth	Ithaca
Bangkok	Damascus	Kabul
Belgrade	Dardanelles	Kandahar
Blue Nile River	Doha, Qatar	Kingstown (Ireland)
Brunswick	Dubai	Lisbon
Brussels	Dunkirk	Lucerne
Bucharest	Florence	Milan
Cologne	Geneva	Moscow

Munich
Naples
Nuremberg
Olympus
Prague
Rhodes
Rome

Sinai, Mount
Sofia
Sparta
Taipei
The Hague
Tiber River
Tibet

Turin
Tyre
Venice
Vesuvius, Mount
Vienna
Warsaw

Regions

1. In the broadest sense, *America* refers to North and South America, and *American* to any resident of the continents. But the narrower meanings of the words — the United States and its citizens — are acceptable in informal and unambiguous contexts.

2. **North America**: Canada, the United States, Mexico, Greenland, Central America, the tiny French islands of St-Pierre-Miquelon and, in broad contexts, the islands of the Caribbean.

Central America: Belize, Costa Rica, El Salvador, Guatemala, Honduras, Nicaragua and Panama.

3. **South America**: Argentina, Bolivia, Brazil, Chile, Colombia, Ecuador, Paraguay, Peru, Uruguay, Venezuela, plus French Guiana, Guyana and Suriname on the northeastern coast which regard themselves as Caribbean countries.

4. **Latin America**: the parts of Central and South America where Spanish or Portuguese is the dominant language. Most countries south of the United States are included. Exceptions are French Guiana, Suriname and areas with a British background: the Bahamas, Barbados, Belize, Grenada, Guyana, Jamaica, Trinidad and Tobago and the smaller islands in the West Indies.

5. **British Isles**: Britain and all Ireland and the islands near their coasts.

United Kingdom: England, Scotland, Wales and Northern Ireland.

Britain: England, Scotland and Wales, but *British* encompasses the United Kingdom.

Ireland: The island is divided into Northern Ireland (part of the United Kingdom) and the independent republic of Ireland.

6. **Scandinavia:** Geographically, the peninsula occupied by Norway and Sweden. Culturally, the countries of Norway, Sweden and Denmark and sometimes Iceland, Finland and the Faroe Islands.

7. **Middle East** or, less desirably, **Mideast**: usually taken to include Afghanistan, Bahrain, Egypt, Iran, Iraq, Israel, Jordan, Kuwait, Lebanon, Oman, Qatar, Sudan, Saudi Arabia, Syria, Turkey, the United Arab Emirates and Yemen. Do not use *Near East.*

8. **Far East**: China, Japan, North and South Korea, Taiwan and the eastern Soviet Union. **Note:** Hong Kong and Macau are now part of China.

9. **Southeast Asia**: Cambodia, Indonesia, Laos, Malaysia, Myanmar, New Guinea, the Philippines, Singapore, Thailand and Vietnam.

10. **South Asia**: India, Pakistan, Bangladesh, Sri Lanka, Nepal and the Maldives. **Note:** Natives of these countries are **South Asian**, not East Indian.

People and places

1. Shorten *Great Britain* to *Britain* in news stories. Write *Briton*, not *Britisher.*

2. Refer to the British capital, both in placelines and the body of a story, simply as *London.* Use *London, England,* only if ambiguity would otherwise result; for example, if two Londons appear in the same story.

3. For the people, prefer *Scot, Scots(wo)man,* not *Scotch(wo)man.* Use *Scottish* as the usual adjective, meaning pertaining to Scotland: **Scottish Highlands, Scottish thrift.** Use *Scotch* of food, drink, plants, animals and things originating in Scotland: **Scotch broth, Scotch tweed, Scotch thistle, Scotch terrier.** But **scotch** (whisky).

4. Where necessary, specify *the republic of Ireland* or *Northern Ireland.*

5. *Ulster* is acceptable as an informal name for Northern Ireland, though the original Ulster comprised the present Northern Ireland and the counties of Cavan, Donegal and Monaghan, now part of the republic of Ireland.

6. *Eire* is the former name of the republic of Ireland.

7. Israel declared Jerusalem its capital in 1950 despite Arab protest. Many countries, including Canada, do not recognize it as such. They maintain their ambassadors in Tel Aviv, which may be referred to as the administrative capital.

➤ See **Placelines**, page 275; **People, places**, page 268.

Plurals of nouns

In general, form the plural of a noun by adding *s* to the singular; add *es* if the singular ends in *s, x, ch, sh* or *z*.

taxis, lenses, complexes, stitches, lashes, topazes

The plurals of the following words often cause problems.

Nouns ending in *f, fe* and *ff*

1. Most nouns in this category have a plural in *s*.

beliefs, briefs, chiefs, griefs, mischiefs, roofs, safes, skiffs, tariffs, tiffs

2. Some have a plural in *ves*.

calves, elves, halves, knives, leaves, loaves, selves, shelves, thieves, wives, wolves

3. A few have two plurals; CP style is shown.

dwarfs, handkerchiefs, hoofs, scarves, still lifes, wharfs

Write **staffs** (poles), **staves** (music).

Nouns ending in *o*

1. Nouns ending with an *o* preceded by another vowel usually have a plural in *s* (not *es*).

cameos, folios, kangaroos, patios, portfolios, radios, ratios, rodeos, studios, tattoos, zoos

2. Nouns ending in *o* preceded by a consonant have a variety of plurals.

a) Some end in *es*.

dominoes, echoes, embargoes, heroes, mementoes, mosquitoes, mottoes, Negroes, noes, potatoes, tomatoes, tornadoes, volcanoes

b) Some end in *s*.

albinos, avocados, cantos, contraltos, dittos, dynamos, Filipinos, gauchos, ghettos, gigolos, octavos, pianos, piccolos, provisos, quartos, silos, solos, tangelos, tobaccos, twos, tyros, zeros

c) Some have two forms; CP style is shown.

banjos, buffaloes, cargoes, concertos, Eskimos, frescoes, innuendoes, lassos, salvoes, sopranos

Nouns ending in *y*

1. Nouns ending in *y* preceded by a vowel have a plural in *s*.

alloys, attorneys, chimneys, days, forays, keys, monkeys, storeys

But soliloquies; prefer moneys to monies.

2. Nouns ending in *y* preceded by a consonant have a plural in *ies*.

armies, authorities, beauties, bodies, caddies, categories, cherries, cities, communities, companies, cries, flies, ladies, parodies, skies

But drys (prohibitionists), standbys

Nouns ending in *ics*

Nouns of this type are singular or plural depending on use. They are singular when denoting the science or a course of study, plural when denoting an activity or quality.

Classics means Latin and Greek. The classics are neglected nowadays. Ethics is defined as a moral philosophy. His ethics are questionable.

➤ See **Singular or plural**, page 307.

Proper nouns

1. Proper nouns usually form the plural by adding *s*.

Drapeaus, Elizabeths, Germanys, Kansas Citys, Kennedys, Little Italys, Marys

Note: Some follow the *ies* rule: Johnnies, Tommies, the Alleghenies (Allegheny Mountains), the Rockies (Rocky Mountains)

2. Proper nouns ending in *ch, s, x* and *z* have a plural in *es*.

Finches, Joneses, Foxes, Heinzes

Compound words

1. Most compounds form the plural by changing the principal word to its plural form.

ambassadors at large, assistant surgeons general, attorneys general, chiefs of staff, commanders-in-chief, consuls general, courts martial, editors-in-chief, fathers-in-law, goings-on, governors general, lieutenant-governors, ministers-designate, ministers without portfolio, notaries public, secretaries general, solicitors general, trade unions

But Trades Union Congress

2. If both nouns are of about equal weight, both take the plural.

men employees, menservants, women writers

3. If no word is significant, the final word usually takes *s* or *es*.

forget-me-nots, hand-me-downs, no man's lands, pick-me-ups, will-o'-the-wisps, Johnny-come-latelies

4. Compounds ending in *ful* add *s*.

armfuls, cupfuls, handfuls, spoonfuls

Foreign nouns

Nouns of this type sometimes have an English as well as a foreign plural. CP style is shown.

addendum, addenda
adieu, adieus
alga, algae
alumna, alumnae (fem.)
alumnus, alumni (masc.)
analysis, analyses
antenna, antennas (aerials),
  antennae (feelers)
apparatus, apparatuses
appendix, appendixes
aquarium, aquariums
automaton, automatons
axis, axes
bacterium, bacteria
basis, bases
beau, beaus
bureau, bureaus
cactus, cactuses
census, censuses
cherub, cherubs
coccus, cocci
crisis, crises
criterion, criteria
curriculum, curricula
datum, data
dilettante, dilettantes
dogma, dogmas
ellipsis, ellipses
erratum, errata
focus, focuses
formula, formulas
fungus, fungi
genius, geniuses
genus, genera
gladiolus, gladioli
helix, helixes
hypothesis, hypotheses

impetus, impetuses
index, indexes
larva, larvae
larynx, larynxes
madam, mesdames
  (madams for brothel-keepers)
matrix, matrixes
maximum, maximums
medium, media
  (mediums in spiritualism)
memorandum, memorandums
millennium, millenniums
minimum, minimums
minutia, minutiae
monsieur, messieurs
nucleus, nuclei
oasis, oases
opus, opuses
parenthesis, parentheses
phenomenon, phenomena
plateau, plateaus
prospectus, prospectuses
radius, radii
referendum, referendums
sanatorium, sanatoriums
seraph, seraphs
sinus, sinuses
stadium, stadiums
stimulus, stimuli
stratum, strata
syllabus, syllabuses
symposium, symposiums
tableau, tableaus
terminus, terminuses
thesis, theses
vertebra, vertebrae
virtuoso, virtuosos

Nouns with the same singular and plural

aircraft, alms, amends, bellows, bison, chassis, corps, counsel, deer, fish, forceps, goods, grouse, head (of cattle, etc.), headquarters, insignia, means, moose, offspring, pains, precis, proceeds, rendezvous, remains, series, salmon, shambles, sheep, species, sweepstakes, swine, trout, United States, wheat, whereabouts

Note: But when more than one kind or species is referred to, a regularly formed plural is sometimes used.

Many fishes, ranging from salmon to eel, are netted. New wheats — crosses of Thatcher and Selkirk — continue to be developed.

Nouns plural in form, singular in meaning

checkers, dominoes, measles, mews, mumps, news, rickets, shingles (disease), works (factory)

Dos and don'ts

Such expressions form their plurals normally.

no ifs, ands or buts; yeses and noes; all the ins and outs

But words being discussed as words form the plural by adding 's.

Some writers mistakenly leave out the the's. He filled his speech with like's and you know's.

➤ See **Punctuation**, page 289.

Possessives

1. Singular and plural nouns not ending in *s* take an apostrophe and *s* to form the possessive case.

father's pipe, women's lib, people's food, the kibbutzim's leaders, alumni's donations

Note: It looks careless to err on words like **children's** (not **childrens'**) shoes, **women's** (not **womens'**) issues, **men's** (not **mens'**) salaries.

2. Plural nouns ending in *s* take an apostrophe alone.

teachers' apples, the two peoples' history, the Joneses' daughter

3. Singular nouns and names ending in *s* (or an *s* sound) normally take an *'s*.

Chris's sandwich, Burgess's novel, Butz's statement, the witness's testimony, Strauss's opera

But names ending with an -*iz* sound often take only an apostrophe. And classical names ending in *s* traditionally take the apostrophe only.

Lansens' foot, Moses' laws, Bridges' plays, Mars' laws, Socrates' plays

4. Names ending in a silent *s* or *x* take an apostrophe and *s*.

Duplessis's cabinet, Delibes's Coppelia, Malraux's paintings, Francaix's symphony

Note: A few French names end in an *s* sound and follow normal rules for the possessive.

Saint-Saens' music, de Lesseps' canal

5. For company and institutional names, follow the organization's preference.

Professional Golfers' Association, Canadian Forces Headquarters

6. Where the usage is more descriptive than possessive, omit the apostrophe.

an autoworkers spokesman, a board of directors meeting, the carpenters union, citizens band radio, a Leafs defenceman, a 1940s car, the UN website

7. Use a single apostrophe for joint possession, separate apostrophes for separate possession.

Smith and Cusak's pharmacy, Pierre and Marie's children, Pierre's and Marie's shoes

8. A group of words used to express a single idea takes an apostrophe on the last word only, although many such phrasings can and should be avoided.

the mayor of Calgary's speech; the government of Canada's policy; her mother-in-law's car; Dodd, Mead's latest books

➤ For plurals of compound words, see **Plurals of nouns**, page 283.

9. In general, inanimate objects take an *of* phrase rather than an apostrophe.

the colour of the coat, not **the coat's colour**
the incidence of flu, not **the flu's incidence**

Note 1: But many idioms, particularly expressions of time and measure, take an apostrophe even though there is no actual ownership.

a stone's throw, the law's delay, a couple of dollars' worth

Note 2: To test whether an apostrophe is needed in such expressions as **two weeks(') pay** and **six months(') pregnant**, mentally substitute the singular and the correct answer will appear: **a week's pay, one month pregnant**.

10. Compound nouns with built-in apostrophes are generally singular.

arm's length, baker's dozen, confectioner's sugar, cow's milk, debtor's prison, farmer's market, fool's paradise, fuller's earth, printer's ink, traveller's cheques, writer's cramp

11. Most pronouns are written without an apostrophe.

hers, its, ours, yours, theirs, whose

But **anyone's guess, another's hopes, others' feelings, each other's view, nobody's fool, anyone else's house, no one else's**

Note: Beware the careless confusion of **its** and **it's** (it is), **theirs** and **there's** (there is), **your** and **you're** (you are), **whose** and **who's** (who is).

Punctuation

General

Punctuation brings order to writing. It helps make the message of a sentence immediately clear. But don't overdo it. A sentence littered with clauses set off by commas, dashes and semicolons can look like a word jungle and chase the reader away.

Apostrophe

1. Use an apostrophe to denote possession.

Davis's car, the Davises' house, Marx's Capital, children's toys, the media's problem, Jesus' name

➤ See **Possessives**, page 287.

2. Use an apostrophe to indicate the omission of letters or figures.

she'd, it's (for it is), couldn't, rock 'n' roll, fo'c's'le, Where E'er You Walk, "Give 'em hell!", the early '30s, the class of '80, "We'll 'elp 'im for 'is mother, an' 'e'll 'elp us by-an'-by." — *Rudyard Kipling*

Note: Contractions are acceptable, but avoid such forced contractions as it'd, should've, Tom'll go; use only readily recognized forms: won't, shouldn't, he'd.

3. Use an apostrophe with verbs formed from capitals.

OK's, OK'ing, KO'd, MC'ing, X'd out

4. Use an apostrophe in plurals of lowercase letters.

Mind your p's and q's. Dot your i's and cross your t's.

5. In general, do not use an apostrophe with plurals of capital letters or numbers.

She graduated with straight As, the three Rs, the ABCs, two VIPs, a formation of F-18s, the Dirty '30s

Note 1: Use an apostrophe with plurals of capital letters if necessary to avoid ambiguity.

A's in math and physics are hard to come by.

Note 2: Whether to write a single letter as a capital or lowercase in a particular context depends somewhat on personal taste; logic favours **with a capital S** and **with a small s**.

6. Do not use an apostrophe to form the plurals in expressions like **the whys and wherefores.**

Here are a few dos, don'ts and maybes. I don't want any ifs, ands or buts. Just give us straight yeses or noes.

Note: Use the apostrophe to form the plurals of words being discussed as words.

three as's, too many is's, not enough the's

7. Do not use an apostrophe with shortened forms that have become accepted as complete words.

cello, copter, flu, gym, phone

Brackets (parentheses)

1. In general, try to use brackets sparingly, when other punctuation won't do the job.

Their biggest difficulties were the heat (temperatures were in the high 20s) and clouds of blackflies.

2. Use brackets to insert fuller identification in proper names, direct quotation and such.

the Moose Jaw (Sask.) Times-Herald. Use commas when no proper name is involved: **the Moose Jaw, Sask., daily.** But prefer **the daily in Moose Jaw, Sask.,** or some such.

"When you ask how (Finance Minister Ellen) McFadden can survive, you are asking the wrong question."

3. Use brackets to enclose a nickname within a name.

William (Bible Bill) Aberhart

➤ See **Names, nicknames, initials**, page 260.

4. Use full brackets in numbering or lettering a series within a sentence.

The union pressed for (a) more pay, (b) a shorter work week and (c) better pensions.

➤ See **Period**, paragraph 6 note, below.

5. Use brackets to enclose political affiliations.

Senator Iva Villman (PC-Man.)

6. Use brackets to enclose equivalents and translations.

"We can expect two more inches (five centimetres) of rain."
The measure now goes to the Bundestag (the lower house of parliament).

7. If a punctuation mark applies to the whole sentence, put the mark after the closing bracket.

Words must be reputable (not socially frowned on). "I tell you this" (turning to the jury): "I am innocent."

8. If a punctuation mark applies only to the words inside the parenthetical section, put the mark inside the closing bracket.

Most employees learned the new system quickly. (It helped to have supervisors on hand.)

"After I gave the alarm (by shouting 'Fire!'), I slid down the rope."

9. In general, a parenthetical sentence takes a capital only if it is a direct quotation.

"We couldn't meet today (she had an appointment), but arranged to have lunch tomorrow."

His comment ("Wow, you're not exactly tall") had annoyed her.

Colon

1. Use a colon, rather than a comma, to introduce a direct quotation longer than a short sentence.

Winston Churchill said in 1942: "This is not the end. It is not even the beginning of the end. But it is, perhaps, the end of the beginning."

2. Use a colon in lines introducing lists, texts and tables.

VICTORIA (CP) — Highlights of the throne speech:
— The creation of 10,000 jobs . . .

3. Use a colon to introduce an amplification, an example or a formal question or quotation. It takes the place of **for example, namely, that is.**

It was a mixed cargo: iron ore, wheat and coal. Various solutions were possible: sell the herd, try to renew the loan, take a partner.

4. Generally do not capitalize the first letter of a sentence that follows a colon; but a capital may be used if emphasis is desirable.

Their learning is like bread in a besieged city: every man gets a little, but no man gets a full meal. — *Samuel Johnson.* This is the rule: Write in easy, conversational English. Verdict: Not guilty.

Note: Capitalize the first word of a quoted sentence: **The prince cried: "Too late! Help came too late."**

5. Use a colon to mark a strong contrast.

Man proposes: God disposes. Eating isn't just a necessity: it's a pleasure.

6. Use colons in question-and-answer formats and for interviews. Quotation marks are not used.

Q: When do you expect an agreement?
A: Before Christmas.

Tatje: Why are you a critic?
Papadakos: One must live.

7. Use a colon to separate hours, minutes and seconds in clock and elapsed times, and periods before fractions of a second.

7:30 p.m.   a record time of 1:25:15.4

Note: Write 8 a.m., not 8:00 a.m.

8. Use a colon after a formal salutation.

Madam Speaker: Gentlemen: Dear Mrs. Odisho:

Note: Informal salutations may take a comma.

Dear Jack,   My dear Puran,

9. Use a colon to indicate chapter and verse, act and scene and other citations.

A soft answer turneth away wrath. — *Proverbs 15:1*
There's daggers in men's smiles. — *Macbeth 2:3.147*

10. Use colons to separate titles and subtitles unless the author's or publisher's form differs.

The Chinese: Portrait of a People

11. Put colons outside closing quotation marks.

Paisley said of the charge of "bigot": "It's a lie."

She was referring to "the most serious of all charges": murder.

Comma

1. Put commas between the elements of a series but not before the final **and, or** or **nor** unless that avoids confusion.

men, women, children and pets

The major decided he must either attack at once, await fresh troops or withdraw.

Breakfast consisted of oatmeal, fried eggs, and bread and butter.

2. Use commas before clauses introduced by the conjunctions **and, but, for, or, nor** or **yet** if the subject changes.

We are all in the gutter, but some of us are looking at the stars. — *Oscar Wilde*

Note: The comma may be omitted when the clauses are short or the subject of both is the same.

The gun boomed and the race was on. The twins shouted and waved and finally managed to attract the driver's attention.

3. Use commas to set off an introductory clause or long phrase that precedes the main clause.

If God did not exist, it would be necessary to invent Him. — *Voltaire*

Note: Even if the introductory clause or phrase is short, a comma may be used for emphasis: **Even so, the vote was close.**

4. Put a comma after the main clause only if the clause that follows is parenthetical.

I'm selling you this gold brick because I like your face. The doctor bought a ticket, though she didn't expect to win.

5. Use commas to separate adjectives before a noun when the commas represent **and**.

a frank, open face; a vigorous, genial, popular man; well-meaning, enthusiastic, immature novices

6. Omit commas if the adjectives could not be separated by **and** and still make sense.

a cold marble floor; Tom's new 10-speed racing bike; her old brown winter coat; an aristocratic French family

Note 1: As another rule of thumb, if the order of the adjectives could not be changed (as in these examples), omit the commas.

Note 2: When in doubt, err on the side of too few commas.

7. Do not put commas around an identifying word, phrase or clause if it is essential to the meaning of the sentence. Do use them if the phrase could be omitted without changing the meaning of the sentence.

The Queen was accompanied by her son Prince Edward.
But: The Queen was accompanied by her youngest son, Prince Edward.

The girl who is singing is my daughter.
But: The girl, who was alone, got into the cab.

They drove to a village where they had seen bandits.
But: They drove to a village, where they bought bread.

8. Use a comma to separate an introductory clause from a short, complete sentence in quotations.

The prime minister replied, "I have nothing to add to what I said in the House."

Note: Do not use a comma if a quotation is extremely short or is an integral part of the clause.

Stop saying "I told you so."

She heard a voice yelling "Baby needs new shoes!" and there was her husband shooting craps.

"A guy comes up to me and says 'Oh, yeah?' and I say 'Oh, yeah?' and slap his face."

9. Use a comma to set off a paraphrased question or statement.

The question is, How can it be done? She said, No, she hadn't seen the boy.

But: She said no.

10. Use commas to set off parenthetical expressions, direct address and the like.

That's right, isn't it? Come into the garden, Maud.
Madam Speaker, I deny that.

Note: Commas are used with transition words like **besides, meanwhile, indeed, of course, too, in fact, as a result** and **consequently** if the sentence reads better with a pause.

11. Use a comma to separate words and numbers when confusion might otherwise result.

He who can, does. He who cannot, teaches. — *G.B. Shaw.* Ralph waxed the floor, and his sister dusted. All day, workers had been preparing the field. Some time before, the Plateans had surrendered. Instead of 20, 50 came.

12. When words readily understood are omitted for brevity, use commas to mark the omission, unless the sentence reads smoothly without them.

To Rolf he gave $5; to Mohammed, $2; to Darrin, nothing.
One child received $5, another $2 but the third nothing.
Let your yea be yea and your nay, nay.

13. Use commas to separate geographical elements.

The tour bus runs from Basel, Switzerland, to Milan, Italy, with frequent stops.

Note 1: Do not omit the second comma.

The runner left St. John's, N.L., last week.

Note 2: Do not put a comma before **of**, indicating place.

Tom Stoddard of Mission, B.C., was first.

Note 3: Avoid this clumsy construction: **a Prince George, B.C., lawyer.**
Prefer: A lawyer in Prince George, B.C.

14. Use commas to set off the year from the month plus day.

March 31, 1949, was the date that Newfoundland joined Confederation.

Note: Do not use commas when the day is not included.

January 1998 was mild in Victoria. Clark died at Easter 1835.

15. In general, use commas to set off thousands but not in years, street addresses or page, phone or serial numbers.

13,250 kilometres	$1,450,250	page 1235
2000 (year)	1530 Rose St.	serial 76543
416-364-0321		

16. Use commas to set off a person's age, degrees, awards and affiliations.

Jean Tateyama, 48, Brandon, Man.; René Tremblay, PhD, faced Alex Dodd, VC, in the debate.

17. Do not use commas with **Sr.** or **Jr.**, or with numerals that can similarly be regarded as an integral part of a name.

Maurice Leblanc Sr. spoke first. Pope John XXIII was popular. Albatross II finally reached port.

18. Do not use commas with multi-unit dimensions, measures, weights or times.

two feet four inches by three feet 10 inches, 10 pounds 12 ounces, two hours 30 minutes 25 seconds

But: a four-foot-11, 90-pound youngster

19. Put commas inside closing quotation marks.

Barb said, "I don't want any," but the pedlar only smiled. The clue consisted of four words: "spinner," "blackbird," "watchman" and "maple." "It sounded like 'gorp,'" he said.

Note: Occasionally, such punctuation is not needed. **More than 1,600 protesters chanting "We're anti-violent people" marched along Portage Avenue.**

20. A comma follows a bracket if sentence structure requires it.

The speech was long, hard to hear (people were coughing), uninspired and uninspiring.

21. Use a comma or a dash but not both.

Not: Wilfred was, — like all the Clutterbucks, — a man of striking personal charm.

Dash

1. The dash is an effective tool but can easily be overused. Many times it can be avoided by breaking a long sentence into two shorter ones.

2. Use dashes to set off mid-sentence lists punctuated by commas.

The ministers will discuss common problems — trade, tourism, immigration and defence — before going to the summit talks.

3. Use dashes when commas (generally preferable) would create confusion.

The pies — meat and fruit — were cheap.

4. Use a dash in placelines after the service logo.

HALIFAX (CP) — An oil . . .

5. Use a tight boldface dash to introduce sections of a list.

OTTAWA (CP) — Highlights of the federal budget Tuesday:
—About 12,500 homeowners are expected to qualify for mortgage assistance.
—Employee benefits . . .

6. Use a dash to mark a sharp break in a word or sentence.

"I've been laughed at, ignored — but I'm boring you."

Note 1:   When a sentence breaks off, no period is used after the dash.

"Really, Madam Speaker, I must —"
"Order!" the Speaker shouted.

Note 2:   When a quotation simply trails away, use three spaced periods.

"Maybe if I had tried harder . . . "

7. Use dashes to mark off interpolations.

"Besides" — he tapped me on the knee — "you're wrong."

8. Use a dash to introduce a phrase or clause that summarizes, emphasizes or contrasts what has gone before.

Quiet, respectful, deferential, even obsequious — those were Mulliner's chief characteristics.

Our army is composed of the scum of the earth — the mere scum of the earth. — *Duke of Wellington*

The English country gentleman galloping after a fox — the unspeakable in full pursuit of the uneatable. — *Oscar Wilde*

9. Use a dash to attribute a quotation.

Pedantry is a misplaced attention to trifles which then prides itself on its poor judgment. — *Jacques Barzun*

10. Do not use dashes with colons, semicolons and commas.

11. Write dashes with spaces before and after but not with agate sports summaries and the exceptions noted above.

Ellipsis (. . .)

1. Use three spaced periods to indicate an omission from a text or quotation.

The decision . . . rests solely with your elected representatives, not with pollsters or the news media.

Note: Put spaces before, between and after the periods.

2. In condensing a text, use an ellipsis at the beginning, inside or at the end of a sentence.

The decision . . . rests solely with your elected representatives. . . .

. . . But the government won't ignore thoughtful suggestions, no matter what their origin.

3. In news stories, use an ellipsis only inside a sentence, not at the beginning or end.

"The decision . . . rests solely with your elected representatives," the prime minister said.

After a reference to comments of delegates, he added, "But the government won't ignore thoughtful suggestions."

➤ But see **Dash, No. 7**, above for one exception.

4. When condensing texts, put other required punctuation before the ellipsis. Thus four periods end a sentence.

But the government won't ignore thoughtful suggestions. . . .

Similarly: **What is the answer?** . . . **We must strive harder,** . . . **produce more,** . . . **lower our expectations.** . . .

Note: Guard against distortion that might result from putting together statements that were not together in the original. The solution may be to interrupt the sequence by starting a new paragraph or renewing the attribution.

5. Ellipses may be used to separate entries in the *Notes* section at the bottom of sports game copy.

Jays Notes — The roof at the Rogers Centre was open to start the game but was closed during the third inning with rain threatening. . . . Pitcher Ken Dayley, sent to Florida on a 30-day rehabilitation stint after overcoming a problem with dizziness, returned Thursday with a sore left forearm. . . . Roberto Alomar extended his consecutive-game hit streak to eight with a seventh-inning single.

Exclamation mark

1. Do not overuse this strong mark of punctuation. Use it to denote great surprise, a command, deep emotion, emphasis and sarcasm.

We won!   "Take aim! Fire!"   Ouch!   Never!   Oh, sure!

Note: If a one-word exclamation rates heavy emphasis, put it in a separate sentence; otherwise treat it as part of another sentence.

"Oh! She almost fell." "Oh! you frightened me!" or "Oh, you frightened me!"

2. Use an exclamation mark with questions that are exclamatory in form.

"You mean we won!"

"How could she do that to him!"

3.   Do not use an exclamation mark to end a mildly exclamatory sentence.

Hurry along, please. Have your tickets ready.

4.   Do not use a comma or period after an exclamation mark.

"Fire! Fire!" the janitor shouted.

Someone cried "She's drowning!"

5.   Put an exclamation mark inside quotation marks when it is part of the quoted material, outside when it is not.

"That's a lie!" a backbencher shouted.

Imagine calling a cabinet minister a "liar"!

Hyphen

1.   Compound words may be written solid (**sweatshirt**), open (**oil rig**) or hyphenated (**white-haired**).

➤ See **Compound Words**, page 232.

2.   Write words as compounds to ease reading, to avoid ambiguity and to join words that when used together form a separate concept.

a once-in-a-lifetime chance, a hit-and-run driver, voice-over-Internet-protocol technology, a used-car dealer, a small-business tax, an extra-high collar, light-year, first-fruits, man-hour, blackbird, streetcar, airbrush

3.   In general, hyphenate compound modifiers preceding a noun, but not if the meaning is instantly clear because of common usage of the term.

the third-period goal, three-under-par 69, a 5-4 vote, multimillion-dollar projects, 40-cent coffee

But **the acid rain threat, the United States dollar, a savings bank deposit, a sales tax increase, the task force landing**

4.   Adverbs ending in *-ly* are not followed by a hyphen. The *-ly* alerts readers that the word that follows is modified: **a brightly lit room, an eagerly awaited speech.**

5.   Hyphens are seldom needed with proper nouns (**a United Kingdom custom**), established foreign terms (**a 10 per cent drop**) or established compound nouns (**a high school principal**).

6.   Certain word combinations are often hyphenated even when standing alone.

noun plus adjective (**fire-resistant, fancy-free**), noun plus participle (**blood-stained, thought-provoking**), adjective plus participle (**sweet-smelling, hard-earned**), adjective plus noun plus *-ed* (**open-handed, red-faced**)

7. Use a hyphen to indicate joint titles and to join conflicting or repetitive elements.

secretary-treasurer, writer-editor, musician-painter, comedy-tragedy, drip-drop, walkie-talkie

8. Hyphenate most well-known compounds of three or more words.

happy-go-lucky, good-for-nothing, Johnny-come-lately, forget-me-not, mother-in-law, a two-year-old

But **coat of arms, next of kin, no man's land**

9. Use a hyphen with certain compounds containing an apostrophe.

bull's-eye, mare's-nest, cat's-paw

10. Use a hyphen to avoid doubling a vowel, tripling a consonant or duplicating a prefix.

co-operate, re-emerge, anti-intellectual, doll-like, brass-smith, re-redesign, sub-subcommittee

But **readjust, reaffirm, reinstate, reopen,** etc.

11. Use a hyphen to join prefixes to proper names.

anti-Trudeau, pro-Communist

But **transatlantic, transpacific**

12. Use a hyphen to join an initial capital with a word.

T-shirt, V-necked, X-ray, S-bend, H-bomb

13. Use a hyphen with fractions standing alone and with the written numbers 21 to 99.

two-thirds, three-quarters, fifty-five, ninety-nine

14. Use hyphens with a successive compound adjective (note spacing).

18th- and 19th-century fashions; 10-, 20- and 30-second intervals

15. Use a hyphen in aircraft identification and such, between the symbols for make or type and model number, but not after the number.

DC-10, DC-8L, MiG-25

But **Boeing 767**

16. Use a hyphen to connect dates except when preceded by **from** or **between**.

the 1982-83 tax year, from January to May (not from January-May), between 1970 and 1976 (not between 1970-76)

Note: Don't drop the first two digits if the numbers are not the same: **1998-99**, but **1998-2002**.

17. Use a hyphen to differentiate between words of different meanings but the same or similar spellings.

correspondent (letter writer), **co-respondent** (in divorce); **resign** (quit), **re-sign** (sign again); **recover** (regain health), **re-cover** (cover again)

18. Use a hyphen to avoid awkward combinations of letters.

cave-in, not **cavein**; **co-star**, not **costar**; **de-ice**, not **deice**; **non-native**, not **nonnative**; **re-ink**, not **reink**; **set-to**, not **setto**; **sit-in**, not **sitin**

19. Use a hyphen for the minus sign in temperatures and with bracketed political affiliations.

-10 degrees, Joan Singh (Con-Man.)

Parentheses ➤ See **Brackets**

Period

1. Use a period to end a declarative or a mildly imperative sentence.

The wind blew and the ground began to dry. Give me the book. Let them have their say.

Note: For greater emphasis, use an exclamation mark, advisedly.

"Stick 'em up!"

2. Use a period to end an indirect question, a request phrased as a question, or a rhetorical question.

The reporter asked how many were killed. Would someone answer my question. What do I care.

3. Use a period with decimals, including decimal currencies.

3.25 $9.50

4. Use a period after certain abbreviations.

➤ See **Abbreviations and acronyms**, page 191.

5.   Put periods inside quotation marks.

The writer said, "This is the end." Her brother said, "I don't know why she said 'This is the end.'"

6.   Omit periods after headings, figures, roman numerals, single letters (except initials) and scientific and metric symbols.

Pope, unionist meet; $52; Chapter 2; Albatross II; E flat; Au (for gold); 15 cm; 20 C

Note: But use periods, as an alternative to brackets, after a letter or number denoting a series.

To improve readability: 1. Don't be too formal. 2. Organize before you start to write. 3. Be active, positive, concrete.

7.   Omit periods after letters used as names without specific designation.

Suppose A takes B to court for damages.

➤ For the use of periods to indicate omission, see **Ellipsis** above.

Question mark

1.   Use a question mark after a direct question, but not after an indirect one.

What day is this? The nurse asked what he wanted.

Note: When a question occurs within a question, both ending at the same time, use only one question mark.

Who asked "Why?"

2.   Use question marks to express more than one query in the same sentence.

Reporters must ask themselves, How does it look? sound? feel? taste? smell?

Note: If a question is not complete until the end of the sentence, use a question mark there.

Do you want coffee, tea or milk?

3.   Use a question mark to express doubt or uncertainty.

The dates of the English dramatist John Heywood are given as 1497(?)-1580(?).

4. Do not use a question mark if the person addressed is expected to act rather than answer.

Would you mind spelling the second name.

5. Question marks go inside or outside quotation marks, depending on meaning.

The Speaker asked, "What was the question?" Did the prime minister say "fuddle-duddle"? He asked, "Did the prime minister say 'fuddle-duddle'?"

6. A question mark supersedes the comma or period that usually ends a quotation.

"Who goes there?" the sentry shouted.

Quotation marks

1. In general, always use double quotation marks except for headlines and quotes within a quote.

2. Use quotation marks to enclose direct quotations.

The lawyer said, "I don't think the police should be paying suspects for information."

3. Use quotation marks to begin and end each part of an interrupted quotation.

"We can't hear you," the girl said. "The radio is on."

Note: Capitalize the first word of the second part of an interrupted quotation only if the second part begins a new sentence.

4. Alternate double and single marks in quotes within quotes.

"I heard her say, 'I only hit him when he sneered and said "Never."'"

5. Capitalize the first word of any mid-sentence quote that constitutes a sentence.

The woman said, "He sneered and said 'Never.'"

This has the same effect as the brush-off used in theatrical circles of "Don't call us. We'll call you."

The trainmaster gave the order to "Get the hell out!"

5. Put each speaker's words in a separate paragraph to make it immediately clear that the speaker has changed.

Vilmik laughed. "Who gave him the quarter?"
"Not me," said his wife. "I'm broke."
"I know," said Vilmik. "Let's ask your mother."

6. When a quote by a single speaker extends more than one paragraph, put quotation marks at the beginning of each paragraph but at the end of only the last.

"As I said earlier, my father was always reasonable about things like that.
"But when it came to money, he could be totally unreasonable. An out-and-out miser.
"Still, on the whole, he was fair-minded."

However, if the quote in the first paragraph is a partial one, use quotation marks at the beginning and end of the partial quote.

He said the argument was "remarkably bitter."
"I didn't know two people could hate each other so much."

7. Provide the speaker's identity quickly if a quotation is unusually long. It should either precede the quotation, follow the first sentence (or the second if it is short and closely linked to the first), or be interpolated.

"This is the best time to call an election," Lumie said. "There is a tremendous momentum going to us. Waiting can only cost us votes. It's now or never."

"We've lost. We've lost," wailed another bystander. "The British have won. Our army has been lying to us."

"The Puritan hated bear-baiting," Macaulay adds, "not because it gave pain to the bear, but because it gave pleasure to the spectators."

8. Use quotation marks to set off a pungent or significant word or phrase but not around routine words or phrases.

His first ship was an old "rustbucket."

Not: The minister replied that the economy is "improving."

Note: Fragmented quotes are justifiable only when the words are controversial, add colour or give the flavour of an event or the style of a speaker.

9. Use quotation marks around unfamiliar terms on first reference.

The fluid was named "protoplasm" by a Czechoslovak.

10. Put quotation marks around words used ironically.

The "friendly" soccer game ended with two players booked.

11. In partial quotes, do not put quotation marks around words the speaker could not have used.

Not: Ali boasted "he was rarin' to go."

12. CP and other news agencies cannot replicate italics for technical reasons and so for clarity put quotation marks around the titles of compositions, including books, computer games, movies, operas, plays, TV programs and songs. (If technically possible, italics are recommended instead.)

Random House will publish "How to Get Rich" in April, to coincide with the show's live season finale.

The Cowsills recorded a series of hits between 1967 and 1970, including "The Rain, the Park and Other Things" and "Hair."

Do not use quotation marks (or italics) around the names of reference books, catalogues, newspapers and magazines or the Bible.

The Bible is a bestseller throughout the country.

Maclean's magazine publishes its university guide every year.

➤ See **Capitalization**, sections **Compositions**, page 209, **Music**, page 217, **Quotations**, page 223.

13. Do not use quotation marks to enclose slogans and headlines.

The pickets carried signs that read Cut Taxes, Not Jobs and Cut Government Spending. The article was headed Drug Squad Flouts Gun Rules.

14. Do not use quotation marks in question-and-answer formats.

Q: Do you recognize this man?
A: Yes.

15. Do not use quotation marks on texts, transcripts or editorial excerpts in symposiums.

OTTAWA (CP) — Text of Gov. Gen. Rhoda Mann's New Year's message:
The mood at the dawn of a new year . . .

St. John's (N.L.) Telegram: The real needs of Canadians . . .

Note: In editorial symposiums, the name of the paper is in boldface, followed by a colon, not a dash.

16. Do not use quotation marks around single letters.

She got a B on the test. He wore the captain's C on his shirt.

17. Periods and commas always go inside closing quote marks; colons and semicolons outside. The question mark and exclamation mark go inside the quote marks when they apply to the quoted matter only; outside when they apply to the entire sentence.

18. When a sentence ends with single and double quotation marks, separate them by a space.

19. Use single marks for quotations in headlines.

Semicolon

1. Use a semicolon to separate statements too closely related to stand as separate sentences.

"I never read a book before reviewing it; it prejudices a man so." — *Sidney Smith*

2. Use a semicolon to separate phrases that contain commas.

Best actor, Robert De Niro, Raging Bull; best actress, Sissy Spacek, Coal Miner's Daughter; best film, Ordinary People.

3. Use a semicolon to precede explanatory phrases introduced by **for example, namely, that is** and the like when a comma seems too weak.

Some pleasures cost next to nothing; for example, reading.

4. Semicolons go outside quotation marks.

Police finally cornered the "bear"; it was a poodle.

Slash

1. Use a slash mark to separate alternatives.

and/or, either/or

But use a hyphen for joint titles and to join conflicting elements.

secretary-treasurer, comedy-tragedy

2. Use a slash mark to replace **per** in measurements.

80 km/h (80 kilometres per hour)

3. A slash is also used to separate the numerator and denominator of a fraction.

3 5/8, 1 7/8, 17 2/3

Singular or plural?

1. In general, a subject singular in form takes a singular verb; a subject plural in form takes a plural verb.

An outbreak of bombing and shelling was heard. On each side of the road were drifts of trilliums.

2. A collective noun (a group of people or things) takes a singular verb if it is seen as a unit, a plural verb if thought of more as a collection of individuals. The singular is more common.

The audience was silent. The audience were stamping their feet. Her family is sending money. Her family are all ill.

This also applies to proper collective nouns, such as the names of sports teams and performing groups.

The Jazz is the first western team to win the championship. The Clash say the key to their songs is complex harmony.

It is important to be consistent once the decision is made.

Not: The Clash are playing its greatest hit.

But: The Clash is playing its greatest hit.

3. When two parts of a compound subject are separated by **with, together with, including, besides, no less than, in addition to, plus, as well as** or **likewise**, the verb agrees with the first part.

The ship with all its crew was lost. Gray as well as his wife and son was in the car. The meat plus packaging weighs about a kilogram.

4. **All, a lot, any, half, majority, more, most, per cent, remainder, rest** and **some** take either a singular or plural verb depending on whether the noun is singular or plural.

Is all the money accounted for? All the cars are new. The government's majority makes it safe from defeat. A majority of Canadians favour wage control.

5. **Anybody, anyone, another, anything, each, either, every, everybody, everyone, many a, neither, no one, nobody, somebody** and **someone** take a singular verb.

Everyone wants his money back. No one knows the future. Neither of the teams stands a chance. Each of the three students comes from a different country.

6. When a sentence contains **not only . . . but also, either . . . or** or **neither . . . nor**, the verb agrees with the nearer subject.

Either the sergeant or the troops are out of step. Either the troops or the sergeant is out of step. Not only the children but also the babysitter was asleep.

7. **None** takes a plural verb when it stands for *not any;* it takes a singular verb when it is followed by a singular noun or when the idea of *not one* is to be emphasized.

None of the passengers were Canadian. None of the furniture was dusted. Ten climbers have tried but none (preferably **not one**) has succeeded.

8. In general, **acoustics, economics, gymnastics, politics, mathematics** and other words ending in *-ics* are singular when they are referred to as a science or course of study and plural when referred to as a practical activity or a quality.

The acoustics are bad. Acoustics is on the curriculum. Her politics are left wing. Politics is a dirty business. My mathematics are weak. Mathematics, rightly viewed, possesses not only truth, but also supreme beauty. — *Bertrand Russell*

Note: When in doubt, use the singular.

9. When **number, total** and **variety** are preceded by *the*, they take a singular verb. Preceded by *a*, they take a plural verb.

The number of unemployed rises monthly. A number of unemployed have found jobs. The total stolen has topped $1 million. A total of 21 people were involved.

10. When **couple** is used in the sense of two persons, it almost always takes a plural verb and plural pronouns.

The couple were hurt when their car crashed.

Note: Couple in this sense is singular on the rare occasion when it is treated as a unit.

A couple pays $5 a ticket.

11. A numerical statement may be singular or plural depending on whether the number is thought of as a unit or as a collection of items.

Three weeks is a long time. Six feet of earth is enough for any man. There was two minutes left in the game. Two days of spring make winter seem almost worthwhile.

12. Subjects plural in form but singular in effect take a singular verb.

Great Expectations has been made into a movie. Jarndyce and Jarndyce is literature's most famous lawsuit.

13. When two subjects form one idea, the verb is singular.

Bread and butter is included. The tumult and the shouting dies. — *Rudyard Kipling*

14. **Data** and **media** are plural. Treat **agenda** as singular.

The media were blamed. The data support this theory. The agenda was short.

Note: Data is sometimes treated as a collective noun: **This is vital data**, a use disliked by conservative writers, who prefer **These are vital data**.

15. When a sentence begins with an introductory **there**, the number of the verb is determined by the delayed subject.

There is much to be seen. There are many beautiful sights.

16. **One of those** takes a plural verb when the phrase introduces a clause.

The clerk is one of those people who are always right. It must be one of the longest sentences that have ever been written.

Note: To confirm that the verb must be plural, reverse the sentence: **Of the longest sentences that have** (not **has**) **ever been written, it must be one.**

Slang and jargon

Slang and its cousins, jargon and buzzwords, riddle our spoken language and often make the leap onto the page. They can enliven stories, giving them colour and flavour in a brief word or phrase. Slang can also help express emotions effectively. But too much or unfamiliar terms can also make copy impenetrable to all those readers not familiar with it. Or it can offend those who regard it as too informal or even improper.

Adding to the challenge is the fact that it is virtually impossible to define slang. Many words in the English language started out as so-called slang and now are respectable nouns and verbs. It has been a sizable part of our language for a good 400 years, commonly used by all ages and social groups. The problem is that by definition it derives from a particular subgroup and as such may not be familiar to everyone.

The subgroup may be as small as the TV audience of a show such as *Seinfeld*, whose members will immediately understand the meaning of such phrases as "shrinkage" or "low talker." Others will just scratch their heads in confusion. Slang is also by nature faddish — what is understood today may not be next week. And it can get stale very easily. Yesterday's **groovy** and **yuppie** seem very dated today.

Some tips

1. Slang, as long as it is not vulgar or otherwise offensive, works well in quotes if the context helps define its meaning.

Thousands of teen girls crowded around actor Orlando Bloom as he made an appearance at MuchMusic in downtown Toronto on Thursday. "Ohmigod, he's so hot," screamed one, tears running down her face.

2. To confirm whether slang is widely known or considered offensive, check the *Canadian Oxford Dictionary*. Be cautious of using slang that is not in the dictionary.

3. Use when appropriate. Sometimes it is not.

Not: The children's dad was led away in handcuffs after their blood-spattered bodies were found in the basement.

Better: The father of the three children was led away in handcuffs after their blood-spattered bodies were found in the basement.

Not: Police are finding girls as young as 12 working as hookers on the streets of Canada.

Better: Police have found girls as young as 12 working as prostitutes on Canadian streets.

4. There is a great temptation to use truncated words in today's

English: **veggies** or **veg** (vegetables); **photo op** (photo opportunity); **PR** (public relations); **porn** (pornography). Again, it can be appropriate in the proper context or if a particular casual effect is desired. Otherwise, avoid.

5. Some writers are particularly fond of turning nouns into verbs: **Klein gaffed while trying to defend his plans to reform health care.** Avoid unless the word has made the jump into common usage as a verb.

6. Don't use quote marks around slang unless it is likely to be a new term for most readers.

NOT: Canada is full of "couch potatoes," a new study of TV watching habits suggests.

Jargon

Inside language of a profession or any other specialist group should be translated into understandable English. But the translation needs care.

Not: "The bullet lodged in the cerebrum," the doctor said.

But: The bullet lodged in the upper front part of the brain, the doctor indicated.

Not: There was "a severe loss of separation" between the two aircraft, the air traffic controller said.

But: The two planes nearly collided, the air traffic controller suggested, explaining that is what he meant when he used the term "a severe loss of separation" in his report.

Not: Police withheld his identity pending notification of next-of-kin.

But: Police withheld his name.

Abstract nouns, especially ones ending in *-ion* and strung together with prepositions, often signal foggy writing. Passive verbs can be culprits as well.

Short words tend to be concrete, standing for people, places, objects and acts.

Not: Medically speaking, the inhalation of the toxic substance is considered capable of the creation of psychological compulsions resulting in his criminal behavior.

But: Doctors said breathing the poison may have affected his mind and driven him to kill.

➤ See **Government jargon**, page 244.

Spelling

General

Is there any subject more controversial for editors than Canadian spelling? Spelling issues bring more mail to the *CP Stylebook* editor than anything else.

Many Canadians are passionate about spelling words "Canadian" – but there are many opinions on what exactly is Canadian. That's because the Canadian style has been to borrow from both Britain and the United States. For some words Canadians opt for a spelling that may have originated in the United States (or more accurately, North America). For other words we follow the British style. On some words, we never use the British variant (**tyre** for **tire**, **gaol** for **jail**); on others we never use the American version (**check** for **cheque, maneuver** for **manoeuvre**).

CP's general philosophy is to use the spelling most commonly found across the country. Our authority for spelling is the *Canadian Oxford Dictionary*. Exceptions are listed in *Caps and Spelling*.

Despite the hybrid nature of our spelling roots, there are some general spelling rules that Canadians seem to accept. Like Americans, we prefer **ize/yze** endings for words such as **criticize** and **rationalize**. Like the British, we prefer **-ce** endings instead of **-se** endings on nouns like **defence** and **offence**; we double the l at the ends of words when adding a suffix: **travelled, rivalled, medallist**; and most Canadians use **-our** endings for words such as **honour** and **favour**.

Some specifics

1. Where Oxford gives alternative spellings — **amok/amuck, judgment/judgement** — CP style is the first, unless shown otherwise in *Caps and Spelling*.

2. When the spelling of the common-noun element of a proper name differs from CP style — **Primary Colors** (book), **Lincoln Center, Canadian Paediatric Society** — use the spelling favoured by the subject.

3. When a verb has two forms for the past tense — **kneeled/knelt, leaped/leapt** — CP uses either one without preference.

4. CP prefers the *sh-* spelling for Yiddish words: **shlemiel, shlock, shmatte**. This is a departure from Oxford's *sch-*.

5. Unless Oxford shows otherwise, the plural of a noun is formed normally, by adding *-s* or *-es*: **shaman/shamans,**

box/boxes. If the plural is irregular, it is given in parentheses: **man (men)**. Where there is a choice — **mango (-es** or **-s)**, **virtuoso (-i** or **-os)** — CP uses the first spelling: **mangoes**, except when *Caps and Spelling* says otherwise: **virtuosos**.

6. For words in common use, CP style is **e** rather than the diphthongs **ae** and **oe**. So it is **archeologist, encyclopedia, fetus, gynecologist, hemorrhage, medieval** and **pediatrician**. Generally, proper names retain the diphthong: **Caesar, Oedipus, Phoebe**.

➤ See **Plurals of nouns**, page 283; see also *(CP) Caps and Spelling*.

When not to use CP spelling

When the spelling of the common-noun element of a proper name differs from CP style, CP uses the spelling favoured by the subject. This applies to all geographical places and the titles of books, movies and so on.

Thus it is **Lincoln Center** (not Lincoln Centre); **Bar Harbor, Me.** (not Bar Harbour); **Color Your World** paint store (not Colour Your World); the book or movie **Primary Colors** (not Primary Colours).

One exception is names of government departments and agencies. CP uses the **U.S. Defence** (not Defense) **Department**, for example, and the **U.S. Labour** (not Labor) **Department**. In such stories, references to the U.S. labour secretary and the defence minister, or defence spending and labour rates are also likely to be found. This exception will avoid having these words spelled two ways in similar usages in the same story. Otherwise, it would be **Defence Secretary Donald Rumsfeld said the Defense Department would increase spending**.

➤ For further details on spelling and an alphabetical listing of words, see *(CP) Caps and Spelling*.

Technical terms

General

1. Avoid unfamiliar scientific, medical, technological and technical terms. When they must be used, give a simple, accurate explanation.

She acted oddly because she had Tourette's syndrome, a nervous disorder characterized by involuntary movements and vocal sounds.

2. Explain the unfamiliar in terms of the familiar.

A centrifuge acts like a cake mixer or merry-go-round, forcing objects outward from the centre.

Keratin is the main protein in fingernails, tiger claws, alligator scales, rhinoceros horns and feather quills.

3. Technical language can be less intimidating if the explanation is given first.

The medical team said a study of the mammoths' white blood cells, called leucocytes, shows them to be perfectly preserved.

4. An everyday term is generally preferable to a scientific one. For example, use **evergreen** instead of **coniferous, marijuana** instead of **cannabis**.

5. Because of the rapid pace of change, it can be difficult to know where to draw the line with terms in communications technology stories. One useful general rule is to avoid abbreviations and acronyms that are used only by industry insiders. If in doubt, err on the side of caution by including an explanation: **Wi-Fi, a wireless network.**

Scientific names

1. The name of a family or genus is capitalized: **Branta**. Use lower case for the species, even when derived from a proper name like Canada: **Branta canadensis** (Canada goose).

2. The genus may be shortened if the reference is a common one:

Brucella abortus (aborts cows, causes undulant fever in people)	Br. abortus
Escherichia coli (intestinal bacterium)	E. coli
Staphylococcus aureus (causes boils)	S. aureus

Drugs

1. In general, refer to a drug by its generic name, not its brand name: **a tranquillizer, diazepam; a pain reliever, ASA**.

2. If an unfamiliar brand name has to be used, follow it with the generic name and a description: **Antabuse, a brand of disulfiram used to discourage the drinking of alcohol.**

When allied news agencies use the term **aspirin**, change it to **ASA** in most cases. In Canada, Aspirin is a trademark and it must be capitalized.

➤ See **Capitalization**, page 231; **Trade names**, page 327; **Business terms**, page 45.

Medical

1. Prefer a common term to a medical one:

bleed to hemorrhage	chickenpox to varicella
broke to fractured	whooping cough to pertussis
clot to embolism	German measles to rubella
indigestion to dyspepsia	bad breath to halitosis
cut to laceration	scarlet fever to scarlatina
scrape to abrasion	shingles to herpes zoster
injury to lesion	stitch to suture

2. In general, don't capitalize diseases, conditions, symptoms, tests and treatments:

legionnaires' disease, scarlet fever, infarction, barium X-ray, cobalt therapy, severe acute respiratory syndrome (SARS)

But capitalize proper names that are part of the term:

Alzheimer's disease, German measles, Parkinson's disease, Down syndrome, Lassa fever, Pap smear, Heimlich manoeuvre.

3. Unless there's a compelling reason to give the precise cause of death, it's usually enough to say a person died, say, of **a stroke, a heart attack** or **in childbirth**, rather than of **cerebral hemorrhage, coronary thrombosis** or **puerperal fever**.

4. Similarly, say **Belfour sprained his right thumb**, instead of **Stress X-rays taken on Belfour, under local anesthetic, showed a tear of the ulnar collateral ligament of the metacarpal-phalangeal joint of the right thumb.**

5. Widespread interest justifies giving more details in reporting the illness or death of a prime minister, president, pope, movie star or other major figure.

➤ See **Obituaries**, page 68.

Condition

1. Descriptions used by hospitals to report a patient's condition are often vague. It helps if a story explains that a patient is **conscious, allowed to sit up** or **receive visitors, is being fed intravenously,** and so on.

2. Here are four common descriptions of conditions, with the meanings some hospitals attach to them:

Good: The pulse, breathing and other vital signs are normal and stable. The patient is comfortable and conscious, and the outlook for recovery is good.

Fair: The pulse, breathing and other vital signs are near normal and the patient is conscious, but he or she is uncomfortable or may have minor complications. The outlook for recovery is favourable.

Serious: The patient is acutely ill and the chance of recovery is uncertain. The pulse, breathing and other vital signs may be abnormal or unstable.

Critical: Death may be imminent. The pulse, breathing and other vital signs are abnormal and unstable and there are major complications.

Burns

There are four degrees of burns, but most hospitals refer to only three: *first, second* and *third* — the third being the most severe.

First degree means the skin is red; *second*, it's blistering; *third*, skin has been destroyed along with underlying tissue and won't heal without grafting.

In a *fourth*-degree burn, muscle and bone have also been damaged.

Hospitals may also refer to partial and full burns. Ask specifically about the extent of tissue damage and the need for skin grafts and other measures.

AIDS

Acquired immune deficiency syndrome (or acquired immunodeficiency syndrome) is a breakdown of a person's immunological system, the body's natural defences against disease. Someone is said to have AIDS if a life-threatening infection or cancer results from failure of the defence system.

It's inaccurate to say someone has died of AIDS. Give the actual cause of death — pneumonia, perhaps — and add that it was complicated by AIDS or was AIDS-related.

AIDS is believed to be spread through the exchange of blood, semen and vaginal secretions in the following ways: through sexual activity; use of HIV-infected syringes; transfusion of HIV-infected blood; and from an infected mother to her fetus.

Although much research is still being conducted into the onset of AIDS, researchers generally agree that HIV, the human immunodeficiency virus, must be present. Therefore, it is permissible to say that **HIV causes AIDS**.

Remember, however, that HIV can cause several infections or diseases, not just AIDS. In some contexts, it may be better to use the more inclusive **HIV**, rather than **the AIDS virus**.

➤ See **Obituaries**, page 68.

Influenza

Influenza, often called by its nickname flu, is a highly contagious viral infection that attacks the respiratory tract. Rapid onset of symptoms is characteristic of influenza. They include severe cold-like symptoms, muscle aches, fever and lethargy. Because it is caused by a virus, influenza is not treatable with antibiotics.

Flu does not target the gastrointestinal tract and does not cause vomiting and diarrhea, except occasionally in young children. The often-seen term "stomach flu" is a misnomer and should not be used.

Richter scale

The Richter scale is an open-ended gauge of ground motion recorded on a seismograph during an earthquake. Every increase of one number means that the ground motion is 10 times greater.

However, science has refined the art of comparing earthquakes since 1935 when Charles Richter helped develop a scale that measured quakes in southern California. Modern seismology equipment is more sensitive and can measure a wider range of quakes than the original Richter scale, although newer scales have been designed to meld with Richter's model. Don't automatically use the phrase **on the Richter scale** when writing about earthquake magnitudes. General references, such as **a quake of 5.2 magnitude**, are usually sufficient.

A quake with a magnitude of 2 is the smallest normally felt by humans. One of magnitude 4 can cause moderate damage in a populated area, one of 5 considerable damage, one of 6 severe damage, and one of 7 widespread heavy damage. A quake of magnitude 8, a "great" earthquake, is capable of tremendous damage.

Time

Introduction

At one time the wire service news day was divided into two cycles – **AMs** (2 p.m. to 2 a.m.) for morning newspapers and **PMs** (2 a.m. to 2 p.m.) for afternoon newspapers.

But the publishing world is not so clear-cut anymore. The deadline of PMs papers is often almost as early as AMs. And newswire stories are often read or published the minute they appear, by online or database customers or 24-hour news channels.

In recognition of this, many news agencies have gone to a 24-hour news cycle. A fresh day, or cycle, begins in the early morning hours.

What day is it?

1.   CP doesn't use **yesterday** or **tomorrow** and only uses **today** if needed in QuickHits — urgent copy intended for broadcast and online clients. (These items are updated later, with the day of the week added, for newspaper and other print media.) Otherwise, to avoid confusion, the day is always named.

2.   Name the day if it falls within seven days of the current date: **on Tuesday** or **next Sunday** or **last Friday**.

3.   For more distant dates, use the date: **May 5**.

4.   For significant events and in sports schedules, give the day and the date: **The budget will be presented Friday, Nov. 4**; or **Saturday, May 13 Toronto at Montreal**.

5.   Place the day in a sentence where it would fall normally in conversation: not **The premier Thursday announced** but **The premier announced Thursday**.

6.   Use **on** when it helps readability or to break up a series of capitalized words:

The measure passed in the House of Commons on Monday. The Edmonton Oilers defeated the Vancouver Canucks on Friday.

7.   Don't wrench a lead out of shape trying for a weak or phoney current-day angle. Bury the time element if necessary, and get the news in the lead.

8.   Avoid putting an obsolescent angle in a lead: **The vote was expected Tuesday**. The event may have occurred by the time the story is read. Instead, concentrate on getting the latest information in the lead and bury the time element so it can be

dumped if necessary. Get a new Writethru out as soon as possible after events overtake the story.

9. Don't write that an event has taken place if the story is written beforehand in anticipation of the event.

➤ See **Advances,** page 412.

What time is it?

1. The exact time of an event is usually unnecessary. Instead, give the reader a sense of the time by describing the scene.

Not: A spectacular collision between two commuter trains occurred at 9 a.m. today.

But: A spectacular collision between two commuter trains caused chaos in downtown Montreal during the morning rush hour.

2. But give a specific time for important announcements, key votes, space launches, ransom deadlines or other events in which the time is a vital component. Give the time in the placelined community, with the equivalent in eastern time in brackets if necessary: **The volcano erupted at 8 a.m. local time (4 p.m. EDT).**

3. Specify the time zone in undated stories.

4. Specify time zones in stories involving the time of live radio and TV programs broadcast nationally. In cases of recorded or delayed broadcasts, provide the eastern time. Each newspaper can provide information on local broadcasts if need be.

5. Time is written in figures. However, write **noon** or **midnight,** not **12 noon** or **12 midnight.**

6. Write **5 a.m.,** not **5:00 a.m.**

7. A colon separates hours, minutes and seconds when figures are used. A period separates seconds from tenths of seconds: **7:32 p.m.** or **Her time was 3:45:20.6.** When written out it would be: **Her time was three hours 45 minutes 20.6 seconds.**

What zone is it?

1. Use abbreviations for time zones with a clock reading: **11 a.m. MST** or **midnight Sunday night PST.** Spell out time zones when they are not accompanied by a clock reading: **Newfoundland daylight time.**

2. Capitalize Newfoundland, Atlantic and Pacific time zones when spelled out. Other time zones – eastern, mountain and central – are lowercase: **Atlantic daylight time** but **eastern standard time.**

3. Greenwich mean time is five hours ahead of eastern standard time and four hours ahead of eastern daylight time. From April through October, when Britain is on **summer time** — their equivalent of **daylight time** — London is one hour ahead of GMT.

➤ See **Abbreviations and acronyms,** page 191.

Source: National Research Council Canada   CP

Titles

General

1. For rules on capitalization of titles, ➤ see **Capitalization**, page 228.

2. With few exceptions, a person's given name is used with surname on first reference.

Note: Famous authors, composers and the like may be referred to by surname only: **Dickens's Bleak House, Beethoven's Fifth, Darwin's theory of evolution.**

3. Front-loading — piling nouns in front of a name — is hard on the reader. Instead, use *of*, *the* and *a*, and set off long titles with commas.

Not: RPM Records of Canada president Gerry Lacoursiere . . .

But: **The president of RPM Records of Canada, Gerry Lacoursiere, attended the news conference.**

Not: **Deputy external affairs minister Jacques Martin was the main architect of the program.**

But: **Jacques Martin, the deputy external affairs minister, was the main architect of the program.**

4. False titles are best avoided.

U.S. modern dance innovator Margaret Mason, retired Yukon judge Roger Kimmerly

A phrase in apposition, preceded by *the*, is proper English.

the U.S. modern dance innovator Margaret Mason, the retired Yukon judge Roger Kimmerly

5. Use titles on first reference but seldom after that.

Ambrozic (not Archbishop Ambrozic) also attended the mass. The size of the deficit startled Landry (not Premier Landry). Berger (not Sgt. Berger) was first ashore. The next in line is William (not Prince William).

But when a story is long or filled with names, repeat a title rather than risk losing a reader.

6. Use such titles as **Dr.** and **Rev.** only when those named are dealing with their speciality. A doctor in the Commons speaking about the environment is simply **Martha Singer, the Regina Conservative.** Speaking about medicare, she becomes **Dr. Martha Singer, the Regina pediatrician and Conservative.**

7. Use **chairman** or **chairwoman**, **spokesman** or **spokeswoman** as appropriate. **Chairperson** and **spokesperson** can be used if the sex of the person is not known. But use substitutes for awkward constructions (**councillor** instead of **alderperson**) whenever possible.

Courtesy titles

1. In general, do not use the courtesy titles **Mr.**, **Mrs.**, **Miss** or **Ms.**

Justice (not **Mr. Justice**) **Ian Binnie wrote the ruling. Murray said she enjoys singing. Campbell said abortion should be illegal.**

When it is necessary to use **Mrs.**, **Miss** or **Ms.**, follow the woman's preference.

2. If appropriate, refer to a couple on first reference by their first names and their common last name: **William and Jane Levinski.** If their relationship is not that of husband and wife, explain: **Wayne Gretzky and his sister, Kim.**

3. When married people do not use a common surname, an explanation can be added for clarity.

Adrienne Clarkson and her husband, John Ralston Saul

4. To distinguish between persons of the same last name on second reference, repeat first names.

Professional titles

1. In general, use **Dr.** for licensed health care professionals. Where pertinent specify.

Dr. John Lucyk; Lucyk, an orthodontist. Dr. Sonya Chong; Chong, a chiropractor. Dr. Bert Clifford; Clifford, a veterinarian. Dr. Catherine Clarke; Clarke, a psychologist.

Note: Each province decides which of its health care practitioners may use **Dr.** If in doubt, check.

2. Do not use **Dr.** for people with doctorates outside the health-care field. If pertinent, say a person has an earned or an honorary degree and give the discipline.

Lynch, a doctor of divinity. Callaghan received an honorary doctorate of letters from the University of Moncton.

Religious titles

1.   Use a religious title before a person's name on first reference. Subsequently use either the surname alone (in most instances), the title preceded by *the*, or a general description.

Archbishop Adam Exner; Exner, the archbishop. Rabbi David Silverstein; Silverstein, the rabbi. Rev. Keith Wallace; Wallace, the priest

Note: Write **Rev.**, not **the Rev.** Never write **Rev. Wallace.**

2.   All popes and some Eastern Orthodox archbishops and bishops, as well as some Roman Catholic and Anglican nuns and brothers, are known by a title and given name only. In such instances, the title is usually retained in subsequent use of the name.

Pope Benedict, Metropolitan Andrew, Archbishop Volodymyr, Mother Mary, Sister Agatha, Brother Jude

Note: It is not necessary to include **XVI** in first references to **Pope Benedict.** It is also acceptable to refer in subsequent refernces to **Benedict** rather than **Pope Benedict** in subsequent references.

3.   The name of the office (**Bishop, Canon, Deacon,** etc.) is preferred as the title before the name: **Archbishop John Somers.** But such forms as **Most Rev. John Somers, Archbishop of New Westminster, B.C.,** are acceptable on occasion.

4.   Write **John Cardinal Brown,** not **Cardinal John Brown.**

5.   Some of the more common identifying titles that apply to various levels of Christian religious office include:

Roman Catholic:
The Pope - **His Holiness**
Cardinal - **His Eminence**
Archbishop - **Most Rev.**
Bishop - **Most Rev.**
Monsignor - **Right Rev.** (but usually **Msgr.**)

Anglican:
Primate - **Most Rev.**
Archbishop - **Most Rev.**
Bishop - **Right Rev.**
Dean - **Very Rev.**
Canon - **Rev.** (**Rev. Terry Scott** or **Canon Scott**)

United Church:
Moderator - **Right Rev.**
Ex-moderator - **Very Rev.**

Presbyterian:
Moderator - **Rev.**

6.   Some religions lack a formal hierarchy, with leaders chosen by the congregation or community. In such cases use descriptive terms such as **holy man** or **priest**, as in **Hindu priest Sharad Rao** or **Sikh priest Satinder Singh**.

7.   Forms of address familiar to the clergy but not to others should be avoided except when in direct quotation:

His Holiness, His Eminence, His Grace, Lord Bishop, His Lordship, His Excellency

8.   Unfamiliar titles should be explained.

Primate Michael Peers, the head of the Anglican Church of Canada; Imam Muhammad Nasim, minister of the Jami Mosque; Kazi Muhammad Abdul, a Muslim religious judge.

9.   **Rev.** precedes the full name of most ministers and priests, including Buddhists. It is not used by Christian Scientists, Mormons, Jehovah's Witnesses or Seventh-day Adventists, among others. Muslims use the title **Imam** for leaders of their mosques.

Note: Do not use **Rev.** as a noun meaning clergyman: **The reverend reads murder mysteries**.

10. Unless it is immediately obvious from the context, do not use **Catholic Church** on first mention for the **Roman Catholic Church**. Several other communions maintain the Catholic tradition in varying degrees while rejecting papal infallibility and other dogmas. These include Eastern Orthodox, Anglican, Old Catholic, Polish National Catholic, Lusitanian (Portugal), Spanish Reformed Episcopal and Philippine Independent Catholic.

Hereditary, honorary titles

1.   The honorary titles **right honourable** and **honourable** are used only when they appear in direct quotation.

2.   **Right Hon.** applies for life to the Governor General, prime minister, chief justice of Canada, and members of the British Privy Council.

3.   **Hon.** is applied for life to members of the Canadian Privy Council and lieutenant-governors. With royal assent, it may be used **for life** by retired judges of superior courts and some others. It is applied **during office** to senators, Speakers of the Commons and legislatures, judges of the Supreme and Federal courts of Canada and corresponding courts in the provinces, and members of provincial cabinets. Also applied to most peers' children.

4.   The rules regarding the use of hereditary titles are complex and vary from country to country. In general, use the title as it is commonly used in the country of origin.

5.   In Britain, the order of rank begins with the Royal Family. Use **King, Queen, Prince** and **Princess** before first names: **Princess Anne, Prince William, Queen Victoria**. It is usually sufficient to refer to the reigning monarch as simply **the Queen** or **the King**. After the Royal Family are these (usually) hereditary titles, in descending order (females or wives in brackets): **duke (duchess); marquess (marchioness); earl (countess); viscount (viscountess); baron (baroness); baronet (baronetess)**.

6.   Dukes are referred to by their full title in first reference: **Arthur, Duke of Wellington**, the **Duke of Wellington**.

7.   Although the full titles of marquesses, earls, viscounts and barons and their female counterparts can serve as alternative names (**Marquess of Bath**), they are more commonly identified as lords: **Lord Bath, Lady Bath**.

8.   **Lady** is used before the first names of the daughters of dukes, marquesses and earls: **Lady Jane**. **Lord** is used before the first name of the son of a duke, marquess or earl, although this person may also hold his own title.

9.   A baronetcy is similar to a hereditary knighthood and holders of the title are called sirs, not lords: **Sir Jeffrey Allen**. A baroness is **Lady Allen**, not **Lady Jane**.

10.   There are also life peerages granted by the Crown, with the most common being a life baron. A life peerage offers all the privileges of a hereditary title except it cannot be passed on to the recipient's descendants. If the title is relevant, use it as granted: **Lord Black of Crossharbour**. But if the person is better known by his birth name, use it: **Conrad Black**.

11.   The titles of knight and dame are honorary and do not make a person a member of the nobility. In these cases, make it **Paul McCartney**, not **Sir Paul McCartney; Taylor**, not **Dame Elizabeth**.

Paul McCartney shows off his medal after receiving his knighthood from the Queen at Buckingham Palace in March 1997. Such titles are honorary and do not make a person a member of the nobility.

(AP Photo)

Trade names

1. Capitalize trademarks: names (and symbols) used by organizations and protected by law.

Frigidaire, Skor bars, Tamiflu

Note: Brand name is a non-legal term for **trademark** or **service mark**.

2. Variety names and names of market grades are capitalized.

Golden Delicious apples, Choice lamb, Grade A beef

3. Common-noun elements of trademarks are generally lowercased.

Pears soap, Harris tweed, White Owl cigars, Mott's Clamato juice, Spic and Span cleaner

4. In general, follow an organization's capitalization. But for readability, capitalize the first letter of lowercase names.

TelePrompTer, SkyDome, Toys "R" Us, Adidas (not adidas) sportswear, EBay (not eBay)

5. For all-caps promotional names, capitalize only the first letters.

Scrabble (not SCRABBLE), Via Rail (not VIA Rail), Oxfam (not OXFAM)

6. The use of a trademark is easily avoided by substituting a general term.

soft drink/pop for Coke, adhesive bandage for Band-Aid, flying disc for Frisbee

7. Use a brand name when it gives point, colour or impact to a story.

She wore Jimmy Choo shoes that had seen better days.

The children were playing a board game using Smarties as counters.

The robbers escaped in a Volkswagon Bug.

➤ See **Capitalization**, page 231.

8. **Aspirin** is a trademark in Canada. Generic alternatives include **acetylsalicylic acid**, **ASA pills** and **a painkiller**.

9. Trademarks not guarded by their owners from being used as generics may lose the protection of the law.

cellophane	kerosene	raisin bran
corn flakes	lanolin	shredded wheat
cube steak	linoleum	trampoline
dry ice	milk of magnesia	yo-yo
escalator	nylon	

10. Sources of information about trademarks include the *Canadian Trade Index* and reference books on drugs. Do not follow the capitalization in the *Canadian Oxford Dictionary*.

11. Here are trademarks often encountered in news stories, with generic alternatives.

Baggies plastic bags
Band-Aid adhesive bandage
Bic ballpoint pen
Caterpillar tractor
Chiclets chewing gum
Coca-Cola, Coke cola drink
Cream of Wheat cereal
Crisco shortening
EpiPen epinephrine injector
Fiberglas glass fibre, fibreglass
Fig Newton cookies
Frigidaire appliances
Frisbee flying disc
Fritos corn chips
Fudgsicle ice cream on a stick
Gravol travel-sickness medicine
Hamburger Helper dinner
Hawaiian Punch fruit drink
Hush Puppies casual shoes
Javex bleach
Jaws of Life extraction equipment
Jeep vehicles, but **jeep** for the military vehicle
Jell-O gelatin dessert
Jet Ski personal watercraft
Kleenex tissues
Levi's jeans
Lycra spandex fibre
Lysol disinfectant
Miracle Whip salad dressing

Mott's Clamato tomato-clam cocktail
Muzak background music
Novocain anesthetic, but **novocaine**
Pablum baby cereal, but **pabulum**
Pepsi-Cola, Pepsi cola drink
Plexiglas acrylic plastic
Polaroid camera, sunglasses
Popsicle flavoured ice on a stick
Pyrex oven glassware
Q-Tips cotton swabs
Realtor (a member of the National Association of Realtors, prefer **real estate agent**)
Scotch tape adhesive tape
Stetson hat
Styrofoam plastic foam
Tabasco pepper sauce
Taser stun gun
Technicolor coloured movies
Teflon non-stick coating
TelePrompTer cueing device
TV Dinner frozen dinner
Vaseline petroleum jelly
Velcro tape fasteners
Xerox photocopier

Weather

Introduction

Weather affects everyone. It's almost impossible to write too much about the weather. But write about it in human terms.

The heavy snowfall that is commonplace in northern Ontario during the winter months — closing schools, stranding motorists, generally disrupting life — is news to Vancouver residents basking in 20 degree sunshine. It is certainly news to anyone planning to travel through the region.

Endless rainfall on the Prairies while farmers are trying to bring in their fall harvest not only causes the farmers major concern but affects the commodity markets as well.

Write about weather in terms of its effects on people. Numbers help but prefer descriptions: **ankle-deep puddles, knee-deep snow, winds turning umbrellas inside out and bending small trees, a downpour causing wading pools to overflow and soaking through clothing.**

Weather knows no boundaries. A storm in Halifax affects those in Truro to the northeast and fishermen off the Atlantic coast. Did the storm originate in Maine and sweep through New Brunswick? Are Prince Edward Island and Newfoundland in the storm's path?

Add Canadian content to any story about weather problems in the northern United States.

Where warranted, use comparisons of other recent storms or those that caused major damage.

Consider a regional weather roundup to provide a proper perspective of what the weather pattern has done.

National weather stories should be considered whenever there is a thread to tie everything together.

Weather in metric

Temperatures are expressed in degrees Celsius, with **0 C** the freezing point of water and **100 C** the boiling point. Do not use **below zero**; use **–5 C** (minus five degrees C). **C** is commonplace; it is not necessary to write out Celsius each time.

For everyday comparison: **30 C** is swimming weather, **20 C** room temperature, **–10 C** skating weather.

Wind speed is measured in kilometres an hour: **light**, up to 20 km/h; **moderate**, 21-40 km/h; **strong**, 41-60 km/h; **gale**, 61-90 km/h; **whole gale**, 91-116 km/h; **hurricane**, over 117 km/h.

Rainfall is given in millimetres and **snowfall** in centimetres. A centimetre of snow equals a millimetre of rain.

Light shower	2.5 mm/h rainfall.
Heavy downpour	25 mm/h rainfall.
Good base for skiing	100 cm of snow

Atmospheric (barometric) pressure is measured in kilopascals. Normal pressure ranges from 98 to 103 kPa.

Terminology

Following are terms that may appear in weather forecasts from Environment Canada. Temperatures are Celsius.

acid rain: Rain mixed with sulphur dioxide, nitrogen oxide and other industrial and automobile pollutants to form acids, at times as strong as lemon juice or vinegar.

air mass: A large body of air with uniform temperature and moisture in a horizontal plane. The transition zone between different air masses is called a **front**. In a **cold front**, cold air is replacing warm; in a **warm front**, warm air is replacing cold.

atmospheric (or **barometric**) **pressure:** The pressure exerted by the atmosphere as a result of gravity. A rapidly falling barometer generally heralds a storm; when the barometer is rising, fair weather can usually be expected.

blizzard: A fierce storm with winds of more than 40 kilometres an hour, temperatures of less than −10, visibility less than half a kilometre.

chinook: A warm, dry wind which mainly affects the foothills of the Rockies. Can raise temperatures 20 degrees within minutes.

cyclone: A wind system rotating counterclockwise around a calm central area. In North America the term is sometimes used for a tornado or storm, in the Indian Ocean region for a hurricane.

flash flood: A sudden flood caused by heavy rain or the rapid melting of snow. A **flood crest** is the highest level reached before the water recedes.

freezing rain, freezing drizzle, ice storm: Rain or drizzle that freezes on impact with objects.

gale warning: Issued when winds are expected to be 34 to 48 knots (about 63 to 89 km/h) over water.

heavy snow: The definition varies from region to region. Heavy snow in Vancouver may be five centimetres, in Montreal 15.

high: An area of high pressure with winds moving clockwise, which often brings fine weather. Used interchangeably with anticyclone (a term not widely understood, however).

humidex: An index that combines the effects of summer temperatures and humidities:

Humidex	Degree of comfort
20-29	Comfortable
30-39	Varying degrees of discomfort
40-45	Most people uncomfortable
46 and over	Some outdoor work must be restricted

humidity, relative: The amount of water vapour in the air expressed as a percentage of the maximum amount the air can hold at that temperature and pressure.

hurricane or **typhoon:** A tropical storm with wind speeds of over 117 kilometres an hour. The hurricane eye is the relatively calm centre. Hurricanes develop east of the international date line. Typhoons develop west of the line; in the Indian Ocean they are called cyclones.

inversion: Instead of decreasing with height as is normal, the temperature remains constant or increases.

knot: A unit of speed: one nautical mile (6,080 feet) an hour is about 1.85 km/h.

low: An area of low atmospheric pressure that has an air circulation counter-clockwise in the Northern Hemisphere.

marine warning: Alerts mariners and shoreline residents of dangerous winds or freezing spray.

nearshore waters, coastal waters: Within five to 10 kilometres of shore.

offshore waters: Up to 400 kilometres from shore.

probability of precipitation: The chance of rain, snow and so on for a specified period, expressed in increments of 10 per cent, from zero (none expected) to 100 (a certainty).

ridge: An elongated area of relatively high pressure extending from the centre of a high-pressure region.

severe thunderstorm: Damaging winds usually with gusts to more than 60-80 kilometres an hour, heavy rain and possibly hailstones, frequent lightning and occasionally a tornado.

small craft warning: A warning issued for pleasure boaters when winds are expected to maintain speeds of 20-35 knots (37-63 km/h).

snow pellets: Tiny balls of snow that rebound on striking hard ground.

thundershower: Rain lasting 10-15 minutes, associated with a thunderstorm.

tornado: A destructive rotating column of air with a funnel shape touching the ground and accompanied by a loud roar. Sometimes called a twister.

tropical storm: A weather system one step below a hurricane; winds from 62 to 117 km/h.

trough: An elongated area of relatively low pressure extending from the centre of a low-pressure region.

typhoon: ➤ See **hurricane**.

UV index: A measure of the intensity of ultraviolet rays. The index ranges from 9.0 or higher, which is considered extreme (takes less than 15 minutes to get sunburn), to less than 4.0 (takes an hour or more).

weather advisory: Alerts the public that weather conditions, though not dangerous, may cause general inconvenience.

weather warning: Alerts the public to conditions that may endanger life, property and the public welfare.

whiteout: Dense blizzard and total obscurity of physical features. Commonest in the Arctic and on the Prairies.

wind chill index: An index of the effects of wind velocity and low temperature that measures how cold it feels. For instance, if the temperature is -10 but the wind chill is -20, the winds make it feel as cold as -20 on a calm day.

wind direction: The direction from which the wind blows: an east wind blows toward the west.

wind shear: A swirling current of air produced at the junction of two horizontal air streams of greatly differing speed or direction. A possible hazard to aircraft landing or taking off.

It's not the heat...
It's the humidity

Hot summer days feel worse when the humidity is high. The humidex chart shows how hot, humid weather feels to the average person. For example: If the temperature is 29 degrees C and the relative humidity is 50 per cent it feels like 34 degrees C.

Humidex	Degree of Comfort
20-29	Comfortable
30-39	Varying degrees of comfort
40-45	Almost everyone uncomfortable
46 and over	Many types of labour must be restricted

Temp. in Celsius	Relative humidity							
	30%	40%	50%	60%	70%	80%	90%	100%
34	37	41	43	47	49	52	55	58
33	36	38	42	44	47	50	52	55
32	34	37	39	42	45	47	50	52
31	33	35	38	40	43	45	48	50
30	31	34	36	38	41	43	46	48
29	30	32	34	37	39	42	44	46
28	28	31	33	35	37	39	41	43
27	28	29	31	33	35	37	39	41
26	–	28	29	31	33	35	37	39
25	–	27	28	30	32	33	35	37
24	–	26	27	28	30	32	33	35
23	–	23	25	27	28	30	32	33

Source: Environment Canada

Jeremy Agius - **CP**

Words

This chapter is designed to demonstrate some tricky distinctions in the meanings of words and some rulings on correct or preferred usage in the CP news report.

according to	Avoid in attributions if it seems to cast doubt on the source's credibility.
adventuresome	ready to take risks
adventurous	fond of adventure
adverse	unfavourable
averse	opposed
affect (verb)	influence, have an effect on
effect (noun or verb)	a result; bring about, accomplish
aggravate	make worse
irritate	annoy, exasperate
allude to	suggest without naming
refer to	name
allusion	a casual or indirect reference
illusion	a false impression
altercation	a noisy dispute or quarrel (not a fistfight)
alternate(ly)	in turns, first one and then the other: **The raiders lay alternately watching and sleeping.**
alternative(ly)	providing a choice (usually the word wanted): **an alternative route.**
ambiguous	having two or more meanings: **The large lady's hat** is ambiguous.
ambivalent	having mixed feelings: **He was ambivalent about arms spending, recognizing the need for defence but wishing the money better spent.**
amiable	friendly, of people
amicable	friendly, of situations and agreements
amount	How much? (weight and money)
number	How many? (individual items)
antagonist	➤ See protagonist.

apparent

Write He died apparently of a heart attack, not He died of an apparent heart attack.

apparently
  obviously

seemingly, presumably
plainly, unmistakably

apt
  liable
  likely

customarily inclined; naturally fit
open to something unpleasant
probable, expected

arbitrate
  mediate

render a binding decision in a dispute
help settle a dispute

as

meaning *since* or *because* should be used with care. It can sometimes be mistaken for *while* or *during the time that*: As he was going out, she asked him to buy a paper.

as

  like

introduces clauses: It tastes good as a cigarette should.
introduces a noun or pronoun not directly followed by a verb: He smokes like a chimney.

as if, as though

may be used interchangeably to connect clauses.

assume
  presume

accept for the sake of argument
take for granted

assure

➤ See ensure.

at present

➤ See presently.

audience
  spectators

watches or listens.
watch.

avenge
  revenge

retaliate for another
retaliate for oneself

averse

➤ See adverse.

avocation
  vocation

a hobby, diversion
a career, occupation

awhile

➤ See while.

bait
  bate

lure (a baited hook); torment
hold in (bated breath)

barely   ➤ See **hardly**.

beg the question   assume the truth, usually unjustifiably, of the thing to be proved: **The worthless Senate should be abolished.** Beg the question doesn't mean evade a straight answer.

begin   is the general word.
  commence   sounds formal.
  start   usually applies to physical motion.

beside   at the side of
  besides   in addition to

bi-   is ambiguous in **biweekly, bimonthly, biennial,** etc. Prefer **twice a week, every two weeks, semi-weekly, semi-annual, half-yearly,** etc.

blatant   offensively noisy, obtrusive
  flagrant   shameless, brazen

bloc   a combination of people, countries or organizations to foster a shared interest
  block   a group of things: shares, seats, tickets

blond (adjective)   **She has blond hair.**
  blond (noun)   a male or female

boat   a small craft propelled by oars, sails or motor; also a submarine, motor torpedo boat, ferry
  ship   a large craft with sails or engine
  vessel   a ship or a boat bigger than a rowboat

born   come into being by birth
  borne   carried, endured

breach   break a contract or a wall
  broach   open a barrel or a topic

breech birth   baby born buttocks first

can (could)   denotes ability or power to do something.
  may (might)   suggests doubt; also expresses permission to do something.
cannon   a gun
  canon   a church decree; a clergyman

canvas	coarse cloth
canvass	solicit
catch-22	a dilemma from which there is no escape. Note the lowercase.
celebrator	one who celebrates, a partygoer
celebrant	an officiating priest
cement	powder used in making concrete
concrete	rocklike material for roads, buildings, etc.
centre (verb)	is followed by **on** or **in.**
revolve (verb)	is followed by **round** or **around.**
childish	silly, puerile
childlike	innocent, confiding
chord	used in musical and mathematical senses: **The name struck a chord.**
cord	used in anatomical senses: **spinal cord, vocal cord, umbilical cord**; also: **nylon cord, cord of wood.**
client	uses the services of a professional person other than a doctor, or of a business.
customer	buys goods from a shop or a business.
climactic	of a climax
climatic	of climate
climax	➤ See **crescendo.**
commence	➤ See **begin.**
communique	Use for official communications, not for terrorists' threatening notes and the like.
compare to	liken to: **The staff compared (likened) him to Hitler.**
compare with	show similarities and differences (the term usually wanted): **He cannot compare with Ruth Rendell as a writer of mysteries.**
contrast with	show differences
complementary	completing; supplying needs
complimentary	praising; free

composed of	made up of
comprise (no of)	contain all the parts
include	contain some of the parts
concrete	➤ See cement.
connotation	➤ See denotation.
consensus	agreement, majority view (**general consensus of opinion** is redundant)
contagious	passed on by contact
infectious	passed on by contact or some other means
contemptible	despicable
contemptuous	scornful, insolent
continual	frequently repeated (a dripping tap)
continuous	uninterrupted (Niagara Falls)
controversial	is not needed when it is clear from the context that the subject is contentious: **The Opposition let the legislature bells ring for three hours Monday in its fight against a (controversial) housing bill.**
convict	➤ See inmate.
convince	is followed by **of** or **that**, but not **to**.
persuade	is followed by **of, that** or **to**.
cord	➤ See chord.
council (noun)	an assembly
counsel (n. or v.)	advice, a legal adviser; to advise
country	➤ See nation.
couple	almost invariably plural in reference to people: **The couple were hurt when their plane crashed.** But **A couple pays $5.**
credible	believable
creditable	praiseworthy
credulous	gullible
crescendo	increasing in strength or loudness
climax	highest point, top of a crescendo

customer	➤ See client.
debate	Write debate **something**, not **someone**.
defective 　**deficient**	faulty lacking, incomplete
definite 　**definitive**	firm, clear final, absolute
defuse (verb) 　**diffuse** (adjective)	to render harmless scattered
demolish, destroy	**completely** is redundant. (Avoid as synonym for **defeat** in sports stories.)
denotation 　**connotation**	what a word specifically means: **Pig denotes a swine.** what a word suggests: **Pig connotes dirt, greed, the little pig who went to market and other storybook characters.**
deny	➤ See rebut, refute.
dependant (noun) 　**dependent** (adj.)	one who depends on another depending on
deprecate 　**depreciate**	express disapproval of lose in value; belittle
desert 　**dessert**	barren; something deserved; to abandon a sweet
different from 　**different than**	is used with a noun or pronoun. introduces a clause.
dilemma	a choice between two equally pleasant or unpleasant things (not a synonym for **difficulty**)
disc 　**disk**	in such references as **a compact disc, a disc jockey, a slipped disc** of computers only: **disk drive, a floppy disk**
discomfort 　**discomfit**	make uncomfortable, uneasy embarrass, thwart
disinterested 　**uninterested**	impartial not interested

dissatisfied   ➤ See unsatisfied.

draft   current of air, sum of money, rough plan, military service, hauling, beer drawn from a barrel (never **draught**)

due to   Use only if *caused by* or *ascribed to* could be substituted: **The crash was due to ice.** Not: **Due to ice, the plane crashed.** Try **because of, owing to.**

eatable   can be eaten because not revolting
  edible   can be safely eaten

economic   relating to economics
  economical   thrifty

-ee, -er   In general, *-ee* denotes the recipient of an action: **employee, examinee, trainee;** *-er* denotes the doer of the action: **employer, examiner, trainer.** But *-ee* sometimes applies to a person who behaves in a certain way: **absentee, debauchee, escapee, refugee.**

effect   ➤ See affect.

effective   having an effect; coming into operation
  effectual   answering its purpose

elder, eldest   used to denote seniority in a family

elicit (verb)   to draw out, evoke
  illicit (adjective)   not legal

emigrant   leaves the country.
  immigrant   enters the country.
  migrant   moves from one place to another.

eminent   prominent
  imminent   near at hand

ended   Use of past: **week ended (last) Jan. 1.**
  ending   Use of future: **week ending (next) May 1.**

enormity   monstrous wickedness, serious error
  enormousness   great size

ensure   to make sure
  insure   to provide insurance

assure	to remove worry or uncertainty
especially	➤ See **specially**.
execute	describes judicial or politically motivated killings, not gangland murders.
exhausting	causing exhaustion
exhaustive	complete
expedient	suitable for a particular purpose; advantageous
expeditious	quick
extradite	hand person to another country; obtain such person for trial
extricate	disentangle, release
farther	denotes physical distance: **farther down the road.**
further	everything else: **to slip further into debt.**
female	refers to sex of human beings, animals or plants: **female servants.**
feminine	applies to qualities said to be characteristic of girls and women: **feminine charm.** ➤ See **gender**.
fewer	Use with plurals: **fewer bills.**
less	Use with singulars: **less sugar, a man less.**
figuratively	means in an allied but not exact sense: **She (figuratively) broke his heart.**
literally	means exactly as stated. Wrong: **She literally broke his heart.**
find	➤ See **locate**.
first, firstly	Write either **first, second, third** or **firstly, secondly, thirdly,** but not a mixture.
flagrant	➤ See **blatant**.
flair	aptitude, knack
flare	a flame; a widening
flaunt	show off
flout	mock, scoff at

flounder	move clumsily
founder	fill with water and sink; fail
following	Prefer **after** as a preposition.
foot, feet	In compounds before a noun, use **foot**: **a six-foot pass**. In more formal and precise contexts, use **feet**: **six feet three inches**. In informal usage, **inches** is omitted and **foot** is usual: **six foot three**.
forbid	is followed by **to**: **The captain forbade them to go ashore.**
prohibit	is followed by **from**: **Government workers were prohibited from striking.**
forego	precede
forgo	abstain from
fortuitous	by chance
fortunate	lucky
fulsome	disgusting, loathsome, excessive
gambit	a chess opening in which a player sacrifices a piece to secure an advantage; any opening move
gamut	a whole series or scope of anything
gas	may be used for **gasoline** if there is no confusion with manufactured or natural gas.
gender	refers to words: **A noun or pronoun that denotes a male is in the masculine gender: boy, brother, he, him.** ➤ See **Popular usage,** page 7.
sex	refers to humans, plants and animals: **athletes of both sexes** (not **genders**).
generation	about 30 years
genius	➤ See talent.
gibe	➤ See jibe.
Gothic	of architecture: **a Gothic cathedral**
gothic	all other uses: **a gothic novel**

gourmand	a heavy eater
gourmet	a connoisseur of food
greeted by	used with people
greeted with	used with things
grill	a metal frame for cooking; question closely
grille	grating, screen
grisly	gruesome, horrible
grizzly	greyish, of bears and beards
hail	greet, call to
hale	take forcibly (as to court). But avoid.
hanged	killed by hanging
hung	suspended
happen	➤ See transpire.
hardly, barely, scarcely	1. These are used without a negative: I can (not can't) hardly read the small print. 2. They are followed by **when**, not **than**: Scarcely had they got home when (not **than**) the phone rang.
historic	important or famous in history
historical	about or based on history
hoard	an amassed store (often of money)
horde	large group, pack
homosexual	either male or female
lesbian	a female homosexual
gay	used for both sexes
human (adjective)	used for both good and bad traits of humanity
humane	merciful, kind
humans	used in contrast to animals. In other cases, **human beings** is more appropriate.
hurting	normally requires object. **Poor sales hurt the company** (not **The company was hurting**); **Guy Carbonneau has been playing with knee problems** (not **Guy Carbonneau has been hurting**).

if and when	Use one, not both.
if, whether	are interchangeable when they make sense and are not ambiguous.
illusion	➤ See **allusion**.
immigrant	➤ See **emigrant**.
imminent	➤ See **eminent**.
imply	suggest or hint at; speakers or writers imply.
infer	deduce or conclude; hearers or readers infer.
inapt	unsuitable
inept	clumsy
infectious	➤ See **contagious**.
inflammable,	Used interchangeably to mean capable of
flammable	being set on fire. Prefer **flammable**.
inmate	occupant of a hospital, home, prison or other institution
prisoner, convict	occupant of a prison
insure	➤ See **ensure**.
irritate	➤ See **aggravate**.
it's	abbreviation for **it is** (or **it has**)
its	belonging to it (**held its own**)
jibe	agree or be in accord with
gibe	jeer, mock
judicial	of a judge or law court
judicious	sound of judgment
jurist	a person versed in law (not necessarily a lawyer or a judge)
laden	a truck **laden with melons** implies it is weighed down.
loaded	a truck **loaded with melons** is simply carrying melons.

lay (laying, laid, laid) to lay something down (takes a direct object): The boy laid the towel on the sand.
lie (lying, lay, lain) to recline (does not take a direct object): Then he lay on the towel.

lead (noun and verb) metal; present tense of **to lead**
led (verb) past tense of **to lead**

lectern ➤ See **podium**.

lend (lent, Use as the verb: **Lend me your ears. Lend**
not **loaned)** **me $10.**
loan Use as the noun: **a $100 loan**

lesbian ➤ See **homosexual**.

less ➤ See **fewer**.

lighted, lit Used interchangeably in the past tense, though **lit** is more common: **The lamps were lighted/ lit.** As an adjective before a noun, **lighted** is preferable: **a lighted cigarette**; except when the adjective is preceded by an adverb: **a brightly lit room.**

like Normal usage for examples is **Mother Teresa helped rescue people like the poor, the sick and the abandoned.**
such as is often used to introduce examples set off with commas: **Several famous composers, such as Mozart and Schubert, died young.**

like - as ➤ See **as - like**.

likely, liable ➤ See **apt**.

linage number of lines
lineage ancestry, descent

lit ➤ See **lighted**.

literally ➤ See **figuratively**.

loaded ➤ See **laden**.

loath reluctant
loathe to detest

locate fix the position of (a downed aircraft)
  find discover without reference to a particular setting (a missing child)

luxuriant lush
  luxurious costly, rich

madam a polite form of address: "No, madam"; a brothel-keeper
  madame a French title of respect: Madame Jules Benoit

male refers to sex of humans, animals or plants: a male lion.
  masculine applies to qualities said to be characteristic of boys and men: masculine vigour. ➤ See gender.

masterful domineering
  masterly expert, skilful

may (might) ➤ See can (could).

me, I To, with, from and other prepositions are followed by me, him, her, us and them, not I, he, she, we or they: Mother gave it to Jack and me (not I). Put your trust in him (not he) who knows best. Many of us (not we) voters are tired of promises.

media takes a plural verb: The media are blamed.

mediate ➤ See arbitrate.

meter a measuring machine
  metre a measure of distance; a verse rhythm

meticulous careful about small details
  scrupulous conscientious, thorough

migrant ➤ See emigrant.

momentarily ➤ See presently.

momentary short-lived, for a moment
  momentous important

moral virtuous; a lesson from a story
  morale mental attitude

more than	is followed by a singular verb when the noun is singular: **More than one tank was hit.** ➤ See **over**.
myself	is properly used to intensify: **I myself wouldn't have gone.** Do not use it instead of **I** or **me**: **Gord and myself (I) weren't invited. The bride didn't invite Gord or myself (me).**
naked	the general word meaning without clothing or covering
nude	often a synonym for **naked**; otherwise usually restricted to artistic or pornographic contexts
nation	the people of a country
country	a nation's territory
nauseous	causing nausea, feeling nausea, nauseated
noxious	harmful, unpleasant
negligent	careless
negligible	small, unimportant
noisome	harmful, foul-smelling
no sooner	is followed by **than**, not **when**.
notable	worth noting
noticeable	easy to see, prominent
nude	➤ See **naked**.
number	➤ See **amount**.
O	is usually restricted to invocations: **O God, help me.** It is always capitalized and is written without a comma.
oh	is an exclamation: **Oh God, he's back. Oh, did he?** It is capitalized only at the start of a sentence. Write **oh-oh**, not **oh, oh**.
observance	obeying, paying heed to
observation	noting, looking at
obsolete	no longer in use
obsolescent	becoming obsolete

obviously	➤ See **apparently**.
official **officious**	connected with an office; authorized meddlesome, bossy
oh	➤ See **O**.
one another	➤ See **each other**.
one of those who	is followed by a plural verb.
oral **verbal**	spoken spoken or written
over	In the sense of *in excess of,* used interchangeably with **more than**: **Creasey and Simenon have each published over (more than) 500 books.**
pair	generally plural: **The pair were seen with their son.** But **A pair receives a smaller pension.**
paramount **tantamount**	supreme equal to
parliamentarian	an expert in parliamentary procedure; a skilled debater; not a synonym for **MP**
peddle **pedal**	sell; a **pedlar** sells. cycle; a **pedaller** pushes pedals; to **softpedal** is to play music with the soft pedal down.
people	In general, use **people**, even if the number is small or precise: **Two people died.** Better: **A man and a woman died.**
persons	Use for formality or occasional variety: **Persons over 21 are eligible.**
perquisite **prerequisite**	special privilege, advantage (a perk) a necessary condition
persuade	➤ See **convince**.
podium **lectern**	the platform a speaker stands on the reading desk a speaker stands behind
practicable	able to be done

practical	useful, sensible, functional
precede	to go before
proceed	to go along, continue
prerequisite	➤ See perquisite.
presently	soon, in a moment (**avoid**: usually misunderstood)
at present	now
momentarily	for a moment
presume	➤ See assume.
principal	chief, most important; capital sum; school head
principle	basic truth or rule; code of conduct
prior to	Use before.
prisoner	➤ See inmate.
prohibit	➤ See forbid.
prone	➤ See supine.
protagonist	chief actor, champion of a cause
antagonist	opponent
punctilious	attentive to detail
punctual	prompt
quartet	➤ See trio.
rack (noun)	framework: **hat-rack**
rack (verb)	to trouble, torture, destroy: **nerve-racking**
wrack (noun)	wreckage, seaweed
rampage	➤ See spree.
rankle	A thing **rankles**; it does not **rankle someone**. Right: **The insult rankled.** Wrong: **The insult rankled Joe.**
ravage	damage badly, devastate
ravish	delight, enrapture; rape
reason	is followed by **that** or **why**, not **because**: **The reason for the loss was that taxes rose.**

rebut, refute   prove to be false: She refuted the charge of theft by producing a sales receipt.

deny   declare to be false: He denied the charge but had no alibi.

regretful   full of regret
regrettable   the cause of regret

reign   monarch's rule
rein   harness

reluctant   unwilling, grudging
reticent   sparing of words, reserved

repetitive   characterized by repetition: a repetitive beat

repetitious   characterized by unnecessary or tedious repetition: repetitious arguments

revenge   ➤ See avenge.

revolve   ➤ See centre.

rob   A person or place is robbed, not the thing stolen: A company was robbed of a payroll. Not: A company's payroll was robbed.

rush   Do not use when the idea of speed is implicit, as in stories involving ambulances, fire trucks and police cruisers. Not: She was rushed to hospital. Write taken or some such.

scarce   of things normally available
rare   of things seldom found at any time

scarcely   ➤ See hardly.

scrupulous   ➤ See meticulous.

seasonable   suitable to the occasion or season
seasonal   occurring at a particular season

sensual   arousing or satisfying bodily appetites or sexual desire: the sensual pleasures of eating; a sensual striptease

sensuous   appealing to the senses, sometimes the mind: a ballet dancer's sensuous movements; a sensuous passage of Mozart

sex	➤ See gender.
ship	➤ See boat.
shot	Use the specific **shot and wounded** or **shot and killed** as appropriate.
situation	Avoid the practice of putting other nouns or phrases before **situation**: **a crisis situation, a classroom situation, a bad-debt situation.**
some	meaning *about* is proper: **some 20 years later, some 500 troops.**
spare	scanty, frugal; thin: **a spare diet, a spare style of writing; a spare man**
sparse	thinly scattered, not thick: **a sparse population, a sparse beard**
specially	for a particular purpose
especially	to a great degree, outstanding
spectators	➤ See audience.
spree	a frolic; a drinking or shopping bout; not violent behaviour
rampage	violent behaviour, a bout of violence
start	➤ See begin.
stationary	unmoving
stationery	writing material
stimulant	drug, etc. (not alcohol, a depressant)
stimulus	incentive, spur
strait	narrow, confined (**straitjacket, Davis Strait**)
straight	unbent, direct
strategy	refers to the overall campaign.
tactics	the art of moving forces; adroit management
such as	➤ See like.
supine	face upward (but **avoid**)
prone	face downward
tack	course of action or policy
tact	ability to deal sensitively with others; sensitivity

tactics	➤ See strategy.
talent **genius**	special ability exceptionally great talent
tantamount	➤ See paramount.
that	As a conjunction, *that* may be omitted if no confusion results: **King said (that) she would go.** It is often needed after such verbs as **assert, declare, estimate, make clear, point out, propose, state, warn: She warned that the committee would oppose the plan.** It may be needed with time elements (**White said** that **in 1950 he was destitute**) and before such conjunctions as **after, although, as, because, before, in addition to, when: Green said** that **when she heard the shot, she was asleep.**
that **which**	often introduces an essential clause — one that defines the noun it is attached to and cannot be omitted: **The house that is painted white is mine.** introduces a non-essential or parenthetical clause — one that adds information that could be omitted without changing meaning: **The house, which was built in 1940, is white.**
that-who	➤ See which-who-that.
the	Do not drop *the* from the beginning of sentences or wherever idiom or grammar demands it. Not: **Terms of the contract were secret; Police would not reveal names of the injured.**
then	Avoid putting *then* as an adjective before a noun if it sounds equally well or better in its normal position. Not: **the then prime minister, Lester Pearson.** But: **the prime minister then, Lester Pearson.**
transpire **happen**	become known occur
trio, quartet	Use only in the musical sense, not of any casual grouping of three or four.

troops	In general, **troops** describes a body of soldiers: **The troops were flown in by helicopter.** It is not used of small numbers of individuals: **30 troops**. But idiom permits its use with large numbers, say in the hundreds: **Some 250 troops surrounded the prison.**
try to	try to (not and) understand
uninterested	➤ See **disinterested.**
unsatisfied **dissatisfied**	falling short of satisfaction discontented
upcoming	Write **coming, approaching** or **forthcoming** if an adjective is needed.
urban **urbane**	of a town or city well-bred, suave
verbal	➤ See **oral.**
vessel	➤ See **boat.**
veteran	one who served in the military; person of long experience. Avoid such descriptions as **five-year police veteran** and **a veteran of four NHL seasons.**
vocation	➤ See **avocation.**
waive **waver**	give up, forgo falter, move to and fro
-ward, -wards	Americans prefer the **-ward** form: **toward, backward, afterward**; Britons prefer -wards: **towards, backwards, afterwards**; Canadians use both forms.
was **were**	simple past tense Use **were** when expressing a wish or a condition contrary to fact, and after **as if** and **as though**: **I wish I were you. She spoke to him as if he were a fool.**
whether, if	➤ See **if, whether.**
whether or not	Retain the *or not* when an alternative is emphasized: **I will go whether you like it or not.**

which-that	➤ See that-which.
which	normally refers to things but may be used of people in a body: **She spoke to the crowd, which grew silent.**
who	usually refers to people but sometimes to animals, especially those with names: **Snip, who is 14, is a toy poodle.**
that	refers to people or things: **It was the pilot that** (or **who**) **spoke.**
while (noun)	**They had to wait for a while.** (note the **for**).
awhile (adverb)	**They had to wait awhile.** (no preposition).
who-whom	Who stands for **he-she-they**, **whom** for **him-her-them**. When in doubt, break the sentence in two: **She met a man who she thought was her brother.** (She thought **he** was her brother, so **who** is correct.) **She met a man whom she took for her brother.** (She took **him** for her brother, so **whom** is correct.)
wove	the normal past tense of **weave**: **His daughter wove him a scarf.**
weaved	the past tense of **weave** means to avoid hitting something: **The forward weaved through the defence**; or to tell an involved story: **The old man weaved a chilling plot.**
wrack	➤ See rack.
yoke	wooden crosspiece
yolk	yellow of an egg

Illustrating the news

Pictures

Pictures sell stories.

A strong photo can promote a story that does not offer other compelling visual elements. This unusual photo of Prime Minister Paul Martin and U.S. President George W. Bush was taken at a routine "photo op" during Bush's visit to Canada in 2004.

(CP—Tom Hanson)

A good picture can carry a story onto page 1; lack of a picture can take a good story off the front page – and right out of the paper. CP aims to illustrate every worthwhile story with photos, maps or graphics.

Having that happen depends on awareness. All editors, writers and photographers need to be alert to illustrating the story, whether it is a rewrite or the germ of an idea for a staff-written series. The story without pictures and graphics won't get the play it deserves.

Good CP work involves developing an understanding of what makes a good illustration and the mechanics of getting it from the photographer or artist to the network of receiving newspapers, magazines, television networks and websites.

CP Picture Service began in 1948 as an exchange of mailed photos. The first Wirephoto network based on an analogue or sound signal transmitted over telephone wires began in Ontario and Quebec in 1954 and 10 years later was coast-to-coast. Wirephoto became LaserPhoto in 1978, when new transmission equipment using a laser beam was introduced. The network name was changed to PhotoNet in 1991 after digital transmission by satellite began.

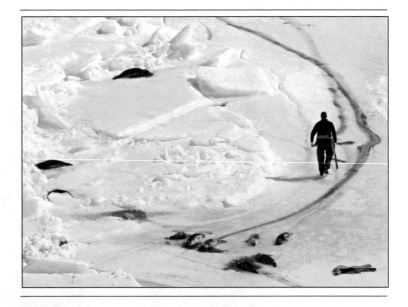

A seal hunter walks along a path of blood in the Gulf of the St. Lawrence during the 2005 hunt. The contrast in colours of the blood and snow makes this photo unusually dramatic.

(CP—Jonathan Hayward)

PhotoNet delivers an average of 600 photos a day to Canadian daily newspapers, websites and other media. One-quarter of the photos originate in Canada, with about a quarter of these coming from newspaper photographers. CP staff photographers and freelances hired by CP provide the rest. The Associated Press and its photographers around the world provide the international content, about 450 photos a day.

Every newspaper subscribing to the photo network – three-quarters of the CP membership – is obligated to provide its local photos from spot news events to CP. Each newspaper subscriber has the capacity to transmit pictures directly to CP by FTP.

AP and CP graphics, in French and English, are also delivered on the same satellite system.

Good illustrations

Good photos have similarities to good stories. They:

1. Are new and in some way unusual.

2. Show action the instant it happens.

3. Portray people and appeal to the emotions.

4. Relate to some important person, event or place.

5. Wrap up a story or provide an overall view of it.

6. Tie in with a current story, the season, the weather, a fad.

A good illustration will be marked by attention to **quality, content, composition, lighting** and **timing.**

Quality

A karate trainer does his routine in the early morning on the Toronto beach by Lake Ontario. The unusual, dramatic lighting and backdrop grabs the reader's attention.

(CP—Frank Gunn)

1. The main subject has clear, sharp details.

2. There are bright, natural colours or a gradual range of grey tones between black and white.

3. Skin tones for light-skinned people are a natural colour or light grey against a white shirt. There must be definition in the facial shading of people with darker skins.

A poor-quality picture might be slightly out of focus – look at the eyes. It might have heavy blacks and brilliant whites, or have an overall grey cast with no blacks and whites. Colours may be washed out or too dark.

The sole exception to these demands for quality is a shot of such outstanding news value that it will get into print despite poor quality.

Follow these basic rules when scanning negatives or acquiring and enhancing digital camera images to ensure maximum quality:

1. Start with an acknowledgment that "less is more" when enhancing images.

2. Do as many enhancements as possible in the pre-scan or when acquiring a digital image.

3. Keep enhancements in PhotoShop to a minimum. Often an unsharp mask is added in the pre-press handling of the image, making excessive use at the scanning stage unnecessary.

When toning, use levels or curves to adjust colour and tone rather than colour balance or brightness/contrast.

Content

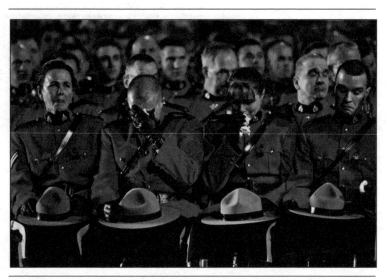

1. Does the photo tell a story?

2. Is its subject important?

3. Is it appealing, well-composed and striking?

4. Is there outstanding human interest or some other quality that overrides minor news value?

Any newsbreak that is visually important or interesting makes the good-quality photo worth distributing. A window cleaner suspended in mid-air by his braces makes a good shot; a minor auto wreck usually doesn't because all wrecks tend to look much the same. A 20-car pileup, multiple deaths or trapped passengers can give an accident photo the news value needed to get it on the network.

Picture judgment is partly personal and partly a matter of experience. A photo is almost certainly worthwhile if an editor experienced in handling news finds it eye-catching. A newspaper photo editor's recommendation is usually a valid reason for selecting a picture.

Composition

1. Are the main subject and its surroundings arranged so as to be attractive and cohesive? The right camera angle often allows information such as signs, buildings and other people to line up with the main subject, making the photograph informative and interesting.

2. Does the entire frame contain relevant content? Large empty areas that add little useful information limit the impact of the photograph.

3. Is the picture cropped to make the subject stand out clearly?

Standup group shots are not wanted, although sometimes the personalities involved create exceptions. The Queen with

Commonwealth prime ministers or a new cabinet is usually newsworthy. In the best such photos, the group's attention is not centred on the camera and a side angle is used "to stack up" the subjects.

Be careful that the "arranged" photo does not turn into a picture that is contrived or set up by the photographer. There is no objection to cleaning up a cluttered background or moving the company president from behind his desk to stand in front of his widget-stamping machine.

The photo becomes contrived when elements or interpretations are added or subtracted to make a point that would not normally have been there. Spot news pictures should not be arranged.

Michael Phelps of the United States surfaces in a heat at the world acquatics championships in Montreal in 2005. This photo is an excellent example of how an unusual perspective – in this case the photographer caught the trail of bubbles produced by the swimmer – can create a memorable image.

(CP—Frank Gunn)

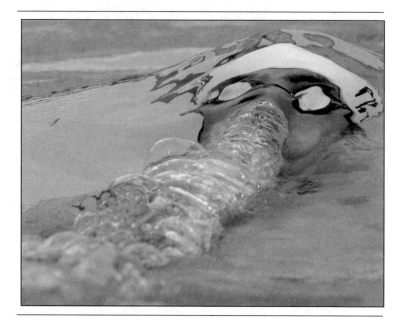

Lighting and timing

1. Lighting gives two-dimensional photographs depth and contributes to the mood and impact of the picture or subject. Avoid flat, full front lighting or direct flash; they do nothing to emphasize the shape of a person or subject. Soft window light that strikes a person on an angle provides excellent light for an environmental portrait. Strong backlight will separate a subject from a dark background and early morning or late afternoon light makes architectural or wide scenic pictures dramatic. Good lighting can make a plain, information-only photo special and move it from the inside pages to a section front or home page.

2. Photographs that are a blend of compelling content and good composition that are made at the precise moment when the action peaks should be every photographer's goal. Timing is more than just pressing the shutter button when the ball is about

to be grasped by a football player. It is the instant when all the other information around or behind the player is arranged and captured at the same time as the peak action. It is often characterized as the "decisive moment."

Photo manipulation

CP does not alter the content of photos. Pictures must always tell the truth – tell what the photographer saw happen. Nothing can damage our credibility more quickly than deliberate untruthfulness. The integrity of our photo report is our highest priority.

PhotoShop is a sophisticated editing tool that allows photographic images to be manipulated easily. It's technically possible to change their content and impact on the reader, whether by accident or design.

Use of this tool must follow the long-established chemical darkroom standards of photo printing. Simple *burning* (making light portions of a print darker), *dodging* (making dark portions lighter), c*olour balancing, toning* and *cropping* are acceptable. Exaggerated use of these features to add, remove or give prominence to details in the photo is not acceptable.

Retouching is limited to removal of dust spots, film scratches or abnormal marks and patterns.

Colour adjustment is to be minimal. Adjustments can be made to ensure honest reproduction of the original when the scanning and transmission processes alter colours.

Consult the Picture Editor first on any question of photo manipulation.

PhotoNet

CP PhotoNet can get a picture across Canada in time to illustrate any breaking story if CP photographers and newspapers move fast.

The large number of Internet sites and web portals dependent on CP for news pictures adds even greater urgency. Pictures must be transmitted as soon after an event starts as possible. The decades-old wire service saying "there is a deadline every minute" has never been more true. For newspapers, pictures that don't move in the same cycle with the story they illustrate will likely not be used, unless the content is exceptional or they illustrate a continuing story.

When a story breaks CP immediately co-ordinates coverage plans with its staff photographers, its member newspapers and AP. The most important consideration while setting up coverage is that a photographer must be at an event when it happens. Coverage must be lined up quickly.

Every paper uses photos to accompany local stories that could have wider interest. To get these on the network in the same cycle for use by others, papers should send their best pictures to the CP Picture desk as soon as they are available.

But what pictures should be sent?

1. Ask yourself whether you would be interested in printing it if you were the editor of a newspaper 100 kilometres away. If the answer is yes, transmit it.

2. Send it if there is a story to go with it.

3. Does it pique your interest in any way?

The most frequent request from newspaper editors is for more news photos that can be used on their inside national pages. On a slow day for spot-news photos, even pictorially interesting weather and feature photos will help fill this demand. Watch for them.

Sending photos

Pictures sent to the Toronto Picture Desk for transmission must be of the highest possible quality. Full captions and relevant International Press Technical Committee (IPTC) field information – used to find and sort archived pictures – must be written and saved with the JPEG file before being transmitted.

Preparing pictures for transmission:

CP photographers and newspapers use digital cameras to make pictures and at times scan older negatives to digitize file photos. In both cases the pictures are imported into PhotoShop software for conversion to JPEG files. These are transmitted on PhotoNet.

Images should be scanned/acquired at a minimum 200 dpi. More and more newspapers and magazines are asking for 300 dpi originals. With higher-quality cameras now in use, the longest dimension should be set to 25 centimetres or more. keep the phoThe longest dimension should not exceed 25 centimetres. Keep the photograph in the RGB mode. Conversion to CMYK from RGB results in the loss of colour information that cannot be recovered. Images should only be converted to CMYK as a final step before going to press.

Pictures should be compressed in standard JPEG format, at a ratio that results in an average one megabyte file. When the file dips below 700 kilobytes it is clear they have been compressed too much.

Images downloaded from the CPimages Archive (*www. cpimages.ca*) must be checked for size before they are transmitted on the network. Many files, including historical material, are stored at a much higher resolution and low compression and must be resized if they exceed the above guidelines.

IPTC fields

Take care when filling out IPTC fields, especially the caption field, which is publishable. CP member newspapers are able to read all IPTC information fields by using their picture browsers or opening the image *File Info* viewable in PhotoShop.

Captions are written in the same style used by most newspapers under the published picture. They should not include information from other IPTC fields.

These are the descriptions of the IPTC fields, and the information that should be placed in them:

Object name: This lists the story slug associated with the photo. For photos without stories, or when a slug is not available, photographers and editors should use a slug that would be a logical search criterion for a story that moves later. Use either the subject's last name, the name of the event, or a word that generally describes the photo.

Original transmission reference: This field lists a call letter-number combination associated with the photo. It includes an originating point's call letters and a picture number; for example, CPT105 would be used for the fifth picture originating in Toronto.

Caption field: A standard CP caption would look like this:

Prime Minister Stephen Harper gestures during a speech to the Canadian Club in Toronto on Tuesday, Feb. 13, 2006. Harper said that child-care funding would be addressed in the next federal budget. (CP PHOTO/Fred Chartrand)

Regular captions have no **overlines** – all-caps descriptions detailing the type of picture. But instructive overlines should be used on file photos and specials as in these examples:

FILE – Roger Clemens of the Toronto Blue Jays clenches his fist in victory in this Aug. 15, 1998, file photo during a game against the New York Yankees. (CP PICTURE ARCHIVE/Frank Gunn)

SPECIAL TO LE JOURNAL DE MONTREAL – Montreal native Bianca Lallito, 13, poses for a photograph on Tuesday, Feb. 7, 2006 in Toronto. Lallito has won a trip to Turino, Italy, for the 2006 Olympic Winter Games (CP PHOTO/Nathan Denette)

The full date – day of the week, date and year – should appear in the body of all captions. If only the month and year are known, use that. In file photos use the date the photo was originally shot. If the date is not known, use the year. If there is no known date, state **date of photo unknown** in the body of the caption and in the *special instructions file* of the IPTC header.

The sign-off for a CP staffer or freelancer is in parentheses: **(CP PHOTO/Frank Gunn)**. If the name of the photographer is not known or needs to be withheld, the sign-off is **(CP PHOTO)**.

Include the name of the newspaper for a member photo sign-off: **(CP PHOTO/Toronto Star-Peter Power)**.

For a handout, use **(CP PHOTO/General Motors)**. If the photographer is known, add the name: **(CP PHOTO/General Motors-John Smith)**. **Note:** Handout photos should also use the code **HO** in the *byline title field* of the IPTC header, but do not put it in the sign-off.

For a pool photo sign-off, use **(CP PHOTO/Peter Jones-Pool)**. Do not name the newspaper or agency that shot for the pool in the caption sign-off. Note: The name of the organization that shot the pool and the word **POOL** should be included in the *source field* and the word **POOL** should be in the *byline title field*.

For a Specials photo sign-off for a photo made by CP, use **(CP PHOTO/Tom Hanson)**. If it was made by a member's own photographer the sign-off is **(Montreal Gazette/Pierre Obendrauf)**.

A file photo sign-off is **(CP PICTURE ARCHIVE/Doug Ball)**. If the name of the photographer is not known, the sign-off is: **(CP PICTURE ARCHIVE)**.

For a CP Graphic sign-off: **(CP GRAPHIC/Sean Vokey)**.

A TV frame grab photo sign-off is **(CP PHOTO/CTV)**. **Note:** TV frame grab photos use the byline title code **TEL** in the byline title field, but do not put it in the caption sign-off. Also, a mandatory credit is often required when using a frame grab. This instruction should be included in the *special instructions field*: **MANDATORY CREDIT REQUIRED WITH THE USE OF THIS PHOTO.**

Date: Date the photo was taken.

Filename: Name originally given to the file when it was saved.

Caption writer: This lists the initials of all the people who wrote or edited the caption, header fields or image file. This includes any toning of the photo file.

Headline: Lists keywords to aid in a more detailed search for a photo. It typically lists who is in the photo.

Special instructions field: Lists any special notations that apply uniquely to a photo such as CP Picture Archive, correction, outs, or mandatory credits.

Byline: Lists the name of the person who made the photo.

Byline title: Lists the title of the person who made the photo. Pick one of these categories:

STF – CP photographs by staff photographers, including Associated Press photographers.

FRL – CP photographs by freelance photographers.

MBR – Photographs from member photographers.

SUB – Photographs picked up by foreign subscribers.

MAG – Photographs provided by magazines.

TEL – Frame grabs from television.

POOL – Photographs by pool photographers.

HO – Handout photographs.

Credit: The name of the service transmitting the photo; almost always CP or AP.

Source: Lists the copyright holder or the original provider of a photo, such as CP, AP, a CP member, pool photo provider, or handout provider.

Category: Lists codes that aid in a more detailed search. Categories are:

A – U.S. news or features

C – Canadian news and features

F – Financial

I – International

S – Sports

V – Advisories

Supplemental categories: Lists codes that aid in a more detailed search for a photo. For example: **HKN** will show all NHL hockey photos. A list of categories is in the AP guide.

City, province, country: Lists the city, province or state and country where the photo was made. For file photos, do not use the transmitting point's city, province or country.

Keywords: Used by CPimages archive staff to add additional search terms.

Writing captions

Captions are always written in the present tense. They tell the reader, briefly and clearly, the basic details of the picture and tie it to the story it illustrates. Remember that photos attract even the most casual reader, so captions are probably the most-read words in the paper or web page, after headlines. Like headlines, captions must be crisp. Like stories, they must be readable and informative, interesting and lively.

Some reminders to make caption-writing easier:

1. Does the caption say when and where?

2. Does it identify, fully and clearly?

3. Are the names in the right order? List people in a group shot from the left, and specify position (left or front row, second from right).

4. Use at least two short, snappy sentences. One long, involved sentence is boring.

5. Stick primarily to explaining the action in the picture, but don't speculate. The prime minister's "grin" may be teeth-gritting anger. The "dozing" legislator may be reading a paper on his desk. Be sure or leave it out.

6. Watch attribution and don't let libel creep in.

7. Read what you've written. Are all the questions answered? Count the people in the picture and the number of names. Are the left-to-right designations correct? Is the action mentioned in the caption really shown?

Credit the photographer in the body of the caption if the picture has exceptional merit or the circumstances in which it was shot were very unusual. Say so when abnormal techniques such as multiple exposures or time exposures were used.

A bagpiper continues his job while surrounded by mayhem at the Summit of the Americas in Quebec City in 2001. Cutlines should give basic background about the news event – in this case, the fact that groups were targeting the summit to protest the effect of globalization.

(CP—Tom Hanson)

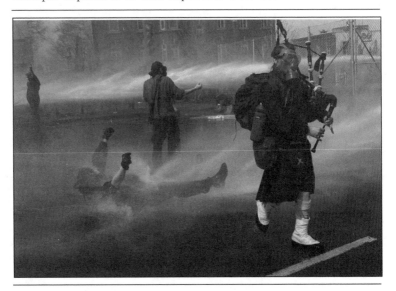

Kills and corrections

All picture kills and corrections are handled by the Toronto Picture Desk, which knows the exact distribution of a picture.

If you see an error in a caption or a graphic, phone the Picture Desk immediately.

Kills and corrections are transmitted on the same photo networks that carried the original. The style differs slightly from the style on news circuits.

CORRECTION: A CP caption correction is moved when a simple and non-libellous error occurs in a caption. Examples would be a misspelled name, or wrong hometown, sports score or slug. The procedure CP uses to file a caption correction form on PhotoNet is to point out the information that is being corrected in the *instructions field* of the IPTC header and write a corrected caption in publishable form. The word CORRECTION and the original photo's number are added to the object name field of the IPTC header. The photo follows the form with a corrected publishable caption noting so in the *instructions field* of the IPTC header.

ADDITIONS: A CP caption addition is moved when the original caption is incomplete, but otherwise accurate. It may add the name of someone in the photo or other important background information. The procedure for a CP caption addition is the same as that for a correction.

ELIMINATIONS: A CP caption elimination is moved when an acceptable photo has a caption that misrepresents the photo or is in bad taste. When this occurs a CP caption elimination form is moved alerting members. Then the photo is retransmitted using the same procedure as a correction.

KILLS: A CP photo KILL is moved on PhotoNet for a photo that is objectionable and presents the possibility of legal action, libel or copyright infringement. Photo kills move in consultation with the Toronto photo supervisor and senior management.

Pictures and the law

The **Legal** section of the stylebook applies equally to the Picture Service. Ensure that neither the caption nor the contents of a photo violate the law or individual rights.

When photographing people in Quebec, take extra care not to violate the Quebec Charter of Human Rights and Freedoms as it relates to a person's right to privacy. The Supreme Court of Canada ruled in April 1998 that an individual's right to privacy under the Quebec charter includes the ability to control use of his or her image.

Although the ruling dealt with Quebec alone, its effect has been to change the way photos are handled in several other provinces with privacy statutes: Newfoundland and Labrador, British

Columbia, Manitoba and Saskatchewan. It means care must be taken with some photos that feature identifiable people in them. Consent must be obtained from the subjects of such photos unless one of the following applies:

a) The people are incidental to the photo.

b) The identifiable person is not the subject of the photo but is one of a group in a public place – a crowd scene, for example.

c) The photo is part of coverage of a legitimate news event that the subject has a role in – a trial, for example.

d) The subject is a public figure.

e) The subject's success in her profession depends upon public opinion.

Otherwise, consent for use of the picture should be obtained and the subject's name and age must be included in the caption transmitted with the photograph.

Privacy is not the only consideration that should be taken into account when handling images of people in the news. In all jurisdictions, a picture of a person accused of a crime could prejudice the outcome of the court hearing if there is a question of identity. And there usually is. If in doubt, consult the editor before transmitting a picture.

Withhold immediately any picture questioned after transmission by sending a news-circuit advisory and a note on all photo networks that received the original. Send a followup advisory and note killing or releasing the picture as soon as the question is resolved.

Copyright photos

CP owns the copyright of photos made by its staff and freelance photographers working on direct assignment for CP. A freelance photographer who shoots a picture before selling it to CP retains the copyright. CP can use it only for the purpose agreed to when it was bought – usually unlimited editorial use by CP and AP member newspapers and magazines.

Any unusual restrictions that the freelance demands must be noted in the *special instructions field* to avoid inadvertent violation of a copyright picture. These restrictions could include:

1. **One-time use only.** The photo can be used once with the current news story.

2. **Magazines out.** The photographer hopes to sell the picture separately to that market.

3. **Copyright photo, credit mandatory.** The newspaper must credit the photographer.

Photos provided by public relations firms or businesses may not be legally available for CP transmission other than at the time they illustrated a specific story. Always check with the photographer or the source before reissuing a picture of this type.

The CP Picture Service contract requires newspaper subscribers to include CP in copyright release of photos by their staff and regular freelances. Be especially careful of occasional freelance photos picked up from newspapers or borrowed later from their libraries. The libraries file every picture used, no matter what the source. Rights may not have been obtained for CP use and must be checked. Do not use a photo if the source is not indicated or cannot be determined from the newspaper's own publication.

Picturing money

It is generally against the law to picture in print any Canadian banknote or a recognizable portion of one. Such photos cannot be carried on PhotoNet. It's prohibited by Section 457 of the Criminal Code.

This does not apply to the printed likeness of a banknote if the length or width is less than three-quarters or greater than 1.5 times the length or width of the real one. Neither does it apply if the likeness is in black and white only or features just one side of the banknote. This gives photographers a fair amount of leeway in illustrating stories about money without breaking the law.

Occasionally the Bank of Canada will provide a replica of a banknote and agree to waive prosecution, usually to promote a newly issued note. These replicas may be transmitted.

It is generally against the law to picture Canadian money in print. But photographers have some leeway. Showing only one side of the bill, as in this photo, is permitted.

(CP—Tom Hanson)

Cartoons

CP picks up cartoons for use with news stories in special circumstances – for example, when a cartoon becomes the subject of political controversy, or to illustrate a story about a cartoonist.

Cartoons may also make good illustrations for a situational or analysis if they offer fair comment. Where there is controversy, more than one cartoon may be needed to reflect opposing views.

Newspapers are not obligated to provide CP with their cartoons, and most editorial cartoonists retain and syndicate the rights to their work. Permission for the use of each cartoon must be arranged in advance with the newspaper or the cartoonist.

The use of any cartoon must be approved in advance by the Chief of Picture Service. Requests for such approval should include the name of the newspaper editor or cartoonist authorizing use.

Graphics

Readers have changed. Busy lives, lightning-fast telecommunications and 20-second TV news items are only a few factors shaping the demands being made upon newspapers. Alert editors and designers have responded with dynamic changes in newspaper presentation. The online environment also presents its own challenges and opportunities for unique presentations of news and information.

In both print and screen environments, sophisticated, information-intensive graphics can help readers understand complex stories or difficult concepts.

Graphics can effectly give the reader a snapshot of a complex story that has many numerical elements.

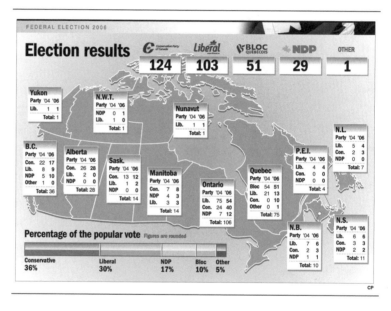

The best graphic artists research, design and construct graphics that show readers the HOW of a story.

The artist can manipulate drawings, take graphs apart and store bits of them in computer memory for later use in another graphic, vary text styles and sizes, and apply colour electronically. The slow mechanical work done in typesetting shops or separation labs is a thing of the past.

CP's **GraphicsNet** service delivers graphics created by CP and Associated Press artists to Canadian newspapers by satellite. At the newspaper, they can be further manipulated to change typestyles, colour or size. CP's graphics service is not limited to single graphics, but includes full pages organized around one topic, such as a major news story or trend, and containing both words and pictures. These pages allow CP writers and graphics artists to work closely together to present a story in the most illuminating way possible.

CP artists also create CP Interactive Graphics for websites. These graphics are almost like little documentaries; they can feature text, pictures, sound and even animation that help explain a story. Readers can select from various menus within the graphic according to what interests them or what they would like to check out first – that's the interactive part.

An interactive graphic can contain a lot more information than the traditional "flat" graphic: a text account of the story, an album of pictures, audio from people involved, relevant maps and chronologies. Each element can also be loaded up with more information than a flat graphic. For instance, a map done in an interactive environment can contain a lot more information that appears as the user rolls his cursor over it.

Staffers everywhere should suggest ideas for graphics. They are often the best way to locate an event, explain a complicated statistical trend or compare products. A good graphic, like a good photo, can help editors squeeze a story into today's tight news holes.

The average news day is full of material that can be made into a graphic. The letterhead on an accreditation application might make a good standing logo for continuing stories on a coming sports tournament. The diagram in the back of the press release that helps reporters understand a new product might be just as helpful for readers. Audio of the Queen's first radio speech will make a memorable addition to an interactive graphic on her Golden Jubilee. A car company's website might have a helpful diagram on the new plant it is building or images of the car models it is eliminating. Give the graphics department a heads-up on what is available.

Information, please

The first element in producing any news graphic is always the same: information. Reporters need to gather this detail in their contacts with news sources.

If a plane crashed on takeoff, find out what runway it was using. How are the runways configured? How far did it go past the runway? Did it crash in trees or a field? What buildings are in the area? Reporters can get this information on the phone. Often, those on the scene – reporters or sources – can sketch a rough drawing for the graphics artist. It's the kind of detail the artist needs, and it's the kind of detail readers are demanding.

From the Montreal massacre, a reporter learns that the gunman used a Ruger Mini-14 rifle. A graphics artist in Toronto, using that information, researches the rifle on the Internet. The result is a graphic that gives the reader the details of the rifle's size, power, ammunition, etc.

A business reporter who hears that a company's sales have been climbing steadily since 2000 can get a graphic going if the annual sales figures can be obtained. Specific numbers are required to produce a graphic, obliging sources to back up their statements with precise facts. The numbers might show that sales are up from 2000, but there have been a number of ups and downs in the period. The fact-digging needed for a graphic is often important in getting an accurate understanding of the story.

Graphics can highlight sidebar material and aid understanding with diagrams.

Ship traffic a danger to whales

Today's bigger, faster and more powerful ships leave less time for whales to avoid them at sea. Whales are increasingly being struck and killed by ships, and authorities are considering rerouting shipping channels or reducing speed limits in whale habitats.

Bulbous bow

The "bulb" on the front provides less resistance for the ship, but whales can get stuck on them.

Whales may also get caught in the draft and pulled into the propellers.

Whales at risk

Surfacing to breathe every few minutes, whales often spend time on the surface dozing or mating. Here are three types of whales that are more commonly struck by large ships.

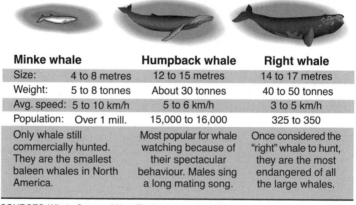

	Minke whale	Humpback whale	Right whale
Size:	4 to 8 metres	12 to 15 metres	14 to 17 metres
Weight:	5 to 8 tonnes	About 30 tonnes	40 to 50 tonnes
Avg. speed:	5 to 10 km/h	5 to 6 km/h	3 to 5 km/h
Population:	Over 1 mill.	15,000 to 16,000	325 to 350
	Only whale still commercially hunted. They are the smallest baleen whales in North America.	Most popular for whale watching because of their spectacular behaviour. Males sing a long mating song.	Once considered the "right" whale to hunt, they are the most endangered of all the large whales.

SOURCES: Whale Center of New England; Associated Press   **CP/AP**

Press kits, catalogues, guidebooks, instruction manuals and program books are often the source of overlooked material that can be turned into a news graphic. However, it is important to only use authoritative sources.

The artist needs reference images. A graphic about the new offshore oil project requires a depiction of the rig as seen by the planners. The artist can't just dream something up. Details are important and are known by somebody familiar with the story. Find the person. That detail included in the graphic ensures accuracy and conveys a sense of heightened realism for readers.

If the jackknifed tractor-trailer has four axles, the graphic is wrong if it shows only three. Sometimes a photographer's pictures will help with detail, but many times graphics portray action that can't be seen by photographers, like the inside of a mine that's collapsed. Get it from an expert.

E-mail or fax machines get information to artists quickly. A scientist at the other end of the country can sketch something fast, fax it to the artist and discuss the graphic as it develops. Information available as a computer file is also easy to incorporate into a static or interactive graphic.

Cautions

Although visual interest is important in a graphic, it comes second to accuracy. A few tips:

1. Do not project, surmise or estimate in a graphic. Only work with what you know.

2. Confirm the location before moving or posting a locator map.

3. Make sure the information is clear and concise. If you don't understand it, the reader won't.

4. Create charts in a perspective that gives an accurate representation of data. Do not skew or alter data to fit a visual need.

5. Credit sources on every graphic, including graphics for which CP journalists have created the data.

6. Graphics often combine various photographic elements, which necessarily means altering portions of each photograph. But there is a limit on what is allowed. The background of a photograph, for example, may be removed to leave the headshot of the newsmaker. This may then be combined with a logo representing the person's company or industry, and the two elements may be layered over a neutral background.

Such compositions must not misrepresent the facts and must not result in an image that looks like a photograph — it must clearly be a graphic.

Similarly, when photos are used in online graphics, the integrity of the image should be retained. Limit changes to cropping, masking and adding elements like logos.

Corrections

Graphics, like stories and pictures, must be corrected immediately. Any graphic being corrected must carry the word FIX in the slug and an explanation of the correction in the replacement graphic.

The incorrect graphic must be removed from the archives to prevent further use.

The CP news report

Main Desk and bureaus

Main Desk in Toronto is the minute-by-minute guardian of the overall quality of the CP news report. Quality originates in the skills of the editors at department desks and regional bureaus countrywide.

Main Desk

Main Desk is staffed by senior editors who co-ordinate coverage and ensure that copy meets CP standards.

Main Deskers:

• See that the CP moves quickly and effectively on major breaking stories, tip deadlining members to important developments, consult with Broadcast News and CP Pictures and alert the Editor-in-Chief or the President as warranted.

• Guard against, and act fast to remove, libel or other legal concerns in copy, usually by dealing personally with legal counsel and the bureau involved.

• Approve the content and format of Correctives and Clarifications before they are transmitted and later fill out a relay report confirming they have moved to all outlets that received the erroneous original.

• Ensure that copy is complete, interesting, well-written and properly edited.

• Suggest significant improvements in stories, perhaps asking a bureau to sharpen a lead by bringing key facts or interesting details higher.

• Watch for regional stories that can be developed for a national audience by a change of approach or addition of background detail — noting similar legislation in another province, for example.

• Consult bureaus by message or phone with a view to building the next-cycle News Budget (➤ See **Advisories**, page 380), suggesting story angles if necessary. Prepare and relay the News Budget advisories.

• Field requests, queries and problems from newspapers or the public, or direct them to the appropriate person or department.

• Proofread CRAFT stories — concerning the newspaper and broadcast industries — for style and content before they are transmitted.

• Mark and relay nightly synopses of the TV newscasts, indicating the status of CP coverage of each story.

- Prepare the twice-daily Page 1 advisory, in consultation with senior editors, and update as necessary with developing stories. (➤ See **Advisories**, page 384.)

- Oversee marking of the Toronto newspapers, chasing matchers to stories from outside their coverage areas. Scan the front-page advisories sent by bureaus, looking for prominently played stories that rate pickup or chasing.

- At least once a day, prepare and distribute to bureaus and departments via the message wire a Developing Sked, which details the status of major stories.

- Assemble and relay the Calendar and Look-Hhead List from bureau contributions (➤ See **Advisories**, page 387).

Bureaus

The deskers at each bureau are charged with the overall goal of explaining their region to the rest of Canada.

Among other things, this demands that bureaus be alert to the kind of context, background information, local colour or other news elements that make a regional story of interest to a broader audience.

The mark of a good bureau is development of its regional news.

Anticipating and planning for news is critical. This starts with a carefully kept datebook of future events; with thorough checks of regional newspapers for news and background information; and with intelligent guidance of newspaper and string correspondents on story development.

Each bureau is responsible for the copy it files, whether written by staff or by travelling staffers assigned to special events. Bureau deskers working alone, or inexperienced deskers, may call upon Main Desk in Toronto to proof important stories before relay.

Cultivating co-operation with the papers is a constant preoccupation. Politeness and helpfulness on the phone are where this starts, and it extends to notifying them promptly on major breaks, especially on Canadian stories that may merit staffing or picture orders.

Stories provided to meet a regional paper's request are pointed out in a bureau phone call to the person who asked.

Duties

Bureau duties include efficient dispatch of certain routine designed to keep members, fellow staffers and other bureaus abreast of coverage:

- Front-page advisories on major papers in the region (➤ See **Advisories**, page 389).

- Marking papers: Desk editors should leave over for their reliever the latest editions of local papers with stories and pictures marked to indicate handling.

At the same time, staffers watch for major play of CP copy and pictures and follow bureau routine to make sure clips and tearsheets are exchanged.

These are the usual markings:

NO — Not carried by CP, with the reason briefly noted (e.g., LOCAL on stories of strictly local interest). Reasons for not carrying prominently played or controversial stories and pictures should be detailed on the Developing Sked. Rejected stories likely to attract other papers' interest may warrant an advisory to spell out the reasons after consulting Main Desk.

NO ASKED — Not carried, CP checking (with arrangements made for matching spelled out in the Developing Sked).

OLD — Fully covered previously.

NCP — Not CP copy but covered by CP; ensure CP copy covers all significant and interesting points in the newspaper's version.

PU — Picked up for CP use.

- Developing Sked: Essentially a memo from a desker going off shift to the desker who follows, although schedules are also sent on the message wire for the reference of Toronto Main Desk and other supervisors.

Format varies to reflect bureau needs but a DevSked's purpose remains the same: an essential at-a-glance guide to incoming deskers on the status of major stories, on outstanding requests, and on staff assignments and coverage plans, with reminders of new standing orders and changes in routine.

A properly assembled DevSked will be the first thing a seasoned desker consults at the start of a shift and the last thing left at the end of a shift. If the DevSked is just a time-consuming chore to all concerned, it's not being done properly.

Keeping editors advised

"Extra! Extra! Triple murder!" Like an old-time newsboy hawking papers on the corner, CP knows that to move news, you have to get the paying customers' attention.

Readers of the wire want to know:

• About the news that's coming 10 minutes from now, and in the cycle ahead.

• What's happening tomorrow? Next week? Next month?

• Will there be pictures and graphics?

• Anything special in the CP report that will be worth saving space for?

• How did other media play the news?

These questions and others are answered by means of *advisories* — notes to editors transmitted along with the news copy.

Some are improvised, pounded out as a hot story breaks and develops. Some are routine — **Fronts**, the **News Budgets**, **Calendar** items and **Page 1** advisories, the weekly **Look-Ahead List**. Others are issued in advance of major events such as elections to detail CP coverage plans. Still others commend editors' attention to special projects that CP has undertaken.

All are driven by the same rationale: customers expect information from an information company.

Advisories

Editors say the most helpful thing CP can do is keep them fully and quickly informed. Not only when big news breaks but as it develops, situations change and deadlines approach.

If a story expected at 9:30 a.m. is going to be delayed, send an advisory. Explain the delay if possible.

Don't be shy with **Top Copy** notes. These give editors an early tip that major unbudgeted stories are coming.

But editors also need to know about CP's plans beyond the day's top news. They want advisories as early as possible on major long-range plans for enterprise series, foreign assignments, advance stories leading up to a political leadership convention and the like.

And make no mistake: these advisories translate directly into play.

Note: Most advisories, including all routine ones, move with message — or **M**-type — designators. One exception is when the advisory concerns copy already sent. It takes the same designator as that on the story: **G** for General, **W** for World, **S** for Sports, etc.

Advisories on immediately upcoming stories with a specific designator should also carry that same designator. This ensures the advisories are routed to the desk that is handling or will be interested in the story.

Spot breaks

1. The phone rings. A major break seems to be in the making. But there is no immediate official confirmation. Remember: editors somewhere are waiting for the story – either on air, online or in a newspaper. They want a message like this:

Tornado, Advisory
CP checking report of major tornado near Olds, Alta.
  Eds: CP is checking a report that a major tornado has touched down near Olds, Alta., about a 40-minute drive north of Calgary. Official word is expected from police shortly. There are no confirmed reports of injuries or damage at the moment.
  CP EDMONTON

Once the information has been confirmed and a story moved, update the advisory with a Writethru:

Tornado, 1st Writethru Advisory
CP confirms tornado causes damage at Olds, Alta.
  Eds: The town clerk at Olds, Alta., has confirmed a tornado has caused severe damage in the town north of Calgary. See Tornado 1st Writethru at 9:59 MDT. CP-BN reporters Sylvia Strojek and Bill Graveland and a photographer are en route to the scene and are expected to arrive at about 10:45 a.m. A 2nd Writethru will move within 10 minutes.
  CP EDMONTON

---

2. Keep editors up to the minute as coverage plans take shape. Don't wait until an eyewitness account or other strong sidebar is fully written before sending a tip. Send fast word on the timing of a news conference or official police statement. Move an immediate advisory if a scheduled briefing is delayed or cancelled. Advisories take seconds to write and send. One advisory may save a dozen phone calls, crucial during a major breaking story.

Tornado, 2nd Writethru Advisory
Media briefing in Olds, Alta., on tornado damage
  Eds: The town clerk of Olds, Alta., will brief reporters on the tornado that struck today, killing at least seven people and causing severe damage throughout the area north of Calgary. The briefing will be held in the town office at 4911 51st Ave. at 11:45 a.m. CP is staffing.
  CP EDMONTON

---

3. Give editors as full a rundown as possible on plans for copy, CP Graphics and CP Photos. This can be done in either the Budget message or with a separate advisory:

> Eds: Besides the budgeted stories **Tornado, Tornado-Victims** and **Tornado-Rebuild**, there will be separates on past tornadoes in the West (**Undated—Tornado-Past**) and how tornadoes are formed (**Undated—Tornado-Profile**), a first-person account by a man who saw the tornado strike (**Tornado-Eyewitness**), a QuickSketch, QuickQuotes, CP Graphics and CP Photos.
> **CP EDMONTON**

Co-ordinate advisory handling with Head Office or another bureau when appropriate:

> Eds: A list of major Canadian disasters this century will move shortly.
> **CP TORONTO**

> Eds: The prime minister is expected to comment on today's tornado in southern Alberta at 3:45 p.m. EDT. CP's Dennis Bueckert is covering.
> **CP OTTAWA**

➤ **See** Breaking News, page 144.

Planned events

1. Expected timing of copy on staged events is vitally important as well. Editors want to know whether copy will move in time for final deadlines. Tell them:

> **Lord, Advisory**
> **New Brunswick premier holds media briefing on labour laws**
> Eds: Premier Bernard Lord is to hold a media briefing on New Brunswick's new labour laws at the legislature in Fredericton at about 10:40 a.m. ADT. CP reporter Chris Morris is covering. First copy is expected by 11:05. It will be followed by updates as needed, as well as QuickFacts and a CP Graphic on the major changes in the law. There will be a later Writethru incorporating reaction.
> **CP HALIFAX**

2. Give advance notice on major announcements whenever possible, even if details are sketchy:

Harper-Economy, Advisory
Announcement by prime minister on economy expected at 2:40 p.m.
Eds: Expected shortly — in advance for release by advisory — is an announcement by the prime minister on the economy. He is expected to start speaking in the Commons at 2:40 p.m. EDT but other business may cause a delay. An urgent release note will move as soon as he starts to speak. Guard against premature use.
CP OTTAWA

Coverage advisories

Some departments and bureaus regularly let folks know what is happening in their backyard with a staffing advisory. Such an advisory is a complete look at that corner of the news service, including stories already on the wire and those in the works.

Biz-Staffing, Advisory
CP Business Coverage Plans
BUSINESS EDITORS: Here are CP Business staffing plans as of 10:15 a.m. ET. Plans may change as circumstances warrant. An updated staffing advisory will move at approximately 2:30 p.m. Queries should be addressed to Business Editor John Valorzi at 416-507-2146 or to James Dalziel on the business desk at 416-507-2138. To contact CP Business by e-mail, send messages to business@cp.org. All copy moves by 6 p.m. ET unless otherwise specified.
SURREY, B.C. — Federal Finance Minister Jim Flaherty signals he will not eliminate the capital gains tax in his first budget. The Conservative government had campaigned on eliminating the tax for individuals on the sale of assets when proceeds are reinvested within six months. By Camille Bains. Flaherty, 2nd Writethru. Moved.
MONTREAL – SR Telecom Inc. (TSX:SRX) says it is eliminating 70 jobs as it outsources some of its Montreal-based manufacturing. The maker of high-capacity wireless data transmission products said it will take $2.2 million in charges for the closure, which it hopes will help it return to profitability. By Allan Swift. SR-Telecom, 1st Writethru. Will be budgeted update.

Publishable and non-publishable notes

Advisories carried on the top of stories fall into two general categories: publishable and non-publishable. The former are aimed at the reader. The latter are for editors' information.

Publishable:

NHL-Preview-Red-Wings, Bgt
Budget
NHL Preview: Detroit Red Wings offer "new look"

The following story is one in a series by Canadian Press sports writers previewing the new National Hockey League season. Neil Stevens of Toronto reports on the "new-look" Detroit Red Wings and their chances of improving their strong finish in the Central Division last season.
By Neil Stevens
DETROIT (CP) — Gordie Howe may have put it best . . .

And at the end of the story:

. . . nowhere to go but up."
Next: Jim Morris of Vancouver looks at the Vancouver Canucks.

Non-publishable:

Eds: Petr (not Peter) in the following is correct. Macdonald is lowercase "d."

Page 1 advisories

The CP Main Desk moves an advisory listing possible Page 1 story choices at 5 p.m. and 4 a.m. It includes a top photo, three top news stories and a "buzz" story – something that may be the topic of conversation at the coffee shop or water cooler.

Follow this style:

Page-1, Advisory
Page 1 Advisory for Monday, Aug. 12
Eds: CP suggests the following stories for front-page consideration:
TOP PHOTO
OTTAWA — New security personnel line the hall outside the office of Prime Minister Harper at the House of Commons on Monday.
MOUSSAOUI SAYS HE AND SHOE-BOMBER WERE TO ATTACK WHITE HOUSE

ALEXANDRIA, Va. — In a startling admission to a jury that is weighing whether he lives or dies, al-Qaida conspirator Zacarias Moussaoui testifies that he and would-be shoe bomber Richard Reid were supposed to hijack a fifth airplane on Sept. 11, 2001, and crash it into the White House. 850 words. See AP Photos. Moussaoui, 3rd Writethru. Moved.

HARPER TO SHOW AMERICANS A WARMER APPROACH
OTTAWA — Prime Minister Stephen Harper meets later this week with U.S. President George Bush and Mexican President Vincente Fox in Cancun. It's the first opportunity for Harper to show off his government's warm new approach towards Canada-U.S. relations. But Harper will also have to push his American counterpart on lingering irritants such as softwood lumber and a new plan from Washington to require Canadians to use passports at the border. 500 words. By Jennifer Ditchburn. Harper-Bush-Meeting, 2nd Writethru. Moved.

LONEY'S FAMILY KEPT HIS SEXUALITY A SECRET AMID SAFETY FEARS
UNDATED — The family of freed Christian peace activist James Loney kept his sexual orientation quiet out of fear for his safety while in captivity, Christian Peacemakers Teams co-director Doug Pritchard said Monday as the northern Ontario city of Sault Ste. Marie continued its preparations for Loney's arrival home. 600 words. By Gregory Bonnell and Keith Leslie. See CP Photos. Cda-Iraq-Hostages, 3rd Writethru. Moved.

The buzz . . .
BATTLE HEATING UP BETWEEN MEDIA AND PMO
OTTAWA — Security on Parliament Hill barred reporters from attending a pair of Stephen Harper photo opportunities Monday as the Prime Minister's Office flexed its media messaging muscles. It was a skirmish in a battle that may start to resonate beyond the cosy precincts of the Peace Tower as the Conservatives threaten to hold secret cabinet meetings and withhold information about visiting heads of state. 600 words. By Bruce Cheadle. Harper-Media-Battle. Moved.

Long-range advisories

1. Advance billing on special projects, foreign travel and other major assignments means better play for CP stories. Editors will look for the copy and use the advance notice to block out space in editions days ahead of time. A CP advance advisory also gives papers a chance to plan local follows, often a key selling point. An example:

VE-Day, Advisory
CP series planned for 60th anniversary of VE-Day
MANAGING EDITORS, NEWS EDITORS, FEATURE EDITORS, SPECIAL SUPPLEMENT EDITORS:
CP has begun moving stories and features to mark the 60th anniversary of Victory in Europe during the Second World War.

Since Thursday, Feb. 24, a weekly historical countdown to May 8, designed for use in weekend editions, has been moving. Slugged VE-Day-Countdown, it is a chronological list of the major war news from 60 years ago the following week. For instance, the item that moves this Thursday, March 31, covers the week of April 3-9. Each Countdown is accompanied by an archival photo.

Beginning Thursday, March 31, a series of weekly newsfeatures that focus on a specific aspect of the end of the war will move. All will be accompanied by pictures. The lineup includes:

— March 31: The war so far: a look at Canada's role in the fight to free Europe from the Nazis. By John Ward. With Chronology. VE-Day-Scenesetter.

— April 7: The Nazi atrocities hit home. Canadians liberate concentration camps in Holland. By Lorraine Turchansky. VE-Day-Camps.

— April 14: The conscription controversy. A shortage of trained infantry brings forward yet again a divisive issue just months before the war's end. By Les Perreaux. VE-Day-Conscription.

— April 21: Hope on the homefront. Canadians look forward to peace. By Michelle MacAfee. VE-Day-Homefront.

— April 28: The Dutch connection. The Canadian military's long campaign in Holland has lasting effects at home when 1,800 Dutch war brides emigrate to Canada. By Chris Morris. VE-Day-War-Brides.

— May 2: Soldiers on the front lines in Holland remember what it was like when the guns were finally silent. By John Ward. VE-Day-End-of-War. Disaster on the homefront: VE-Day celebrations turn ugly in Halifax. By Keith Bonnell. VE-Day-Riots. With original CP stories from Germany reporting the troops' reaction to the end of the war; and another from France covering the scene of the German military surrender.

Another advisory will move later detailing our plans for covering the commemorative services associated with VE-Day.

If you have questions, requests or suggestions, please call or e-mail Senior Supervising Editor Patti Tasko (416-507-2153, ptasko@cp.org)

CP TORONTO

Other advisories

The range of potential advisories is unbounded.

There is a simple test: If an editor was on deadline or planning ahead, would a CP advisory help?

By no means complete, here is a selection of other advisories:

Top-Copy-Terror-Bill
Top copy: Ralph Klein says he's no Darth Vader on public health care

Eds: Please note the following top copy to move by 16:00 PST:

VANCOUVER — Alberta Premier Ralph Klein denies he is

the Darth Vader of health care, setting out to destroy the public system. But he told a Vancouver audience change is necessary. 500 words. By Terri Theodore. Klein-B.C.

Cda-Iraq-Hostages, Advisory
Arrival in Toronto of hostage freed in Iraq delayed until Sunday
Eds: The flight of Christian Peacemaker Teams member James Loney, recently freed after nearly four months in Iraq, has been delayed. His flight now is believed to be arriving at 1:07 p.m. EST Sunday at Pearson International Airport, Terminal 1. The group says Loney will have a private visit with relatives, then make a brief statement to media at the airport.
CP reporters and photographers are staffing.
CP TORONTO

Brownwich, Advisory
Trial of former P.E.I. cabinet minister resumes at 10 a.m. AST Monday
Eds: The trial of former P.E.I. cabinet minister Ethel Brownwich resumes at 10 a.m. AST Monday with testimony from her secretary. CP's Derrick Toth is staffing and expects to file a story by noon AST, depending on the testimony.
CP HALIFAX

Aboriginal-Occupation, Advisory
First Nations news conference in Maycroft, Alta., cancelled
Eds: The Maycroft, Alta., budget item Aboriginal Occupation will not be available. A news conference scheduled for 2 p.m. MDT Thursday was cancelled. An unbudgeted 250-word story will move by 5 p.m. MDT, and if there are further developments later in the day an advisory will be sent outlining coverage plans.
CP EDMONTON

Calendar and Look-Ahead

Few features of journalism can match the exhilaration of covering a sudden, fast-breaking story. Few frustrations can match trying to catch up with a major story that could have been foreseen and planned for if it hadn't been for neglected datebooking.

Every CP bureau and department seeks out hints of news to come in the reams of news releases, newsletters, e-mails, press kits and other material that are directed its way.

CP keeps track of coming events for its own coverage planning and to inform its newspaper and broadcast customers. There are two main advisories focused on scheduled news events, the weekly **Look-Ahead** list and the daily **Calendar**.

The Look-Ahead is assembled by Toronto Main Desk from a central electronic datebook maintained by bureaus and departments. It moves each Friday morning at about 5 a.m. eastern time.

Each Look-Ahead covers events, by date, from the Sunday of the coming weekend through two weeks down the road. The Calendar, also prepared by Main Desk, lists events for the following day and is transmitted at about 3:30 p.m. eastern time with updated versions at about 6 p.m. and 3:30 a.m. The Calendar sent Fridays covers events through Monday.

The format for contributions to both these lists is the same: a brief description of the event, time, place and any other information useful to regional newspapers or broadcasters who may plan to cover. An **x-** in front of the placeline denotes that CP is staffing the event; a **y-** denotes picture coverage; and a **z-** denotes graphics coverage.

Examples:

> HALIFAX — Nova Scotia standing committee on human resources to discuss appointments to agencies, boards and commissions. (9 a.m. at Room 1, 3rd floor, Dennis building, 1740 Granville St.)

> x-MONTREAL — Maurice (Mom) Boucher, leader of the Hells Angels in Quebec, faces two counts of first-degree murder and one count of attempted murder for allegedly ordering the deaths of two prison guards in 1997. (9:30 a.m. at Courthouse, Room 5.01.)

> MONT-STE-ANNE, Que. — Standards Council of Canada organized the first-ever national Standards System conference, featuring delegates from the World Bank, Hydro-Quebec and the international Organization for Standardization. (Chateau Mont-Ste-Anne Resort and Convention Centre.)

- Specify when times, places are unavailable. But such detail, or an explanation for its absence, is essential when the event carries an **x-**. Newspapers and broadcasters find such information helpful and the stories they get are shared with CP.

- Description of the event should be brief but still spell out its news interest.

Not: Joe Saxon appears in court.

But: Joe Saxon, accused of attacking a neighbour with an electric weed trimmer, stands trial for first-degree murder.

- Follow format with care. Reworking entries to conform is time-wasting.

- Entries are in full – no in-house abbreviations such as newser for news conference. Full names and titles are required, as they would be in a news story.

Calendar updates and changes

When it is necessary to update, correct, delete or add a Calendar item, include a word specific to the topic in the slug. It should be **Calendar-Inuit** so editors can easily pinpoint what is being changed:

Calendar-Inuit
Inuit meeting postponed until May 13
Eds: Please note that the Calendar item from IQALUIT, Nunavut, on the meeting of Inuit leaders is incorrect. The meeting has been postponed until May 13.
CP EDMONTON

Fronts advisories

Readers of the CP news service are naturally interested in what newspapers and broadcasters are doing with the major national and international stories of the day. And they like to know what local or regional stories are getting big play in papers elsewhere.

A routine item called a **Fronts Advisory** is CP's method of letting people across the country know about the front-page picture and news choices of newspapers in most major cities. Each bureau is responsible for preparing and sending these advisories as soon as local papers are available.

As well, the advisories include brief notes on major play for CP's work — especially section fronts and op-ed pages — as a form of instant feedback on how staff's work is received.

Advisories follow these formats:

For a newspaper:

Advisory-Fronts-Globe
Globe and Mail fronts for Tuesday, March 28
WASHINGTON (Staff) — Zacarias Moussaoui stuns court with testimony. (COVERED)
TP-01, Mexico (Staff) — Mexican leader urges Canada to open door to "guest workers." (PICKING UP)
UNDATED (Staff) — Foreign labourers shown the door. (MAIN ELEMENTS COVERED PREVIOUSLY)
UNDATED (Staff) — Hostage's private life kept hidden. (COVERED)
PARIS (Staff) — A bitter end to Europe's lifetime jobs? (NOT MATCHING)
MAIN PHOTO:
WASHINGTON (AP) _ Court; artist's rendering.

For a TV news broadcast:

CBC-News-Advisory
CBC National News, Sunday, March 27

JERUSALEM — Voter turnout expected to be weak in this week's Israeli election; there's no standout, strong candidate, although analysts say the election is crucial because the main issue is how to make peace with the Palestinians. COVERED.

RAMALLAH, West Bank — Palestinians watching this week's Israeli election closely, but they are also preoccupied with local politics, as the untried Hamas government moves ahead and donor countries threaten to cut off aid if Hamas does not change its stance on Israel. COVERED.

VANCOUVER — Inderjit Singh Reyat, currently serving time for his role in the Air India bombings, goes on trial for perjury after testifying that he knew nothing about a plot to blow up the plane; meanwhile, lawyers for Ripudaman Singh Malik were also in court on Monday; he is suing the a B.C. government agency after he was banned from running a credit union. COVERED.

ALEXANDRIA, Va. — Zacarias Moussaoui tells jury he knew in advance of the Sept. 11 plot and deliberately kept the information from federal investigators; he says he and co-conspirator Richard Reed had been supposed to take a fourth plane and crash it into the White House; minutes before making the admissions he denied knowing anything about the plot. COVERED.

KANDAHAR, Afghanistan — Air base where Canadians are stationed came under mortar fire Monday night; no one hurt. COVERED.

SAULT STE. MARIE, Ont. — Family and friends of Christian Peacemaker Teams member James Loney welcome his safe return; Christian Peacemakers plan to pull out the three members it has left in Iraq. COVERED.

MONTREAL — Three separate attacks are made against Jewish properties. COVERED.

NORTH HATLEY, Que. — One of the oldest inns in Quebec's Eastern Townships is destroyed by fire. COVERED.

ST. JOHN'S, N.L. — Province hit by 30 centimetres of snow; schools and businesses closed for the day and flights are cancelled; forecast calls for snow and wind into Tuesday. COVERED.

NEW YORK — Sinkhole caused by broken water main swallows SUV. COVERED.

• A scan of story queues in the computer usually reveals whether national or international stories are covered. If in doubt, consult Toronto Main Desk.

• Notations such as **COVERED** are not needed on stories credited to CP or AP.

• Some variation of **COVERED PREVIOUSLY** is acceptable for backgrounders and features. But consult archives and include a day or date for hard-news stories that CP has covered before.

- Fronts advisories are sent with **M**-type message headers.

- Credits of syndicates or supplementary services are not abbreviated (e.g. **Knight-Ridder**, not **K-R**).

- Placelines are not boldfaced.

- Do not use unfamiliar abbreviations and insider lingo in fronts advisories. They are read by people who do not work in the industry.

News Budgets

Putting together a newspaper, newscast or online news site without a clue of what will be available would be like ordering dinner without a menu. Surprises are certain but so is a sense of queasy uncertainty.

CP tells editors and other readers of the wire what's cooking four times a day with an advisory called the **News Budget**. It details the top stories in sight, grouped in the categories of domestic, world, business, lifestyles, entertainment, travel and sports news.

The budget is considered essential reading as editors across the country convene news meetings to plan story play. It is also of great interest to the CP clients who subscribe to the wire for business reasons. Each budget entry provides:

- A summary of the story's content and approach, phrased attractively.

- Expected wordage to help plot a paper's space needs.

- Writer's byline, if applicable.

- What developments are expected that could change the story.

- What illustrations and Quicks will be provided.

- Whether sidebars are planned, whether other current stories are related.

- Whether the story might interest other departments.

- The keyword slug under which the story can be found in computer queues.

Putting together the budget starts with bureau desk staff, news editors and department editors, who consider the top stories of the day in their regions and specialties and how they can be presented to qualify for the budget.

Staff-written spot stories, analyses, backgrounders and features almost always rate a place. So do the best pickups from newspapers.

Breadth of interest and the quality of the copy are the major criteria. Good writing, background information and local colour can elevate a story from strictly regional interest to a place on the News Budget.

Budget lines are updated as often as four times during a 24-hour cycle. From Monday to Friday, general news, world and sports lines are updated at 1 p.m., 3 p.m., 7:30 p.m. and 1 a.m. ET (midnight on Fridays). Business lines move at 1 p.m., 3 p.m., 7:30 p.m. and 10 p.m., while life-entertainment lines are moved at 1 p.m., 3 p.m. and 6 p.m. (5 p.m. on Fridays). Lines usually move twice a day on Saturdays and three times on Sundays, more if needed.

Lines from the sports, business, life-entertainment and world queues are handled within those departments, while all general Canadian news lines are messaged to Toronto Main Desk. For news, the 1 p.m. advisory focuses on the top stories that CP is covering that day as known at that hour. Slugs and placelines are identified to the extent they are known. At 3 p.m. Main Desk moves a 1st Writethru, which updates and expands on the items in the first advisory. A 2nd Writethru moves by 7:30 p.m., adding any new budgeted top stories that have developed since 3 p.m. and any major changes to major stories, either on the wire or anticipated. The final Writethru at 1 a.m. reviews all top copy that still stands, plus any fresh items anticipated in the next couple of hours. Then, at 1 p.m. the next day, the slate is wiped clean and the budget begins again, itemizing only items that have moved since 1 a.m. The other departments follow a similar format.

Main Desk should be messaged any additions and updates at least 30 minutes before the News Budget is scheduled to move. It may be possible to squeeze in items after that, but this should be reserved for late-breaking material. A top copy advisory can be sent if the development misses the News Budget.

Here is how this works on a typical story, as it might change through the day. At 1 p.m., the line is written from the information in the Calendar because nothing new is known:

> **OTTAWA** – Health Minister Tony Clement meets with counterparts from other major western countries Wednesday to discuss preparations for controlling the spread of the deadly bird flu virus H5N1. 550 words. By Helen Branswell. See CP Photo. Countries-Fight-Flu.

At 3 p.m., the budget line is updated with Clement's comments as the meeting breaks up. There is already an item on the wire, but a Writethru is in the works, so the line notes this:

> **OTTAWA** – After meeting with his counterparts from other major western countries Wednesday, Health Minister Tony Clement said they had productive discussions on how they could cope with expected outbreaks of the H5N1 influenza virus. 550 words. By Helen Branswell. See CP Photo OTT105. Countries-Fight-Flu, 1st Writethru. Early story has moved.

At 7:30 p.m., more details can be included. If another Writethru is anticipated this should be added:

> **OTTAWA** – Health Minister Tony Clement and his counterparts from other major western countries agreed Wednesday on protocols for fighting the spread of the H5N1 influenza virus. Critics, meanwhile, noted the supply of anti-flu medicine is not nearly enough to cover even 20 per cent of the populations of these countries. 675 words. By Helen Branswell. See CP Photo OTT105. Terrorist-Bioterror, 2nd Writethru. Has moved; 3rd Writethru expected by 20:00.

At 1 a.m., an updated version of the 7:30 p.m. line is carried again because the item is still a top one of interest to afternoon papers publishing later that day.

Budget lines should be organized as follows:

- The placeline, capped and boldface.

- A descriptive line. This requires as much care as the lead sentence of the story – both are intended to attract interest and convey information. Simply using the lead paragraph as a budget line doesn't always work.

- Wordage of the story or the best possible estimate.

- **CP Backgrounder, CP News Analysis, Newsmaker** or **Roundup** can also be used here to signify the nature of the story.

- Byline.

- Photos and Graphics that are to be sent. Include the number (e.g. **CPT102**) if available.

- Related stories, or sidebars, QuickFacts or QuickQuotes are pointed out, as well as any other specific information (**Business interest, Out slug,** for instance).

- Keyword slugline, which newspaper editors will look for when seeking the copy. It must be identical on the story.

- After the slugline, include information about the timing of the story and the wires it will move on: **Moves Business (B) and General (G) Datafile only after 8 p.m. ET news conference.**

More examples:

> **PRINCE GEORGE, B.C.** – British Columbia's forest industry delivers an update Wednesday on a devastating pine-beetle infestation said to be the worst in the province's history. The pest is damaging billions of dollars worth of timber. 550 words. By Steve Mertl. Business interest. B.C.-Pine-Beetle. Moves Regional (D) after 9 p.m. ET news conference.

- Although this budget line was submitted before the news conference, it helpfully includes context on why it is expected to be newsworthy. Something lame – **B.C. foresters hold news conference** – does nothing to encourage use of the story.

- The possible interest of this story to another newspaper department – business in this case – is noted. Variations include **Lifestyles interest, Entertainment interest, Sports interest**. Or **Newspage interest** for stories budgeted under any of those categories.

OTTAWA – Parliament concludes a passionate debate about same-sex marriage with a vote. 500 words. By Stephen Thorne. See CP Photos. With Vars Same-Sex. Same-Sex-Vote. 1st Writethru moves after debate resumes at 18:00; early story moved.

- Developments at a specific time that will result in an update to a budgeted story are noted, especially if copy is likely to be late or the developments fall when key newspaper deadlines are approaching.

TORONTO – The Ontario government has reached a deal that will allow thousands of teachers to retire at an earlier age, clearing the way for the hiring of younger – and cheaper – replacements. 450 words. With QuickFacts and Teachers-Pensions. TOR OUT. Teachers. Moves Regional (C).

- Pickups from newspapers that are subject to **locals OUT** codes – protection from a competitor's use of the story – are noted, as are any embargoes.

- Stories that will move with a regional designator are also noted.

Sometimes CP is aware of events that will produce news but is uncertain whether the developments will rate a budgeted story. Tip lines can be used to highlight such news. Tip lines can also be used to promote secondary stories that have already moved. Follow budget line style, though by necessity they often have less information and sometimes even lack a slug.

CP is also following:
EDMONTON – Alberta Premier Ralph Klein and caucus meet to discuss options to resolve teachers strike. Alta-Teachers-Dispute. Copy develops following end of meeting, likely 19:00 ET.

If a tip line on a budget advisory notes that the story has moved, and if the story is not developing further, it can be dropped from the next advisory.

Stories that are not worth budgeting but accompany other budgeted stories, as well as routine items such as basketball roundups, can be included in the budget lines under a **See also:** slug.

See also:
– Budget-Seniors
– Budget-Agriculture
– Budget-QuickFacts

See also:
– NBA-Rdp

A particularly important news event can produce a number of related stories for the budget. They should be grouped under an appropriate subhead: Federal Budget, Stanley Cup Final.

Sometimes stories don't pan out as expected. When this happens, or copy for some reason is not available, an advisory is issued to delete the story from the budget.

For example:

Budget-Klein, Advisory
Ralph Klein speech cancelled
   Eds: Please delete Edmonton-placelined Klein from the News Budget. Speech cancelled due to minor illness.
   CP Edmonton

Quicks and formatted items

The traditional sentence and paragraph is not always the most effective way to present data, especially to time-strapped readers.

Many publishers, including newspapers, websites and magazines, have moved to using summaries, capsules and other digests of information — often along with eye-catching graphics — that can be absorbed quickly. It is usually possible to present information in such ways without sacrificing the detail that readers look for.

There is virtually no limit on the different formats that can be employed to help present information in a cohesive and accessible way. On the CP Wire, some of the more common instruments are **At-a-Glances, Q and A's, Highlights** and **Quicks**. Each has a different look but offers the same thing: fast access to information that is important, helpful or just plain interesting. These techniques can be embedded as well into a traditional story format through the use of bullets.

This packaging of information can also provide material for CP's print graphics, for use in newspapers, and interactive graphics, which are featured on websites. Graphics offer a dynamic way of presenting factual and background material.

See **Graphics**, page 370.

Information contained in a Quick can be transferred into an attractive graphic that gives editors visual content for their news pages.

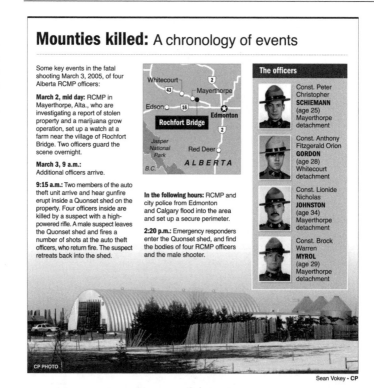

Mounties killed: A chronology of events

Some key events in the fatal shooting March 3, 2005, of four Alberta RCMP officers:

March 2, mid day: RCMP in Mayerthorpe, Alta., who are investigating a report of stolen property and a marijuana grow operation, set up a watch at a farm near the village of Rochfort Bridge. Two officers guard the scene overnight.

March 3, 9 a.m.: Additional officers arrive.

9:15 a.m.: Two members of the auto theft unit arrive and hear gunfire erupt inside a Quonset shed on the property. Four officers inside are killed by a suspect with a high-powered rifle. A male suspect leaves the Quonset shed and fires a number of shots at the auto theft officers, who return fire. The suspect retreats back into the shed.

In the following hours: RCMP and city police from Edmonton and Calgary flood into the area and set up a secure perimeter.

2:20 p.m.: Emergency responders enter the Quonset shed, and find the bodies of four RCMP officers and the male shooter.

Whitecourt · 43 · 2 · Mayerthorpe
Edson · 16 · Edmonton
Rochfort Bridge · 2
Jasper National Park · Red Deer
B.C. · ALBERTA

The officers

Const. Peter Christopher **SCHIEMANN** (age 25) Mayerthorpe detachment

Const. Anthony Fitzgerald Orion **GORDON** (age 28) Whitecourt detachment

Const. Lionide Nicholas **JOHNSTON** (age 34) Mayerthorpe detachment

Const. Brock Warren **MYROL** (age 29) Mayerthorpe detachment

CP PHOTO

Sean Vokey - CP

Bullets

Simple, yet effective formatting can be done within the body of a story with bullets. They can be either long or short, but should always follow a parallel structure.

Punctuation and capitalization in short bullets of a few words can be eliminated without hampering readability:

> The symptoms of a heart attack include:
> — dizziness
> — shortness of breath
> — confusion
> — chest pain
> — numbness in the left arm

But if the material is longer or would stand on its own as a sentence, uppercase the first letter of the first word in each bullet and use periods at the end of each one:

> The leaders of the Asia-Pacific Ecoonomic Co-operation forum outlined measures to combat bird flu at the end of their summit Saturday. The measures include:
> — Committing member countries to effective surveillance to prepare for and reduce the effects of a human pandemic.
> — Supporting the avian flu preparedness efforts of the World Health Organization.
> — Compiling lists of experts who could respond to the early stages of an outbreak.
> — Enhancing public awareness.

At-a-Glance

When a major story is breaking here, there and everywhere, the occasion calls for an At-a-Glance:

> **Terrorism-Glance ❶**
> **Terrorism-at-a-Glance**
> **By The Canadian Press ❷**
> Major developments Thursday related to the war on terrorism:❸
> – ❹ Canadian military mission is to be operating by the weekend if everything goes according to plan in Afghanistan, commanding officer says.
> — — — ❺
> – Canadian soldiers use beige paint, brushes and sand bags to adapt their forest-green camouflage for the desert environment of Kandahar.
> — — —
> – President **George W. Bush❻** says Geneva Convention

applies to Taliban prisoners but not to captured al-Qaida terrorists; he refuses ❼ to classify either as prisoners of war.

— — —

– 1,300 people give notice they may sue New York City for a total of $7.18 billion for alleged negligence during recovery and cleanup of World Trade Center site. ❽

— — —

– Plane carrying 28 detainees lands at Guantanamo Bay❾ naval base in Cuba...❿

❶ **Keyword** slug is variation of the slug on the main story the Glance accompanies **(Terrorism)**.

❷ Not bylined except for the **CP credit**, boldface, centred.

❸ Glances accompany rapidly developing stories. They are frequently **updated** to keep pace with events.

❹ Each paragraph is indented and preceded by a boldface **dash** and a **space**. It ends with a period, not a semicolon.

❺ Each paragraph is separated by **three dashes**, boldface, centred.

❻ **Names** are boldfaced.

❼ Entries are written in the **present tense** whenever possible to lend immediacy. Avoid headline writing that drops articles and auxiliary verbs. Each paragraph should be constructed in the same pattern for ease of reading.

❽ Paragraphs should not exceed **30 words**. Sentences are kept concise but not to the point where reader understanding or significant detail is sacrificed.

❾ **Location** is noted where the entry concerns a development away from the centre of the action.

❿ An At-a-Glance includes material that is dealt with at least briefly in the **main story**. But a Glance of more than eight entries likely includes secondary material that should be trimmed.

Highlights

When complex elements of a story need summarizing, use Highlights.

Fedbudget-Highlights ❶
URGENT
Federal budget highlights ❷
　❸OTTAWA (CP) — Highlights of the federal budget
presented Thursday: ❹
　— ❺ About 50,000 new home-buyers are eligible for loan
guarantees of up to $3,000.
　　　　　　　　　　　　— — — ❻
　— Builders are offered❼ interest-free loans of up to $7,500
for each rental unit constructed in tight-market areas. ❽
　　　　　　　　　— — —
　— One-third of Canada's 16 million income-tax payers will be
taxed less but few will save more than $100. ❾
　　　　　　　　　— — —
　— Farmers facing bankruptcy ❿ . . .

---

❶ **Keyword** slug is a variation of the slug on the main story the Highlights accompany **(Bgt)**.

❷ Carries **headline** but no **byline**.

❸ Usually **placelined** because it pulls together the key points of a major story focused in a single centre.

❹ Usually accompanies fully developed stories. **Rarely requires updating.**

❺ Each paragraph is indented and preceded by a boldface **dash** and a **space**. It ends with a **period**, not a semicolon.

❻ Each paragraph is separated by **three dashes**, boldface, centred.

Note: Short sections of Highlights included in the text of a story — often referred to as **bullets** — are not separated by dashes.

❼ Entries are written in the **present tense** whenever possible to lend immediacy. Avoid headline writing that drops articles and auxiliary verbs. Each paragraph should be constructed in the same pattern for ease of reading.
— Sales tax rises to eight per cent Sept. 1.
— Single parents get child-care deduction up to $2,000.

❽ Paragraphs should not exceed 25 words. Sentences are kept concise but not to the point where reader understanding or significant detail is sacrificed.

❾ Highlights emphasize the key points of a story most closely affecting readers' lives, give specific examples and avoid jargon.

Not: Benefit eligibility for involuntary job-seekers reduced by one week.

But: Laid-off workers get unemployment pay after two weeks instead of three.

❿ Highlights include material that is dealt with at least briefly in the main story. Secondary items are not included. There should be no more than six entries.

Quicks

Almost every good story presents an opportunity for a **QuickFacts, QuickList, QuickSketch** or **QuickQuotes**, whether hard news or feature.

Quickly defined, Quicks are short, sharp collections of information — facts, figures, trivia, biographical snapshots, memorable quotations.

These features are boxed for display or brightened by an accompanying CP Graphic to break up fields of grey type and offer interesting highlights, sidelights or insights into the news.

There is no real limit on what can go into a Quick.

Among other things, Quicks can:

• Provide a tight summary of main points from a high-profile meeting.

• Explain technical language from any kind of specialized get-together.

• Provide a calendar of main events at a multiple-day conference.

• Recite a selection of worthwhile jokes from a comedy festival or one-liners from an entertainer's news conference.

And especially, never neglect a Quick when it can give readers news they can use:

• What a new innovation means to you.

• How to tell if you've got the problem.

• What you can do about it.

• How the program works.

• Where to go for information.

• Pitfalls to watch for.

A Quick should rarely consist only of information already reported in the main news story. It may blend elements of the story with supplementary material from reference works or other sources. Or it may be a collection of related snippets not found anywhere else. It is also a good way to carry essential information that would bog down the main story. In a story, for instance, on the Canada's worst roads, the names of the roads can belisted in a Quick, leaving room in the story for quotes, comments and background.

Formats are highly adaptable. Informative, interesting and amusing are the main criteria. Question-and-answer formats are especially useful for complicated subjects.

Some guidelines:

• Quicks can be either placelined or undated. They are not bylined apart from CP credit.

• Quicks should be snappy. Bare-bones, not story form. Unlike At-a-Glances and Highlights, complete sentences not required. Nor detailed tie-ins to main story. **Here are** not a mandatory introduction.

Not: **Here are some facts and figures about Yugoslavia, where civil war has claimed hundreds of lives in recent days:**

But: Facts and figures on Yugoslavia, embroiled in civil war:

Not: Early career: Born in 1920 to vaudeville entertainers, Rooney made his first stage appearance at 15 months. He made his film debut in silent-era short subjects at six and went on to star as perpetual juvenile Andy Hardy in a popular MGM series that ran from 1936 to 1946.

But: Early career: Born 1920 to vaudevillians. Stage debut at 15 months, on screen from age six. Top box-office draw in Andy Hardy series 1936-46.

• Quicks should be brief; 100 to 250 words is ideal. Anything longer should be packaged as something else.

• As in regular news copy, prefer the specific to the general. In some circumstances, Quicks can be used to provide detail that would clutter up the main story, such as province-by-province comparisons or statistical data.

Not: Showed interest in politics from early age.

But: At nine, insisted on joining father at Pierre Trudeau campaign rally.

Not: Union seeks 11 per cent pay increase over two years.

But: Union wants 76 cents hourly in first year and 67 cents in second half of two-year contract, net rise of 11 per cent over average hourly wage of $12.79.

• Try to include something offbeat in each Quick. A funny or shocking statement is a good lead-in to a collection of otherwise sober QuickQuotes or a good kicker to close a straightforward QuickSketch. An oddball statistic can enliven a businesslike QuickFacts (e.g. **stacked in a pile, copies of the committee's reports would reach higher than the 100-metre Parliament Building Peace Tower**). Don't overlook colourful personal traits in QuickSketches (e.g. **Jean Chrétien's deliberately folksy English, George Burns's trademark cigar**).

- QuickQuotes can expand on statements that appear in the main story. They can offer more direct quotes on statements that are treated briefly, or actual words for paraphrased material, or new quotes that weren't essential to the story. Quotes are separated by **three-em dashes**, boldfaced, centred. Limit the selection to four or five, whether from a single person or several principals in an event. Where essential quotes run too long for the Quick format, adopt a different slug (**Trudeau-Quotes**).

- QuickTips can offer practical information for readers: five steps to healthier meals, seven ways to organize cupboards, etc.

- Don't use all-caps in headings.

Some examples:

Visiting-Elders-QuickFacts
By The Canadian Press
Some tips from the Baycrest Centre on visiting older relatives:
—Show respect in everything you say or do.
—Place yourself at eye level. If your relative is in a wheelchair, sit on a chair.
—Engage in an activity that is comforting, such as storytelling.
—Animate your discussion with gestures. For example, touch the person's hair as you say, "Your hair looks pretty."
—Use a normal conversational tone.
—Be patient. Your relative may need time to absorb what you are saying before responding.
—If talk is difficult, communicate in another way, perhaps by combing hair, massaging hands with lotion or giving a hug.
On the Net: www.baycrest.org

TV-Gemini-QuickQuotes
By The Canadian Press
Some of what was said at Sunday night's Gemini awards for Canadian television:
"I have to thank Paul Haggis for being clinically insane." – Paul Gross thanking Due South's producer after winning his best actor award.

— — —

"No matter how much time I'm forced to live in exile I'm always first, last and foremost a Canadian. This land is your land, this land is my land, from the big snowy part to the other big snowy part." – Stephen McHattie, who won a best actor award for Life With Billy.

Note: Prefer the quote, then the attribution and context, if appropriate.

Cabinet-Day-QuickSketch

By The Canadian Press

A sketch of Stockwell Day, named federal minister of public safety on Monday: ordon Lightfoot's career:

Political history: Served in Alberta legislature for 14 years, held three cabinet posts. First leader of the Canadian Alliance in 2000. Lost leadership to Stephen Harper in 2002.

Private career: Counsellor and administrator at Christian school in Alberta.

Political views: Promotes traditional conservative policies of tax cuts, increased military spending, tougher law-and-order measures.

Famous for: Arriving at a news conference on a personal watercraft while Alliance leader.

Quote: "If you're looking for dinosaur politics, you need to look at the Liberals." — Day following revelations he believed the earth was only 6,000 years old, suggesting dinosaurs existed alongside man.

Editorial symposiums

Some cynic once defined editorial writers as bandits who descend from the hills when a battle is over to shoot the wounded.

But at their best, newspaper editorial pages are in the thick of the fray, armed with argument, reason, wit and not-so-common common sense.

A selection of excerpts from well-turned editorials can reflect the depth of debate and range of opinion at play on important national and world issues — federal elections, key developments in the constitutional arena and the like.

Such selections are provided by CP in an **Editorial Symposium**, a sampling of what newspapers countrywide have to say.

Symposiums are most often started by Head Office, via Toronto Main Desk, but bureaus and departments are welcome to suggest appropriate topics. Requests for symposiums from member newspapers should always be referred to Toronto.

Providing a truly national, representative selection is essential. Metropolitan newspapers aren't alone in having opinions worth reading; a small-town view of events can be equally provocative.

Bureaus should actively solicit contributions from newspapers in their region, delivered electronically or by fax. The timeliness of a symposium effectively ends about 24 hours after it starts, so waiting for mailed copies of papers is not practical.

Here's what the first selection looks like:

FedBgt-Symposium
Editorial Symposium on federal budget
                              By The Canadian Press
   Selections from newspaper editorials and columnists, with headlines, following Monday's federal budget:
New budget misses mark
   Timmins Press: Finance Minister Jim Flaherty wanted to ...

For subsequent contributions:

FedBgt-Symposium, add
Add Editorial Symposium on federal budget

Government performs fiscal exorcism
   Toronto Star: Call it a budget of penance for 20 years ...

•   Keep excerpts brief. They should rarely exceed 100 words. Choose sentences that fairly summarize the editorial position.

• Use *ellipses* (three periods) to indicate material omitted. But give preference to blocks of comment that can be run without ellipses, since too many of them can create a poor typographical effect.

• Any citations must be exactly as printed. Paraphrasing isn't allowed.

• Newspaper names are boldface, uppercase and lowercase and followed by a colon.

• Contributions take a G-type designator and are sent on the same circuits normally used for general news copy.

Headlines

General

Headlines are the hidden weapons of writers and editors. More than any other element, a strong headline can grab the attention of readers and lure them into a story. A good headline – specific, lively and concise – should tell a reader everything he needs to know about the story, but still make him want to read more.

Headline writing is a special art. Some editors seem to have a natural knack for it. Others have to work at it. It is kind of like solving a crossword puzzle – practice makes it easier because you learn the little tricks. But accuracy always comes before cleverness. Many readers stop at the headline; if it gives them a misleading impression of the story, they will take that with them. Headlines must face the same tests of accuracy and fairness as all other publishable copy. The headline can't say Five Dead in Prison Riot if this is based on unconfirmed TV reports quoting unnamed sources. Such information must be qualified in a headline the same way it would be in the body of the story. Headline style allows statements to be condensed but not by sacrificing accuracy on crucial points.

Headline writing is strongly influenced by the amount of space an editor has to work with. For a newspaper editor, this can vary greatly depending on layout. For a news agency or online editor, the space is usually the same on each story. No matter what the length, a good headline should use short, punchy words that accurately and vigorously sell the story.

Headline writing tips

Writing a good headline takes time. Allow enough. And try the following:

1. Draft or edit the headline before you write or edit the story. This may help you to identify the essential elements that must be included. After you have written or edited the story, you may be too familiar with it to easily spot headlines that are incomplete or hard to understand.

2. Think about what information must be included in the headline. Will it need a locator? What are the key elements of the story? Do you need to signal what sort of story it is? This applies mostly to departmental copy, such as sports, business or entertainment.

3. Write a working headline that includes all the essential information. The headline should really be a précis of the story, with enough detail that the reader can take away a complete idea or thought without needing further information.

4. Try to improve the language in your working headline to make it snappier, breezier, more colourful and definitive. Look at the words you have used. Can you pump up the language and create stronger images? How about a wordplay – not a bad pun, but a twist of phrasing? Techniques such as rhyming words and alliteration can brighten up a headline. On a story about the untimely death of Wiarton Willie a few days before his starring role on Groundhog Day, one headline read: **Dead Willie? Cynics Smell a Rat.**

5. Verbs are vital! A strong, active verb can help create a mental picture. And write in the present tense. Make it **Pilots OK Airline Merger to Save Jobs**, not **Pilots Have Oked Airline Merger to Save Jobs.**

6. Does the headline encapsulate the emotion or drama in the story?

7. Look to quotes for inspiration. Is there a great quote that sums up the story? Can it be used or paraphased in the headline?

8. Are there enough specifics in the headline? Vague headlines leave no impression with the reader. Many everyday headlines can be jazzed up with just a few more details. The specific **Headless Torso Found in Topless Bar** is much more attractive than the generic **Body Found in Bar.** On CP's first report that former prime minister Pierre Trudeau was seriously ill, the headline was: **Ex-prime minister Pierre Trudeau not feeling well.** This was not detailed enough to be useful to the reader, and the source of the news should also have been included. Much better: **Pierre Trudeau 'not well'; receiving medical care, his sons say.**

9. Watch for times when a description or title is better than a name. While it is OK to refer to the prime minister only as **Harper** in a headline, don't use a name-only reference with people who are not well-known. Try to judge how immediately recognizable the names are across Canada.

10. Avoid long phrases that can't be easily split – newspaper headlines usually run two or three lines.

11. Avoid headlines that can be read two different ways – **Iraqi Head Seeks Arms.**

12. Freshness is important. A big story that breaks early in the afternoon presents a challenge to editors writing headlines for the next day's papers. Most readers will already know something about the story from radio and TV by the time the newspaper arrives. Something creative or the promise of fresh information is needed. For instance, when

13. Make sure the headline is updated every time a Writethru changes a story in a substantial way.

Headline style

1. Only the first letter in the first word of the headline is uppercase. All other words in the headline follow normal CP style for capitalization. However, the principal words of headlines are capped when they are quoted within the body of a story (as they are in this chapter).

2. The usual CP rules on abbreviations apply, with some additions. For Canadian provinces, it is OK to use **B.C., P.E.I., N.B., N.L., N.S.** and **N.W.T.** in all references (nouns and adjectives) in headlines. **Sask., Alta., Ont., Man. and Que.** can also be used. Use these abbreviations only if space constraints require it. Don't shorten **Yukon** and **Nunavut**. Do not load up a headline with numerous abbreviations – reading a headline should not be an exercise in decoding a foreign language.

3. Use numerals – **8** instead of **eight**, **1st** instead of **first**, etc. – for numbers under 10.

4. Use **%** instead of **per cent**.

5. It is OK to use **M**, capped, for **million** after a numeral: **$2M in funding**.

6. On business stories, business quarters can be represented as **Q1, Q2, Q3** and **Q4**.

7. Use single, not double, quotation marks in headlines. This is the style most newspapers follow.

8. On CP copy, headlines should be flush left and in boldface. They should be between 60 and 77 characters long.

Headline glossary

More short synonyms can be found in the Plain Words chapter of *Caps and Spelling*.

Instead of	Use
abandon	quit, leave
abolish	end, scrap
acknowledge	admit
administer	direct, control
advise	tell
agreement	pact, deal
amalgamate	join
amendment	change
approves	OK's
arrest	bag, bust, nab
assist	aid
attempt	try
bargain	deal
cancel	nix
catch, apprehend	nab

Instead of	Use
celebrate	mark
child(ren)	kid(s)
collision	crash
company	firm
comparable	like
competitor	rival
conclude	end
Conservative	Tory
consult	ask
consume	eat, use up
currently	now
decrease	cut, drop, fall
explosion	blast
father	dad
federal government	Ottawa
former	ex-
frequently	often
friend	pal
fundamental	basic
guerrilla	rebel
implement	do, set up, begin
increase	boost, up, rise, grow
inform	tell
injunction	ban, order
inquire	ask
Liberal	Grit
looking for	seek
manufacture	make
marijuana	pot
mother	mom
numerous	many
obtain	get
occasion	event
offer	bid
oil and gas industry	oilpatch
persuade	coax, sway
physician	doctor
pickup truck	pickup
police	cops
position	job
prohibit	ban
promises	vows
proposal	plan
purchase	buy
prime minister	PM
principal	main, chief
procedure	way, method
project, proposal	plan
provide	give
reduce, lay off	cut
reduction	cut

Instead of	Use
replace	swap
rescue	save
resign, retire	quit
Statistics Canada	StatsCan
stop	nix
Toronto	T.O.
transport	ferry, tote
treaty	pact, deal
unemployment rate	jobless rate
versus	vs.
were supposed to be	slated

Newspage copy

1. Newspage copy or *the newspager* is most often tied to a major break in Sports or Business news. These stories fall into two main categories:

a) Short items that capture the key elements of the event and their impact. These items are written to whet the appetite for fuller coverage on sectional pages: for example, a story on the Toronto Maple Leafs winning the Stanley Cup. The top of the newspage story should be complete enough to flag fuller treatment inside.

b) Longer stories that take a non-specialist approach to a specialist event: how Edmonton celebrates a Grey Cup win; how employees in a small town react to a big-city decision by their only employer to go out of business after 80 years; how consumers will be affected by the merger of two meat-packing plants that have long been competitors. Strong human elements are essential in looking behind the game score, job-loss statistics and other hard-news angles.

2. In either case, plain English and the absence of jargon are essential. Sports-page copy on the Leafs winning the Cup can talk about goals-against average and assume the reader knows all about Mats Sundin and Tie Domi, but newspage stories must go back to basics. Technical terms should be explained, issues presented in terms of their impact on the public or readers and leading figures in the story seen in human terms.

3. Advisories tipping editors that newspage copy is planned are essential and should be carried as early as possible. But even short notice about a newspager on a late-breaking development can help editors planning front and section pages.

Advances

General

Texts of speeches, reports and other material are routinely provided to the media in advance of their delivery to the public. That allows reporters to treat the material more carefully and organize background or explanations as needed.

Some of this material can be distributed early by a news agency, embargoed for release when the speech or whatever is delivered. Through coding, CP often limits the relay of advance copy to its newspaper clients only, so they can process the material in time for their next deadline. Advance material is not sent to online and database services, since this would mean instant publication.

Once such stories have been distributed with embargoes — or with internal phrasing that suggests the copy was prepared in advance – editors must be kept informed. Was the speech delivered or the report presented? Send advisories. If the stories need to be modified for any reason, do it promptly.

Speeches

1. Stories about speeches distributed before the speech is made need a phrase such as **in a speech prepared for delivery to**. A separate paragraph can say **A text of the governor's address was provided to the news media before delivery.** The paragraph can be easily deleted if a newspaper wishes; it should not include material essential to the story.

2. Divergences from the prepared speech, audience reaction and circumstances surrounding the event can give life to the bare text.

3. Corrections or additions to update a story moved in advance must be transmitted promptly. An important addition by the speaker is indicated by saying **Madhani digressed from her prepared speech and . . .** On occasion, the divergence may rate a new lead. If there is an important omission, say so and indicate in the story the wording of the original text.

4. When a speech has been checked and the advance stands, advise editors with a note.

Madhani, Advisory
   EDS: See Ottawa Madhani. A check shows Madhani did not depart from the text released in advance.
   CP Ottawa

The paragraph referring to an advance text may be deleted and the reference to **prepared for delivery** changed to **in a speech to . . .**

5. When a text contains controversial or spectacular statements, every effort should be made to confirm the statements were indeed made. If CP cannot staff the speech, arrangements should be made for a fast check with an assigned newspaper or broadcast reporter.

6. When a speaker drops a controversial statement from a speech, this is sometimes more important than the speech itself if it indicates a change in policy or a moderation of tone. The speaker must always be questioned about the reason for the omission. As warranted, CP should also seek reaction from others involved in the issue.

Broken embargoes

1. CP editors should tell the source of embargoed material that we will abide by the release time only as long as others do. We will release the material immediately if someone else is found to have broken the embargo.

2. CP will take no account of the size or importance of the newspaper or broadcaster that broke the embargo.

Royal, Release Advisory
   EDs: Toronto Royal-Bank on the Royal Bank of Canada's annual report, moved in advance for release at 10 a.m. EDT, is now available for publication. The embargo has been broken by other media.
   CP Toronto

Advance slugs

1. Advance items carry cautionary slugs. Style examples follow.

2. In copy relayed by Toronto deskers, embargo times are converted to eastern time. Specific times in the body of a story, however, are not changed to their eastern equivalent.

3. To avoid misunderstanding, sources issuing important releases should be encouraged to provide specific release times. They should also understand the newspapers need lead time in order to print the story; a release time of 6:30 p.m., for instance, means the article won't be published in a newspaper until the next day.

Style for slugs

Follow these styles for advances.

1. On copy for a specific time today:

Prisons, Advance
ADVANCE — Embargoed for 12:30 p.m. EDT TODAY, June 11

2. On copy for a specific time the following day:

Prisons, Advance
ADVANCE — EMBARGOED until 10 a.m. ET THU Feb. 12

3. On copy moved more than 24 hours in advance:

Awards, Advance
ADVANCE — EMBARGOED until 9 p.m. ET THU Oct. 12
NOTE FUTURE DATE

4. On AP feature copy that is embargoed for online use only:

Vonnegut, Advance
ADVANCE — EMBARGOED for online use until Sunday,
May 12

5. On copy to be held for release by an advisory:

Throne-General, Advance
ADVANCE — EMBARGOED AND NOT TO BE USED UNTIL
RELEASED BY ADVISORY, POSSIBLY ABOUT 2:15 P.M.
EDT TODAY JUNE 12. GUARD AGAINST PREMATURE USE

Use this form to release copy moved in advance for indefinite-
time release:

Fedbudget, Release Advisory
URGENT
    OTTAWA — Release all advance copy on federal budget.
    CP Ottawa

Advance advisories

1. On major announcements to be released in advance, an
advisory should be sent where possible.

Economy, Advisory
Major economic statement by the prime minister expected at
2:40 p.m.
    EDS: We expect to move shortly in advance for release by
advisory an important announcement by the prime minister on
the economy. He is expected to start speaking at 2:40 p.m. EDT
but other Commons business may cause delay. An urgent
release note will be sent immediately when he starts to speak.
Guard against premature use.
    CP Ottawa

---

2. CP subscribers must be kept informed of changes in the prospects for release by advisory. If we have said a release is possible at 2:40 p.m. and it does not develop, a cautionary note slugged Urgent and accompanied by five unspaced bells must be carried at 2:40 p.m. or earlier.

Economy, Advisory
URGENT
PM's economic statement delayed by procedural wrangle in Commons

EDS: The prime minister's statement about the economy, originally expected to be released about 2:40 p.m. EDT, is delayed by a procedural wrangle in the Commons. Meanwhile, the embargo on Ottawa Economy continues until the prime minister begins his announcement. Release will be by an urgent advisory.

CP Ottawa.

3. Use this form for the release:

Economy, Release Advisory
URGENT

OTTAWA — Release the prime minister's statement about the economy.

CP Ottawa

4. Once the embargo is lifted, retransmit the story on all services, adding the following note in the slugging: **Eds: Repeat of earlier embargoed story.**

Bylines and credit lines

General

Bylines recognize a reporter's original contribution and diligence on a story. When a CP byline is preserved by a newspaper, it sends a public signal of a job well done.

Bylines shouldn't be misused. They aren't normally warranted for a rewrite of someone's news release, the monitoring of a telecast or other task involving minimal imagination and enterprise. Solid original reporting and bright writing can rate a byline.

CP staff with full-time specialist beats should let editors and readers know about their expertise. Such identifications are used whenever department heads or specialist writers are reporting about their areas of speciality.

Newspapers are loath to credit more than two people for a single story. Multiple bylines can look awkward. Consult Toronto Main Desk before sending a story with more than two bylines.

Basic guidelines

1. Bylines are used on top stories, outstanding features and stories by specialist writers.

2. A byline may be removed at the request of a writer if extensive changes are made to the story. In the case of Analyses or first-person material, which should not be distributed without a byline, the writer may request that the story be ditched if a dispute over editing changes cannot be resolved.

3. Desk editors may remove the byline when a story requires exceptionally heavy editing and the writer's approval is not available for the changes.

4. Bylines are not used from placelines where the writer has not been to collect the information reported. Where a reporter's diligence with the phone and other resources has helped produce a story that deserves recognition, or if the story has been gathered from a variety of locations, consider moving the story without a placeline. Or a credit line can be used.

5. Department heads and specialist writers drop their titles when their position or speciality is irrelevant; for instance, if the CP Business Editor covers an axe murder next door.

6. Aside from columns, first-person writing is normally reserved for a vivid, dramatic experience involving the writer: **As I watched, the avalanche roared down on the village, flinging trees and rocks aside.** The first person is also justified when a staffer is an expert on the subject in the news: as a former Olympic sculler commenting on a world record in the event, for instance.

7. Always obtain consent (written consent on major events) before using any non-staffer's byline on a first-person descriptive story.

8. Bylines are set uppercase and lowercase, boldface and centred. No other slug intervenes between them and the story.

Style

For staff of CP and AP:

1. For most stories with a placeline:

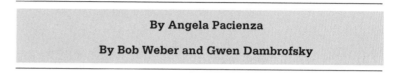

> **By Angela Pacienza**
>
> **By Bob Weber and Gwen Dambrofsky**

Note: For double bylines, both writers must be in the location of the placeline.

2. For most stories without a placeline:

> **By Les Perreaux**
> **The Canadian Press**
>
> **The Associated Press**

3. For department heads and specialist writers with job titles:

> **By Anne-Marie Tobin**
> **CP Life-Entertainment Editor**

4. For reviews by staffers without job titles but with special knowledge of a particular field, use the byline and add a note at the end of the review under three dashes centred:

> — — —
> CP reporter Chris Morris studies the banjo.

5. For Notes packages and other collections of material from a variety of sources, put together with originality, add a note at the end under three dashes centred:

> — — —
> Compiled by Judy Creighton.

For non-staffers:

1. For string correspondents, use only the byline on stories with a placeline:

By Fred Weir

But on stories without a placeline, add the service:

By Fred Weir
Canadian Press Correspondent

---

2. For stories picked up with few if any changes from member newspapers and used with the byline:

By Walter Smith
Hamilton Spectator

Note: On the rare occasion when a story from a member newspaper carrying a byline and newspaper credit must be Undated, use the boldface credit line **Distributed by CP** at the end of the story, on a separate line.

3. For experts writing about their speciality, use the byline alone and add the credentials in a boldface note, usually at the end of the story under three dashes centred.

— — —
Eleanor Shu is a professor of economics at the University of British Columbia.

Note: If further detail is needed, the expanded note may go above the byline in boldface and above three dashes centred.

4. For arts reviews from papers or freelance writers, use the byline alone and add the identification in a boldface note at the end of the review under three dashes centred:

— — —
Michael Walsh is a theatre critic for the Calgary Herald.

Barbara Dumont, a graduate of the National Ballet School, is a freelance dance critic.

5. Similarly for travel stories and other material by freelances:

> **— — —**
>
> **Joan Hanright is a freelance writer based in Darmouth, N.S.**

6. For unplacelined copy by freelances, experts and so on, follow this style:

> **By Jim Holt**
> **For The Canadian Press**

Add the identification, if necessary, in a boldface note at the end under three dashes centred:

> **— — —**
>
> **Jim Holt is a freelance writer based in Los Angeles.**

7. For stories written especially for CP, such as a first-person account by an eyewitness, always preceded by a publishable editors note:

> **Jim Anderson was working in the fields of his 100-hectare farm Friday when a twin-engine jet crashed less than a kilometre away, killing 10 people. Here is his eyewitness account.**
> **Written for CP**
> **By Jim Anderson**
> BRADFORD, Ont. (CP) — It was the high-pitched whine of the engine that first caught my attention . . .

For unbylined stories:

1. For stories without placelines:

   a) From a single service:

> **By The Canadian Press**
> **By The Associated Press**

   b) From two or more services:

> **From AP-CP**

Note: It is *From,* not *By.*

2. For stories with placelines:

   a) From a single service, use an agency credit in the placeline:

HALIFAX (CP) — Six . . .

---

   b) The placeline credit AP-CP indicates CP has extensively rewritten or added material to an AP story.

TOKYO (AP-CP) — At least 50 people, including six Canadians, . . .

Credit lines

1. On rare occasions, a credit line is appropriate for a reporter who has written or made a significant contribution to a story, but is not in the location of the placeline:

—By Michelle MacAfee in Winnipeg.

—With files from Michelle MacAfee in Winnipeg.

Note: Credit lines should not be used for routine contributions. It should meet the same criteria that would be required for a byline.

2. On roundups, the byline goes to the writer. A notable contribution from another writer can be acknowledged with a credit line. A notable contribution in a roundup would be material that is used in the lead or that makes up a sigfnificant chunk of the story.

Member newspaper credit

All stories picked up from member newspapers, even if they carry a byline, should carry a bracketed credit at the bottom of the story. If the story was combined from items from more than one member, list them according to the amount of material contributed:

(Toronto Star, Globe and Mail)

Corrections

CP uses the following forms to make important changes to stories:

WRITETHRU — makes a change in fact or wording, including any error in the lead.

WITHHOLD — puts a hold on publication of questionable or erroneous material.

KILL — eliminates a story that is wrong, legally dangerous or damaging.

SUB — replaces an earlier story in its entirety; particularly used for a story that has been killed.

1. Explanations or information provided to justify the **WRITETHRU, WITHHOLD, KILL** or **SUB** slugs must be clear and easily understood.

2. All stories carrying any of these slugs get top priority on news circuits where the erroneous or suspect copy was previously transmitted. The slugs are all-caps and boldface, except the Writethru slug.

➤ See **Slugs and coding**, page 427.

3. **WRITETHRU** — Used to correct errors and recast unnecessary or superseded material. Also used to update material. When it is correcting a previous story, the word CORRECTS, all caps, must be in the Update Note. Do not use descriptions such as recasts, clarifies, fixes or changes when correcting errors of fact. And be specific about the error.

Not: fixes name.

But: CORRECTS Eve to Eva in para 3.

➤ For an example see **Slugs and coding**, page 430.

Writethrus containing important corrections, such as those which substantially change the lead of a story, are moved as Urgents and flagged with five unspaced bells. The slug !!!!**URGENT** or !!!!**BULLETIN** is sometimes used.

Truck-Crash, URGENT 1st Writethru
!!!!URGENT
Update: CORRECTS criminal charges in para 1.
Two downtown Regina storefronts demolished; driver charged with dangerous driving
    REGINA (CP) — A Saskatoon driver was charged with dangerous driving and leaving the scene of an accident today after his pickup truck jumped a curb and demolished the fronts of two downtown stores.

Note: The five bell characters, inserted directly after !!!!URGENT

CORRECTION or !!!!BULLETIN CORRECTION and on the same line, must be unspaced to trigger alarms at some papers.

4. WITHHOLD — Used to warn editors that a story may be erroneous, dangerous or premature and that it must not be published pending a check.

Withhold notes are sent as bulletins, with bells. They identify the story by placeline and slug, and detail the reason for the Withhold.

> **Truck-Crash, BULLETIN WITHHOLD**
> **BULLETIN WITHHOLD**
>   Editors: Withhold from publication Regina Truck-Crash. The identity of the driver charged has been questioned.
>   CP Edmonton

5. RELEASE WITHHOLD — Used to notify editors that a story previously withheld has been cleared for publication. Notes releasing a withheld story are sent as bulletins.

> **Truck-Crash, BULLETIN RELEASE**
> **BULLETIN RELEASE**
>   Editors: Release Regina Truck-Crash previously withheld because identity of the driver was questioned. Police have confirmed the identity of the driver.
>   CP Edmonton

6. KILL — Used to eliminate an erroneous or unnecessary story, whether or not it has been previously withheld. Kills are sent as bulletins. They identify the story by placeline and slug, specify the reason and say whether a substitute story is planned. They move with bells.

> **Truck-Crash, BULLETIN KILL**
> **BULLETIN KILL**
>   Editors: KILL Regina Truck-Crash previously withheld, which identified the driver of the pickup truck. Legal counsel confirms it is possibly dangerous. Will be sub.
>   CP Edmonton

7. SUB — Used on a story that supersedes an erroneous item. It rates an urgent slug.

A sub repeats the story but with the erroneous material corrected. It is flagged at the top with an explanatory note to editors.

> **Truck-Crash, URGENT SUB**
> **URGENT SUB Regina Truck-Crash**
> **Eds: Subs for Regina Truck-Crash previously killed. It eliminates the possibly dangerous identification of the driver.**
>   REGINA (CP) — A Saskatoon driver . . .

Correctives

Mistakes happen. Misinformation gets reported. When it does, the first priority is always to get it fixed, quickly and properly.

The CP **Corrective** is used to catch up with an error that has probably already been published. It is specifically designed to face the error head on and set the record straight frankly.

It deals *only* with information shown to be in error, when enough time has passed for the mistake to get into print. If the error is caught in the same news cycle in which it is made — within a few hours, in other words — move a **Writethru** with an Update note that explains the problem.

Always go back to the original story when writing a Corrective. Focus on the precise words that are wrong and deal only with the erroneous information. But deal with it fully and openly. Never try to *interpret* the original. If it is wrong, it is wrong.

Here is a sample Corrective when the mistake is CP's alone:

Hockey-Pond-Championship, CCTV
CORRECTIVE
    HUNTSVILLE, Ont. (CP) — The Canadian Press erroneously reported Jan. 29 that the Shoot for the Cure campaign raises money for cancer research. In fact, the program raises money for spinal cord awareness, prevention and research.

When the mistake originates with a newspaper story, the Corrective should say that CP *distributed* an erroneous report. In all but extreme cases (see No. 7 in the *General guidelines* below), consult the newspaper before carrying a Corrective based on a pickup. Put out a **Withhold** (see page 417) if the paper cannot be reached immediately. Advise a CP supervisor so that further steps may be taken to reach newspaper staff.

CP believes that readers should be given both the correct version and the erroneous version together, to make clear what was wrong. It is not enough to present the correct information while acknowledging only that *erroneous information was reported previously.*

When an error originates with a government announcement, a company news release or some other official source, a followup story should be done if there is a legitimate news angle. For example, a followup to a story based on erroneous mortgage rates released by a bank might be tied to the angle that bank branches were flooded with calls.

If there is no legitimate news angle, then a Corrective should be moved. Do not state that CP *erroneously reported* or *distributed an erroneous report*, but do explain how the error originated.

> **NS-Taser-Assault, CCTV**
> **CORRECTIVE**
>   DARTMOUTH, N.S. (CP) — A Canadian Press story March 19
> that was based on a police release said that a Nova Scotia man
> was facing charges after an assault involving a Taser. However,
> police later said the assault involved a stun gun, but not one
> manufactured by Taser International Inc.

General guidelines

1. When a mistake is discovered, send a proposed Corrective to Main Desk immediately, with a full explanation of how the error was made and who made it. Make sure it fully corrects what was wrong in the original. The Corrective *always* includes a reference to The Canadian Press erring or distributing an erroneous report. It also includes the date of the error. It carries a boldface **Corrective** slug.

2. When facts and figures are involved, simply admit the error and give the correct information.

3. Consult counsel if there is a chance libel or contempt may be involved. Seek advice also if a Corrective might hurt CP's legal position or aggravate the damage caused to a potential complainant.

4. Add regrets or an apology where there has been obvious damage to the reputation of a person or corporation. Such a story should be approved by counsel. It must be headed by a boldface note asking newspapers that published the original error to give equal prominence to the Corrective. (See page xxx.)

5. Never try to fudge a mistake in a developing story by overtaking it with a Writethru that includes a clarifying statement or skates around the original error completely. An Update note at the top should specify that the Writethru corrects a previous mistake. If there was time for the error to be published, a Corrective is called for.

6. If a member of the public with a vested interest disputes a story, and if CP itself or an originating newspaper stands by it, carry the person's denial along with a statement that CP or the paper stands by its report. Main Desk may need to check counsel on the appropriate wording.

7. Consider an immediate Corrective if the weight of evidence suggests the original was wrong, even when the originating newspaper cannot be reached. But keep pushing to reach newspaper staff. Consult Main Desk.

8. Correctives carry a placeline, almost invariably that of the original story.

9. Correctives must be sent on all services that carried the original item, using the same Index categories. Main Desk

compiles a relay report to ensure that a Corrective reaches every newspaper and client that received the original story. Main Desk must make specific checks with CP Montreal to establish whether the original was used on the French-language service; and with CP Online and electronic databases to make sure the faulty original is removed or updated as necessary. The Corrective may also be carried on these services.

➤ See **Writing for and About the Internet**, page 180.

Style

The following forms are for the guidance of editors preparing Correctives for Main Desk approval:

1. Specific reference:

OTTAWA (CP) — The Canadian Press erroneously reported Nov. 28 that oil exports during the first eight months of 2001 declined by 17 per cent. In fact, oil exports fell by 27 per cent.

2. Correcting serious or legally dangerous errors:

Eds: Papers that published the St. John's, N.L., Elwood Hatcher slaying story of Sunday, June 1, dealing with the arrest of two suspects, are asked to give equal prominence to the following CORRECTIVE.

3. Apology for serious error:

The Canadian Press regrets its error and apologizes for any embarrassment or inconvenience caused John Doe or Margaret Roe.

Clarifications

1. A Clarification is carried when a story is not essentially wrong but is incomplete or may have left room for a possible misunderstanding. It is a brief placelined item with the boldface slug **CLARIFICATION** and follows the handling steps set out for Correctives.

2. A Clarification should make clear that the original CP story — or in the case of a pickup, the story distributed by CP — left out important information or could be misinterpreted. The Clarification would then provide a fuller version or straighten out the possible misunderstanding.

3. A Clarification would be appropriate, for example, if a CP story gave only one side of an issue, or if the wording could be read two ways, or if someone felt unfairly treated, even though there were no errors of fact.

Suspensions, Clarification
CLARIFICATION

WINNIPEG (CP) — The Canadian Press reported July 15 that Winnipeg city council had ordered two municipal employees suspended from their jobs for going fishing when they should have been inspecting sewage lines.

The story may have left the impression that the suspended workers had not disputed council's action. In fact, both workers have been supported by their union and are contesting the suspensions.

They maintain they were on accumulated leave when they were spotted with fishing equipment on the banks of the Red River just outside Winnipeg.

Slugs and coding

Slugs are labelling lines that help editors figure out at a glance what the story is about. They indicate whether the story is for news or sports pages, what the topic is, whether this is a new story or a variation of an old one, whether there are illustrations to accompany the story, and other information editors should have.

Coding tells computers what material to send where. It can be used to shorten stories automatically or prevent some stories from going to specific receiving points.

Consistency in slugging and coding is important since, in many cases, computers are auto-sorting stories into specific queues based on an exact code.

CP has an elaborate coding system that can change quite often, given software developments. This section provides only an overview of slugging and coding. Practices can vary from bureau to bureau and desk to desk. For details and updates, consult desk books.

For the sake of brevity, coding lines have been left off most of the examples in this chapter and others.

Priority coding

One set of codes that has contributed to the folklore of news agencies, not to mention the vernacular of "newspeak", is based on how editors in the old days used to rank stories for transmission based on their urgency. This was necessary because slow technology meant it could take 15 or 20 minutes to transmit one long story. A way was needed to ensure an urgent story could "jump the queue." Today, with high-speed data transmission, stories are transmitted so quickly that priority codes are seldom necessary. But it is still a time-honoured tradition at news agencies to put a bulletin code on the prime minister's resignation and a regular code on the hog sales report.

These priority codes, which go on the first line of a story, include:

f — Flash. The highest priority, only for news of overwhelming urgency. Breaks into news flow and into any other story being transmitted.

b — Bulletin. For one-paragraph items of hot news, Kill advisories or NewsAlerts. Supersedes all but a flash in the computer queue.

u — Urgent. Used on high-priority copy of more than one paragraph.

r — Regular priority. Used on the longer stories that are the backbone of the CP news report.

d — Deferred priority. Used for copy that can be delayed while more important material is transmitted.

c — Cycle priority. These stories are transmitted continuously. Used only for cable television news service.

Departmental designators

Departmental designators help sort copy into categories and into different queues in computer systems.

The file name created at the originating point in the CP news network contains two (uppercase) letters and three or four numbers.

The first letter refers to the bureau or department of origin and is invisible to papers receiving the material.

The second letter is the departmental designator, based on the type of story: Canadian general news, world news, sports and so on.

These are the departmental designators:

A — **Atlantic** regional general news
B — **Business**
C — **Quebec-Ontario** regional general news
D — **Western** regional general news
E — **Entertainment**
F — **Financial** routine
G — National **general** news
H — **Quebec-Ontario** regional **sport**
I — **Atlantic** regional **sport**
J — **Travel**
K — **Agriculture**
L — **Lifestyles**
M — Service **messages** and advisories
Q — **Photo** service captions
R — **Sport** scores, summaries and other tabular sports copy
S — **Sports** in general
V — **Western** regional **sport**
W — **World** general news
X — **Spare** category for **sport**, such as Olympics
Y — **Spare** category for **news**, such as elections
Z — **Spare** category

Slugs

The first slugline of an item contains one or more words that describe the contents of the story. All elements are separated by hyphens. The exact same keyword(s) should be used any time the story is changed by later developments, or when other stories are related to the same topic: **Avalanche; Avalanche, 1st Writethru; Avalanche-Survivors.**

Uniqueness in slugging is important to avoid confusing two or more stories: **OBIT-Peter-Gzowski,** not **Died.** Intriguing or snappy slugs can also go a long way to selling a story to an editor: **Pigs-on-Road,** not **Accident.**

Slugs go boldface and most are in uppercase and lowercase.

Slug order

Here is the proper lineup for slugs:

Keyword-Slug, version field
code:
Out code
URGENT
Update note
Budget
With, Espy
See CP Photo, Graphics
INDEX:
SYMBOL:
HL:A headline of between 60 and 77 characters goes here
By The Canadian Press

Keyword slug line

The first line under the coding instructions to the computer is the keyword slug line, consisting of the keyword or keywords, and the version field:

Toxic-Ban, Bgt

Keep slugs tight, yet descriptive. One-word slugs are preferred when possible. International news agency standards limit the slug length to 24 characters, although they may appear longer in receiving databases.

An all-caps word is sometimes used to designate copy intended for specific pages or sections of a newspaper. This word appears at the beginning of the slugline: **BOOKS-John-Irving**.

All-caps slugs include: **ART; BOOKS; BRITE** (for amusing or lighter stories); **CRAFT** (media industry news); **CRIME; FASHION; FILM; FOOD; GAMES** (computer and video games); **GARDEN; HEALTH; HOMES; MUSIC; OBIT** (for obituaries); **ODDITY; RELIGION; SCIENCE; THEATRE; TRAVEL; TV; WEA** (for weather items); **WKND** (repeats of features intended for weekend editions).

Version field

The version field provides more detailed information for newspaper editors using directory displays to search for copy. This information helps editors link the various components of a story.

The version field is separated from the keyword field by a comma and a space. Some examples:

Canadian-Lords, Bgt

NAC-Yashin, Urgent 1st Writethru

Canadian-Lords, BULLETIN KILL

NAC-Yashin, 2nd Writethru

Clandestine, Advance

FILM-Sundance, Rpt

Anniversary-Queen, Advisory

Material in the version field is listed in the following order:

— Flash, BULLETIN, KILL, Withhold, Urgent, Rpt, Writethru, Advance, Advisory, Bgt

In the version field, **Budget** may be abbreviated to **Bgt**. However, it should be written out in a lower slug line.

Words within the version field are separated by spaces, not by commas or hyphens.

The combined keyword-version field should be kept to a maximum of 45 characters, including punctuation, to allow for proper display in newspaper computer systems.

Specific slugs

This section outlines the main story slugs and the forms in which they are written by CP editors and writers. To save space, not all the coding lines are included in all examples.

FLASH — An emergency signal to editors that outstanding news is breaking. Limited to one sentence, a flash has transmission priority and can break into any other story being transmitted before it. It is extremely rare and must be followed immediately by a Bulletin.

The word **FLASH** is sent all caps, centred and flagged with five unspaced bells. The text is indented and boldface. The item has a placeline but no service logo.

Plane-Crash, Flash
FLASH
BLANDFORD, N.S. — A jet with 227 people aboard has crashed in the Atlantic Ocean.

NewsAlert — Used for most newsbreaks — important government announcements, court decisions and the like. In one sentence, it alerts editors that a Bulletin or an Urgent is on its way within five minutes.

It carries the identifier **CP NewsAlert**, flush left, and is flagged with five unspaced bells. The item has a placeline and a CP service logo. It can be headline style or one sentence. It moves on an urgent priority.

> **Bomb-Explodes, NewsAlert**
> **CP NewsAlert**
>   BAGHDAD (CP) — Car bomb explodes in front of police station, say witnesses.

BULLETIN — Used on the first publishable paragraph — usually not more than 50 words — of important breaks. It should be followed almost immediately by an URGENT add. The word BULLETIN is sent all caps, centred and carries five unspaced bells. It is publishable and immediately precedes the headline.

> **Plane-Crash, Bulletin**
>   **BULLETIN**
> **Swissair jet crashes off Nova Scotia coast**
>   **By Steve MacLeod**
>   BLANDFORD, N.S. (CP) — A Swissair jetliner carrying 227 passengers and crew has crashed in the Atlantic Ocean near this tiny fishing village.

URGENT — Used on stories of Bulletin or near-Bulletin character running more than 50 words or so. Urgent stories are kept short for fast relay.

The word **URGENT** is sent all caps, flush left, and carries five unspaced bells. It is not intended for publication and comes immediately after the keyword slug line.

An urgent lead would be slugged like this:

> **Bush, Urgent**
> **URGENT**
> **U.S. President George W. Bush to convene peace talks in Middle East**
>   WASHINGTON (AP) — U.S. President George W. Bush ...

QuickHit — Used on an urgent story that is being filed to all services (print, broadcast and online). It generally carries the story only during the first hectic minutes. When developments slow down, the broadcast and print streams separate so copy can be written with the specific needs of each service a priority. However, the QuickHit format can be resurrected should events start happening quickly again.

A **QuickHit** carries basic CP slugging. (The slugging is automatically reformatted for broadcast wires.) The writing is a combination of print and broadcast styles. It should be no more than six paragraphs long, has one sentence per paragraph and uses a conversational style that can be read by newscasters. **Today** is OK but days of the week are used for other time references. Quotes should be avoided and paraphrased instead, and attribution should be at the beginning of a sentence. But like a CP story, it has a placeline and also uses CP style for numbers, abbreviations (**CBC**, not C-B-C), titles and the like. Pronouncers should be included when needed, but in the **Update** line:

Klein-Throws-Booklet
Alberta premier loses temper and throws booklet at legislative page

EDMONTON (CP) — Premier Ralph Klein has apologized for throwing a booklet at a page in the legislature during an emotional debate over Alberta's health care reforms.

The 17-year-old page had delivered a soft-covered, 80-page booklet of Liberal policy proposals to Klein's desk in the assembly, when he grabbed it and tossed it at her.

The premier was heard to say, "I don't need this crap," referring to the booklet that was sent to him by the opposition as they fired questions over the Third Way health reforms.

The page refused comment to the media and there was no confirmation that the booklet actually hit her.

Speaker Ken Kowalski was clearly miffed over the incident and Klein later rose and apologized to the page and to the liberals for calling their policy booklet "crap."

The premier said he was simply frustrated over health care, but Liberal Leader Kevin Taft described the incident as "appalling" and said it shows the premier is "out of control."

1st Writethru — Used on a story superseding a previous story in the same cycle. When warranted, it is followed by **2nd Writethru**, **3rd Writethru** and so on.

A Writethru repeats the story in its entirety, with any changes incorporated and described in a detailed **Update note** at the top of the item. Update notes always begin **Update:** and should explain changes that are being made. Include paragraph numbers so editors do not have to read through the story looking for the changes. Update notes should be considered publishable, as they appear on some of CP's electronic services. Do not use unfamiliar abbreviations or newsroom lingo.

Changes fall into four broad categories: updates, corrections, inserts and precedes.

When the story is being updated with new material, be specific about what is new. Use an urgent slug if the material significantly changes the story.

Plane-Crash, Urgent 1st Writethru
URGENT
Update: Coast Guard confirms in paras 2-4 that wreck of the jet has been found
See CP Photos, Graphics
Jetliner crashes off coast of Nova Scotia; 229 aboard
By Steve MacLeod
   PEGGY'S COVE, N.S. (CP) — The wreckage of a Swissair jet that crashed with 229 people aboard has been located in the dark ocean waters off the coast of Nova Scotia.

If the story is being corrected, the word **CORRECTS**, all caps, must be in the Update note:

Plane-Crash, 2nd Writethru
Update: CORRECTS number aboard plane to 229 from 227; fixes destination to Geneva in para 2.
See CP Photos, Graphics
Swissair jet crashes into ocean off Nova Scotia with 229 people aboard
By Steve MacLeod
   BLANDFORD, N.S. (CP) — Ships and aircraft were searching the ocean early today for a Swissair jet carrying 229 passengers and crew that crashed near this tiny fishing village.
   The MD-11 jet, en route from New York to Geneva, was attempting an emergency landing at Halifax airport, said Andrew Ereau of search and rescue in Halifax.

Note: Writethrus containing important corrections must also be slugged URGENT CORRECTION or BULLETIN CORRECTION.

➤ See **Corrections**, page 421.

If the placeline of the story is changing, the word **PRECEDES**, all caps, should appear:

Plane-Crash, 3rd Writethru
Update: PRECEDES BLANDFORD, N.S. with exact location of Peggy's Cove; ADDS comments from search and rescue; edits throughout.
See CP Photos, Graphics
Debris spotted in ocean off Nova Scotia after Swissair jet carrying 229 people crashes
By Steve MacLeod
   PEGGY'S COVE, N.S. (CP) — Debris, lights and an oil slick were spotted in the Atlantic Ocean early today where a Swissair jet carrying 229 passengers and crew is believed to have crashed just off the southwest coast of Nova Scotia.

When an insert is needed, the word **INSERTS**, all caps, appears:

> **Plane-Crash, 4th Writethru**
> **Update: INSERTS after para 14 toll-free numbers for victims'**
> **relatives.**
> **See CP Photos, Graphics**
> **Debris spotted in ocean off Nova Scotia after Swissair jet**
> **carrying 229 people crashes**
> **By Steve MacLeod**
> PEGGY'S COVE, N.S. (CP) — The wreckage of a Swissair jet
> that crashed with 229 people aboard has been located in the
> dark ocean waters off the coast of Nova Scotia.

With — Used on a sidebar from another point in either news
cycle. The slug is upper and lower.

> **Plane-MD-11**
> **With Peggy's Cove Plane-Crash**
> **Plane model that crashed off Nova Scotia being phased out**
> TORONTO (CP) — The Swissair MD-11 that crashed off Nova
> Scotia on Wednesday night is a highly sophisticated wide-body
> jetliner model that is being phased out by Boeing, putting 600
> Canadians out of work.
> The jetliner, which first flew in January 1990, was the first
> jet with three engines to be introduced since the Douglas DC-
> 10 and Lockheed L-1011 lifted off in the 1970s.

Espy — Used on a story aimed at a particular community or region.
The slug is upper and lower, flush left. **Espy Mtl, Espy West.**

Headlines

Almost every piece of information on CP's wires needs a line of
sluggng at the top that stands as a headline. This may be the
tradiitonal news headline: **Bomb explodes on London subway**;
or it may be a line that identifies the content of the item:
Friday's Probable Pitchers. This line is the final one before the
first paragraph of the story, unles there is a byline.

Catchlines

Extremely long items, such as Look-Aheads and sports statistics,
sometimes moves in 'takes" to break up copy to ensure it can be
sent and received by all systems. Slugging on these Adds should
include a line that describes what the item is so the item is easily
identifiable in a database or directory.

> **Look-Ahead, 1st add**
> **1st add CP News Look-Ahead List for Sunday, April 16 to**
> **Saturday, April 29**

Computer sorting codes

CP has an elaborate coding system that sorts and ranks stories and automatically routes them to the proper subscribers. There are three main sorting codes:

1. **OUT** – Used on a story based on a pickup from a newspaper in a city with more than one paper. The slug prevents the story from entering the computer of the competing paper. It is also used to keep embargoed items from appearing on websites.

CGY OUT CQQ (Calgary); **EDM OUT EQQ** (Edmonton); **HFX OUT HQQ** (Halifax); **MTL OUT ZZZ** (Montreal English); **MTL OUT ZZZ F** (Montreal French); **OTT OUT QQQ** (Ottawa); **QUE EXCLU QEX** (Quebec City); **TOR OUT YYY** (Toronto); **VCR OUT VQQ** (Vancouver); **WEB OUT WZZ** (Online use); **WPG OUT WQQ** (Winnipeg)

2. **CODE** – Ranks stories from one to eight, which determines which CP services carry the story. The ranking is produced when the story is categorized according to its type (news, feature, routine item) and its importance (high, medium, low).

3. **INDEX** – Identifies stories based on their content, mainly intended to help with autorouting and sorting in receiving databases. CP editors can select one or more as appropriate.

Advisories, Agriculture, Arts, Automotive, Banks, Beverages, Books, Business, Celebrity, Chemicals, Construction, Defence (includes aerospace), **Economy, Education, Entertainment, Environment, Film, Finance, FinServices, Fisheries, Food, Forestry, Hardware, Health, Insurance, International, Justice, Labour, Manufacturing, Media, Metals, Mining, Music, Oil&Gas, Politics, Pharma, Radio, RealEstate, Religion, Retail, Social, Software, Sports, Telecom, Television, Trade, Transport, Travel, Utilities, Video**

Note: Coding requirements can change frequently. Check deskbooks for details and updates.

4. **STOCK SYMBOLS** – A line that lists the stock symbols of publicly listed companies mentioned in the story or affected by it. ,

➤ See **Stock symbols,** page 52; **Slug order,** page 429.

Sports news and statistics

For general information on covering sports issues, see **Sports**, page 84.

Slugs

1. Slugs must be informative. A well-chosen slug can whet the appetite of an editor and also simplify the search for a specific story.

2. The second element of the slug — all caps and no longer than five characters — identifies major sports. Secondary sports are grouped under the generic **MISC** slug, with the specific sport identified in subsequent slug words. For game copy involving established leagues, the league abbreviation substitutes for the sport designator. Here are the major sports and leagues and their keyword slugs:

Sports

AUTO	auto racing
BBL	baseball
BKBL	basketball
BOX	boxing
CANOE	canoeing
CRKT	cricket
CURL	curling
CYCLE	cycling
DIVE	diving
EQUE	equestrian
FTBL	football
GOLF	golf
GYM	gymnastics
HARN	harness racing
HKY	hockey
LACR	lacrosse
RODEO	rodeo
ROW	rowing
RUGBY	rugby
SAIL	sailing
SKTG	skating (figure and speedskating)
SKI	skiing
SOC	soccer
SWIM	swimming
TEN	tennis
THBRD	thoroughbred racing
TRACK	track and field (athletics)
VLBL	volleyball
MISC	all other sports

Leagues

AHL	American Hockey League
AMN	American League (baseball)
CFL	Canadian Football League
CIS	Canadian Interuniversity Sport
MLS	Major League Soccer
NAT	National League (baseball)
NBA	National Basketball Association
NFL	National Football League
NHL	National Hockey League
NLL	National Lacrosse League
WNBA	Women's National Basketball Association

Multi-sport events

OLY   Olympics

GAMES   Other multi-sport events such as the Pan Am, Commonwealth or Canada Games

4.   The next elements of the slug identify specific subject matter. For example, a story aimed at morning papers and dealing with a world-record swim by Canadian Nancy Sweetnam might be slugged: **SWIM-Sweetnam-Record**. Or, a feature on Canadian table tennis champion Gideon Joe Ng might carry a **MISC-Table-Tennis-Ng** slug.

In game stories, the second element of the slug identifies the league and the third and fourth elements the two competing teams (the visiting team listed first). For example, an NHL game with the Vancouver Canucks visiting the Toronto Maple Leafs would be slugged: **NHL-Vcr-Tor.**

Agate

As the design and focus of sports sections continue to evolve, the demand for agate increases.

Agate, or scoreboard, pages allow newspapers to present the essential aspects of a game or competition concisely. In many instances, they provide the option of not carrying a story on the event. These pages also satisfy the appetite among sports readers for more background statistics and comparison tables.

Reporters and editors should think constantly of ways to supplement stories with agate tables, fact boxes and graphics.

All CP-tabulated material carries a **Tab** identifier in the slugline immediately following the cycle designator. Unedited AP tabular copy does not take the Tab slug.

Consult desk books for details on tabulating material.

Results formats

Most results are presented in one of three formats: **bare score**, **basic summary** or **head-to-head result**. An example of each is given here for fast reference. Individual sports sections will specify which format is appropriate.

Canadian results in international competitions are boldfaced. Home towns for Canadians are provided; others are listed by country.

Bare score

The winning team is listed first, with the exception of European soccer results where the home team is listed first, regardless of the outcome.

Tab-HKY-Rslts
Wednesday's list
　　　　　　　　By The Canadian Press
NHL
　Toronto 3 Montreal 3

Later scores go as follows:

Tab-HKY-Rslts, add
Add Wednesday's list
Add NHL
　Calgary 6 Vancouver 4

Basic summary

Tab-TRACK-World-Cup-Rslts
　EDMONTON (CP) — Results Sunday from a World Cup track meet (distances in metres):
　　　　　　　　WOMEN
　　　　　　100 Hurdles
　　　　　　Semifinals
Heat 1: 1. Perdita Felicien, Pickering, Ont.,, 12.75 seconds; 2. Joanna Hayes, U.S., 12.75; 3. Nichole Denby, England, 12.79.

　　　　　　　　MEN
　　　　　　High Jump
　　　　　Qualifyiing
　　　(q-advanced to next round)
Group A: 1. q-Mark Boswell, Brampton, Ont., 2.29 metres; 2. q-Yaroslav Rybakov, Russia, 2.25; 3. q-Mickael Hanany, France; 2.20; 4. (tie), Jacques Freitag, South Africa, and Kyle Lancaster, U.S., 2.15.

Note: Where the field is particularly large, such as in a marathon, results are broken into paragraphs, approximately of equal length.

For example, a 20-member field would be broken into two paragraphs of 10 competitors each. Paragraphs end with periods.

Head-to-head result

Tab-TEN-Wimbledon-Rslts
LONDON (CP) — Results Wednesday from the Wimbledon tennis championships (seedings in parentheses):
MEN
Singles
Final
Goran Ivanisevic, Croatia, def. Pat Rafter (3), Australia, 7-6, 3-6, 6-3, 2-6, 9-7.

Athletics   ➤   See **Track and field.**

Auto racing

1. Report Grand Prix racing in kilometres, but stock-car, Indy-car and drag racing in miles.

2. Results use the field format.

Tab-AUTO-Cdn-GP-Rslts
MONTREAL (CP) — Results and grid positions after qualifying Saturday for the Canadian Grand Prix at the 4.42-kilometre Gilles-Villeneuve Circuit (with name, country, team and time):
1. Michael Schumacher (Germany), Ferrari, one minute 15.782 seconds (average speed 210.018 km/h); 2. **Jacques Villeneuve, Iberville, Que., BAR-Honda, 1:17.035**; 3. Eddie Irvine (Britain), Jaguar, 1:18.033 . . .

Baseball

1. Write **American League, National League, American League East**, etc.

2. In sluglines on game stories, use **AMN** (all caps) for the American League and **NAT** for the National League, followed by the abbreviations of the teams involved, visiting team first.

NAT-NY-Mtl
MONTREAL (CP) — A ninth inning homer ...

For non-game stories, use the generic **BBL** as the keyword in the slug.

3.   Use these team abbreviations:

American League: **Bal** (Baltimore), **Bos** (Boston), **ChiW** (Chicago White Sox), **Cle** (Cleveland), **Det** (Detroit), **KC** (Kansas City), **LAA** (Los Angeles Angels), **Min** (Minnesota), **NYY** (New York Yankees), **Oak** (Oakland), **Sea** (Seattle), **TB** (Tampa Bay), **Tex** (Texas) and **Tor** (Toronto).

National League: **Ariz** (Arizona), **Atl** (Atlanta), **ChiC** (Chicago Cubs), **Cin** (Cincinnati), **Col** (Colorado), **Hou** (Houston), **LAD** (Los Angeles Dodgers), **Fla** (Florida), **Mil** (Milwaukee), **NYM** (New York Mets), **Pha** (Philadelphia), **Pgh** (Pittsburgh), **StL** (St. Louis), **SD** (San Diego), **SF** (San Francisco) and **Wash** (Washington).

4.   Scores are normally carried as part of standings. In instances where stand-alone scores are warranted, use the bare scores format.

5.   The first linescore of the day follows this style:

Tab-BBL-Linescores
Thursday's list
By The Canadian Press
AMERICAN LEAGUE
Anaheim   000 000 000— 0   9   1
Toronto   000 000 11x— 2   6   0

   Schoeneweis (L,2-2), Levine (8), Holtz (8), Hasegawa (8) and BMolina; Parris (W,1-2), KEscobar (8), Koch (S,7) (9) and Fletcher, ACastillo (9). **HR:** Tor — Frye (1), Green 2 (13); Cle — Ramirez (15).

Note 1: A *thin space* is inserted after every three innings to break up the figures and make them more readable.

Note 2: There is no spacing around the dash in the team lines, but there is when listing the home runs.

Note 3: Team abbreviations may be necessary for extra-inning games to avoid team lines spilling over.

Subsequent linescores do not carry specific add numbers, such as **1st add**, **2nd add**, and do not carry catchwords.

Tab-BBL-Linescores, add
Add Thursday's list
Add AL etc.

6. In boxscores, the visiting team is on the left. Each player is shown in the last position he played. Figures in parentheses are the player's total in that category for the season.

Note: CP relays AP boxscores in unedited form.

Tab-BBL-AMN-Box-Tor-Bal
BLUE JAYS 8, ORIOLES 2

TORONTO	ab	r	h	bi	BALTIMORE	ab	r	h	bi
Stewart cf	4	2	1	1	Surhoff lf	5	1	2	1
Grebeck 2b	5	1	2	2	Davis dh	4	0	1	1
Canseco dh	4	1	2	0	Bordick ss	5	0	3	0
Green rf	4	0	2	3	Mouton rf	1	0	0	0
Delgado 1b	2	0	2	1	Ripkin 3b	4	0	1	0
Fernandez 3b	4	1	0	0	Hoiles c	3	0	0	0
Fletcher c	5	1	1	0	Palmeiro 1b	1	0	0	0
Cruz Jr. lf	3	0	0	0	Alomar 2b	4	0	1	0
Gonzalez ss	5	1	3	1	Anderson cf	3	1	2	0
Totals	**36**	**7**	**13**	**8**	**Totals**	**30**	**2**	**10**	**2**

Toronto	001 000 060—7
Baltimore	002 000 000—2

E—Grebeck (1), Fernandez (6). DP—Toronto 2, Baltimore 1. LOB—Toronto 10, Baltimore 9. 2B—Delgado (5), Green (7), Canseco (7), Ripken (4). 3B—Surhoff (2). HR—Palmeiro (9). SB—Stewart (11), Alomar 4 (18). CS—Gonzalez (2).

	IP	H	R	ER	BB	SO
Toronto						
Clemens W,9-2	7	9	1	2	2	3
Quantrill	1	0	0	0	0	1
Persons	1	2	1	2	1	0
Baltimore						
Mussina	7 2-3	8	2	2	4	4
Rhodes	1-3	0	0	0	0	0
Coppinger L,0-1	1-3	2	4	4	2	0
Mills	2-3	2	2	2	2	0

Umpires — Home, Ford; First, Clark; Second, Barnett; Third, Kosc. T—3:21. A—25,569.

Note: For weekend games, the day of the week is included in the slugging to assist editors in differentiating between the Saturday and Sunday games.

Tab-AMN-Box-Tor-Bal-SAT

7. Standings for major league baseball are transmitted throughout the night — after eastern games for early morning editions and at the conclusion of play — and are slugged accordingly (**Early** and **Final**).

Standings follow this style:

Tab-BBL-AMN-Stdgs-Final
Sunday's standings

By The Canadian Press
(All times EDT)
AMERICAN LEAGUE
East Division

	W	L	Pct.	GBL
Toronto	92	63	.594	—
Boston	90	65	.581	2
Detroit	81	73	.526	10½

etc.

Sunday Results
Toronto 7 Cleveland 6 (11 innings)
Boston 4 Detroit 1

Saturday Results
Toronto 4 Cleveland 0
Detroit 5-4 Boston 3-6

Note: In doubleheaders, combine the two scores for each club, listing the opening game score first.

Monday Games
No games scheduled.

Tuesday Games
Toronto at Baltimore, 7:35 p.m.
Boston at New York, 8:35 p.m. . . .

8. **Leaders**

At the conclusion of play each day, the Leaders feature, listing the hitting and pitching leaders in each league, is carried. This item lists the top 10 hitters graded by average, in tabular form, plus the top players in 10 separate categories, listed in paragraph form.

Tab-BBL-NAT-Leaders
NATIONAL LEAGUE LEADERS
By The Associated Press

	G	AB	R	H	Pct
LWalker Col	68	270	46	95	.352
Helton Col	61	214	37	72	.336
Berkman Hou	64	267	51	88	.330
Alou Hou	68	275	46	90	.327

. . .

Runs — SSosa, Chicago, 134; Helton, Colorado, 130; . . .
RBIs — SSosa, Chicago, 158; Helton, Colorado, 147; . . .
Hits — Aurilia, San Francisco, 219; Pierre, Colorado, 210; . . .
Doubles — Berkman, Houston, 51; Helton, Colorado, 48; . . .
Triples — Rollins, Philadelphia, 12; Uribe, Colorado 10; . . .
Home runs — Bonds, San Francisco, 70; SSosa, Chicago, 66; . . .
Stolen bases — Pierre, Colorado, 58; Rollins, Philadelphia, 50; . . .
Pitching (19 decisions) — Schilling, Arizona, 17-3, .850, 2.90;
R.D. Johnson, Arizona, 20-6, .769, 2.47; . . .
Strikeouts — RDJohnson, Arizona; 300; Schilling, Arizona, 257; . . .
Saves — Nen, San Francisco, 53; Benitez, New York, 51; . . .

9. **Probable Pitchers**

This feature, moved for AMs editions, lists the pitchers expected to start and the times of major league games. It is carried one day in advance.

Tab-BBL-Pitchers
Monday's Pitchers
              By The Canadian Press
Probable pitchers, with won-lost records, for major league baseball games Monday (all times EDT):
              AMERICAN LEAGUE
Cleveland (Sabathia 3-3) at Boston (Lowe 4-10), 1 p.m.
Toronto (Escobar 6-1) at Detroit (Cornejo 4-5), 1:30 p.m.
Texas (Bell 7-1) at Baltimore (Johnson 4-3), 1:30 p.m.
Anaheim (Wise 4-6) at Oakland (Lidle 6-3), 4 p.m.
N.Y. Yankees (Mussina 8-4) at Seattle (Garcia 4-4), 4 p.m.

---

10. Roundups are written for PMs papers on both the American and National leagues. When play in one league consists of only one or two games, a combined major league roundup may be considered. If such a roundup is contemplated, inform members by advisory as soon as possible.

Basketball

1. Write **National Basketball Association (NBA** also acceptable on sports pages), the **Pacific Division of the Western Conference**, the **Central Division of the Eastern Conference**, etc. On subsequent references: **the NBA West**, etc.

2. Use these NBA team abbreviations in slug lines and the like: **Atl** (Atlanta), **Bos** (Boston), **Cha** (Charlotte), **Chi** (Chicago), **Cle** (Cleveland), **Dal** (Dallas), **Den** (Denver), **Det** (Detroit), **GS** (Golden State), **Hou** (Houston), **Ind** (Indiana), **LAC** (Los Angeles Clippers), **LAL** (Los Angeles Lakers), **Mia** (Miami), **Mil** (Milwaukee), **Mem** (Memphis), **Min** (Minnesota), **NJ** (New Jersey), **NO** (New Orleans), **NY** (New York), **Orl** (Orlando), **Pha** (Philadelphia), **Pho** (Phoenix), **Por** (Portland), **Sac** (Sacramento), **SA** (San Antonio), **Sea** (Seattle), **Tor** (Toronto), **Utah** (Utah), **Wash** (Washington).

3. For results, follow the bare score format.

4.   Standings follow this style:

Tab-NBA-Glance-Final
National Basketball Association
At-A-Glance
By The Associated Press
(All Times EDT)
Eastern Conference
Atlantic Division

	W	L	Pct.	GB	
Miami	51	9	.850	—	
New York	44	17	.721	7½,	etc.

Central Division

	W	L	Pct.	GB	
Chicago	41	21	.661	—	
Indiana	32	31	.508	9½,	etc.

Western Conference
Midwest Division

	W	L	Pct.	GB	
Utah	39	25	.609	—	
San Antonio	34	30	.531	5,	etc.

Pacific Division

	W	L	Pct.	GB	
Seattle	45	16	.738	—	
Phoenix	37	26	.587	9,	etc.

Friday Results
New York 107 Seattle 98
Atlanta 110 Vancouver 93, etc.

Saturday Games
Portland at New York, 7:30 p.m.
Cleveland at Milwaukee, 8:30 p.m.

Sunday Games
New York at Boston, 7:30 p.m.
Cleveland at Milwaukee, 8:30 p.m.

Note: Some leagues use a format that includes a games column and award two points for a win and one for a tie. For such leagues, follow the format for hockey standings.

Bobsleigh, luge, skeleton

Use a basic summary format.

Men's Two
(individual run times in brackets)
   1. Canada 1 (Pierre Lueders (pilot), Edmonton; Lascelles Brown, Calgary), one minute 50.54 seconds (55.34, 55.20); 2. Germany 1 (Andre Lange, Martin Putze), 1:50.57 (55.21, 55.30); 3. Canada 2 (Serge Despres, Cocagne, Alta., David Bissett, Edmonton), 1:50.88 (55.40, 55.48).

Boxing

1. These are the Olympic weight categories: *light flyweight* (to 48 kg), *flyweight* (48-51 kg), *bantamweight* (51-54 kg), *featherweight* (54-57 kg), *lightweight* (57-60 kg), *light welterweight* (60-63.5 kg), *welterweight* (63.5-67 kg), *light middleweight* (67-71 kg), *middleweight* (71-75 kg), *light heavyweight* (75-81 kg), *heavyweight* (81-91 kg), *super heavyweight* (more than 91 kg).

2. These are the major pro weight categories: *flyweight* (to 112 lb.), *bantamweight* (113-118 lb.), *featherweight* (119-126 lb.), *lightweight* (127-135 lb.), *welterweight* (136-147 lb.), *middleweight* (148-160 lb.), *light heavyweight* (161-175 lb.), *cruiserweight* (176-195 lb.), *heavyweight* (196 lb. or more).

3. Use a revised head-to-head results format, stating whether the victory was by **decision, knockout (KO)** or **referee stopped bout.**

Note: In pro bouts, the **technical knockout (TKO)** is used instead of **referee stopped bout.**

> **Light flyweight (48 kg):** Ivalio Hristov, Bulgaria, def. Michael Carbajal, U.S., 4-1; **Scott Olson, Edmonton,** etc.
> **Welterweight (67 kg):** Robert Wangita, Kenya, def. Laurent Boudouani, France, bout stopped, 0:44 second; etc.
> **Heavyweight (91 kg):** Ray Mercer, U.S., def. Baik Hyun-man, South Korea, KO, 2:16 first; etc.

Canoeing

Use a field result format. Categories are listed as *C-1* (canoe singles), *K-2* (kayak pairs), etc.

> **Tab-CANOE-Rslts**
> NOTTINGHAM, England (CP) — Results Tuesday at the world canoeing championships:
> **WOMEN**
> **K-1 500 metres (Heat 1):** 1. Sharon Smith, Britain, two minutes 7.35 seconds; 2. **Margaret Langford, Lions Bay, B.C., 2:08.55**; 3. etc.

Cricket

International cricket competition generally consists of Test matches and one-day international matches. Test matches last five days and involve teams given Test status by the International Cricket Council. The current Test-playing countries are Australia, Bangladesh, England, India, New Zealand, Pakistan, South Africa, Sri Lanka, West Indies and Zimbabwe.

Test matches take daily breaks at lunch and tea before the end of day's play (sometimes called at stumps). In moving copy, take care to ensure the story covers the day's play and not just a portion.

An explanation of some common cricket terminology:

Innings — An innings (singular) is completed when: (1) 10 of a team's batsmen have been dismissed; (2) the batting captain "declares" (voluntarily ends the innings); or (3) a specified number of overs have been bowled.

Overs — consisting of six balls delivered from alternate wickets.

Wickets — three stumps topped by crosspieces (called *bails*) situated at either end of the pitch (field) and from which the ball is bowled.

Curling

1. Rinks are named in this order: *lead, second, third* (or *vice-skip*), *skip*.

2. Do not write *curling bonspiel*.

3. Abbreviations when necessary in linescores are: **Alta, B.C., Man, N.B., N.L., N.Ont, N.S., Ont, P.E.I., Que, Sask** and **Terr** (Territories).

4. Linescores follow this style:

Tab-CURL-Women-Rslts
　　MOOSE JAW, Sask. (CP) — Linescores Tuesday at the Canadian women's curling championship:

	Round 10
P.E.I.	001 010 201 1 — 6
Manitoba	200 101 010 0 — 5

Later scores go as follows:

Tab-CURL-Women-Rslts, add
MOOSE JAW, Sask.— add women's curling linescores

	Round 11
Nova Scotia	103 021 010 x — 8
Newfoundland	020 200 101 x — 6

　　Bye: Territories.

---

5. Standings follow this style:

Tab-CURL-Women-Stdgs
　　MOOSE JAW, Sask. (CP) — Standings after the 11th round at the Canadian women's curling championship Wednesday:

	W	**L**	
Alberta	7	0	
B.C.	7	1	
Ontario	7	1	
Nova Scotia	6	2	
N. Ontario	5	3	etc.

Cycling

Use a field result format.

Tab-CYCLE-Tour-Que
QUEBEC (CP) — Results Sunday from the Tour de Quebec men's cycling series:
220-kilometre third stage: 1. Czeslaw Lukaszewicz, Chateauguay, Que., three hours 32 minutes 10 seconds; 2. Gord Fraser, Nepean, Ont., same time; 3. Mark Walters, Toronto, five seconds behind; 4. John Harris, New Zealand, 0:17 behind; . . .
Overall standing: 1. Fraser, 5:51:05; 2. Walters, 5:51:10; 3. Mark Anand, Calgary, 5:51:41; . . .

Diving

Use a field result format.

Tab-DIVE-Cda-Rslts
WINNIPEG (CP) — Results Sunday in Canadian World Cup diving:
WOMEN
Three-metre: 1. Emilie Heymans, Montreal, 877.05 points; 2. Myriam Boileau, Montreal, 876.36; . . .

Equestrian

1. Identify events as *show jumping, dressage* or *three-day event.*

2. Use basic field result format.

Fencing

1. Identify events as *épée, foil* or *sabre.*

2. Use head-to-head result format.

Figure skating

1. Most figure-skating competitions comprise *men's singles, women's singles, pairs* (man-woman) and *ice dance* (man-woman). *Singles* consists of two segments — a short program of required elements and a free-skating long program. The short program is worth one-third and the free-skating segment two-thirds. In the short program, skaters must attempt predetermined jumps or movements in not more than two minutes 40 seconds. In free skating, competitors put together their own combination of jumps, spins and steps, with time allowed varying between three and 4 1/2 minutes depending on whether it's a men's or women's competition and on the age group. Skaters select their own music for both the short and long programs. Judges assign two marks, one for technical merit and one for artistic impression.

Pairs skating consists of a short program in which several elements (jumps, spins, lifts, etc.), announced in advance, must be attempted, and a free-skating portion which contains moves similar to singles skating but executed simultaneously by both competitors. Free skating accounts for two-thirds of the final mark and varies in length from three to four minutes, depending on the age group.

Ice dancing, in simple terms, is ballroom dancing on ice. It is easily distinguished from *pairs* skating in that there are no jumps or lifts above the waist. The couple seldom separate. The program has three elements — compulsory dances (variations of such dances as the waltz, tango and foxtrot) skated to designated rhythms and patterns; the original dance (three repetitive sequences of steps), and the free dance in which competitors select their own moves, steps and music.

2. Some of the more common jumps (named after their inventors and, therefore, capitalized):

Axel: Skater, facing forward, takes off on the outside edge of either foot, rotates up to 3 1/2 times and lands on the outside edge of the other foot, facing backward.

Lutz: Skater starts with a lengthy glide backwards down the ice, then takes off on the outside edge of either foot and, after up to three rotations, lands on the outside edge of the other foot, facing backward.

Salchow: Skater, facing backward, takes off from the inside edge of either foot and, after up to three rotations, lands on the outside edge of the other foot, facing backward.

3. Use a field result format.

Football

1. Avoid **major** as a synonym for touchdown. A major was an old scoring play worth five points. Use **touchdown** or, in subsequent references, **TD**.

2. For results, use a bare score format.

3. Style for game summary:

Tab-CFL-Sums-Tor-Ham
    HAMILTON (CP) — CFL Thursday night:
                              SUMMARY
                        First Quarter
    Tor — TD Clemons 15 run (Chomyc convert) 0:45
    Ham — TD Winfield 27 pass from McPherson (Osbaldiston convert) 2:10
                        Second Quarter
    Tor — Single Ilesic 55 7:18
    Tor — Safety McPherson tackled 13:15
                        Third Quarter
    Ham — FG Osbaldiston 47 4:15
    Ham — TD Zatylny 95 kickoff return (two-point convert failed) 12:12

Tor — TD Harding blocked punt in end zone (Chomyc convert failed) 13:42
Tor — Safety Osbaldiston conceded 15:00
Fourth Quarter
No scoring.

Toronto	7	3	8	0—18
Hamilton	7	0	9	0—16

Attendance — 16,485.

---

4. Style for game statistics:

Tab-CFL-Stax-Edm-Wpg
WINNIPEG (CP) — Statistics from the Edmonton-Winnipeg CFL game Friday night:

	Edm	Wpg
First downs	14	22
Yards rushing	156	88
Yards passing	255	280
Total offence	411	368
Team losses	25	15
Net offence	386	353
Passes made-tried	20-37	21-37
Returns-yards	5-95	2-22
Intercepts-yards by	0-0	2-22
Fumbles-lost	0-0	0-0
Sacks by	2	1
Punts-average	6-41	5-44
Penalties-yards	7-70	4-25
Time of possession	26:45	33:15

Net offence is yards passing, plus yards rushing, minus team losses such as yards lost on broken plays.

Individual
Rushing: Edm — Foggie 11-84, Marshall 13-54, Smith 1-11, Soles 1-8, Walling 1-minus 1; Wpg — Richardson 11-55, Dunigan 7-26, Hudson 4-7.
Receiving: Edm — Smith 8-131, Brown 4-46, Cyncar 2-24, Soles 2-17, Wright 1-11, Walling 1-10, Smith 1-8, Marshall 1-6; Wpg — House 6-17, Tuttle 3-70, Hudson 4-66, Hull 2-26, Streeter 2-17, Richardson 1-14.
Passing: Edm — Ham 20-37, 253 yds, 1 TD, 3 int; Wpg — Dunigan 18-31-286-3-0, McManus 2-2-66-1-0, Garza 1-4-15-0-1.

---

5. Style for rosters provided before the opening of the season, or as game lineups for the Grey Cup:

Tab-CFL-Grey-Cup-Rosters
Rosters for the CFL Grey Cup game Sunday between the Montreal Alouettes and the B.C. Lions (x-denotes Canadian, y-denotes import):
Montreal Alouettes
1. x-Kelly Wiltshire, lb
2. x-Davis Sanchez, cb
3. x-Sylvain Girard, wr
4. y-Thomas Haskins, rb
5. y-Stanley Jackson, qb . . .

Injured List

7. y-Jamie Barnette, qb . . .

B.C. Lions

1. y-Nate Sparks, qu
2. y-Eric Carter, cb
5. x-Lui Passaglia, k
6. y-Mike Fletcher, db . . .

Injured List

10. x-Jason Crumb sb/db . . .

Golf

1. Write par 4, par-4 hole, five-iron or No. 5 iron, three-wood or No. 3 wood, 1 over par for the round, shot a 1-over-par 73, parred, birdie, birdied, bogey, double-bogey, triple-bogey 7, bogey-free (not bogey-less), bogeyed.

2. There are two basic types of play: *match* and *medal* (or *stroke*).

In *match* play, the individual or team wins a hole by taking fewer strokes than the opponent. The entry winning the most holes wins the match. Stroke totals are not kept.

In *medal* play, the individual or team keeps a running total of strokes taken at each hole. The one taking the fewest strokes overall is the winner.

3. Match-play tournaments follow this style in head-to-head results:

Bill Richardson, Creston, B.C., def. Ian MacDonnell, Antigonish, N.S., 3 and 2.

(Richardson had an insurmountable lead of three after 16 holes. As a result the final two holes were not played.)

Bill Richardson, Creston, B.C., def. Ian MacDonnell, Antigonish, N.S., 1-up.

(Richardson led by one after 18 holes or after extra play. If two players are tied after 18 holes, play continues until a hole is won.)

4. Medal-play tournaments follow this style for results (lowest scores are listed first; home towns are listed, indented on a second line, for major national tournaments):

For first round:

Cheryl Richardson	33-35—68
Creston, B.C.	
Heather MacDonnell	36-34—70
Antigonish, N.S.	

For second round:

Cheryl Richardson	68-69—137
Creston, B.C.	
Heather MacDonnell	70-68—138
Antigonish, N.S.	

	For third round:
Heather MacDonnell Antigonish, N.S.	70-68-69—207
Cheryl Richardson Creston, B.C.	68-69-71—208
	For fourth round:
Heather MacDonnell Antigonish, N.S.	70-68-69-70—277
Cheryl Richardson Creston, B.C.	68-69-71-71—279

5. In professional tournaments, prize money is included and golfers' first names are reduced to initials to accommodate a single column results format. Some unusually long surnames may also require abbreviation.

G. Norman, $250,000	70-73-72-70—285
A. Forsb'd, $175,000	74-72-70-72—288

6. Team standings for men's and women's interprovincial competitions follow this style:

ST. JOHN'S, N.L. (CP) — Final interprovincial team standings after play Thursday at the Canadian amateur women's golf championship (top three individual scores each day are counted):

NEW BRUNSWICK

Marilyn Smith Campbellton	70-72—142
Jennifer McDougall Sackville	68-74—142
Sandy Garson Shediac	75-75—150
Heidi Green Moncton	76-81—157
Total: 434	

SASKATCHEWAN

Bev Richards Saskatoon	73-74—147
Sally Oneschuk Prince Albert	75-72—147
Pamela Gordon Regina	79-77—156
Rosemary Hart Moose Jaw	80-77—157
Total: 450	

Gymnastics

1. Identify events as *side horse, floor exercises, vault, rings, parallel bars, high bar, uneven bars, balance beam, team, all-round,* and

ensure it's clear whether it's *team, individual combined* or *individual competition*.

2.   Use a field result format.

WOMEN

All-round: 1. Yvonne Tousek, Cambridge, Ont., 38.250 points; 2. Michelle Conway, Toronto, 37.650; 3. Julie Beaulieu, Montreal, 36.950; . . .

Hockey

1.   A three- or four-letter abbreviation is used to identify teams in slug lines and in the *penalties* section of the game summary. For team bench penalties, spell out the team name.

For the NHL, use: **Ana** (Anaheim), **Atl** (Atlanta), **Bos** (Boston), **Buf** (Buffalo), **Cal** (Calgary), **Car** (Carolina), **Chi** (Chicago), **Col** (Colorado), **Clb** (Columbus), **Dal** (Dallas), **Det** (Detroit), **Edm** (Edmonton), **Fla** (Florida), **LA** (Los Angeles), **Min** (Minnesota), **Mtl** (Montreal), **Nash** (Nashville), **NJ** (New Jersey), **NYI** (New York Islanders), **NYR** (New York Rangers), **Ott** (Ottawa), **Pha** (Philadelphia), **Pho** (Phoenix), **Pgh** (Pittsburgh), **SJ** (San Jose), **StL** (St. Louis), **TB** (Tampa Bay), **Tor** (Toronto), **Vcr** (Vancouver), **Wash** (Washington).

2.   For results, use the bare score format.

3.   Style for game summaries:

Tab-NHL-Sums-Ott-Cal-SAT
   CALGARY (CP) – NHL Saturday night:
                              First Period
   1. Ottawa, Heatley 34, 0:54
   2. Ottawa, Chara 11 (Smolinski, Sperra) 8:19 (pp)
   3. Ottawa, Alfredsson 32, 12:49 (penalty shot)
   Penalties – Kobasew Cal (tripping) 2:04, Varada Ott (obstruction-hooking), Regehr Cal (diving) 5:45, Amonte Cal (goaltender interference) 7:32, Hasek Ott (delay of game; served by Fisher) 17:59.
                              Second Period
   4. Calgary, Iginla 25 (Langkow, Phaneuf) 2:52 (sh)
   5. Calgary, Regehr 5 (Amonte, Phaneuf) 6:22 (pp)
   6. Ottawa, Havlat 9 (Phillips, McGrattan) 6:35
   7. Calgary, Iginla 26 (Huselius, Ference) 8:00
   Missed penalty shot – Lagnkow Cal, 16:45.
   Penalties – Hamrlik Cal (holding) 2:11, Chara Ott, (double roughing), Lombardi Cal (roughing) 5:04, Calgary bench (too many men; served by Yelle) 14:06, Kelly Ott (slashing) 19:42.
                              Third Period
   8. Ottawa, Vermette 12 (Eaves) 8:11
   9. Calgary, Leclerc 9, 12:29
   10. Calgary, Huselius 13 (Nilson, Donovan) 19:15
   Penalties – Ference Cal (holding stick) 2:31, Smolinski Ott (fighting), Meszaros Ott (roughing, hitting from behind major, game misconduct), Fisher Ott, Spezza Ott, Donovan Cal, Regehr Cal (roughing, fighting, misconduct), Kiprusoff Cal (leaving the crease; served by Yelle), Lombardi Cal (roughing, fighting), Simon Cal (instigating, fighting, game misconduct) 16:45.

Overtime

No scoring.

Penalty – Chara Ott (cross-checking) 3:21.

Shootout
Calgary wins 2-1

Ottawa (1) – Alfredsson, miss; Heatley, miss; Spezza, goal; Havlat, miss; Redden, miss.

Calgary (2) – Iginla, goal; Kobasew, miss; Langkow, miss, Amonte, miss; Huselius, goal.

Shots on goal by

Ottawa   12 6 9 3–30
Calgary   7 14 9 1–31

Goal (shots-saves) – Ottawa: Hasek (L,23-15-2); Calgary: Kiprusoff (W,21-16-4)(start, 6:35 second)(22-17), Boucher(12:49 first)(8-8).

Power plays (goals-chances) – Ottawa: 2-7; Calgary: 0-4.

Referees – Greg Kimmerly, Dan Marouelli. **Linesmen** – Lyle Seitz, Markk Wheler.

Attendance – 17,242 (17,439).

Note 1: The number after a scorer's name is his season goal total. The *(pp)*, *(sh)* and *(en)* notations designate *power-play, short-handed* and *empty-net* goals.

Note 2: The time of each goal is computed from the start of the period.

Note 3: The winning goaltender is the one in net when the winning goal is scored. The NHL defines the winning goal as the goal which is one more than the opposition's final total. For example, if the final score is 8-4, the fifth goal scored by the victorious team is the winner.

4.   At the end of each night's play, results are grouped by league in descending order of significance. Junior leagues are listed geographically, east to west.

Tab-HKY-Grp-Rslts
Wednesday's List

By The Canadian Press
NHL

Edmonton 4 Colorado 3 (SO)
Montreal 5 Ottawa 3 . . .

AHL

Hamilton 2 San Antonio 1 (OT)
Manitoba 4 Norfolk 2 . . .

ECHL

Victoria 3 Alaska 1 ...

OHL

No games scheduled.

5.   Style for standings:

Tab-NHL-Stdgs-Final
National Hockey League
Standings
At A Glance
By The Canadian Press
All times EST
NHL
EASTERN CONFERENCE
Atlantic Division

	G	W	L	T	F	A	P
Philadelphia	44	24	10	10	135	87	58
New Jersey	44	25	14	5	129	117	55
etc.							

Northeast Division

Toronto	46	27	16	3	152	133	57
Ottawa	45	25	14	6	133	101	56
etc.							

Southeast Division

Carolina	45	20	18	7	116	112	47
Florida	44	17	16	11	110	115	45
etc.							

WESTERN CONFERENCE
Central Division

Detroit	46	23	20	3	135	122	49
St. Louis	42	16	17	9	111	108	41
etc.							

Northwest Division

Colorado	45	22	19	4	114	113	48
Edmonton	44	18	19	7	126	116	43
etc.							

Pacific Division

Dallas	43	27	9	7	127	89	61
Phoenix	41	24	11	6	110	84	54
etc.							

Monday Results
Dallas 5 Phoenix 3
Detroit 1 St. Louis 0 (OT)
Tuesday Games
Ottawa at Boston, 7 p.m.
Florida at N.Y. Rangers, 7:30 p.m.

Horse racing

1.   Terms to watch include *colt* (an uncastrated male aged four or less), *horse* (an uncastrated male aged five or more), *stallion* (an uncastrated male, especially one used for breeding), *gelding* (a castrated male of any age), *filly* (a female aged four or less), *mare* (a female aged five or more), *quarter-horse* (a horse bred to run a quarter-mile), *standardbred* (bred chiefly for harness racing; a pacer or trotter), *thoroughbred* (of pure or pedigree stock; chiefly for flat racing and steeplechase).

Judo

1. Weight categories are *extra lightweight* (up to 60 kg), *half lightweight* (up to 65 kg), *lightweight* (up to 71 kg), *half middleweight* (up to 78 kg), *middleweight* (up to 86 kg), *half heavyweight* (up to 95 kg), *heavyweight* (over 95 kg), *open category* (no weight limit).

2. Use a basic summary format.

Lacrosse

Use the **Hockey** summary style.

Motorcycle racing

Follow the **Auto racing** style.

Rowing

1. A *regatta* is a knockout competition ending with a race or races between two or more finalists. A *repechage* is a second chance to qualify, used only in the preliminaries. The boats used in sculling and rowing are *shells*, not sculls.

In sculling (*singles, doubles* or *four-member crews*), each competitor rows with two oars called *sculls*. In rowing (*pairs, fours, eights*), each competitor uses one oar.

Fours and eights are *crews*, never teams. The competitors are *scullers* or *oarsmen* or *oarswomen*, never rowers. The terms *rowing* and *oars(wo)men* may be used in a general sense referring to regattas and the scullers who take part.

2. Identify events as *single sculls, double sculls, coxless pairs, coxed pairs, coxless fours, coxed fours, coxless eights, coxed eights.*

3. Use a basic summary format.

Rugby

Use a bare scores result format. List the home team first in international matches.

Sailing

1. In Olympic sailing (formerly yachting), races fall into two categories: *fleet racing* and *match racing*. In fleet racing, all competing boats race against each other at the same time. In match racing, two boats compete one on one. All events are fleet races except the *Soling* event, which starts with a series of six fleet races to determine the top 12 competitors, who then advance to a match racing elimination series.

Boats are categorized into classes based on the weights and measurements of the boats. This changes frequently as the popularity of various boats waxes and wanes. In general, the trend is toward smaller boats with fewer crew members. There are men's, women's and mixed events.

2. The America's Cup is a *formula* class event. For a yacht to qualify for this challenge series, its size must not exceed a given limit. That limit, which approximates the length of the boat, is arrived at using a complicated mathematical formula that factors in such things as length, draft and sail area. In 1992 a 24-metre limit was set.

3. Where names of yacht classes include an imperial measure (e.g. *Whatsis 30:* a 30-footer), a sentence of explanation may be necessary if there's a risk of confusion.

4. Some races are still measured in nautical miles. Convert these to kilometres but retain an initial nautical-mile equivalent in parentheses. A nautical mile is equivalent to 1.852 kilometres.

Shooting

1. Identify events as *free pistol, fullbore, rapid-fire pistol, skeet, smallbore rifle* and *trap*.

2. Use a basic summary format.

Skiing

1. Skiing is divided into four categories: *alpine, nordic, biathlon* and *freestyle*. Alpine includes downhill, slalom, giant slalom, super giant slalom and a combined event. Nordic includes cross-country, ski jumping and a combined event. Biathlon combines cross-country skiing with rifle shooting. Freestyle includes acro, moguls and aerials.

2. Use a basic summary format.

Tab-SKI-WC-Women-Rslts
    KITZBUEHEL, Austria (CP) — Results at a World Cup women's downhill ski race Saturday, with finish, starting position in brackets, competitor, hometown or country and time:
    1. (4) Janica Kostelic, Croatia, one minute 29.40 seconds; **2. (11) Emily Brudon, Fernie, B.C., 1:29.62**; 3. (12) Julia Mancuso, U.S., 1:30.04; **4. (17) Brigitte Acton, Mont-Tremblant, Que., 1:30.98.**
    Did not finish: Allyson Forsyth, Canmore, Alta.

Note: When a competitor appears a second time in standings, his first name and country are dropped.

Soccer

1. For scores, the home team is listed first in British and European play.

Results style is as follows:

Tab-SOC-British-Rslts

LONDON (CP) — British soccer results Saturday (home team listed first):

ENGLAND
Premier League

Birmingham 1 Sunderland 0
Blackburn 1 Arsenal 0. . .

Football League Championship

Coventry 1 Burnley 0 . . .

League One

Blackpool 2 Yeovil 0 . . .

League Two

Cheltenham 1 Rochdale 1 . .

Football League Championship

SCOTLAND
Scottish Cup
Fifth Round

Gretna 4 St. Mirren 0 . . .

Premier League

Dunfermline 1 Dundee United . . .

First Division

Ross County 1 Stranraer 1 . . .

Second Division

Alloa 1 Raith 1 . . .

Third Division

Albion 1 Stenhousemuir 2 . . .

---

2. For standings, use this style (note order for *T* and *L* reversed from standard North American tables):

Tab-SOC-British-Stdgs

British Soccer Standings
By The Associated Press
Through Feb. 25
England
Premier League

Team	W	T	L	F	A	P
Chelsea	21	6	3	73	24	69
Manchester United	18	4	9	60	37	58
Liverpool	14	9	6	39	25	51
etc.						

League Championship

Team	W	T	L	F	A	P
Reading	18	7	6	56	33	61
etc.						

Scotland
Premier League

Team	W	T	L	F	A	P
Celtic	20	4	4	59	21	44
etc.						

Speedskating

1. Speedskating consists of *outdoor* (long-track) and *indoor* (short-track) events. Race distances include 500, 1,000, 1,500, 3,000 (women only), 5,000 and 10,000 metres (men only).

2. Scoring is in minutes, seconds and tenths of a second. Extend to hundredths if available.

2. Use a basic summary format.

Squash

Use head-to-head format.

Swimming

1. Identify events as *men's 100-metre freestyle, women's 4x100-metre medley relay*, etc.

2. Use a basic summary format.

Tennis

1. Use head-to-head results format. Grouped results should be graded in order of seedings. See example page xxx.

2. Tiebreakers are used to avoid marathon sets. The first player to win six games wins the set, unless the opponent has won five games. In that case, the player with six games may take the set by winning the next game. If that player loses it, (a) play can continue until either player wins two straight games, or (b) a tiebreaker may be played in which the winner is the first player to score seven points with at least a two-point lead. If the score reaches 6-6 in the tiebreaker, play continues until one player leads by two points.

Track and field   (Athletics)

1. Olympic and other international events are measured in metric, although some imperial distances are still raced in the United States. Distances and heights in such field events as the high jump, long jump, pole vault, shot put, discus, hammer and javelin should be reported in metres. But the 100-yard dash, for example, is not converted to the 91.44-metre dash.

2. Use the metric distance for marathons — 42.195 kilometres (not 26 miles 385 yards).

3. Use a basic summary format. See example page 399.

Volleyball

Use head-to-head result format.

Tab-VLBL-Rslts
Friday's list
By The Canadian Press
WORLD LEAGUE
Canada def. Brazil 3-2 (15-12, 16-14, 8-15, 12-15, 15-10).

Weightlifting

1. Olympic and most other amateur competitions are divided into 10 weight categories: 52 kg, 56 kg, 60 kg, 67.5 kg, 75 kg, 82.5 kg, 90 kg, 100 kg, 110 kg and over 110 kg.

2. Use a basic summary format.

Wrestling

1. There are eight weight categories for men and six for women. The eight men's classes are: up to 54 kg, to 58 kg, to 63 kg, to 69 kg, to 76 kg, to 85 kg, to 97 kg, to 130 kg. The women's divisions are: to 46 kg, to 51 kg, to 56 kg, to 62 kg, to 68 kg, to 75 kg.

2. Identify events as Greco-Roman or freestyle for men. Women compete only in freestyle.

3. Use head-to-head formats.

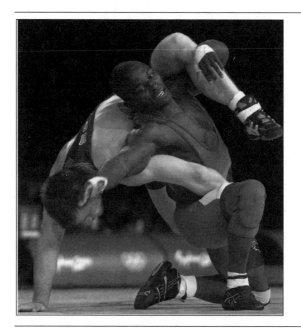

Canada's Daniel Igali throws American wrestler Lincoln McIlravy during their freestyle semi-final bout at the 2000 Summer Olympics in Sydney, Australia. Wrestling events are either Greco-Roman or freestyle.

(CP—Ryan Remiorz)

News releases

Newsrooms are inundated with news releases every day. Most of them go straight into the garbage. But a few will become the basis of a news story, especially if they are announcing genuine news. A well-written news release, like a well-written news story, can help that process by grabbing an editor's attention.

What makes a good news release? Accurate information, clearly presented, that answers all the basic questions a reporter or reader might have. Although the purpose of a news release is quite different from that of a news story, many of the same writing principles apply.

Content

1. Write in everyday English. Forget the bureaucratic or scientific jargon. Explain unfamiliar terms. Prefer **begin** to inaugurate, **best** to optimum, **less than ideal** to sub-optimal, **carry out** to implement, **final result** to bottom line.

2. Don't hide bad news under fancy words. The layoff of 150 workers is just that; it's not consolidation or downsizing. Be specific and save the reporter a phone call.

3. If you must use unusual technical terms, explain them.

4. Try to answer the questions all readers ask: *Who? What? When? Where? Why? How?* What is happening? Who says? Who is involved? When will it happen? And where? How or why is it happening?

5. Don't try to answer all six questions in the first sentence. Put what you consider the most important news in the first paragraph.

> **Not:** At a news conference today, Atlas Mines president John W. Merryweather said he was "happy to announce that the company has signed a $100-million, five-year agreement" with Karasawa Industries of Tokyo to produce coal for the Japanese metallurgical company, which would "necessitate the reopening of the Dovetail mine and the creation of 250 jobs at the coal face and in surface installations."

> **But:** The Dovetail coal mine, which has been closed for 20 years, is to be reopened as part of a $100-million, five-year contract with a Japanese company. Some 250 miners and surface workers will be hired.

The details can be added in subsequent paragraphs.

6. How much detail? That's a matter of judgment. Put yourself in the reader's place and try to answer all pertinent questions. What network will the show be on and when? How soon will the new vaccine be in drugstores? What prize did your prize-winning

author win? The Pulitzer? Or the Grade 10 English award? The union is pressing for $1 an hour more. What is the current rate?

7. Give some background on the organization or company involved in the news. Make sure it is factual and doesn't give the wrong impression. Resist hyperbole. Don't say the company had its highest revenues ever in the last year without also mentioning that profits were down.

8. Include the source of the news. The person quoted should be someone in authority – the company president, the coach, the chief fund-raiser, the researcher who made the discovery. Include phone numbers. Most reporters like to get their own quotes; broadcast reporters will need quotes on tape.

9. Make sure time elements are clearly presented. Specify when the book is going to be released. If it is a tour, provide specific details. If the ballet company is going to Europe, include cities, dates, theatres and hotels so news coverage can be arranged.

10. Include the person's age and birthplace in biographical material. Tracking down such small but important facts can consume a lot of a reporter's time. If people from across the country are involved in a news event, include home towns.

Format

Certain conventions should be followed, no matter if the release is being delivered by fax, regular mail or electronic mail:

1. Put a date at the top of the release. Specify at the top if the news item can be used at once. If it is to be released at a specific time, add that information: For release at 8 p.m. EST Monday, Dec. 23.

2. Headlines can be useful, especially in lengthy announcements. They don't need to be fanciful – just a clear summary of the main news is fine.

Not: Royal Bank president speaks to Canadian Club.

But: Royal Bank president predicts bank mergers won't proceed.

3. At the top or bottom of the release, give the names and titles of people who can be contacted for more information, their phone numbers and the name of the organization and address. Make sure they will be at those numbers when the release is distributed.

4. Gimmicks might get an editor's attention for a minute or two, but they are no substitute for solid information tied to a genuine news event. Samples or other free material are not usually wanted. Exceptions would be cases where the product is needed to write a story – a new book or video, for instance.

Pictures

Pictures are usually a welcome addition to a news release. Like the written information, they should be new or in some way unusual, or relate to a live news topic. They attract attention because of human interest and appeal to the emotions, or they can relate to some important person, event or place.

The print must have a sharp, sparkling quality. Avoid busy backgrounds and low, "artsy" lighting. Colour is preferred. Captions should identify everyone in the picture.

Who gets it?

1. Keep a contacts list up to date. It is always best to direct a release to the beat reporter, but make sure that person is not on holidays or out of town. Next best is the appropriate editor, such as the entertainment editor for an announcement on music awards. An urgent release during off-hours should be directed to the news desk.

2. The president, publisher or other top executives of a news organization rarely attend news conferences or assign staff to cover them, so nothing is gained by sending them a copy of a news release.

3. Don't blanket news organizations with the same release. It is only going to get reported once. The bank president may be taking his speech on a cross-country tour, but a national news organization is only going to carry one story, preferably the first time he makes it.

Bibliography

These works were consulted in the preparation and shaping of the *CP Stylebook:*

Barber, Katherine (ed.). *The Canadian Oxford Dictionary.* Oxford University Press. Toronto, 2005.

Barzun, Jacques. *Simple & Direct: A Rhetoric for Writers.* Harper & Row. New York, 1975.

Bernstein, Theodore M. *The Careful Writer: A Modern Guide to English Usage.* Atheneum. New York, 1973.

Burchfield, R.W. (ed.). *The New Fowler's Modern English Usage.* Oxford University Press. Oxford, 1996.

Chicago Manual of Style. University of Chicago Press, Chicago, 2003.

Collins-Robert French-English English-French Dictionary. William Collins Sons & Co. (Glasgow) and Dictionnaires Le Robert (Paris), 1987.

Copperud, Roy H. *American Usage and Style: The Consensus.* Van Nostrand Reinhold. New York, 1980.

Fee, Margery and McAlpine, Janice. *Guide to Canadian English Usage.* Oxford University Press. Toronto, 1997.

Evans, Harold. *Editing and Design; Newsman's English.* Heinemann. London, 1973.

Goldstein, Norm (ed.). *Stylebook (online edition).* The Associated Press. New York.

Hale, Constance and Scanlon, Jessie. *Wired Style: Principles of English Usage in the Digital Age.* Broadway Books, New York, 1999.

Jacobi, Ernst. *Writing at Work: Dos, Don'ts and How Tos.* Hayden Book Co. Rochelle Park, N.J., 1976.

Manser, Martin H. *Good Word Guide.* Bloomsbury Publishing. London, 1988.

Manual of Style. U.S. Government Printing Office. Gramercy Publishing. New York, 1986.

McFarlane, J.A. and Clements, Warren. *The Globe and Mail Style Book.* McClelland and Stewart. Toronto, 1998.

Messenger, William E., de Bruyn, Jan, Brown, Judy and Montagnes, Ramona. *The Canadian Writer's Handbook.* Oxford, 2005.

Metric Press Guide. Metric Commission Canada. Ottawa, 1981.

Nickles, Harry G. *Dictionary of Do's and Don'ts.* McGraw-Hill. New York, 1975.

Robertson, Stuart M. *Robertson's Newsroom Legal Crisis*

Management. Hallion Press. Dunedin, Ont., 1991.

Rose, Turner. *Stylebook for Writers and Editors.* U.S. News and World Report. Washington, 1984.

Ross-Larson, Bruce. *Edit Yourself.* W.W. Norton. New York, 1982.

Sabin, William. *A Reference Manual.* McGraw-Hill Ryerson. Toronto, 1978.

Shaw, Harry. *Dictionary of Problem Words and Expressions.* McGraw-Hill. New York, 1975.

Skilling, Marjorie E. and Gay, Robert M. *Words Into Type.* Meredith Publishing. New York, 1964.

Strunk, William Jr. and White, E.B. *The Elements of Style.* Macmillan Publishing Co. New York, 1979.

Timmons, Christine and Gibney, Frank (eds.). *Britannica Book of English Usage.* Doubleday. Garden City, N.Y., 1980.

Walsh, Bill. *Lapsing Into a Comma.* Contemporary Books, 2000.

Worth, Sylvia (ed.). *Rules of the Game.* St. Martin's Press. New York, 1990.

Acknowledgments

What more appropriate for a co-operative news agency than a co-operative stylebook? CP staff across the country have traditionally shared in the updating and revising of this book through many editions. For many, it is work fitted around their regular workload. People from every bureau and desk toss in ideas for improvements. All recognize the importance of making the *CP Stylebook* as authoritative and helpful as possible.

The greatest debt for any new edition of the *CP Stylebook* is undoubtedly to the past. The earliest workers and managers at The Canadian Press established the traditions of quality, integrity and consistency for the news agency and gathered them into book form. Senior managers of the past like Gillis Purcell, Charles Bruce and John Dauphinee put their various personal – and sometimes eccentric – stamps on CP style. Later, Bob Taylor contributed an enviable knowledge and a distinctly human touch to regular updatings of the stylebook. Peter Buckley co-ordinated a major revision and his sensible voice on style and ethics issues continues to reverberate throughout the book.

For this edition, the editor turned to the following for their expertise: Lois Abraham, Andrea Baillie, Dean Beeby, Heather Boyd, Bruce Cheadle, Tim Clark, Neil Davidson, Donna Hooper, Paul Loong, Dan McGinty, Donald McKenzie, Ron Poling, Donna Spencer, Anne-Marie Tobin, John Ward and Scott White.

They and the following CP journalists also acted as a sounding board for style decisions: Jim Dalziel, James McCarten, Steve Mertl, Judy Monchuk, Gary Norris, Mary Ann O'Rourke, Colin Perkel, Derrick Toth, Lorraine Turchansky, John Valorzi and Nelson Wyatt.

CP Senior Main Desk Editor Malcolm McNeil, working with the law firm of O'Donnell, Robertson and Sanfilippo, once again ensured our legal advice is current and reflects common journalistic concerns.

A stylebook undergoes the same intense scrutiny as Caesar's wife – and senior editor Mike Fuhrmann kept us on the straight and narrow with his copyediting help, as well as his from-the-frontlines suggestions on additions and changes.

Besides putting the book together, Sean Vokey of CP's Graphics Department also gave us a lively and dynamic new cover. Harold Herschell, CP Graphics Editor, also lent his expertise to the production process, while Graeme Roy, CP Pictures Editor, co-ordinated the pictures.

And Thuy-An Ngyuen of CP's marketing department kept the project almost on schedule, despite the best efforts of the production team to ignore deadlines.

The editor salutes them all and takes full responsibility for any shortcomings or errors in the finished work.

Index